Dirr's Hardy Trees and Shrubs

Taxodium distichum, Common Baldcypress, and *Liriodendron tulipifera,* Tulip Tree, at Milliken Arboretum, Spartanburg, South Carolina

Dirr's Hardy Trees and Shrubs

AN
ILLUSTRATED
ENCYCLOPEDIA

by
Michael A. Dirr

Timber Press

All photographs are by Michael A. Dirr.

Published in 1997 by
Timber Press, Inc.
The Haseltine Building
133 S.W. Second Avenue, Suite 450
Portland, Oregon 97204, U.S.A.
www.timberpress.com
For contact information regarding editorial, marketing,
sales, and distribution in the United Kingdom,
see www.timberpress.co.uk.

Twentieth printing 2005
Printed in Hong Kong

Library of Congress Cataloging-in-Publication Data

Dirr, Michael.
[Hardy trees and shrubs]
Dirr's Hardy trees and shrubs : an illustrated encyclopedia / by Michael A. Dirr
p. cm.
Includes indexes.
ISBN-13: 978-0-88192-404-6
ISBN-10: 0-88192-404-0
1. Ornamental trees—United States—Encyclopedias. 2. Ornamental shrubs—United States—Encyclopedias. 3. Ornamental trees—Encyclopedias. 4. Ornamental shrubs—Encyclopedias. 5. Ornamental trees—United States—Pictorial works. 6. Ornamental shrubs—United States—Pictorial works. 7. Ornamental trees—Pictorial works. 8. Ornamental shrubs—Pictorial works. 9. Landscape plants—United States—Encyclopedias. 10. Landscape plants—Encyclopedias. I. Title.
SB435.5.H37 1997
635.9'77'097303—dc21 96-54032
CIP

To Life's Greatest Treasure . . .
The Dirr Family . . .
Bonnie, Katherine, Matthew, and Suzanne

Contents

Preface
A Few Ruminations from the Author

What the reader sees is the essence of this treatise—a photographic essay that profiles and highlights the most common woody landscape plants adapted to the cooler environments of northern gardens. The principal zone coverage is 3 to 6, although most species will grow into Zones 7 or 8 (using the U.S. Department of Agriculture's Hardiness Zone Map). This book will complement Timber Press's other excellent reference and garden offerings.

A book of this nature requires patience, particularly in regard to the selection of photographs. If a picture is truly worth a thousand words, then extraordinary attention should be afforded each photo selected. All photographs were taken by the author and represent 25 active years in pursuit of the perfect plant specimen. For some species, like *Acer saccharum*, Sugar Maple, I have 300 slides in my collection; for others, like *Heptacodium miconioides*, Seven-Son Flower, there are only five.

For most principal species, a photograph of habit is included. Attendant to this are photos that show the essential ornamental characteristics, such as flower, fruit, fall color, and bark.

The brief text follows a more-or-less defined format for each entry and includes descriptions of habit, foliage and leaf characteristics, flower, fruit, bark, culture, potential landscape use, size, zones of adaptability, and native habitat. Common or more interesting cultivars are presented after the main treatment, often with attendant photographs.

The concept for this book was first discussed in 1983 by me and Mr. Richard Abel, then owner of Timber Press. Mr. Robert Conklin, current owner, has the same zeal for the book as Richard and I. Countless calls, comments, and letters over the years have indicated the need for such a reference. Garden designers, landscape architects, horticulturists, retail garden-center operators, and gardeners have expressed their collective desire for such a book.

It is written by a passionate gardener, plantsman, and observer of the biological world. I hope the book provides a measure of inspiration for the plants and incites the readers to search them out for their gardens and landscapes.

Acknowledgments

Caring is the precursor of excelling. I want to thank Mrs. Betty Johnson, who typed and nurtured the manuscript into readable form. She became part of the creative process and brought the book to fruition.

Also, kudos to Ms. Vickie Waters who provided the organizational skills so necessary when screening 80,000 Kodachromes to a workable quotient of about 1,500. Vickie and the author commiserated over migraines.

To Josh Leventhal and Neal Maillet, editors at Timber Press. Thank you for persisting and fine-tuning the manuscript and photographs.

PART I

A–Z Illustrated Guide to Woody Plants

Prunus ×*yedoensis* 'Akebono'

Abeliophyllum distichum

Korean Abelialeaf, White Forsythia

Many years past, in mid-March I would bundle up my Illinois students and take them south to Bernheim Arboretum, in Clermont, Kentucky, and Cave Hill Cemetery, in Louisville, Kentucky. Consistently, we would find Korean Abelialeaf in full white flower, long before true forsythia ever considered thrusting its yellow head from the buds. Students would ask its identity and then invariably add, "Gosh, it's ugly." True, overgrown specimens and mass plantings of Korean Abelialeaf tend to assume the appearance of an old brush pile. The habit is rounded with arching branches. The white or faintly pink-tinged, four-petaled, fragrant flowers open before the leaves. The 2- to 3½-in.-long, medium to dark green leaves offer no fall color. Plants are easily transplanted and grown. Suitable for massing in full sun. Might be used in a winter-garden border with hellebores, witchhazels, winterhazels, and bulbs. Grows 3 to 5 ft. high, 3 to 4 ft. wide or more. Zones (4)5 to 8. Korea.

Abeliophyllum distichum, Korean Abelialeaf

Abeliophyllum distichum flowers

Abies balsamea needles

Abies, Fir

In the grand scheme of everyday landscaping, the Abies *species are probably utilized less than any other needle evergreens. Their sensitivity to extremes of soil and climate translates to mediocre performance. Where adaptable, they make noble, formal, elegant, aesthetic components to the landscape.*

Abies balsamea

Balsam Fir

A symmetrically pyramidal tree, Balsam Fir has ½- to 1-in.-long, lustrous dark green needles, each with two silver bands on the underside. The 2- to 4-in.-long cones are dark violet when young, turning gray-brown and resinous with maturity. The species requires well-drained, moist, acid soils and some protection from desiccating winds. Use for Christmas tree production, as a specimen, or in groupings. Grows 45 to 75 ft. high, 20 to 25 ft. wide. Zones 3 to 5(6). Labrador to Alberta, south to Pennsylvania.

Abies balsamea, Balsam Fir

Abies concolor

White Fir

No doubt, this is the most adaptable of the firs for landscape work. Under hot, dry conditions, White Fir is the most prosperous fir for general use. The habit is strongly spirelike to narrow-conical, with tiered branches. The 1½- to 2½-in.-long needles vary from green to blue-green to almost silver-blue. In the wilds of Arizona, the silver-blue forms are mixed with the green types. Grows 30 to 50 ft. high, 15 to 20 ft. wide; can grow to 100 ft. or more. Zones 3 to 7. Western United States.

Cultivars and Varieties. 'Violacea' is a silver-blue form of great beauty, especially when the new growth emerges.

Abies concolor, White Fir

Abies concolor 'Violacea' foliage

Abies fraseri

Fraser Fir

Mentioned here only because of its similarity to *Abies balsamea* and its importance as a Christmas tree. The actual differences between this species and *A. balsamea* are minimal, and it could be considered a southern extension. Grows 30 to 40 ft. high, 20 to 25 ft. wide. Zones 4 to 7. Mountains of West Virginia, North Carolina, and Tennessee.

Abies fraseri, Fraser Fir

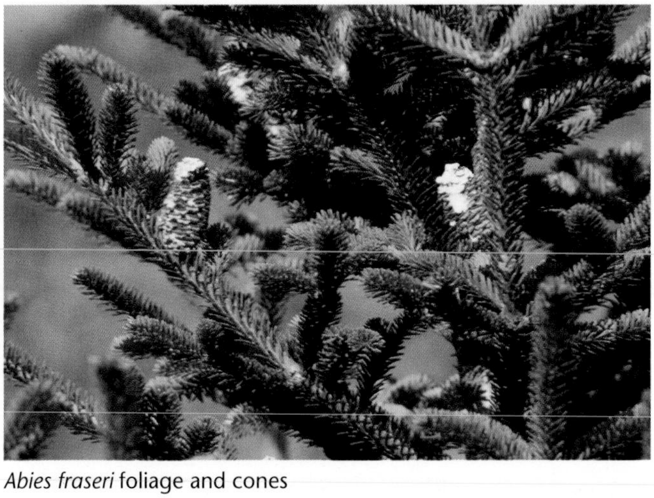

Abies fraseri foliage and cones

Abies homolepis
Nikko Fir

The few Nikko Fir trees that I have observed were quite handsome specimens. It is typically spirelike and conical in habit. Needles are glossy dark green with two white bands on the lower surface. Grows 30 to 50 ft. high; can grow 100 to 130 ft. high in its native Japan. Zones 4 to 6. Japan.

Abies homolepis, Nikko Fir

Abies nordmanniana
Nordmann Fir

A magnificent fir. At its best, this species forms a dense, uniform pyramid of lustrous black-green needles. May be more adaptable than *Abies balsamea* and *A. fraseri* to general landscape conditions. Grows 40 to 60 ft. high in cultivation; can reach 200 ft. high in the wild. Zones 4 to 6. Caucasus, Asia Minor.

Abies nordmanniana, Nordmann Fir

Abies veitchii, Veitch Fir

Abies veitchii
Veitch Fir

Another handsome dark green species that has performed reasonably well in the Midwest. Needles average 1 in. long and have two silver-white bands on the undersides. Grows 50 to 75 ft. high, 25 to 30 ft. wide. Zones 3 to 6. Japan.

Abies veitchii, undersides of the needles

Acanthopanax sieboldianus
Fiveleaf Aralia

This is one of the toughest, most nearly indestructible shrubs available. Almost impossible to locate in commerce, it is frequently found in older landscapes as a hedge or massing plant. By no means dainty, open-grown specimens of *Acanthopanax sieboldianus* become massive, rounded shrubs. The dark green leaves are composed of five to seven 1- to 2½-in.-long, serrated leaflets. The greenish white flowers are undistinguished and the black fruit seldom, if ever, set. Easily cultured, it will prevail in urban situations and appears quite tolerant of air pollution. Grows where little else will. Use in groupings and masses, in shade or full sun, on clay or rock scrabble. Grows 8 to 10 ft. high and wide. Zones 4 to 8. Japan.

Cultivars and Varieties. 'Variegatus', more commonly available than the species, has leaflets with irregular creamy white margins. Good for brightening a shady corner of the garden. Grows more slowly than the species, to 6 to 8 ft. high and wide.

Acanthopanax sieboldianus, Fiveleaf Aralia

Acanthopanax sieboldianus 'Variegatus' foliage

Acer buergerianum
Trident Maple

Small, dapper, handsomely clothed trees are a rarity, and Trident Maple qualifies as one of the best. The habit is oval to rounded. The pest-free, lustrous dark green, 1½- to 3½-in.-wide leaves are three lobed (hence, trident). They change to rich yellow and red in fall. Bark on old trunks is quite striking, coloring gray, orange, and brown and developing an exfoliating, platy, scaly character. This species withstands drought and infertile soils and displays excellent cold and heat tolerance. Unlike many maples, *Acer buergerianum* does not develop leaf scorch under drought stress. A fine choice for the small residential landscape, as a street tree, or under utility wires. Grows 25 to 35 ft. high, 15 to 25 ft. wide. Zones 5 to 8(9). China.

Acer buergerianum, Trident Maple

Acer buergerianum fall color

Acer buergerianum bark

Acer buergerianum in winter

Acer campestre
Hedge Maple

The common name is appropriately derived from the use of this species for hedging purposes, especially in Europe, where it occurs naturally in the famed hedgerows along highways. As a medium-sized lawn tree, it has few rivals. The habit is rounded and dense. The dark green leaves, 2 to 4 in. long and wide, are composed of five rounded lobes. Leaves usually die off late in fall but on occasion turn yellow. Displays excellent tolerance to drought and heat. Good for use along streets, in lawns and parks, and fashioned into a hedge. Grows 25 to 35 ft. high and wide; can reach 75 ft. high. Zones 4 to 8. Europe, Near East, Africa.

Cultivars and Varieties. Queen Elizabeth™ ('Evelyn') is more vigorous than the species. Its branches angle at 45°. The dark green leaves are larger than those of the species and develop yellowish fall color. Matures to a medium-sized tree with a flat top and rounded outline.

Acer campestre, Hedge Maple

Acer campestre, Hedge Maple, pruned as a hedge

Acer campestre in fall

Acer campestre Queen Elizabeth™

Acer ginnala
Amur Maple

This species ranks as one of the most cold-hardy maples, and certainly one of the most adaptable. Grown as a large shrub or small tree, it serves many landscape purposes. In its finest form, the tree is "limbed up," exposing the smooth gray bark and creating an artistic, sculptural element. The three-lobed, 1½- to 3-in.-long leaves change from a rich dark green to excellent shades of yellow, orange, and red in fall. Fragrant, creamy white flowers appear with the new foliage in April and May, and the wings of the fruit often turn handsome red in August and September. It is the first maple, and one of the first woody plants, to leaf out in the spring. Displays excellent tolerance to dry and alkaline soils. Fine plant for raised planters, narrow tree lawns, and difficult sites. Grows 15 to 18 ft. high and wide. Zones 3 to 8. Central to northeastern China, Japan.

Acer ginnala, Amur Maple

Acer ginnala foliage and flowers

Acer ginnala fruit

Acer ginnala fall color

Acer griseum
Paperbark Maple

If more widely available in commerce, Paperbark Maple would be a common plant in American gardens. Its paucity can be related to the difficulty associated with propagation—poor seed quality and very difficult to root. As an element in a winter landscape, however, it has few peers. The rich cinnamon to reddish brown exfoliating bark commands center stage, especially when framed by snow. Habit is that of a small tree, ranging from oval to rounded in outline. The dark bluish green, 3- to 6-in.-long, trifoliate leaves often turn brilliant red in fall, but superior fall color is more common in the East than in the Midwest. The species is extremely tolerant of acid or alkaline clay soils, as long as they are well drained. No two specimens are exactly alike, and such individuality provides for excellent landscape effect. Serves well as a specimen or small lawn tree, in a shrub border, or in groupings. No finer tree could be recommended. Grows 20 to 30 ft. high and wide. Zones 4 to 8. Central China.

Other trifoliate maples that offer excellent fall color and/or bark include: *Acer mandschuricum*, Manchurian Maple, with fluorescent, pinkish red fall color and smooth gray bark; *A. maximowiczianum (A. nikoense)*, Nikko Maple, with yellow, red, or purple (often muted red) fall color and smooth gray bark; and *A. triflorum*, Threeflower Maple, with brilliant orange to red fall color and ash-brown exfoliating bark.

Acer griseum, Paperbark Maple

Acer griseum fall color

Acer griseum bark

Acer griseum in winter

Acer japonicum, Fullmoon Maple

Acer japonicum 'Vitifolium' in fall

Acer japonicum 'Aconitifolium' fall color

Acer japonicum foliage

Acer japonicum

Fullmoon Maple

Although not as popular as its close relative *Acer palmatum*, Japanese Maple, this small, rounded tree offers excellent fall foliage and has several outstanding cultivars. The 3- to 6-in.-wide, rich green leaves are composed of seven to eleven lobes. The sinuses are not as deeply cut as those of *A. palmatum*. In autumn, the leaves change to vibrant yellows and reds. Purplish red flowers, ½ in. in diameter, appear in great numbers on long-stalked, nodding corymbs in April. The smooth gray bark is quite handsome. Culture is similar to that of *A. palmatum*, except *A. japonicum* does not appear to be quite as heat tolerant. Grows 20 to 30 ft. high and wide. Zones 5 to 7. Japan.

Cultivars and Varieties. 'Aconitifolium' has nine- to eleven-lobed leaves that are cut to within ¼ to ½ in. of the petiole. Each major lobe is again divided and sharply toothed, producing a fernlike texture. Fall color is spectacular orange to crimson. Rounded and shrubby in habit. Grows 8 to 10 ft. high.

'Aureum' is a pretty yellow-leaved selection. The color holds quite well, except in intense heat. Fall color is a handsome golden yellow. It has a distinct upright, vase-shaped habit, with the branches suspended in cloudlike strata. Now placed as a cultivar of *Acer shirasawanum*. Grows 10 to 20 ft. high.

'Vitifolium' has grapelike leaves, 4 to 6 in. long and wide, that turn rich shades of yellow, orange, red, and purple in autumn. Grows 20 to 25 ft. high and wide.

Acer japonicum 'Aureum'

Acer negundo
Boxelder

Acer negundo, Boxelder, in fall

For those areas of the country where tree culture is fraught with difficulty, this species can be recommended. The ornamental attributes are limited, but Boxelder's adaptability to dry or wet soils and to inhospitable climatic conditions provide a legitimate basis for utilization. Habit is rounded to broad-rounded, but there is no constancy to this character and *Acer negundo* may appear as an unkempt shrub, a gaunt tree, or a biological fright. The light green leaves are composed of three to five 2- to 4-in.-long leaflets that turn yellowish in fall but are not particularly striking. It is dioecious (sexes separate), and female trees set prodigious quantities of fruit, which leads to supra-optimal quantities of seedlings. Wood is subject to breakage, insects, and diseases. Temperance is the rule when considering this species. Grows 30 to 50 ft. high, variable spread. Zones 2 to 9. United States, Canada.

Cultivars and Varieties. Several variegated cultivars have been described, the best being 'Variegatum', with cream-margined leaves. It is spectacular for summer foliage color, but it requires partial shade. 'Auratum' has yellow leaves, and 'Flamingo' has brilliant pink new leaves that mature to green with a white border.

Acer negundo 'Flamingo'

Acer negundo foliage

Acer negundo 'Variegatum' foliage

Acer palmatum, Japanese Maple

Acer palmatum in winter

Acer palmatum var. *atropurpureum* 'Bloodgood'

Acer palmatum 'Sango Kaku' winter stems

Acer palmatum var. *dissectum* branches and bark

Acer palmatum
Japanese Maple

True aristocrats are rare among people and trees, but Japanese Maple is in the first order. It is difficult to imagine a garden that could not benefit from one of the many forms of *Acer palmatum*. The normal habit is round to broad-rounded, with the branches assuming a layered, almost stratified architecture similar to *Cornus florida*, Flowering Dogwood. The five- to nine-lobed, finely serrated, 2- to 5-in.- long and wide leaves vary from light green to dark green; the variety *atropurpureum* offers shades of reddish purple. Fall color is sensational, for rich yellows and reds develop consistently from fall to fall. The color persists and may be effective as late as November. The winter silhouette is also attractive and, coupled with the smooth gray bark, provides interest during the "off season." Landscape uses for the species and its many cultivars are limited only by the imagination of the gardener. Soils should be evenly moist, acid, organic-laden, and well drained. Grows 15 to 25 ft. high and wide; 40-ft. specimens are known. Zones 5 to 8. Japan.

Cultivars and Varieties. Hundreds of selections have been made. For a detailed and meticulous accounting, refer to J. D. Vertrees's *Japanese Maples* (Portland, OR: Timber Press, 1987).

'Bloodgood' and 'Moonfire' are two of the best var. *atropurpureum* types for retaining reddish purple foliage, particularly in intense heat.

var. *dissectum* offers finely cut leaves and a shrubby habit, with picturesque contorted, twisted, and convoluted branches. Forms a broad, billowy, cloudlike mound. A sight to behold in fall when the foliage is on fire. Grows 6 to 8 ft. high and wide.

'Sango Kaku' is an upright, vase-shaped form. It has green leaves, yellow fall color, and coral orange-red winter stems.

Acer palmatum var. *atropurpureum* 'Moonfire'

Acer pensylvanicum
Striped Maple

This species belongs to a group of maples termed "snakebarks." The unflattering nickname refers to the whitish vertical fissures that develop on the bark, which when set against the greenish background conjure visions of a snake's skin. Habit is upright-oval to oval-rounded. The bright green leaves, 5 to 7 in. long and wide, turn soft yellows in fall and provide a candle glow in the northern woods. *Acer pensylvanicum* occurs as an understory species in the wild and does not compete well when transported to cultivation. The vagaries of domesticated environments often wreak havoc. Cool, evenly moist, acidic soils are optimal. Grows 15 to 20 (to 30) ft. high, similar spread. Zones 3 to 7; use only at higher elevations farther south. Quebec to Wisconsin, south to northern Georgia.

Other species with somewhat similar traits include: *Acer capillipes*; *A. davidii*, David Maple; *A. rufinerve*, Redvein Maple; and *A. tegmentosum*, Manchustriped Maple.

Acer pensylvanicum, Striped Maple, in fall

Acer pensylvanicum foliage

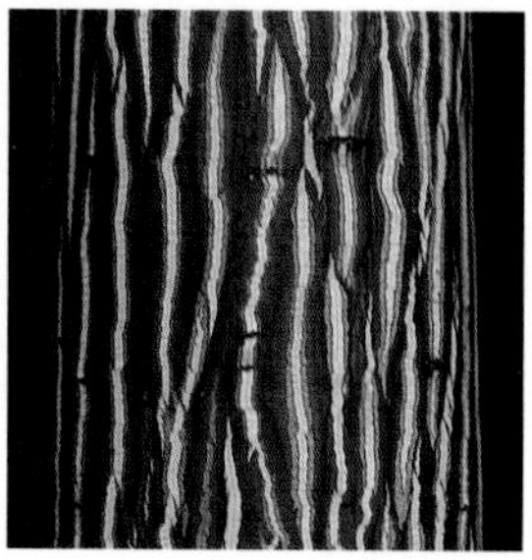

Acer pensylvanicum bark

Acer platanoides
Norway Maple

Commonality breeds contempt, and many gardeners have tired of Norway Maple, long a staple for street and urban use, with street after street planted with this maple species. Stress tolerances of the tree are also now being questioned. The rounded outline is common to young and mature trees. In spring, lovely yellow flowers smother the as-yet-leafless branches. The dark green, 4- to 7-in.-wide leaves may turn rich yellow in fall and, when environmental conditions are optimal, can be spectacular. Generally quite tolerant of extremes of soil and climate. Grows 40 to 50 ft. high, similar spread. Zones 3 to 7. Europe.

Cultivars and Varieties. Numerous cultivars have been selected over the centuries, and some, such as 'Crimson King' (reddish purple leaves) and 'Schwedleri' (reddish purple in spring, fading to green), have become more common than the species. 'Cleveland', 'Emerald Queen', and 'Summershade' offer the greatest hope for the landscape.

Acer platanoides 'Crimson King' foliage

Acer platanoides, Norway Maple

Acer platanoides 'Cleveland'

Acer pseudoplatanus, Sycamore Maple

Acer pseudoplatanus 'Brilliantissimum' foliage

Acer pseudoplatanus 'Leopoldii' foliage

Acer pseudoplatanus

Planetree or Sycamore Maple

A weed in Europe and some portions of the eastern United States, *Acer pseudoplatanus* has never received the acceptance of the native maple species because it lacks their dignity and excellent fall color. The branching pattern is distinctly upright-spreading, the ultimate silhouette approaching oval to oval-rounded. The five-lobed, 3- to 6-in.-wide, dark green leaves seldom display good fall color. Bark on mature trees becomes brown or grayish, with rectangular exfoliating scales exposing the orangish brown inner bark. Tolerates sandy or clay-based soils and saline conditions. Grows 40 to 60 ft. high, 25 to 40 ft. wide. Zones 4 to 7. Europe, western Asia.

Cultivars and Varieties. 'Atropurpureum' has leaves that are purplish on their lower surface.

'Brilliantissimum' is a slow-growing rounded form with shrimp-pink new leaves that turn cream to yellow-green. Widely used in Europe, occasionally seen in New England.

'Leopoldii' has white-speckled leaves in a pattern reminiscent of marble cake.

Acer pseudoplatanus bark

Acer rubrum

Red Maple

A Red Maple from Florida is not the same as a Red Maple from Maine. The name may be the same, but leaf shape, degree of leaf retention, fall color, and cold hardiness are distinctly different. A Red Maple from Florida will die in Maine, and vice versa. In either locale, *Acer rubrum* forms a pyramidal or elliptical outline in youth, becoming ovoid, rounded, or irregular at maturity. Reddish flowers appear in early spring and are followed by red fruit. The smooth gray bark is quite attractive, particularly on young plants. Emerging leaves are reddish tinged, changing to medium or dark green and reaching 2 to 5 in. in length. Foliage often develops glorious yellows and reds in fall. In the wild, a pure yellow fall-colored specimen will rub branches with a rich red plant. The colors of New England autumns are a spectacular mix of Red Maple, Sugar Maple, and birch—no sight is more magnificent or more memorable. *Acer rubrum* is a cosmopolitan species and can be found in swamps, mixed forest situations, and rocky uplands. When correctly utilized, it makes a fine tree for lawns, streets, or parks. Grows 40 to 60 ft. high, variable spread. Zones 3 to 9. Newfoundland to Minnesota, south to Florida and Texas.

Acer rubrum, Red Maple

Cultivars and Varieties. 'Armstrong', 'Bowhall' ('Scanlon'), 'Columnare', 'Karpick', and 'Scarlet Sentinel' are upright, columnar-pyramidal forms. 'Armstrong' and 'Bowhall' are the most common of these and arguably the best.

'Autumn Blaze' is a cultivar of the hybrid *(Acer ×freemanii)* of *A. rubrum* and *A. saccharinum*, Silver Maple. It grows rapidly and displays excellent red fall color.

'October Glory' and 'Red Sunset' are the most widely known and utilized selections, offering excellent orange-red to red fall color.

Acer rubrum 'October Glory' fall color

Acer rubrum in fall

Acer saccharinum
Silver Maple

Once the most widely planted native maple, Silver Maple has fallen into disfavor with nursery people and gardeners. Broken limbs, limited ornamental attributes, and a gross-feeding root system that buckles sidewalks and clogs drains have inhibited its planting. The fastest growing maple species, it is at the same time the most susceptible to breakage in storms. Habit is oval to rounded, with strongly upright, spreading branches. The five-lobed, deeply cut, 3- to 6-in.-long leaves are dark green with silvery backs, creating a rather attractive effect when the wind buffets and exposes the undersides. The flowers often open before those of *Acer rubrum* and range in color from yellowish to a good red. The species is extremely adaptable to varied soils. A reasonable choice where few other species will grow or where there is need for a truly fast-growing shade tree. Grows 50 to 70 ft. high, 30 to 45 ft. wide. Zones 3 to 9. Quebec to Florida, west to Minnesota, Oklahoma, and Louisiana.

Cultivars and Varieties. 'Silver Queen' represents an improvement on the species because of its better habit and its lack of fruit, reducing the nuisances of litter and invasiveness.

Acer rubrum 'Bowhall'

Acer rubrum 'Red Sunset' in fall

Acer saccharinum, Silver Maple, in fall

Acer saccharinum 'Silver Queen'

Acer saccharum
Sugar Maple

The true nobility of fall-coloring trees—challenged by many, rivaled by none. Traveling on a quiet country lane in Massachusetts, Indiana, or Pennsylvania on an October day yields a spectacular experience: the yellow, orange, and red palette of Sugar Maple. The soul is soothed, and one is able to cope with the tribulations of daily life. The habit of this tree is distinctly upright-oval to rounded. Displays attractive gray-brown bark. The five-lobed, 3- to 6-in.- long and wide leaves range from medium to dark green in summer. Greenish yellow flowers emerge before the leaves and from a distance appear as a soft haze. Well-drained, evenly moist, acid soils suit it best. *Acer saccharum* does tolerate less-than-ideal conditions, although it is not a tree for high-stress environments. Makes a great lawn, park, campus, golf-course, or large-area tree. Grows 60 to 75 ft. high, 40 to 50 ft. wide. Zones 3 to 8. Eastern Canada to Georgia, west to Texas.

Cultivars and Varieties. 'Commemoration', 'Green Mountain', and 'Legacy' have thick, waxy textured leaves, rapid growth rates, yellow-orange fall color, and excellent heat tolerance. 'Legacy' has proven the toughest of the cultivars in Kansas and South Carolina tests.

'Monumentale' ('Temple's Upright') is a handsome broad-columnar form.

Acer saccharum, Sugar Maple, in fall

Acer tataricum
Tatarian Maple

In many respects, this species is a carbon copy of *Acer ginnala*, Amur Maple, except the leaves do not develop the strong lobing found in those of the latter. The habit is also more treelike and the fruit more consistently red than those of *A. ginnala*. Fall color of *A. tataricum* is seldom pronounced and does not rival Amur Maple's. Displays tolerance to dry and high pH soils. A good small specimen tree for the residential landscape. Grows 15 to 20 ft. high and wide. Zones 3 to 8. Southeast Europe, western Asia.

Acer saccharum 'Monumentale'

Acer saccharum 'Legacy' fall color

Acer tataricum, Tatarian Maple

Acer tataricum fruit and foliage

Acer tataricum fruit

Acer truncatum
Shantung or Purpleblow Maple

This is another small maple that could be effectively utilized in urban situations. It is a small, round-headed tree with a neat outline and a regular branching pattern. The five-lobed, 3- to 5-in.-wide, lustrous dark green leaves turn yellow-orange and red in fall. Bright yellow flowers emerge before the leaves in April. It is tolerant of acid, alkaline, and dry soils, making it well suited to the rigors of the urban landscape. Fine specimens found in Maine, on the campus of the University of Maine at Orono, and in Iowa attest to the northern adaptability of the tree. In situations where *Acer platanoides* and *A. rubrum* grow excessively large, this is a fine choice. Grows 20 to 25 ft. high, similar spread. Zones 4 to 8. Northern China.

Acer truncatum subsp. *mono*, Painted Maple, is slightly larger than the species, somewhat vase-shaped with a domelike crown at maturity.

Acer truncatum, Shantung Maple

Acer truncatum fall color

Acer truncatum subsp. *mono*, Painted Maple

Actinidia arguta
Bower Actinidia

This vigorous twining vine, with beautiful lustrous dark green foliage, appears restricted only by the structure to which it is attached. I have seen 30-ft.-high plants climbing drain spouts on large buildings and 8-ft.-high plants on small trellislike structures. The 3- to 5-in.-long leaves have undulating surfaces and red petioles. Leaves hold late and seldom develop any fall color. Whitish, ¾-in.-diameter, fragrant flowers develop from the axils of the stems in May and June, after the leaves have emerged, and are essentially hidden from view. Edible, greenish yellow berries, 1 to 1¼ in. long and ¾ in. wide, ripen in fall. This is an excellent vine for difficult sites. Tremendously adaptable to acid or high pH soils, and withstands sun or shade. Obviously a rampant grower and should be considered for large-area use. Requires support. Grows 25 to 30 ft. high. Zones 3 to 8. Japan, Korea, northeastern China.

Actinidia kolomikta
Kolomikta Actinidia

This species is less rampant than *Actinidia arguta* and offers exquisite white- to pink-blotched foliage. The coloration occurs from the middle of the leaf to the tip. The 3- to 6-in.-long leaves emerge purplish tinged and develop the white, pink, and dark green combinations. Young plants do not have the strong coloration of mature plants. Supposedly, males are more strongly colored than females. The vividness of the color is reduced by hot weather, and excess fertility or shade will also reduce coloration. Ideally plants should be purchased in leaf to assure trueness. White, ½-in.-diameter, fragrant flowers appear in the leaf axils during May and June. The fruit are sweet, edible, greenish yellow, 1-in.-long berries that ripen in September and October. *Actinidia kolomikta* is as adaptable as *A. arguta*. Probably better suited to the smaller landscape. Grows 15 to 20 ft. high or more. Zones 4 to 8; plants can survive Zone 2 temperatures (–45°F). Northeastern Asia to Japan, central and western China.

Actinidia arguta, Bower Actinidia

Actinidia kolomikta, Kolomikta Actinidia

Actinidia arguta flowers

Actinidia kolomikta flowers

Actinidia polygama
Silver-Vine

Extremely rare in cultivation, and in all my travels I have encountered the plant on only two or three occasions. It is the weakest growing of the *Actinidia* species presented here. The 3- to 5-in.-long leaves are marked with a silver-white to yellowish color on male plants. White, ½- to ¾-in.-diameter, fragrant flowers open in June and July. The 1-in.-long, greenish yellow berries are edible. The chief advantages of this species are its less-vigorous nature and smaller stature. Like the other actinidias discussed, it is a twining vine and requires support. Grows 10 to 15 ft. high. Zones 4 to 7. Japan, central and northeastern China.

Actinidia polygama, Silver-Vine

Actinidia polygama foliage

Actinidia polygama flower

Aesculus ×*carnea*
Red Horsechestnut

A hybrid between *Aesculus pavia* and *A. hippocastanum* that is superior to either parent species for general landscape use. The habit is rounded to broad-rounded, with the stout, close-knit branches creating a dense canopy. The leaves are composed of five to seven lustrous dark green leaflets. In May, 6- to 8-in.-high and 3- to 4-in.-wide panicles of rose-red flowers cover the tree. For flower effect, it is spectacular. Red Horsechestnuts are susceptible to a blight (fungal disease) that causes a browning of the leaves in summer and fall. This tree prefers moist, deep, well-drained soils, but it is widely adaptable to soil types. Worth considering for parks, campuses, golf courses, and other large-area uses. It is widely planted in Europe in parks, on residential lots, and along streets. Grows 30 to 40 ft. high and wide. Zones 4 to 7.

Cultivars and Varieties. 'Briotii' has flowers that are deeper red and held in longer panicles (to 10 in.).

Aesculus ×*carnea*, Red Horsechestnut

Aesculus glabra
Ohio Buckeye

This native species is commonly found in moist soils and there makes its best growth. As a general landscape plant, it offers limited promise. Mildew, leaf blight, and scorch often disfigure the trees. If native in an area, it should be protected and worked into the framework of the landscape. Generally rounded in habit, the plant appears quite coarse in winter. The dark green leaves are composed of five to seven 3- to 6-in.-long leaflets. Foliage may change to pumpkin-orange in fall, but fall color is variable and seldom consistent from tree to tree. Greenish yellow flowers are borne in 4- to 7-in.-long and 2- to 3-in.-wide terminal panicles during May and are almost lost among the leaves. The fruit are prickly, dehiscent capsules that contain the shiny, rich brown seeds known as buckeyes. Grows 20 to 40 ft. high and wide. Zones 3 to 7. Pennsylvania to Alabama, west to Kansas.

Aesculus ×*carnea* 'Briotii'

Aesculus ×*carnea* foliage

Aesculus ×*carnea* flowers

Aesculus glabra, Ohio Buckeye

Aesculus glabra fruit

Aesculus hippocastanum
Common Horsechestnut

A common species in the Midwest and New England that is seldom planted anymore in the United States. In Europe, it graces parks and gardens and is one of the dominant landscape species. Like *Aesculus glabra*, it is afflicted (at least in the United States) with a blotch that causes an unsightly browning of the leaves by summer. When unadulterated, it can command a kingly presence. Trees vary in shape from upright-oval to rounded. The dark green leaves are composed of seven (occasionally five) 5- to 10-in.-long leaflets that turn a respectable yellow in fall. White flowers are borne in May in 5- to 12-in.-long and 2- to 5-in.-wide terminal panicles. The spiny, capsular, 2- to 2½-in.-diameter fruit each contain one or two rich brown seeds. Grows 50 to 75 ft. high, variable spread. Zones 3 to 7. Greece, Albania.

Cultivars and Varieties. 'Baumannii' is the best of the many cultivars that have been selected. It has double white sterile flowers (no fruit are produced).

Aesculus hippocastanum, Common Horsechestnut

Aesculus hippocastanum flowers

Aesculus hippocastanum foliage

Aesculus octandra
Yellow Buckeye

Of the native tree buckeyes, this species is certainly the most spectacular and, from a landscape standpoint, the most trouble free. In the mountains of north Georgia, 80- to 100-ft.-high specimens can be found in moist coves. In a comparable environment, *Aesculus octandra* appears less prone to disease than *A.* ×*carnea*, *A. glabra*, and *A. hippocastanum*. The habit is upright-oval, and the upper branches develop a slight spreading outline. The dark green leaves are composed of five 4- to 6-in.-long leaflets that turn yellow to pumpkin-orange in fall. Greenish yellow flowers appear in May and, like those of *A. glabra*, are somewhat masked by the foliage. The smooth, pear-shaped, brownish capsules house one or two buckeyes. The bark is a rather curious combination of gray and brown, with large, flat, smooth plates and scales on old trunks. Grows 60 to 75 ft. high, 30 to 50 ft. wide. Zones 4 to 8. Pennsylvania to Illinois, south to Tennessee and northern Georgia.

Aesculus hippocastanum 'Baumannii'

Aesculus parviflora
Bottlebrush Buckeye

Over my career, I have given hundreds of garden and nursery talks, and this species has probably appeared in 90 percent of them. Truly one of the best native shrubs for late-spring and early-summer flower. This broad-mounded, suckering shrub can colonize a large piece of real estate. The wonderful coarse-textured, dark green leaves are composed of five to seven 3- to 8-in.-long leaflets that turn rich butter-yellow in fall. The 8- to 12-in.-long, bottlebrush-shaped inflorescences contain hundreds of white, four-petaled flowers with pinkish white stamens that stand out an inch from the petals. The inflorescences occur at the ends of the branches and are held upright. Interestingly, this species flowers almost as prolifically in shade as in sun. Smooth, 1- to 3-in.-long, pear-shaped, light brown capsules contain one or two shiny, light brown seeds. Bottlebrush Buckeye requires moist, well-drained soils for best growth, although quality specimens are found in every conceivable situation. Transplant balled and burlapped or from a container. Ideal for underplanting in woodlands or for use in shrub borders and large masses. Grows 8 to 12 ft. high, 8 to 15 ft. wide. Zones 4 to 8. South Carolina to Alabama and Florida.

Cultivars and Varieties. var. *serotina* flowers two to three weeks later than the species. 'Roger's' is a selection of var. *serotina* with inflorescences fully 18 to 30 in. long.

Aesculus octandra, Yellow Buckeye

Aesculus octandra bark

Aesculus parviflora var. *serotina* 'Roger's' flowers

Aesculus parviflora, Bottlebrush Buckeye

Aesculus parviflora in fall

Aesculus pavia
Red Buckeye

Another native buckeye that inhabits woodlands and spends its life in the shadows of large trees. When grouped or massed in light shade provided by pines, the effect can be spectacular. The brilliant dark green leaves, each with five to seven 3- to 6-in.-long leaflets, are among the handsomest leaves of the native buckeyes. Rich red flowers appear in April and May in 3- to 6-in.-long and 1½- to 3-in.-wide panicles above the foliage. The smooth brown capsules harbor one or two lustrous dark brown seeds. Habit is rounded, but there is significant variation, and at times the plant appears almost shrublike. This is a fine plant for naturalizing in moist soils and where there is a modicum of shade. Like *Aesculus glabra*, it abhors dry soils and tends to develop leaf scorch or to defoliate, often by August or September. Grows 15 to 20 ft. high and wide. Zones 4 to 8. Virginia to Florida, west to Texas.

Aesculus pavia, Red Buckeye

Aesculus pavia flowers

Ailanthus altissima
Tree-of-Heaven

The tree that grows in Brooklyn could be none other than this species. Tough, persistent, and durable to a fault, it has few redeeming landscape features. Asphalt, sidewalks, or construction seldom deter it from making an appearance. If its genes could be transferred to our agronomic crops, the need for pesticides would nearly disappear. In its finest form, the habit is upright-spreading, open, and coarse, with clubby branches. The dark green, 18- to 24-in.-long, compound pinnate leaves, composed of 13 to 15 leaflets, display no propensity to develop fall color. Yellow-green flowers appear in June, and male flowers have a particularly vile odor. Unfortunately, female plants set prodigious quantities of fruit, and the resulting seedlings can be troublesome. For impossible landscape situations, this might be an acceptable choice. Grows 40 to 60 ft. high. Zones 4 to 8. China, naturalized over much of the United States.

Ailanthus altissima, Tree-of-Heaven

Akebia quinata
Fiveleaf Akebia

Ailanthus altissima flowers and foliage

I have a strong love-hate relationship with this most vigorous twining vine. When restrained by proper pruning, the bronzy purple new leaves, which mature to rich blue-green, the rosy purple flowers, and the purple-violet pods add up to a spectacular ornamental vine. Left to its own devices, however, it will colonize an area, twining around, over, and through other plants, shading them like Kudzu. The leaves, composed of five 1½- to 3-in.-long leaflets, emerge early, often by March, and then persist, often into December. The flowers are hidden beneath the foliage and are curiously interesting. The three-sepaled, 1-in.-diameter, chocolatey purple, slightly fragrant female flowers occur separately from the smaller, lighter-colored males. The 2¼- to 4-in.-long fruit resemble fattened, violet-purple sausages. Fruit set is dependent upon another clone being available for cross-pollination. Adaptable to sun or shade, moist or dry soils, low or high pH, *Akebia quinata* is difficult to kill once in place. It is somewhat stoloniferous, which allows it to colonize and cover large ground areas. On a fence or other suitable structure, it is a respectable plant. I have also observed it as a groundcover. Use with the knowledge that it can transcend the boundaries imposed. There are white- and pink-flowered forms, as well as a white-fruited form. Grows 20 to 40 ft. Zones 4 to 8. Central and northeastern China, Korea, Japan.

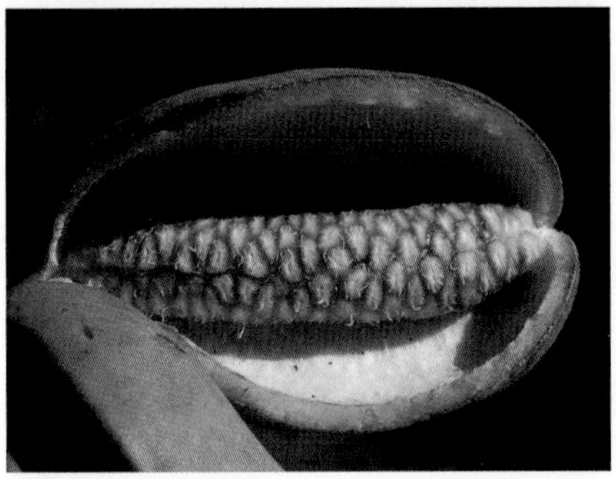

Akebia quinata fruit

Akebia quinata female flowers

Akebia quinata, Fiveleaf Akebia

Albizia julibrissin
Silk Tree, Albizia, Mimosa

Certainly a handsome small tree when the flowers appear like rosy pink brush strokes across a green canvas. Unfortunately, this member of the legume family is extraordinarily susceptible to a wilt disease that causes gradual decline and eventual death. The habit is vase-shaped with a broad-spreading, flat-topped crown. Rich green, almost tropical-looking leaves, to 20 in. in length, hold late in autumn and develop no appreciable fall color. This is one of the last trees to leaf out in spring. The fragrant, pink, brushlike flowers appear in July and August and are followed by 5- to 7-in.-long, gray-brown pods. Extremely tolerant of droughty, alkaline soils. At one time considered a choice small flowering tree, it is questionable in today's landscapes because of its disease susceptibility. Grows 20 to 35 ft. high and wide. Zones 6 to 9; low temperatures around –5 to –10°F result in some stem dieback. Iran to central China.

Cultivars and Varieties. var. *rosea* ('Ernest Wilson') is considerably more cold hardy than the typical species and tolerates –15°F.

Albizia julibrissin, Silk Tree

Albizia julibrissin foliage

Albizia julibrissin flowers

Alnus cordata
Italian Alder

In landscape status, the Italian Alder most assuredly plays second fiddle to its close relative *Alnus glutinosa*, European Alder. Ornamentally, however, this species is superior. The lustrous dark green, 2- to 4-in.-long leaves are attractive throughout the seasons. In early spring, the yellowish brown, pendulous catkins sway in the soft breeze. The large (1 in. long), egg-shaped fruit look like small pine cones. Habit is pyramidal to pyramidal-oval, and after the leaves fall, a clean, finely branched winter silhouette is evident. An excellent choice near water, but it is also at home in drier soils. Withstands infertile, high pH soils. Deserves a longer look by American gardeners. Grows 30 to 50 ft. high, 20 to 40 ft. wide. Zones 5 to 7(8). Corsica, southern Italy.

Alnus cordata foliage

Alnus cordata, Italian Alder

Alnus cordata bark

Alnus cordata fruit

Alnus glutinosa

Common or European Alder

This dark, somber broadleaf tree is often found in the English landscape, especially along watercourses. In America, it has naturalized along stream banks to the point of weediness. In youth the outline is pyramidal and with maturity becomes ovoid or oblong and somewhat irregular. It has often been grown multistemmed and makes an attractive specimen. The dark green, 2- to 4-in.-long, 3- to 4-in.-wide leaves offer no hint of fall color and die off green or brown. One of the best trees for wet soils, it can endure standing water for a time. It fixes atmospheric nitrogen and is able to survive infertile soils. Tent caterpillars can be a problem. Grows 40 to 60 ft. high, 20 to 40 ft. wide. Zones 3 to 7. Europe, western Asia, northern Africa.

Cultivars and Varieties. 'Imperialis' bears finely dissected leaves and provides a much finer-textured imprint on the landscape.

'Pyramidalis' ('Fastigiata') is a distinct columnar form not unlike Lombardy Poplar, *Populus nigra* 'Italica'. It can be used for screening in areas where *Alnus glutinosa* would spread out-of-bounds.

Alnus glutinosa male flowers

Alnus glutinosa foliage

Alnus glutinosa, Common Alder

Alnus glutinosa 'Imperialis'

Alnus glutinosa 'Pyramidalis'

Amelanchier arborea

Downy Serviceberry; also Juneberry, Shadbush, Service-Tree, Sarvis-Tree

One of the finest native North American species for naturalizing at the edge of woodlands. In the wild, it occurs along streams and on rocky slopes as a small tree or a large, multistemmed shrub of rounded outline. The emerging leaves are covered with numerous hairs, which impart an almost pussy-willow effect. Leaves mature to a rich green, 1 to 3 in. long, and in October they color yellow, orange, and apricot to dull, deep, dusty red. White flowers, in fleecy 2- to 4-in.-long racemes, appear slightly before or with the leaves in April. In June, the ¼- to ⅓-in.-diameter fruit mature from green to red and finally to purple-black. The fruit taste much like those of Highbush Blueberry *(Vaccinium corymbosum)* but are slightly sweeter, and they make outstanding pies. Birds are particularly fond of the fruit, so it is often a race between homeowner and feathered creature. With the annual rites of winter, the beautiful smooth, grayish streaked bark assumes center stage and provides an excellent effect. Downy Serviceberry is adaptable to acid and high pH soils, and to moist or relatively dry situations. Many cultivars have been introduced, including several notable selections of the hybrid of *Amelanchier arborea* and *A. laevis*, *A.* ×*grandiflora* (see page 42). Its cosmopolitan nature should endear this species to more gardeners. At home in Chicago, Boston, and Atlanta. Grows 15 to 25 ft. high, variable spread; can grow to 40 ft. Zones 4 to 9. Maine to Iowa, south to northern Florida and Louisiana.

Amelanchier arborea flowers

Amelanchier arborea fruit

Amelanchier arborea, Downy Serviceberry

MORE ➤

Amelanchier arborea continued

Amelanchier arborea in fall

Amelanchier arborea fall color

Amelanchier arborea bark

Amelanchier canadensis
Shadblow Serviceberry

The true *Amelanchier canadensis* is hopelessly confused in the landscape trade. In general, it is an upright, suckering, tightly multistemmed shrub with a dome-shaped crown. The leaves, 1½ to 2½ in. long, are similar to those of *A. arborea*, but the white flowers come in more compact, 2- to 3-in.-long racemes and are held in a more upright position. To this author, the fruit do not have the flavor of those of *A. arborea* or *A. laevis*. In flower, Shadblow Serviceberry is not as dominant as the other species, but it is still an effective landscape element. It occurs naturally in bogs and swamps along the eastern seaboard, but under cultivation, it performs well in drier soils. A wonderful plant to use around ponds, lakes, and streams, or in boggy or marshy ground. It will never disappoint. Grows 6 to 20 ft. high. Zones 3 to 7(8). Maine to South Carolina, along the coast.

Amelanchier canadensis flowers

Amelanchier canadensis, Shadblow Serviceberry

Amelanchier canadensis bark

Amelanchier ×*grandiflora*

Apple Serviceberry

A naturally occurring hybrid between *Amelanchier arborea* and *A. laevis*, it exhibits characteristics intermediate between those of the parent species. Absolute identification is difficult. The newly emerging leaves are purplish tinged and slightly pubescent, a quality that distinguishes the hybrid from its parents. Grows 20 to 25 ft. high, similar spread. Zones (4)5 to 8(9).

Cultivars and Varieties. Several interesting cultivars have been selected. The best of the influx include 'Autumn Brilliance', with red fall color, 'Ballerina', with brick-red fall color, and 'Princess Diana', with red fall color. 'Robin Hill' and 'Rubescens' have pink buds that fade upon opening.

Amelanchier ×*grandiflora* 'Autumn Brilliance' fall color

Amelanchier laevis

Allegheny Serviceberry

Another serviceberry not too different from the other species, especially *Amelanchier arborea*, in flower, fruit, bark, and growth habit. The principal differences are the purplish to bronze color of the emerging leaves and the lack (almost) of hairs on the leaves and flower stalks. When the leaves mature to summer green, it is virtually impossible to distinguish between this and the three previous serviceberries. For most purposes, the species are interchangeable in the landscape. Grows 15 to 25 (to 40) ft. high, similar spread. Zones 4 to 8. Newfoundland to Georgia and Alabama, west to Michigan and Kansas.

Amelanchier ×*grandiflora* 'Rubescens' flowers

Amelanchier laevis, Allegheny Serviceberry

Amorpha canescens, Leadplant Amorpha

Amelanchier laevis flowers

Amorpha canescens flowers

Amorpha canescens

Leadplant Amorpha

Although seldom used in contemporary landscapes, this gray-leaved shrub provides worthwhile summer foliage color. The leaves are composed of 15 to 45 grayish, ⅓- to 1-in.-long leaflets, resulting in a fine texture. Purplish flowers occur in 1- to 2-in.-long, cylindrical terminal panicles during July. Prospers under hot, dry conditions. Grows 2 to 4 ft. high and wide. Zones 2 to 6. Manitoba and Saskatchewan, south to Iowa and New Mexico.

Amorpha fruticosa
Indigobush Amorpha

My first encounter with this shrub provided convincing evidence that I would never use it in the garden. The habit is upright-spreading, rather unkempt and untidy. In winter, the gray-brown stems look as if they were dead. The bright green foliage is rather pleasing and probably the shrub's most noteworthy attribute. Flowers are purplish blue with orange anthers and occur in 3- to 6-in.-long upright spikes in June. Adaptable to infertile, dry, sandy soils. Once planted, it remains for life. Utilize in dry soils and full sun where precious few plants will prosper. Grows 6 to 20 ft. high, 5 to 15 ft. wide. Zones 4 to 9. Connecticut to Minnesota, south to Florida and Louisiana.

Amorpha fruticosa 'Nana' flowers

Ampelopsis brevipedunculata, Porcelain-Vine, fruit

Ampelopsis brevipedunculata var. *maximowiczii* 'Elegans' foliage

Ampelopsis brevipedunculata var. *maximowiczii*

Ampelopsis brevipedunculata
Porcelain Ampelopsis, Porcelain-Vine

As much as this plant is ballyhooed for its excellent yellow to pale lilac to bright blue fruit, the species makes a minimal contribution to the smaller garden. I grew a plant on a downspout of my Illinois home and had to wade through five or six viburnums to even see the fruit of this vine. Porcelain-Vine is exceptionally vigorous and climbs by twining and tendrils. Unless provided a structure, it becomes a viny heap. The dark green, 2½- to 5-in.-long, three- (rarely five-) lobed leaves seldom develop fall color. Greenish flowers open in July and August, followed by ¼- to ⅓-in.-diameter fruit in September and October. Adaptable to varied soils, but site in full sun for best fruiting. Japanese beetles love the foliage. Use in a seminaturalized way by allowing it to scramble over a rock pile or wall, or perhaps a lattice or open fence. Grows 10 to 20 ft. high or more. Zones 4 to 8. China, Korea, Japan, Russian Far East.

Cultivars and Varieties. 'Elegans', which appears to be a selection of var. *maximowiczii*, displays greenish white and pink leaf color when young, maturing to green and white. Not as vigorous as the species.

var. *maximowiczii* has leaves with lobes more deeply cut than those of the species. Often more common in commerce than the species.

Aralia elata
Japanese Angelica Tree

Truly one of the great plants for foliage texture, this species provides a rare opportunity to bring the tropics to the North Temperate Zone. The gigantic compound leaves range from 3 to 5½ ft. in length and slightly less in width. One leaf provides shade for an entire garden party. The 2- to 5-in.-long, dark green leaflets may turn yellow to reddish purple in fall. The habit varies from an irregularly shaped tree to a large, spreading, suckering shrub. White, 12- to 18-in.-diameter flowers appear in August and are followed by purplish fruit. Not particular as to soils and tolerates partial shade or full sun. Grows 20 to 30 ft. high, variable spread. Zones (3)4 to 8. Japan, Korea, China, Russia.

Cultivars and Varieties. 'Variegata', with creamy white leaf margins, and 'Aureo-variegata', with yellow-margined leaves, are great color elements in a shady corner of the garden.

Aralia elata, Japanese Angelica Tree

Aralia elata flowers

Aralia elata 'Variegata' foliage

Aralia elata bark

Aralia spinosa, Devil's-Walkingstick

Aralia spinosa fruit

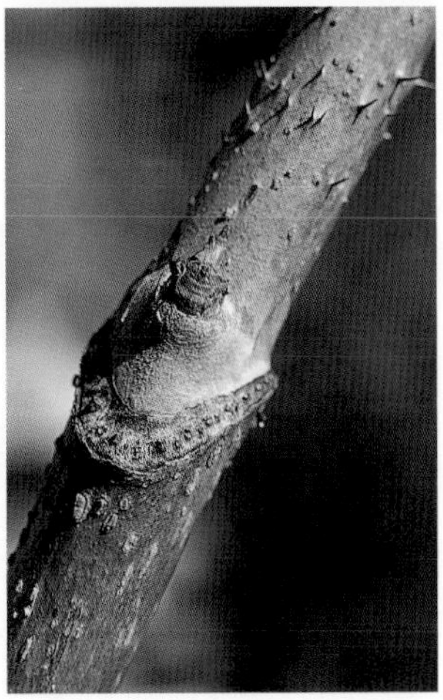

Aralia spinosa stem

Aralia spinosa

Devil's-Walkingstick, Hercules'-Club

Very similar to *Aralia elata*, differing in its smaller size and more vigorous suckering habit. A great plant for textural effect, but it needs to be restrained in the landscape to prevent rampant spread. The rich dark blue-green leaves are free of pestiferous nuances and may turn yellow to purplish in fall. Prominent white flowers occur in 12- to 18-in.-diameter inflorescences in mid- to late summer. The light brown, clubby stems are armed with prominent prickles, providing the basis for the common names. Often seen in the eastern states in moist soils along highways. Grows 10 to 20 ft. high, spreads almost indefinitely unless restrained. Zones 4 to 9. Southern Pennsylvania to eastern Iowa, south to Florida and east Texas.

Aristolochia durior

Dutchman's Pipe

Older residences throughout the Midwest and East often used this vine as a kind of sun shield or venetian blind to shade porches. Typically, a set of strings or trellis was attached to the porch, and the twining nature of Dutchman's Pipe would take the leaves to the top in about six to eight weeks. The 4- to 12-in.-long, dark green leaves may stand out like elephant ears, but it serves a functional purpose. The flowers, which bloom from the leaf axils in May and June, resemble a meerschaum pipe. In order to see the flowers, the foliage must be parted. Extremely adaptable. Withstands full sun or partial shade. Grows 20 to 30 ft. high. Zones 4 to 8. Pennsylvania to Georgia, west to Minnesota and Kansas.

Aristolochia durior, Dutchman's Pipe

Aristolochia durior foliage

Aristolochia durior flower

Aronia arbutifolia

Red Chokeberry

Red Chokeberry labors in obscurity and is seldom available in commerce. The shrub's bright red fruit are long persistent and they are shunned by the birds, as is suggested by the name "chokeberry." A mature specimen or colony can be spectacular in October as the leaves turn brilliant red. The 1½- to 3½-in.-long, lustrous dark green leaves, handsome throughout the spring and summer, are free of serious insects and diseases. White flowers occur in May in 1- to 2-in.-diameter clusters of 9 to 20. The ¼-in.-diameter, rounded, bright red fruit start to ripen in September and persist through winter. Unfortunately, the habit is somewhat

Aronia arbutifolia, Red Chokeberry

leggy, and old specimens appear disheveled. Proliferates in well-drained, acid, and organic matter–laden soils, but it is quite adaptable. Use in borders or masses, or as a bank cover along streams and ponds. Grows 6 to 10 ft. high, variable spread; usually wider at maturity. Zones 4 to 9. Massachusetts to Minnesota, south to Florida and Texas.

Cultivars and Varieties. 'Brilliantissima' has waxier, more lustrous leaves and more vivid red fall foliage. On occasion, it rivals *Euonymus alatus*, Winged Euonymus, for fall color.

Aronia arbutifolia flowers

Aronia arbutifolia fruit

Aronia arbutifolia 'Brilliantissima'

Aronia arbutifolia 'Brilliantissima' fall color

Aronia melanocarpa
Black Chokeberry

This species is generally considered inferior to *Aronia arbutifolia*, although it does offer several worthwhile ornamental attributes, including large, long-persistent, black fruit and wine-red fall color. Habit is similar to that of *A. arbutifolia*, perhaps less leggy. The 1- to 3-in.-long leaves are a rich, lustrous dark green. The small, white flowers do not overwhelm. Adaptable to many soils, in sun or partial shade. Use in borders, masses, or large groupings. Can colonize large areas. Grows 3 to 5 (to 10) ft. high. Zones 3 to 8(9). Nova Scotia to Florida, west to Michigan.

Cultivars and Varieties. var. *elata* is superior to the species from a landscape perspective because of its greater stature—6 to 10 ft. high and wide, with larger leaves, flowers, and fruit. Certainly worth considering where an *Aronia* is to be used.

Aronia melanocarpa fruit and fall color

Aronia melanocarpa, Black Chokeberry

Aronia melanocarpa var. *elata*

Asimina triloba
Pawpaw

Simply a great plant for foliage effect. The droopy, 6- to 12-in.-long leaves provide a sleepy, "shut-eye" aura to the summer landscape. This beautiful native tree is often found as an understory plant in cool, moist, alluvial soils along streams. Lurid purple flowers creep out of hairy, brown buds before the leaves in April and May. They are followed by edible, waxy, irregular-shaped berries, 2 to 5 in. long. The fruit are greenish yellow maturing to black and have a slight banana-like taste. The rich green leaves turn spectacular golden hues in fall. It prefers moist, well-drained soils, in shade to full sun. Difficult to transplant; gardeners should opt for small container-grown seedlings. Will sucker and produce colonies that make an almost eerie, enchanted-forest quality. Unfortunately, this species is virtually unattainable in the retail nursery trade, but it can be obtained from specialty mail-order firms. Grows 15 to 20 ft. high and wide; can grow 30 to 40 ft. in favorable locations. Zones 5 to 9. New York to Florida, west to Nebraska and Texas.

Asimina triloba, Pawpaw

Berberis candidula
Paleleaf Barberry

This diminutive evergreen species makes a handsome addition to any perennial border or rock garden, and it can serve as a functional mass or large groundcover plant. Broad-mounded in habit, the branches are rigidly arching and covered with three-parted spines. The 1- to 2-in.-long leaves are lustrous dark green above, silver below. Bright yellow, $\frac{5}{8}$-in.-diameter flowers appear in May and June. I have never observed fruit set, although it is described as a grayish purple, $\frac{1}{2}$-in.-long berry. Transplant from a container into any well-drained soil, in sun or partial shade. In northern areas, protect from extreme wind and sun. Numerous evergreen barberries are available, but identification is quite difficult. *Berberis candidula* is one of the best. Grows 2 to 4 ft. high, to 5 ft. wide. Zones 5 to 8. China.

The related species *Berberis verruculosa*, Warty Barberry, is similar to and often confused with *B. candidula*. I have studied many specimens and have yet to discover a reliable method of distinguishing the two species. Supposedly, the stems of *B. verruculosa* are warty (bumpy), the undersides of the leaves not as silvery, and the ultimate size larger (3 to 6 ft. tall). Having grown the two plants side by side in my Illinois garden, I know *B. verruculosa* is less hardy than *B. candidula*. Best in Zone 6.

Asimina triloba in fall

Asimina triloba flowers

Asimina triloba foliage

Berberis candidula foliage undersides

Berberis candidula, Paleleaf Barberry

Berberis ×gladwynensis 'William Penn'

A hybrid evergreen barberry that has become popular in the Mid-Atlantic states. The spiny, 1- to 2-in.-long, lustrous dark green leaves turn bronze-red in winter. Yellow flowers open in April and May. The habit is mounded-spreading. Makes an effective groundcover or mass. Grows 3 to 4 ft. high and wide. Zones 6 to 8.

Berberis ×gladwynensis 'William Penn'

Berberis julianae

Wintergreen Barberry

Probably the best-known garden representative of the evergreen barberries, this species develops into a large, rounded, impenetrable mass of heavy, rich dark green leaves and three-parted, spiny stems. Abundant golden yellow flowers appear in April and are followed by rather inconspicuous grayish, waxy coated, small fruit. Easily transplanted and grown. The most common evergreen barberry in gardens on the East Coast. A great foliage and barrier plant, Wintergreen Barberry has kept many college students in bounds on their way to and from classes. Grows 6 to 8 (to 10) ft. high and wide. Zones 5 to 8. China.

Cultivars and Varieties. 'Nana' is more compact and suitable for smaller gardens. It has all the attributes of the species but is half the size. Plants that I have seen are mounded-spreading.

'Spring Glory' has bronze-red new shoots that provide an unusual color addition to the spring garden.

Berberis julianae, Wintergreen Barberry

Berberis julianae 'Spring Glory' foliage

Berberis julianae foliage

Berberis julianae flowers

Berberis koreana

Korean Barberry

I have always wondered why this species was not more abundant in American gardens. Perhaps its rather aggressive, suckering nature is offensive to many gardeners. An upright-branched, colonizing shrub, Korean Barberry requires occasional thinning to keep in bounds. The medium to dark green (almost blue-green) leaves turn rich shades of yellow, orange, and reddish purple in autumn. In the Boston area (Zone 6), the leaves persist into November. The bright yellow flowers occur in 3- to 4-in.-long, pendulous racemes in May and provide a delicate floral beauty that is foreign to the common landscape barberries. The egg-shaped, reddish fruit, ¼ to ⅜ in. long, are effective through fall and into winter. The species is easy to grow and prospers in anything but wet soils. Use in a border, as a barrier, or in a mass. Probably not a good choice for the small garden, where *Berberis thunbergii* cultivars would be more appropriate. Suckering nature may result in large colonies. Grows 4 to 6 (to 8) ft. high, generally less in spread. Zones 3 to 7. Korea.

Berberis koreana, Korean Barberry, in fall

Berberis ×*mentorensis*

Mentor Barberry

I can still remember perusing the old Wayside Garden catalogs as a horticulture student at Ohio State and reading about the best hedge plant ever developed—and that label has stayed with the plant to this day. Mentor Barberry is often used as a hedge or barrier, especially in the Midwest. Purportedly a hybrid between *Berberis thunbergii* and *B. julianae*, it develops into a dense, rounded, spiny shrub. It has heavy textured, 1- to 2-in.-long, dark green leaves that hold later than those of *B. thunbergii* and often turn yellow, orange, and red in fall. Flowers are yellow. Of easy culture, it is a solid, functional performer, never flashy or gauche. Easily pruned into any configuration. Grows 5 to 7 ft. high and wide; I have seen specimens 5 to 7 ft. high and 10 to 12 ft. wide. Zones 5 to 8.

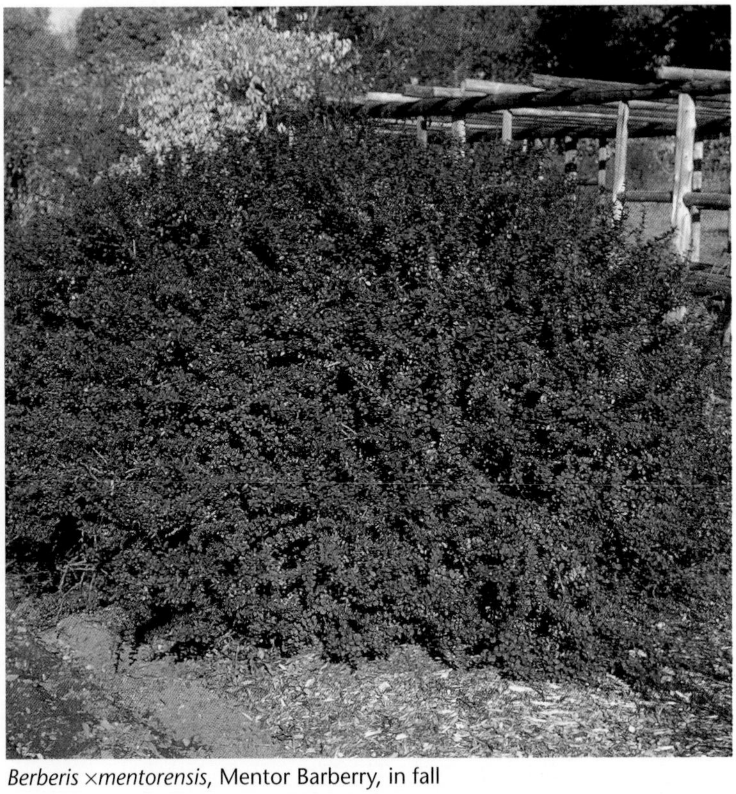

Berberis ×*mentorensis*, Mentor Barberry, in fall

Berberis koreana fall color

Berberis koreana fruit

Berberis ×*mentorensis* fruit

Berberis thunbergii
Japanese Barberry

Worldwide, this is the most popular landscape barberry, and the number of cultivars that originated in Europe, particularly the Netherlands, is astronomical. In my travels through European gardens, I saw selections that I did not even know existed. The species is not an unworthy plant, forming a rather dapper mound of single-spined branches. The spatulate, ½- to 1¼-in.-long leaves have entire margins, a feature that separates this species from *Berberis* ×*mentorensis*. The ⅓- to ½-in.-diameter, yellow flowers occur in small clusters on the undersides of the stems in late April and May. The ⅓-in.-long, ellipsoidal, bright red berries ripen in October and persist through the winter. Quite adaptable. Prefers full sun but will tolerate partial shade. Used as a hedge or barrier in many older gardens. The newer cultivars are utilized in all types of situations. Grows 3 to 6 ft. high, 4 to 7 ft. wide. Zones 4 to 8. Japan.

Cultivars and Varieties. var. *atropurpurea* ('Atropurpurea') has spawned a whole race of purple-leaf forms that are among the most common barberry cultivars. Differing in growth habit and in the intensity of purplish red leaf color, these cultivars generally grow about the same size as the species. Useful in the summer or fall garden for the color of the foliage. For best leaf color, the plants should be grown in sun.

var. *atropurpurea* 'Bagatelle' is a small, compact form. It is similar to 'Crimson Pygmy' but much slower growing, reaching perhaps 2½ ft. in 15 years. Makes a great filler in rock garden or perennial borders.

Berberis thunbergii, Japanese Barberry

Berberis thunbergii fruit

Berberis thunbergii fall color

Berberis thunbergii 'Sparkle'

Berberis thunbergii var. *atropurpurea* 'Rose Glow' foliage var. *atropurpurea* 'Crimson Pygmy' is the most popular of the purple-leaf forms because of its excellent reddish purple leaves and compact, mounded habit. Often used in mass plantings, almost as a tall groundcover. Grows 1½ to 2 ft. high, 2½ to 3 ft. wide.

var. *atropurpurea* 'Rose Glow' may be the best reddish purple form. The first leaves emerge from clustered buds a rich purple, followed by new shoots with rose-pink leaves, mottled and speckled with deeper red-purple splotches. These shoots eventually turn reddish purple. Fall color can be a good red. Grows 5 to 6 ft. high and wide.

'Aurea' provides knockout golden yellow foliage color. Practice restraint when using this shrub; perhaps plant it as a decoy to divert attention away from garbage cans. Grows 3 to 4 ft. high and wide, sometimes larger.

'Kobold' is reminiscent of a green boxwood because of its rich green foliage and densely mounded habit. Makes a good low hedge and has been used in mass plantings with great success. Grows 2 to 2½ ft. high and wide.

'Sparkle' should rank among the leaders of the green barberry revolution but, unfortunately, it has not been promoted like other forms. The plants, even when young, have arching horizontal branches and maintain a dense constitution into old age. The leathery, glossy dark green foliage turns fluorescent reddish orange in fall. Grows 3 to 4 ft. high, slightly greater in spread.

Berberis thunbergii var. *atropurpurea* 'Crimson Pygmy'

Berberis thunbergii 'Aurea'

Berberis thunbergii var. *atropurpurea* flowers

Betula alleghaniensis (*B. lutea*)
Yellow Birch

Truly a native treasure, this species is not in vogue because its bark is not white. In fall, however, the brilliant golden yellow foliage compensates a thousandfold. Summer leaves are dark green and average 3 to 5 in. long. The leaves are highly resistant to leaf miner, a severe problem for many of the white-barked species. The bark on young trees is a polished brown or bronze, with thin, papery, shaggy shreds; with age, the bark becomes gray-brown and breaks into large, ragged-edged plates. Bruised stems emit the heady aroma of wintergreen. The habit on young trees is pyramidal-oval, becoming rounded at maturity. Prefers cool, moist soils and cool summer temperatures. Grows 60 to 75 ft. high and wide. Zones (3)4 to 7. Newfoundland to Manitoba, south to the high peaks of Georgia and Tennessee.

Betula alleghaniensis, Yellow Birch, in fall

Betula jacquemontii, Whitebarked Himalayan Birch

Betula jacquemontii bark

Betula alleghaniensis bark

Betula jacquemontii
Whitebarked Himalayan Birch

Although a certain amount of taxonomic confusion surrounds this tree (it could be *Betula utilis* var. *jacquemontii*), the certainty of its early and pure milk-white bark is absolute. Like *B. pendula*, European White Birch, this species is not heat tolerant, but the distinct pyramidal habit, the dark green leaves (2 to 3 in. long), and the bright yellow fall color, together with the exquisite bark, make it a choice specimen in colder climates. Whitebarked Himalayan Birch has received attention from nursery people as a possible borer-resistant substitute for European White Birch, but unfortunately, it too has proven susceptible. Grows 30 to 50 ft. high, 20 to 35 ft. wide. Zones 4 to 7. Western Himalayas.

Betula lenta, Sweet Birch, in fall

Betula lenta
Sweet, Black, or Cherry Birch

Not unlike *Betula alleghaniensis* in garden attributes and cultural requirements—indeed, side by side, older trees of the two species appear quite similar. This species is possibly more heat tolerant and has performed admirably in the Midwest for many years. The fall color, regardless of environmental conditions, is a consistent rich golden yellow. The reddish brown bark on young branches does not peel like that of *B. alleghaniensis*, but Sweet Birch offers similar mature bark, and the stems emit a wintergreen odor when bruised. A superb birch for naturalizing. Best growth is realized in deep, moist, slightly acid, well-drained soils; however, it is often found on dry, rocky sites. Grows 40 to 55 ft. high, 35 to 45 ft. wide. Zones 3 to 7. Maine to Alabama, west to Ohio.

Betula maximowicziana, Monarch Birch, in fall

Betula maximowicziana bark

Betula lenta bark

Betula maximowicziana
Monarch Birch

This species was touted as the savior of the white-barked birches because of its suspected resistance to bronze birch borer. Unfortunately, when the true species finally arrived in America, the tree was neither uniformly white-barked nor borer resistant. The bark may be whitish to brown and is seldom uniform among seedlings. The habit is coarsely pyramidal to rounded, with perhaps the stiffest secondary branches of any birch. The 3- to 6-in.-long, dark green leaves are the largest of the cultivated birches. In autumn, the leaves turn lovely butter-yellow and have the size and consistency of notebook paper when they fall. Provide deep, moist soils, and avoid heat and drought stress. The Arnold Arboretum has many different seedling accessions, and some are large, robust, thriving trees growing over 30 ft. high in 14 years, while others are riddled with borers. Perhaps this species is best reserved for the collector. Be leery when purchasing the species, for its identity is confused. Grows 40 to 50 ft. high, can be as wide at maturity. Zones 5 to 6. Japan.

Betula nigra
River Birch

Perhaps the most heat resistant of all North American birch species. The habit is pyramidal to oval in youth, often rounded at maturity. Large, multistemmed specimens are inherently more aesthetic than the single-stem specimens because the attractive rich cinnamon-brown exfoliating bark is more visible on the former. In fact, this particular birch is more spectacular without leaves. The medium green, 2- to 3½-in.-long leaves seldom color in fall (at best they turn yellow). In extremely rainy seasons, the leaves may develop significant leaf spot, and under drought conditions, they may drop prematurely, but neither problem is sufficiently serious to discourage use. Found in moist soils along watercourses throughout its native range. For best growth, soils should be moist and acidic; in high pH soils, chlorosis can be serious. River Birch is not afflicted by the bronze birch borer. Grows 40 to 70 ft. high, 40 to 60 ft. wide. Zones 4 to 9. Massachusetts to Florida, west to Minnesota and Kansas.

Cultivars and Varieties. 'Heritage' is an excellent selection with superior vigor, larger leaves, and greater resistance to leaf spot. It displays salmon-white bark, especially in the early years of growth (2 to 5 years).

Betula nigra, River Birch

Betula nigra bark

Betula nigra in winter

Betula nigra 'Heritage' bark

Betula papyrifera, Paper Birch, in fall

Betula papyrifera

Paper or Canoe Birch

This superb white-barked native birch offers greater resistance to the borer than either *Betula pendula* or *B. populifolia*. The loosely pyramidal outline of youth gives way to an oval to rounded crown at maturity. The dark green, 2- to 4- (to 5½-) in.-long leaves turn rich butter-yellow to golden yellow in fall. The chalky white bark is outstanding in the winter landscape. This species is excellent when used in groupings, in groves, or even as a single specimen. Performs best in moist, acid, sandy, or silty loams, but will grow in a wide range of soil conditions. A cool-climate tree that deserves the title "Lady of the North American Forest." Grows 50 to 70 ft. high, 25 to 45 ft. wide. Zones 2 to 6(7). Labrador to British Columbia, south to Pennsylvania, Nebraska, and Washington.

Betula papyrifera in winter

Betula pendula
European White Birch

At one time, this was the most popular white-barked birch because the bark color develops at an early age. Unfortunately, bronze birch borer reduces European White Birch to rubble, especially when the tree is under stress, and now many gardeners and nurseries shy away from the species. In youth the habit is gracefully pyramidal; at maturity, oval to rounded. The triangular to diamond-shaped, 1- to 3-in.-long, dark green leaves turn yellow in fall. Tolerant of extremely moist and dry soils, but the tree should not be stressed—you might as well send a formal dinner invitation to the bronze birch borer. Grows 40 to 50 ft. high, 20 to 30 ft. wide. Zones 2 to 6(7); occasionally Zone 8, but plants look more dead than alive. Europe, especially high altitudes, northern Asia.

Cultivars and Varieties. 'Dalecarlica' has finely cut leaves and gracefully pendulous branches on a full-sized framework.

'Fastigiata' is an erect, columnar form that becomes columnar-oval with age. Foliage holds later than that of other cultivars. Appears to possess some resistance to the bronze birch borer.

'Youngii' has normal leaves but a strong weeping tendency. Grows 15 to 20 ft. high and wide.

Betula pendula, European White Birch

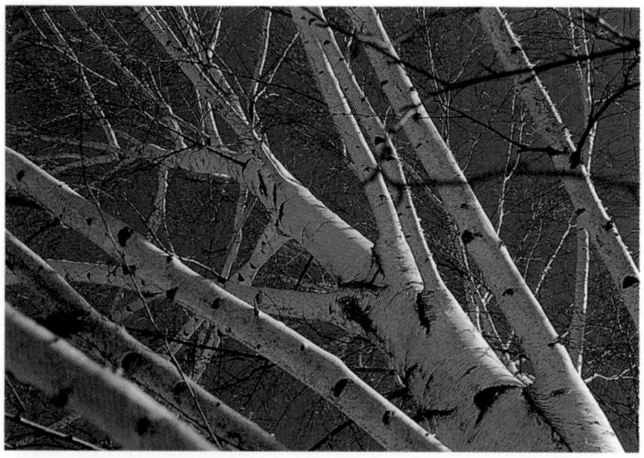

Betula pendula bark

Betula pendula 'Dalecarlica' foliage

Betula pendula 'Youngii'

Betula platyphylla var. *japonica*
Japanese White Birch

Along with the *szechuanica* variety of *Betula platyphylla*, this beautiful variety was hailed as the replacement for *B. pendula* because of early reports of resistance to the bronze birch borer. In 1957, Dr. John Creech, of the U.S. National Arboretum, collected the seed of the original *B. platyphylla* var. *japonica* in a remote alpine meadow in Japan. Only one seedling raised from seeds planted at the University of Wisconsin proved borer resistant, and this selection, 'Whitespire', was introduced. Almost 30 years after the original seed was collected, this promising tree was made available to the gardeners of the world. Variety *japonica* offers a lovely pyramidal outline, leathery, dark green, 1½- to 3-in.-long leaves, and white bark at an early age. It has proven exceptionally adaptable to the vagaries of the midwestern climate. Borers and leaf miners have recently manifested themselves on var. *japonica*. If purchasing a 'Whitespire' clone, make absolutely certain it was not seed-grown but vegetatively produced from the original tree at Wisconsin. Grows 40 to 50 ft. high, 20 to 30 ft. wide. Zones 4 to 7(8). Japan, northern China.

Betula platyphylla var. *japonica* 'Whitespire', Japanese White Birch

Betula populifolia bark

Betula populifolia foliage

Betula platyphylla var. *japonica* 'Whitespire' bark

Betula populifolia
Gray Birch

Always treated as a distant landscape cousin of the more popular *Betula pendula* and *B. papyrifera*, but certainly worthwhile in its native haunts. A weedy species throughout the Northeast, Gray Birch grows in the poorest of acid, sterile soils, from sand and gravel to rock. The narrow, irregularly open, conical crown never reaches the stature of that of the previous birch species. The glossy dark green, 2- to 3½-in.-long leaves turn yellow in fall. The bark drifts to a dirty off-white and does not glisten like that of its rich relatives. Leaf miner can be particularly serious on this species, but it is not as susceptible to the borer as *B. pendula*. Develops leaf chlorosis in high pH soils. Best in cooler areas of eastern North America. Grows 20 to 40 ft. high, 10 to 20 ft. wide. Zones 3 to 6(7). Nova Scotia to Ontario, south to Delaware.

Betula populifolia, Gray Birch

Bignonia capreolata (Anisostichus capreolata)
Crossvine

Although not well known in gardening circles, the Crossvine offers worthwhile attributes. The semievergreen to evergreen, 2- to 6-in.-long leaves are lustrous dark green in summer, turning bronzy red in winter. Broad trumpet-shaped, brownish orange to orange-red flowers, 1½ to 4 in. long and ¾ to 1½ in. wide, open in May. The flowers have a distinct mocha fragrance. Although found in the shade in its native setting, Crossvine achieves best growth in full sun. Prefers moist, acid, well-drained soils, but can also be found along rivers and streams where it is periodically flooded. A true clinging vine, it also twines. A plant in my garden has cemented itself to a wood fence and is climbing toward the heavens. Requires pruning under cultivation to keep it in check. A handsome vine for walls, trellises, and structures. Depending on the support structure, it will climb 30 to 50 ft. Zones (5)6 to 9. Virginia to southern Illinois, south to Florida and Louisiana.

Cultivars and Varieties. 'Tangerine Beauty', with orange-red flowers, and 'Jekyll', with flowers displaying an orange outer corolla and yellow on the interior, are two worthwhile selections.

Bignonia capreolata, Crossvine

Bignonia capreolata flower

Bignonia capreolata climbing a tree trunk in winter

Bignonia capreolata 'Jekyll' flowers

Buddleia alternifolia, Alternate-Leaf Butterflybush

Buddleia alternifolia in flower

Buddleia alternifolia

Alternate-Leaf Butterflybush

This is such a great plant, but so rarely used in modern gardens. To be sure, it can become mammoth, the long supple branches often reaching out to consume precious garden real estate. The overall texture is quite refined because of the gray-foliaged branches that sway in the faintest breeze. The habit is that of a large shrub or small tree. The 1½- to 4-in.-long leaves are dull green above and grayish below, appearing almost willowlike in composition. Bright lilac-purple, fragrant flowers appear in dense clusters from the axils of the previous season's growth, usually in June. Prefers loose, loamy soils and a sunny position. Makes a great addition to the border. Can be used tree-form (single stem). Grows 10 to 20 ft. high. Zones (4)5 to 7. China.

Cultivars and Varieties. 'Argentea' is a fine selection, with appressed silky hairs that impart a silvery sheen to the leaves.

Buddleia alternifolia 'Argentea' flowers

Buddleia davidii
Orange-Eye Butterflybush

This beautiful flowering shrub is culturally adapted to virtually any landscape site. Peering through a bus window in Edinburgh, Scotland, I spied a vacant, rubble-strewn lot alive with seedling butterflybushes; I have also seen this plant growing out of mortar joints in walls. These are old-fashioned garden plants, and their popularity has ebbed and flowed. With a new wave of imported cultivars, the plant is currently in vogue. The habit is rounded-arching with long, slender branches. The 4- to 10-in.-long leaves vary from gray-green to dark green above and are silver and pubescent beneath. The leaves hold late and do not develop any fall color. Fragrant flowers appear in 4- to 10- (to 14-) in.-long panicles on new growth of the season from June and July to fall. The flowers range in color from white, pink, lavender, and purple to near red. Spent inflorescences must be removed to foster new shoot growth and flower development. Easily transplanted from containers. Prefers well-drained, moist, loamy soils. Once established, the plant tolerates heat and drought. If plants become overgrown, cut back to 12 in. from the ground in late winter and fertilize—a handsome flowering shrub will be evident by midsummer. A great border plant. Attracts butterflies and bees in profusion and imparts a pastoral tranquility to the garden. Also makes a good cut flower. Grows 5 to 10 ft. high and wide. Zones 5 to 9. China.

Buddleia davidii, Orange-Eye Butterflybush

Buddleia davidii flowers

Cultivars and Varieties. 'Black Knight' has extremely dark purple, wonderfully fragrant flowers in 10-in.-long panicles. It may be slightly hardier than many other clones.

'Fascination' offers dense, 14- to 18-in.-long, vivid lilac-pink flower panicles on a strong-growing shrub.

'Lochinch' has sweetly scented, violet-blue (lavender-blue) flowers in 12-in.-long panicles. It may be confused in the trade, for I have observed at least two forms: one vigorous, the other less so. The form that I grow is more compact and smaller in all its parts, with attractive grayish, felted leaves. The large form may grow 12 to 15 ft. high; the compact form, half this size.

Nanho Series comprises forms with white, mauve-blue, and purple flowers on a more compact, finely textured framework, 5 to 6 ft. high and wide. In my garden, 'Nanho Purple' is slower growing and has smaller flowers and leaves than those of the species types.

'Pink Delight' has deep pink, fragrant flowers in 12- to 15-in.-long panicles.

'Royal Red' has rich purple-red flowers in 10- to 15-in.-long panicles. The habit is quite large, and a plant can grow as much as 12 to 15 ft. high and wide.

'Sun Gold' ('Sungold') is actually a cultivar of the hybrid *(Buddleia ×weyeriana)* between *B. davidii* var. *magnifica* and *B. globosa*. Yellow-orange flowers occur in interrupted panicles on a large 6-ft. shrub.

'White Bouquet' and 'White Profusion' are among the best of the many white-flowered forms. 'White Bouquet' has fatter panicles than the others. 'Peace', 'Ornamental White', and 'Snowbank' are also worthy white-flowered forms.

Buddleia davidii 'Black Knight' flowers

Buddleia ×weyeriana 'Sun Gold' flowers

Buddleia davidii 'Fascination' flowers

Buddleia davidii 'White Bouquet' flowers

Buxus, Boxwood

For functionality, few broadleaf evergreens approach the boxwoods. The name is synonymous with hedging, and the intricate parterres of many formal European gardens come to mind. Cultivars of Buxus microphylla *and* B. sempervirens *fit numerous geographic and climatic niches. Boxwoods prefer loamy, loose, well-drained soils. Root systems are near the surface and should not be disturbed. Full sun or partial shade situations are suitable.*

Buxus microphylla var. *koreana* 'Wintergreen'

Buxus microphylla
Littleleaf Boxwood

Buxus microphylla is a compact, mounded-rounded, densely branched shrub. The ⅓- to 1-in.-long, oval leaves are medium green in summer and turn yellow, brown, or bronze in winter, especially in cold climates. It is less troubled by insects and diseases than *B. sempervirens*, Common Boxwood, but it is not as handsome in leaf or stature. Utilize for large masses or as accents in borders, rock gardens, and perennial gardens. The numerous cultivars lend themselves to specialized uses. Grows 3 to 4 ft. high and wide. Zones 6 to 8. Japan, Korea.

Cultivars and Varieties. var. *japonica*, although more common in the Southeast and Southwest, is adaptable in Zone 6. The ⅓- to 1-in.-long leaves are almost as broad as those of the species and they are a much darker green color. I have not observed severe discoloration of winter foliage in this variety. Appears more sun and shade adaptable than typical *Buxus microphylla*. Grows 3 to 6 ft. high and wide.

var. *koreana* is the true cold-hardy stalwart and will survive –20 to –25°F or lower (Zones 4 or 5). Leaves are smaller than those of the species, but other characteristics are the same. This variety is the more commonly found form of the plant.

Sheridan Hybrids resulted from crossing *Buxus microphylla* var. *koreana* and *B. sempervirens*, and the hybrids embody the best characteristics of the parents. 'Green Gem', 'Green Mound', 'Green Mountain', and 'Green Velvet' are compact forms of varying growth habits, with excellent dark green winter color reminiscent of that of *B. sempervirens* and cold hardiness paralleling that of var. *koreana*. Somewhat slow growing.

'Wintergreen' represents a seedling selection from var. *koreana* with smaller leaves and green winter color. The leaves are light green, but they hold color reasonably well, even in climates like that of Chicago.

Buxus sempervirens
Common, American, or English Boxwood

One of the most functional plants in garden history, it has been used for screens, hedges, and foundations in the great gardens of the world. In habit, Common Boxwood is a behemoth; specimens 15 to 20 ft. high and wide prospered in Cincinnati, Ohio, until the devastating freezes of 1976–77. Compared to the previous species, this boxwood offers neither outstanding cold nor heat tolerance. The ½- to 1-in.-long, ½-in.-wide

Buxus sempervirens, Common Boxwood

leaves are dark green above, yellowish green below. Prospers in virtually any well-drained soil, in sun or quite dense shade. Plants can become unkempt as the result of climatic and insect problems. Cut older plants in late winter to within 18 to 36 in. of the ground; by the end of summer, the foliage will have covered the exposed stems. Psyllid, leaf miner, mites, and nematodes may cause significant damage. Grows 15 to 20 ft. high and wide. Zones (5)6 to 8. Europe, northern Africa, western Asia.

Cultivars and Varieties. The many cultivars are preferable to the species, although no perfectly cold-hardy forms exist for all conditions. Those most frequently listed or quoted for hardiness include 'Inglis', 'Northern Beauty', 'Northern Find', 'Northland', 'Pullman', 'Vardar Valley' (perhaps best), and 'Welleri'.

Buxus sempervirens 'Vardar Valley'

Callicarpa, Beautyberry

Although the Callicarpa *species are dieback shrubs and may be better suited to Zone 6 and warmer conditions, since they flower on new growth of the season several species are presented here.*

Callicarpa americana
American Beautyberry, French Mulberry

Callicarpa americana, American Beautyberry

Spectacular in fruit but coarse textured in habit, *Callicarpa americana* is suitable for massing in large areas. The 3½- to 6-in.-long, medium green leaves have no appreciable fall color. Dense, lavender-pink cymes develop from the axils of the leaves, and the fruit set that follows is so abundant that the stems are encircled with the brilliant violet to magenta, ¼-in.-diameter, rounded drupes. It is a great thrill to experience the plant in the wild, particularly in September and October when the fruit are at their best. This shrub thrives with neglect. It fruits more abundantly in full sun, but it is probably the best for shade of the species treated here. Grows 3 to 8 ft. high and wide. Zones (6)7 to 10. Southwest Maryland to Arkansas, south to the West Indies and Mexico.

Cultivars and Varieties. var. *lactea* has white fruit and is available from specialty nurseries.

Callicarpa americana foliage

Callicarpa americana fruit

Callicarpa americana var. *lactea* fruit

Callicarpa bodinieri
Bodinier Beautyberry

From a landscape point of view, I do not see great differences between this species and *Callicarpa japonica*, Japanese Beautyberry. The habit is erect, loose, and somewhat unkempt. Admittedly, the rich magenta-lilac fruit are lovely. The fruiting clusters are much more open and loose than those of either *C. americana* or *C. dichotoma*. Leaf color is a dull dark green, and on occasion, the leaves turn pinkish purple in fall. Culture and care are similar to that of the previous species. Grows 6 to 10 ft. high and wide. Zones (5)6 to 8. China.

Cultivars and Varieties. 'Profusion' is a Dutch selection with ⅙-in.-diameter, violet fruit that occur in clusters of 30 to 40. Fruit are more abundant, even on young plants.

Callicarpa bodinieri 'Profusion'

Callicarpa bodinieri 'Profusion' fruit

Callicarpa dichotoma
Purple Beautyberry

Purple Beautyberry is the most refined of the beautyberries. It has a graceful, arching, spreading habit and 1- to 3-in.-long, light to medium green leaves. Small, rather inconspicuous, light lavender-pink flowers emerge from the leaf axils in June, July, and August. The ⅛-in.-diameter, lilac-violet fruit start to ripen in September and persist into November. The fruit are borne in clusters above the foliage, and the branches appear studded with brightly colored jewels. The species will prosper in any well-drained soil and in full sun. If plants become tatty, cut to within 6 in. of the ground in late winter and fertilize. Regrowth is rapid, and flowers and fruit will occur the same year. For maximum effect, use in masses or large groups. Grows 3 to 4 ft. high, slightly greater in spread. Zones 5 to 8. China, Japan.

Cultivars and Varieties. 'Albifructus' is a pretty white-fruited form with lighter green foliage and white flowers. It reaches 6 to 8 ft. in height.

Callicarpa dichotoma, Purple Beautyberry

Callicarpa japonica
Japanese Beautyberry

At one time, I rated this species as my favorite, but after growing and carefully observing all the species described here, *Callicarpa dichotoma* is the new favorite. *Callicarpa japonica* is certainly a fine plant, but it grows much larger and more open than *C. dichotoma*. Habit is bushy and rounded with arching branches. Requires pruning to keep it well groomed. Fruit color varies from violet to metallic purple. Grows 4 to 6 ft. high and wide; can grow 10 ft. high. Zones (5)6 to 8. Japan.

Cultivars and Varieties. 'Leucocarpa' offers attractive white fruit.

Callicarpa dichotoma flowers

Callicarpa dichotoma 'Albifructus' fruit

Callicarpa japonica 'Leucocarpa' fruit

Callicarpa japonica, Japanese Beautyberry

Callicarpa japonica fruit

Calluna vulgaris
Heather

During late summer in England and Scotland, the fields are ablaze with mauve-pink to rose-pink heathers—a sight that both inspires and humbles. *Calluna vulgaris* makes a splendid groundcover in full sun and can be effectively combined with dwarf conifers and deciduous shrubs to produce a magnificent landscape tapestry. The needlelike, soft-textured leaves range from light to dark green in the species, although the many cultivars provide offerings of gray, silver, yellow, and red foliage. Flowers appear in elongated racemes up to 12 in. long. Remove old flowers after they fade. Provide well-drained, acid, sandy soils that are low in fertility. Good drainage is critical, and one authority reported a 20 to 25 percent loss of plants in heavy clay soils and humidity in Zone 7. Grows ⅓ to 2 ft. high, much greater in spread. Zones 4 to 6. Europe, Asia Minor.

Cultivars and Varieties. Within the genetic plasticity of this single species, over 700 cultivars have been selected for foliage, flower color, and habit. Every conceivable foliage and flower color is available. Flowers also come in singles and doubles. Great fun for the collector.

Calluna vulgaris, Heather

Calluna vulgaris 'Silver Knight'

Calocedrus decurrens (*Libocedrus decurrens*)
California Incensecedar

I have always considered this a most elegant and formal evergreen, but it is seldom used in contemporary landscapes. The form typically found in cultivation is possibly 'Columnaris', an upright, telephone pole–shaped, columnar cultivar of *Calocedrus decurrens*; the species form is more broadly conical. The shiny dark green foliage is handsome year-round. The gray-green to red-brown bark is scaly and exfoliating and provides winter interest. Prefers moist, acid, well-drained soils, although based on successful plantings in Massachusetts, Ohio, Georgia, and Oklahoma, the plant is tremendously adaptable. Grows 30 to 50 ft. high, 8 to 10 (to 15) ft. wide; can grow 100 to 125 ft. high in the wild. Zones 5 to 8. Oregon to Nevada and lower California.

Cultivars and Varieties. 'Aureo-variegata' is a rather unusual yellow-variegated form, with variegation ranging from a small splash to an entire spray.

Calocedrus decurrens, California Incensecedar

Calycanthus floridus
Sweetshrub, Carolina Allspice

Calocedrus decurrens 'Aureo-variegata' foliage

One of the great treasures of eastern North America, especially the open-grown specimens that develop into large, roundish shrubs and offer wonderfully fragrant, brown-maroon flowers in April and May. Truly an old-fashioned heirloom plant that I have found in many old gardens. It offers a sense of permanence and purpose. The lustrous dark green, 2- to 5-in.-long leaves turn respectable yellow in autumn. Flowers appear on short stalks from the nodes of naked stems and continue to open as the leaves unfurl. The fragrance is reminiscent of a mélange of ripening melons, strawberries, pineapples, and bananas. Unfortunately, seed-grown plants are unpredictable as to degree of fragrance, and some actually smell like vinegar. Always buy the plant in flower to insure pleasing fragrance. Site in any well-drained soil, in sun or partial shade. Although found in the wild on dry slopes as an understory plant, it performs more satisfactorily in good light. Great for the shrub border, and I have used it as a welcoming plant by the front door. Grows 6 to 10 ft. high, 6 to 12 ft. wide. Zones (4)5 to 9. Virginia to Florida.

Cultivars and Varieties. 'Athens' ('Katherine') is a deliciously fragrant, yellow-flowered clone, with heavier-textured, dark green leaves that turn good golden yellow in autumn.

'Edith Wilder' offers the species' flower color but with guaranteed floral fragrance.

'Michael Lindsey' produces deliciously fragrant maroon flowers and spinach-green leaves on a more compact framework.

Calocedrus decurrens bark

Calycanthus floridus 'Michael Lindsey' flower and foliage

Calycanthus floridus flowers

Calycanthus floridus 'Athens' flower

Calycanthus floridus, Sweetshrub, in fall

Campsis radicans
Common Trumpetcreeper

Campsis radicans, Common Trumpetcreeper

Common Trumpetcreeper is a rampaging, clinging and twining vine that will scale a 60-ft. tree or snake along the ground until it meets something to ascend. In my travels, I have never seen a specimen that did not need pruning. The lustrous dark green leaves are composed of seven to eleven coarsely serrated leaflets, ¾ to 4 in. long. Fall color is at best yellow-green. Orange to red, 2½- to 3-in.-long, trumpet-shaped flowers open from June and July into September on new growth of the season. The 3- to 5- (to 8-) in.-long, podlike capsules contain numerous winged seeds. Trumpetcreeper tolerates virtually any soil condition, except permanently wet. Maximum flowering occurs in full sun. Prune in late winter, since flowering occurs on new growth. Grows 30 to 40 ft. high. Zones 4 to 9. Pennsylvania to Florida, west to Missouri and Texas.

Cultivars and Varieties. 'Crimson Trumpet' is a strong-growing form, with glowing pure red flowers that lack any trace of orange.

'Flava' is a handsome yellow-flowered form (actually more orange-yellow), that displays vigor similar to that of the species. 'Apricot' is similar and may, in fact, be a rename.

Campsis radicans 'Crimson Trumpet' flower

Campsis radicans in flower

Campsis radicans 'Flava' flower

Campsis ×*tagliabuana* 'Mme. Galen'

Mme. Galen Tagliabue Trumpetcreeper

This hybrid between *Campsis grandiflora*, Chinese Trumpetcreeper, and *C. radicans* is less rampant and slightly less hardy than the latter parent, but it offers orange, tuba-shaped flowers, each 2 to 3 in. long and wide, in 6- to 12-flowered panicles. The flowers are spectacular, and the growth habit is more restrained than that of *C. radicans*. I have seen it flowering heavily in full sun or in half shade. Like the previous species, it displays great heat tolerance. Grows 20 to 30 ft. high. Zones (5)6 to 9.

Campsis ×*tagliabuana* 'Mme. Galen'

Campsis ×*tagliabuana* 'Mme. Galen' flower

Caragana arborescens

Siberian Peashrub

Peashrubs crop up in the strangest places, although none are common, and in the great shrub sweepstakes, this plant would never survive the first round of cuts. For impossibly harsh northern conditions and heavy, dry soils, however, it has a place. Siberian Peashrub becomes a massive, wide-spreading, irregularly rounded shrub, with pea-green leaves that develop before or with the yellow flowers in May. The effect is not overwhelming, as some of the flower effect is diminished by the foliage. The 1½- to 3-in.-long leaves are composed of 8 to 12 leaflets. Fruit are narrow, 1½- to 2-in.-long, pencil-like pods that make a popping sound as they open in July and August. Easy to culture. It also fixes atmospheric nitrogen. Useful as a hedge, screen, or windbreak. Grows 15 to 20 ft. high, 12 to 18 ft. wide. Zones 2 to 6(7). Siberia, Mongolia.

Cultivars and Varieties. 'Lorbergii' has feathery leaflets that provide a ferny texture.

'Pendula' is a stiffly weeping form that is often grafted on a standard, resulting in a respectable weeping tree.

Caragana arborescens, Siberian Peashrub

Caragana arborescens foliage

Caragana arborescens 'Lorbergii'

Caragana frutex
Russian Peashrub

This species is an upright, suckering shrub. Unarmed, this plant does not bear the spines that are found on several other peashrub species. The leaves are composed of four $\frac{1}{4}$- to 1-in.-long, dark green leaflets. Bright yellow, 1-in.-long flowers appear in May and June. Grows 6 to 9 ft. high. Zones 2 to 6. Russia.

Cultivars and Varieties. 'Globosa' is a diminutive, globe-shaped form. Grows 2 ft. high and wide.

Caragana frutex, Russian Peashrub

Carpinus betulus
European Hornbeam

In the garden-making process, this species should find a place of prominence. A superb medium-sized, oval to rounded, dapper tree of uniform proportions, it functions equally well as a single specimen, in groupings, as a screen, in the understory, or as a magnificent hedge. Furthermore, the steel-gray, smooth, sinewy bark is a welcome addition to the winter landscape. The deep green, prominently ribbed, 2- to $5\frac{1}{2}$-in.-long leaves hold late in fall and may turn golden yellow, although exceptional fall coloration is rare. The reddish brown buds of *Carpinus betulus* are angular-conical and much larger than those of the next species, *C. caroliniana*, American Hornbeam. Displays excellent tolerance to acid, high pH, moist, or dry soils and withstands full sun or heavy shade. A well-grown specimen is a superb garden treasure. Grows 40 to 60 ft. high, 30 to 40 (to 60) ft. wide; I have seen gigantic 80-ft. specimens in Europe. Zones 4 to 7(8). Europe, Asia Minor.

Cultivars and Varieties. 'Columnaris' maintains a central leader and relatively upright-ascending secondary branches. The branches are so closely spaced that it serves as an effective screen even in winter.

'Fastigiata' is a fine form with upright branching and a pyramidal-oval outline. Grows 30 to 40 ft. high, 20 to 30 ft. wide.

'Globosa' develops a more compact outline than the species, eventually becoming somewhat egg-shaped.

'Pendula' is not well known in the United States, but it is reminiscent of *Fagus sylvatica* 'Pendula', Weeping European Beech. The branches arch, dip, and dive to produce a singularly unique specimen plant. Grows 30 to 40 ft. high, 35 to 45 ft. wide.

Carpinus betulus, European Hornbeam

Carpinus betulus in winter

Carpinus betulus 'Columnaris'

Carpinus betulus 'Fastigiata' in fall

Carpinus betulus 'Pendula'

Carpinus caroliniana
American Hornbeam, Ironwood, Musclewood

The North American counterpart of the European Hornbeam is smaller in size and has distinct brownish black buds. Some of the best gardeners in the world have confused the two species. *Carpinus caroliniana* is distinctly upright-spreading with a round (often irregular) to flat-topped crown. The bark is similar to that of *C. betulus*. The dark green, 2½- to 5-in.-long leaves color yellow to reddish purple in the fall. American Hornbeam usually grows along streams in moist, alluvial soils throughout its range. In the wild, it occurs primarily as an understory tree, but it can be grown successfully in full sun under landscape conditions. Maximum growth is achieved in deep, moist, acid soils, although the species performs remarkably well in the more hostile environments of the Midwest. Great tree for naturalizing along the edges of woodlands and streams. Also makes a fine small street or lawn tree. Grows 20 to 30 ft. high and wide. Zones 3 to 9. Nova Scotia to Minnesota, south to Florida and Texas.

Carpinus caroliniana, American Hornbeam

Carpinus caroliniana bark

Carpinus caroliniana fall color

Carpinus caroliniana male catkins

Carya, Hickory

Hickories are seldom available in the landscape trade because of transplanting difficulties and the public's perception of them as less-than-desirable landscape plants. The large, compound pinnate leaves are dark yellow-green, often lustrous, and on many species turn brilliant yellow to golden yellow in fall. The leaves, as well as the fruit, are messy however, and in general, the tree grows too large for contemporary landscapes. But if hickories are present on a building site or around the home, do not disturb or remove. The assets far outweigh the liabilities. The trees will provide seasonal interest, and several species produce edible nuts. Hickories grow in deep, moist, well-drained soils, as well as dry, upland soils.

Carya cordiformis, Bitternut Hickory, foliage

Carya cordiformis
Bitternut Hickory

Bitternut Hickory is a slender tree, usually with an irregular, cylindrical crown of stiff, ascending branches, often widest at the top. The compound pinnate leaves contain five to nine medium green, 3- to 6-in.-long leaflets that turn yellow in fall. The seeds are bitter, and supposedly even the squirrels ignore them. Grows 50 to 75 ft. high. Zones 4 to 9. Quebec to Minnesota, south to Florida and Louisiana.

Carya, Hickory, in fall

Carya glabra
Pignut Hickory

Generally smaller than *Carya cordiformis*, and when open grown, it develops an oblong to round-headed outline. Usually this species is a tree with a regular, rather open, oval head of slender, contorted branches. The lustrous dark green leaves contain five 3- to 6½-in.-long leaflets, which turn gorgeous, often brilliant yellow in fall. The seeds are bitter and astringent. In the wild, it grows along hillsides and ridges in well-drained to dry, fairly rich soils. Grows 50 to 60 ft. high, 25 to 35 ft. wide. Zones 4 to 9. Maine to Ontario, south to Florida and Mississippi.

Carya glabra, Pignut Hickory

Carya glabra fall color

Carya illinoinensis
Pecan

Economically, this species is a most important member of the genus *Carya*—the production of pecans is a multimillion-dollar industry in the United States—but again there are limitations in the average landscape. This massive, upright-spreading tree can consume an entire city lot. The lustrous dark olive-green leaves, composed of 11 to 17 4- to 7-in.-long leaflets, do not develop appreciable fall color. Additionally, leaf scab can cause premature defoliation. The nuts are outstanding, but they ripen consistently only in the warmer regions of the country. The species is quite difficult to transplant—a 6-ft. tree may have a 4-ft. taproot. Best growth occurs in deep, moist, well-drained soils; it follows the river valleys closely in its native range. Grows 70 to 100 ft. high, 40 to 75 ft. wide. Zones 5 to 9. Indiana to Iowa, south to Alabama, Texas, and Mexico.

Carya illinoinensis, Pecan

Carya illinoinensis in winter

Carya ovata
Shagbark Hickory

Carya illinoinensis fruit

Perhaps the most widely recognized of all hickories because of its large, shaggy strips of exfoliating gray bark that provide the basis for the common name. Shagbark Hickory develops a straight, cylindrical trunk and an oblong crown of ascending and descending branches. The leaves consist of five deep yellow-green, 4- to 6-in.-long leaflets that assume rich yellow and golden brown tones in fall. The seed is sweet and edible. Grows best in rich, well-drained, loamy soils but is extremely adaptable. The closely related *Carya laciniosa*, Shellbark Hickory, differs primarily in that its leaves are composed of seven leaflets. Grows 60 to 80 ft. high, 30 to 40 ft. wide. Zones 4 to 9. Quebec to Minnesota, south to Georgia and Texas.

Carya ovata, Shagbark Hickory

Carya ovata foliage and fruit

Carya ovata bark

Carya ovata in fall

Caryopteris ×clandonensis
Blue-Mist Shrub, Blue Spirea

A valuable shrub for its soft gray-green foliage color and light blue summer flowers. For years, I have grown it in a sandy vein of soil and have never witnessed anything less than excellent performance. It thrives with neglect. Leaves average 1 to 2 in. long, and from the axils arise cymose clusters of soft blue flowers in August and September. Flowers occur on the new growth of the season, and plants should be cut back in late winter to promote vigorous shoot extensions. The habit is mounded-rounded. Great in a perennial border or for foliage effect. In my garden, it grows next to rosemary and santolina in a rather harmonious arrangement. Grows 2 to 3 ft. high and wide. Zones (5)6 to 9.

Cultivars and Varieties. Many cultivars are listed, but their actual differences are slight.

'Kew Blue' and 'Longwood Blue' have dark blue flowers.

'Worcester Gold' offers yellow foliage and blue flowers.

Castanea mollissima
Chinese Chestnut

As a substitute for *Castanea dentata*, American Chestnut, this species is acceptable, but as an outstanding ornamental it falls short. The American Chestnut, once a magnificent and noble tree of the eastern North American forests, was devastated by a blight. *Castanea mollissima* is typically rounded in outline with a short trunk and wide-spreading branches. The lustrous dark green, 3- to 6- (to 8-) in.-long, coarsely serrated leaves assume a respectable yellow to golden brown fall color. The exceptionally foul-smelling flowers appear in May and June and can ruin a late-spring barbecue. The edible nuts are borne two to three together in a prickly structure not unlike a mini-porcupine. The burrs litter the ground, and hence, trees should be located away from trafficked areas. Presents no problems as to culture. Grows 40 to 60 ft. high, similar spread. Zones 4 to 9. Northern China, Korea.

Caryopteris ×clandonensis, Blue-Mist Shrub

Castanea mollissima, Chinese Chestnut

Caryopteris ×clandonensis flowers

Caryopteris ×clandonensis 'Kew Blue' flowers

Castanea mollissima fruit

Castanea mollissima foliage and fruit

Catalpa bignonioides flowers

Catalpa bignonioides 'Aurea' foliage

Catalpa bignonioides

Southern Catalpa, Indian Bean

Ever ask the local nursery for a catalpa? Chances are it has none to offer. Southern Catalpa and the related species nearly qualify for dinosaur status in the landscape world. The flowers are quite attractive, however, and the bold coarseness of the large leaves adds textural interest. *Catalpa bignonioides* is a rounded to broad-rounded tree, with an irregular crown composed of short, crooked branches. The 4- to 8-in.- long and wide leaves are light green and seldom display a hint of fall color. White, tubular-flaring, 2-in.- long and wide flowers occur in 8- to 10-in.- high and wide panicles in June, about two weeks after those of *C. speciosa*, Northern Catalpa. Each flower has two ridges and two rows of yellow spots and numerous purple spots on the tube and lower lobe. The 6- to 15-in.-long, beanlike (capsule) fruit occur in prodigious quantities and provide the basis for the common name "Indian Bean." Tremendously tolerant of adverse soil conditions. Generally, the cultivars are more suitable than the species for contemporary landscaping. Grows 30 to 40 ft. high and wide. Zones 5 to 9. Georgia to Florida and Louisiana.

Cultivars and Varieties. 'Aurea' has leaves of a rich yellow color, and they do not lose all their color in cooler climates.

'Nana' is an old dwarf, bushy form that is grafted on a standard to produce a mushroom or globe shape. It was developed in 1850.

Catalpa bignonioides, Southern Catalpa

Catalpa speciosa

Northern or Western Catalpa

A common sight on farmsteads of the Midwest, and certainly not without merit because of its inherent toughness and adaptability. It differs from *Catalpa bignonioides* in its narrow, open, irregular, oval crown, and its flowers open several weeks earlier. No genuine advantage over Southern Catalpa other than hardiness and size. Grows 40 to 60 ft. high, 20 to 40 ft. wide. Zones 4 to 8. Southern Illinois and Indiana, south to western Tennessee and northern Arkansas.

Catalpa speciosa flowers

Catalpa speciosa, Northern Catalpa

Ceanothus americanus

New Jersey Tea, Redroot

Along I-80 in Pennsylvania on a June day, thousands of *Ceanothus americanus* plants appear as billowy white cushions. Unfortunately, this species has never found its way into commerce, possibly because of transplanting difficulties. The habit is a refined broad-mounded cushion. The rich, glossy green, 2- to 3-in.-long leaves may develop yellowish hues in fall. White flowers appear in 1- to 2-in.-long panicles at the end of the shoots in June and July. Transplant from a container. Will grow in infertile, dry soils. Also has the ability to fix atmospheric nitrogen. Use as a tall groundcover or mass on banks, cuts, and fills and in difficult dry, sunny locations. Grows 3 to 4 ft. high, 3 to 5 ft. wide. Zones 4 to 8. Quebec to Manitoba, south to South Carolina and Texas.

Ceanothus americanus, New Jersey Tea

Cedrela sinensis (Toona sinensis)
Chinese Toon

This Tree-of-Heaven *(Ailanthus altissima)* look-alike is not meant for the everyday gardener, but its environmental adaptability might hold it in good standing for urban plantings. At maturity, it develops a rather coarse, upright-spreading outline. The species also suckers, meaning that one tree may, like a sumac, become a grove. The dark green leaves are composed of 10 to 22 leaflets, each 3 to 6 in. long, that emerge bronzy red in spring. Bruised foliage has an onionlike odor. The brown bark peels off in long strips. Fruit are 1- to 1½-in.-long, woody capsules that look like roses when mature. The species tolerates extremes of soil and climate and might prove beneficial on infertile, eroded, or abused soils. Grows 30 to 40 ft. high, variable spread. Zones 5 to 8. Northern and eastern China.

Cultivars and Varieties. 'Flamingo' is an interesting form with rose- or pink- to cream-colored new foliage that matures to green. Cut back in late winter to induce long, colorful spring shoot extensions.

Cedrela sinensis, Chinese Toon

Cedrela sinensis 'Flamingo' foliage

Cedrela sinensis bark

Cedrela sinensis fruit

Cedrus atlantica

Atlas Cedar

The true cedars are in the first rank of needle evergreens, and the Atlas Cedar is, with maturity, truly magnificent. Variety *glauca* is more common than the species and will be discussed here. The habit in youth is pyramidal and sparsely branched; in 10 to 20 years, denser and acquiring character; by year 50, a grand and noble, broadly horizontal-branched specimen. The $\frac{3}{4}$- to $1\frac{1}{2}$-in.-long needles are rich frosty blue, particularly on the new spring growth. In a crowd, this form shouts for attention. The male cones are 2- to 3-in.-long, finger-shaped structures that release clouds of golden yellow pollen in September. Female cones, on the same tree (monoecious condition), are 3 in. long, 2 in. wide, and egg-shaped. They are glaucous blue-green maturing to rich brown. Female cones take two years to develop and only occur on older trees. Transplant as a container-grown or balled and burlapped plant into any reasonably moist, well-drained soil. It is tolerant of acid and alkaline conditions and, once established, is more tolerant of heat and dry soil than *Cedrus deodara* or *C. libani*. The least cold hardy of the tree cedars. Ideally *C. atlantica* var. *glauca* should be used as a specimen plant where there is ample room for it to spread its feathery, blue boughs; anything less is a sin. Has been used beside lakes, ponds, and reflecting pools, where it appears as blue-green water cascading over rocks—a magnificent sight! Grows 40 to 60 ft. high, 30 to 40 ft. wide; trees over 100 ft. high are common in Europe. Zones 6 to 8. Atlas Mountains of northwest Africa.

Cultivars and Varieties. 'Glauca Pendula' is a weeping form that can be trained and shaped to resemble a daddy-long-legs, a potato beetle, or geodesic dome framework.

Cedrus atlantica var. *glauca*

Cedrus atlantica var. *glauca* female cones

Cedrus atlantica 'Glauca Pendula'

Cedrus deodara, Deodar Cedar

Cedrus deodara
Deodar Cedar

The most popular landscape cedar, principally because of its fast growth and branch density in youth. The habit is fluffy and dense, becoming more open and artistic with age. The 1- to 2-in.-long, sharply pointed, blue-green needles are the longest of the true cedars. Cones are similar to those of *Cedrus atlantica*, only larger. A top decline (possibly from canker or cold) often results in multiple leader formation and, in some cases, severe dieback. The easiest true cedar to transplant. Commonly used as an understock. Extremely adaptable, it has survived on the high, dry, alkaline plains of west Texas. Grows 40 to 70 ft. high. Zones 6 to 8(9). Himalayas.

Cultivars and Varieties. 'Kashmir' and 'Kingsville' are often listed as cold-hardy forms, but they are really no better than –5°F cold tolerant.

'Shalimar', an Arnold Arboretum introduction, displays good blue-green needle color and is hardy to at least Boston, Massachusetts (Zone 6). It survived –15°F in Winchester, Tennessee.

Cedrus deodara cones

Cedrus deodara trunk and branching habit

Cedrus libani
Cedar of Lebanon

Considered the patriarch of the true cedars because of biblical associations and its dominating landscape presence. A fully developed specimen provides cause for reflection and inspiration. In youth the habit is tightly pyramidal; with age it develops horizontally disposed branches and a flat-topped crown. The ¾- to 1½-in.-long needles are lustrous dark green. Culture is similar to that of *Cedrus atlantica*. At the species level, this is the most cold hardy of the cedars. Grows 40 to 60 ft. high. Zones 5 to 7. Asia Minor.

Cultivars and Varieties. var. *stenocoma* is an extremely cold-hardy (–20°F) form, more stiff and rigid than the species. The habit is pyramidal-columnar.

Cedrus libani, Cedar of Lebanon

Cedrus libani male cones

Celastrus orbiculatus
Oriental Bittersweet

Oriental Bittersweet is closely related to *Celastrus scandens*, American Bittersweet, but differs in the flowers and fruit that develop in the axils of the leaves. The leaves are more rounded and slightly larger (2 to 5 in. long). This species is a significant weed in the Northeast and has crowded out native vegetation. Use with caution in any cultivated situation. Grows 20 to 40 ft. high. Zones 4 to 7. Japan, China.

Celastrus orbiculatus, Oriental Bittersweet

Celastrus orbiculatus foliage

Celastrus orbiculatus fruit

Celastrus scandens

American Bittersweet

American Bittersweet offers beautiful yellow-orange and red fruit that have long been a staple of the dried-flower market, particularly for fall arrangements. The species is a vigorous twining vine or scandent shrub. The 2- to 4-in.-long, lustrous dark green leaves turn greenish yellow in fall. Nonshowy, yellowish white flowers open in May and June in 2- to 4-in.-long panicles at the ends of the branches. The species is dioecious, and male and female plants are needed for good fruit set. The ⅓-in.-diameter, three-lobed, capsular fruit open in October to display the yellow-orange inside and crimson seeds. The species is adaptable to a wide range of soils and pH, even dry conditions. Site where the plant will not engulf other plants. Best in a seminaturalized situation on a fence or rock pile. Grows 15 to 20 ft. high. Zones 4 to 8. Quebec, south to North Carolina and New Mexico.

Celastrus scandens fruit

Celastrus scandens, American Bittersweet

Celtis laevigata

Sugar Hackberry

Certainly never on any list of the 10 most desirable trees, but Sugar Hackberry is as handsome as any when properly grown. The city of Savannah, Georgia, has splendid specimens used in street plantings. The habit is distinctly upright-spreading, not unlike that of *Ulmus americana*, American Elm, but without the elegance of the latter. The bark on the best forms is a smooth, rich gray, very similar to that of *Fagus grandifolia*, American Beech. The lustrous dark green, 2- to 3½-in.-long leaves do not color particularly well in fall. The small, ⅓-in.-diameter, orangish to blue-black fruit have a sweet datelike taste and are relished by many birds. *Celtis laevigata* will grow in wet or dry soils. Has been utilized in the South and, to some degree, the Midwest with great success. Selection of superior trees is the key to wider use. Grows 40 to 50 ft. high, similar spread. Zones 5 to 9. Southern Indiana and Illinois, south to Florida and Texas.

Celtis laevigata bark

Celtis laevigata, Sugar Hackberry

Celtis occidentalis
Common Hackberry

The fierce, drying winds of the Midwest and Plains states do not faze this tough hombre. Its tolerance is legendary, and it can be found in flood plains, in open fields, along roadsides, and in fencerows. The best forms approach the dignity of an American Elm; the worst, a worn-out broom. In youth the habit is weakly pyramidal; in old age the broad crown is composed of ascending-arching branches, often with drooping branchlets. The gray bark is covered with corky warts and ridges. Unfortunately, the light to medium green foliage is not particularly attractive and is often covered with a nipple gall. Witches'-broom (clusters of twiggy growths) also often develops in Common Hackberry. Trees with superior characteristics are evident in any population. For areas where few trees will prosper, it is a reasonable choice. Grows 40 to 60 ft. high, similar spread. Zones (2)3 to 9. Quebec to Manitoba, south to Georgia and Oklahoma.

Cultivars and Varieties. 'Prairie Pride' offers good glossy foliage, but no gall or witches'-broom.

Celtis occidentalis fruit

Celtis occidentalis, Common Hackberry

Cephalanthus occidentalis
Buttonbush

In a naturalized landscape where excess moisture is present, the Buttonbush is a reliable performer. Short on ornamental attributes—except for its 2- to 6-in.-long, lustrous green leaves and the curious 1- to 1¼-in.-diameter, rounded, creamy white flowers in August—the plant labors in obscurity. I have observed it growing with its trunks submerged in freshwater ponds on Cape Cod, Massachusetts. The habit is rounded, rather lax and loose, and variable in size. Grows 3 to 6 ft. high and wide; can reach 10 to 15 ft. high and wide. Zones 5 to 10. United States, Cuba, Mexico, eastern Asia.

Cephalanthus occidentalis, Buttonbush

Celtis occidentalis in winter

Cercidiphyllum japonicum
Katsuratree

Cephalanthus occidentalis foliage

Cephalanthus occidentalis flowers

Cercidiphyllum japonicum in fall

Understated elegance is evident in this species through the seasons—never gauche, gaudy, or noisy, always in elegant landscape fashion. Habit is pyramidal in youth, pyramidal-oval to rounded with maturity. Leaves average 2 to 4 in. long and wide, with a uniform crenate-serrate margin. The young leaves emerge a beautiful bronzy purple, fading to light green and then blue-green, and turn rich yellow to apricot hues in fall. The senescing (fall-coloring) leaves give off a delightful, spicy odor reminiscent of cotton candy. The brown, slightly shaggy bark is lovely through the seasons. No serious insect or disease problems, but trunks of young trees may sun-scald or split in cold climates. Requires ample moisture in the early years of establishment. A superb species for large lawns, parks, and streets. Grows 40 to 60 ft. high and wide; often variable in spread. Zones 4 to 8. China, Japan.

Cultivars and Varieties. 'Pendula' is a small, gracefully weeping form. From a graft, it will grow 10 to 15 ft. high and wide in five years. The closely related *Cercidiphyllum magnificum* 'Pendulum' grows taller but exhibits the same weeping characteristics.

Cercidiphyllum japonicum, Katsuratree

Cercidiphyllum japonicum bark

MORE ➤

Cercidiphyllum japonicum 'Pendula'

Cercidiphyllum magnificum 'Pendula'

Cercis canadensis
Eastern Redbud

A treasure in the April landscape when its clustered magenta buds unfold a blanket of rosy pink. No equal, no competitor, can be found among small flowering landscape trees—the stage is reserved for this native species. The flowers appear on leafless branches and are followed by waxy, bronzy to reddish purple new leaves that soon turn dark, almost bluish green and may assume yellow tints in fall. The 3- to 5-in.- long and wide leaves are a unique heart shape. This is a small, dapper, low-branching tree with a spreading, flat-topped to rounded crown. Leaves may develop spotting or discoloration in late summer, and along with the excess baggage of abundant 2- to 4-in.-long seedpods, may prove less than aesthetic. The bark, especially when moist, is glistening black, with rust-colored patches resulting from the exfoliation of the outer scales and plates. Not the easiest plant to transplant, it should be moved balled and burlapped in the dormant season. Adaptable to acid or high pH, moist or dry soils. In highly stressed situations, redbuds may decline from diseases; *Verticillium* wilt and canker are the most troublesome diseases. Can be used for every imaginable landscape situation, from the front yard of a Florida residence to the slopes of a New England freeway. Grows 20 to 30 ft. high, 25 to 35 ft. wide. Zones 4 to 9. Massachusetts to northern Florida, west to Missouri, Texas, and northern Mexico.

Cultivars and Varieties. 'Alba' and 'Royal White' offer white flowers.

'Forest Pansy' has shimmering, reddish purple young foliage that fades with the heat of late spring.

'Oklahoma', a selection of *Cercis canadensis* var. *texensis*, has deeper rosy magenta flowers and waxy, thick-textured, dark green leaves.

Cercis canadensis flowers

Cercis canadensis, Eastern Redbud

Cercis canadensis 'Alba'

Cercis canadensis in flower

Cercis canadensis 'Forest Pansy' foliage

Cercis chinensis
Chinese Redbud

Almost always a strongly multistemmed, upright-rounded to oval-rounded shrub; occasionally it is trained as a small tree. The 5- to 6-in.- long and wide, lustrous dark green leaves possess the typical heart shape, but they are thicker in texture than those of *Cercis canadensis*. Rosy-purple flowers occur up and down the stems about the time forsythia blooms in April. Easy to transplant and grow; unfortunately, it is still rare in American gardens. Makes a wonderful specimen plant, but better used in borders or groupings. A combination with spring bulbs like *Leucojum* would prove lovely. Grows 6 to 10 ft. high and wide; I have encountered 15-ft.-high specimens. Zones 6 to 8(9). China.

Cultivars and Varieties. 'Avondale' is an attractive small tree form with vivid magenta-pink flowers in great profusion.

Cercis chinensis in flower

Cercis chinensis flowers

Cercis chinensis 'Avondale'

Cercis chinensis, Chinese Redbud

Chaenomeles japonica
Japanese Floweringquince

This species is seldom available in commercial horticulture and has been largely superseded by the many hybrids and *Chaenomeles speciosa* cultivars. Frequently a denizen of older gardens, Japanese Floweringquince offers a compact framework of interlacing, often spiny stems, which seems to attract bottles, cans, and paper. Five-petaled, 1½-in.-diameter, orange to orange-red flowers occur on naked stems in late winter and often remain colorful after the leaves have unfurled. The lustrous dark green, 1- to 2-in.-long leaves seldom develop anything more than subdued yellow fall color. The greenish yellow, 1½-in.-diameter, rounded, hard-as-a-bullet fruit make ideal ammunition against the creatures of the garden. Provide moist, acid, well-drained soils, in full sun or partial shade. Use in mass plantings or as a filler in the shrub border. Grows 2 to 3 ft. high and wide. Zones 4 to 8. Japan.

Chaenomeles japonica, Japanese Floweringquince

Chaenomeles japonica fruit

Chaenomeles speciosa
Common Floweringquince

At their best, the flowers are spectacular; at the least hint of winter warmth, however, the buds swell and flowers open, which results in cold-damaged, ugly brown petals. The habit is rather oafish and clumsy, lacking the grace and dignity of the viburnums. Strongly multistemmed with a tangled mass of stems, it requires frequent pruning and tidying. The lustrous dark green leaves, 1½ to 3½ in. long, are susceptible to a disease that causes premature defoliation, usually leaving only the youngest leaves present by summer's end. Flowers range from white to pink to scarlet and every conceivable shade in between, in singles and doubles. The fruit average 2 to 2½ in. long and wide, are yellow to rose-blush in color, and have the firmness of a rock. An adaptable species, but chlorosis in high pH soils is a problem. Use in a shrub border, under pines, or in a mass. Often used as a single specimen, where it can become a hummocky mass of unmanageable proportions. Grows 6 to 10 ft. high and wide. Zones 4 to 8(9). China.

Cultivars and Varieties. Of the hundreds of cultivars, only a few are commercially available.

'Cameo' offers large, double, fluffy, peach-pink flowers in profusion. Holds its foliage into fall better than most other cultivars.

'Jet Trail' is a white-flowered sport of 'Texas Scarlet' with a similar growth habit.

'Texas Scarlet' presents tomato-red flowers on a spreading shrub that matures between 3 and 4 ft. high. Profuse flowers and a long flowering period.

'Toyo-Nishiki' is a strong, upright grower. White, pink, red, and combination-colored flowers appear on the same or different branches.

Chaenomeles speciosa, Common Floweringquince

Chaenomeles speciosa 'Jet Trail'

Chaenomeles speciosa 'Cameo' double flowers

Chaenomeles speciosa 'Toyo-Nishiki' flowers

Chamaecyparis lawsoniana

Lawson's Falsecypress

This species is not common in eastern and midwestern gardens, primarily because of its intolerance to heavy, wet, inadequately drained soils. In Europe and in the Pacific Northwest, it is quite common. Over 250 cultivars have been named. The species develops into a pyramidal to conical tree, with a massive, buttressed trunk and short, ascending branches that droop at the tips and end in flat, glaucous green to deep green sprays. Provide well-drained soils. Although respectable specimens of this species occur on Long Island, New York, for most of the eastern half of the United States, *Chamaecyparis obtusa*, *C. pisifera*, and *C. thyoides* and their cultivars are preferable. It is worthwhile to relate that the two largest West Coast wholesale container conifer producers did not list a single form of *C. lawsoniana* in their catalogs. Grows 40 to 60 ft. high, 10 to 15 ft. wide. Zones 5 to 7. Southwestern Oregon, isolated parts of northwestern California.

Cultivars and Varieties. 'Allumii', with strongly vertical sprays of rich blue-green foliage, shows up more often than any other large, tree-type cultivar in the Midwest and East.

Chamaecyparis lawsoniana, Lawson's Falsecypress

Chamaecyparis nootkatensis

Nootka Falsecypress, Alaska Cedar, Yellow Cypress

A common sight on the West Coast and plentiful in Washington and Oregon. The habit is softly pyramidal-conical with numerous drooping branches and long, flattened, pendulous sprays. The needles range from grayish green to bluish green. The ⅓- to ½-in.-diameter, globose cones are composed of four (to six) scales. The species grows best when both atmospheric and soil moisture are abundant. Grows 30 to 45 ft. high, 15 to 20 ft. wide; larger (100 ft. high) in the wild. Zones 4 to 7. Alaska to Oregon.

Cultivars and Varieties. 'Pendula' is an attractive weeping form with graceful, elegantly arranged pendulous branches. It is reasonably common in the Middle Atlantic states. I have never seen a plant taller than 20 ft.

Chamaecyparis nootkatensis foliage

Chamaecyparis lawsoniana cones

Chamaecyparis nootkatensis, Nootka Falsecypress

Chamaecyparis nootkatensis 'Pendula'

Chamaecyparis nootkatensis cones

Chamaecyparis nootkatensis bark

Chamaecyparis obtusa

Hinoki Falsecypress

The species is virtually an enigma, but cultivars are abundant throughout the landscape. The few that I have seen were softly pyramidal trees with spreading branches and drooping, frondlike branchlets. The needles are dark green above, with silvery markings on the undersides, and the foliage is almost fernlike in overall form and texture. The ⅓- to ½-in.-diameter cones are composed of eight to ten scales. For positive identification of *Chamaecyparis obtusa* as distinct from *C. pisifera*, the cone size is a reliable trait. Soils should be moist, well drained, and acidic, although this species is the most climatically adaptable of the genus. Full sun to partial shade is suitable. Use as an accent or specimen plant or use the dwarf forms in rock gardens, borders, and foundation plantings. Grows 50 to 75 ft. high, 10 to 20 ft. wide. Zones 4 to 8. Japan, Taiwan.

Cultivars and Varieties. Numerous cultivars are known. Consult a specialty reference book, such as *Conifers: The Illustrated Encyclopedia* by D. M. van Gelderen and J. R. P. van Hoey Smith (Portland, OR: Timber Press, 1996), for additional listings.

'Filicoides' is a small tree of open, irregular habit, with long, extended branches clothed in semipendulous sprays of dark green foliage.

'Nana Gracilis' has dark green foliage in artistic clusters. Grows about 6 ft. high, 3 to 4 ft. wide.

Chamaecyparis obtusa, Hinoki Falsecypress

Chamaecyparis pisifera

Japanese or Sawara Falsecypress

Like *Chamaecyparis obtusa*, this species is seldom found in the United States. General characteristics are much like those of *C. obtusa*, except for the smaller, ¼-in.-diameter, globose cones. Prefers cooler climates. Grows 50 to 70 ft. high, 10 to 20 ft. wide. Zones 4 to 8. Japan.

Cultivars and Varieties. 'Boulevard' has silvery blue-green, soft-textured foliage on a tight columnar framework. Grows 10 ft. high or more.

'Filifera' forms a gigantic, pyramidal haystack and displays atypical stringy, green foliage. Can grow 15 to 20 ft. high and has actually prospered in heat and

Chamaecyparis pisifera foliage, showing silvery undersides

Chamaecyparis obtusa foliage

Chamaecyparis obtusa cones

drought. A golden-foliaged form, 'Filifera Aurea', offers the same growth habit.

'Plumosa' is a standard tree type with soft-textured, feathery foliage. Plants in the Midwest have grown over 30 ft. high. A golden form, 'Plumosa Aurea', is also available.

'Squarrosa' is called the Moss Falsecypress because of its feathery, gray-green to blue-green, needlelike foliage. Treelike in habit. Grows 30 to 40 ft. high.

Chamaecyparis pisifera, Japanese Falsecypress

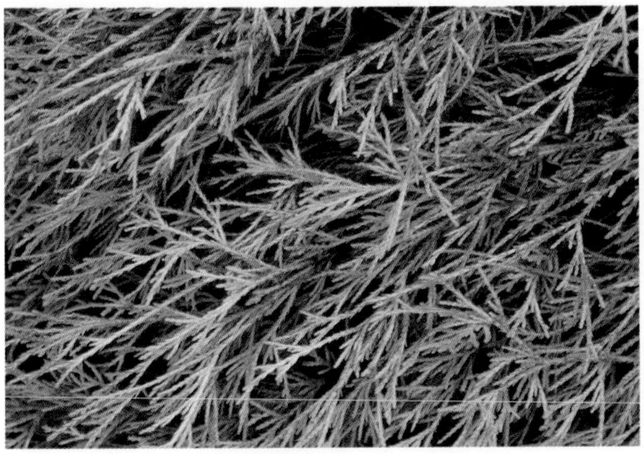

Chamaecyparis pisifera 'Filifera Aurea' foliage

Chamaecyparis pisifera 'Filifera'

Chamaecyparis pisifera 'Squarrosa'

Chamaecyparis thyoides
Atlantic Whitecedar

What a thrill it was to view this tree for the first time in the White Cedar Swamp in Cape Cod National Seashore—the plant was growing in a swamp along with blueberry and clethra. A tall, slender, columnar tree, the plant looks more like a juniper than a falsecypress. The green to bluish green, needlelike foliage may develop an off color (bronze) in winter. The ¼-in.-diameter cones are about the smallest of the genus. Probably does not have great landscape appeal, but for naturalizing in wet areas it is acceptable. Grows 40 to 50 ft. high, 10 to 20 ft. wide. Zones 4 to 8. Maine to Florida along the coast, west to Mississippi.

Chamaecyparis thyoides, Atlantic Whitecedar

Chamaecyparis thyoides cones

Chionanthus retusus
Chinese Fringetree

Like its American cousin *Chionanthus virginicus*, Chinese Fringetree is one of the most beautiful large shrubs or small trees for North American gardens. The habit varies from a large, multistemmed, rounded to broad-rounded shrub to a small, rounded tree. The bark is a pleasing gray and with maturity becomes ridged and furrowed. The 3- to 8-in.-long, lustrous dark green leaves hold late, often into December in southern climes, and may show reasonable yellow fall color. Two forms are in cultivation in the United States: one is shrublike with rounded, leathery, dark green leaves; the other is treelike and has thinner, more elongated leaves. White, lightly fragrant flowers occur in 2- to 3-in.-long and 2- to 4-in.-wide panicles at the end of the current season's growth in May and June. The flowers smother the foliage and create a fleecy, snowlike dome. Fruit are ovoid, ⅜- to ½-in.-long, bluish drupes. Since the species is effectively dioecious, the fruit occur in prodigious quantities only on female plants. Extremely easy to grow. Chinese Fringetree withstands acid or high pH, sandy loam or clay soils. It prospers in sun and also withstands a modicum of shade. Use as an elegant specimen plant, in groupings, in the back of a shrub border, or as a small street tree. I have observed it in gardens from Massachusetts to California to Georgia. Grows 15 to 25 ft. high and wide. Zones 5 to 8. China, Korea, Japan.

Chionanthus retusus, Chinese Fringetree

Chionanthus retusus flowers

Chionanthus virginicus
White Fringetree

Chionanthus retusus fruit

An extremely variable species, no two seedlings are alike in all characteristics. One of the great challenges in my research career has been to propagate this native species from cuttings. To date, the plant has resisted all advances. Found in a variety of habitats throughout the southeastern United States, it is perfectly cold hardy to at least –30°F. Habit varies from an oval or wide-spreading shrub to a small tree. The bark is light gray-brown. The 3- to 8-in.-long leaves vary from medium to dark green, with various degrees of gloss. In fall, leaves turn muted yellow to yellow-brown. Slightly fragrant, strap-shaped, four- to five-petaled, white flowers are borne in 6- to 8-in.-long, fleecy panicles that open on the previous year's wood in May and June. The ½-in.-long, bluish drupes ripen in September. Culturally, it prefers moist, acid, well-drained soils, but like *C. retusus*, it is extremely adaptable. Prospers in full sun to moderate shade. Makes a great woodland or understory naturalizing plant. Flowers at a young age; two- to three-year-old seedlings will produce flowers. Grows 12 to 20 ft. high and wide; can grow larger. Zones 4 to 9. Southern New Jersey to Florida, west to Texas.

Chionanthus retusus bark

Chionanthus virginicus, White Fringetree

Chionanthus virginicus flowers

Chionanthus virginicus in winter

Cladrastis kentukea (C. lutea)

American Yellowwood

The blossoms of American Yellowwood, cascading like white rain from the pea-green shrouded canopy on a spring day, produce one of the most spectacular shows among large flowering trees. This native species, nowhere very common, is a low-branching tree with a broad-rounded crown of delicate branches. The older branches and trunk are smooth and gray—very beechlike in appearance. The emerging leaves are covered with silky hairs, which impart a gray haze, but they soon mature to rich pea-green and turn yellow to golden brown in fall. Fragrant, creamy flowers occur in pendulous, 8- to 14-in.-long panicles in May and June and are followed by small, $2\frac{1}{2}$- to 4-in.-long, light brown pods. Best growth occurs in high pH soils, but splendid specimens throughout the Northeast grow in distinctly acid soils. An excellent specimen tree, it deserves a prominent position in the landscape. Grows 30 to 50 ft. high, 40 to 55 ft. wide. Zones 4 to 8. North Carolina to Kentucky and Tennessee.

Cultivars and Varieties. 'Rosea' is a handsome pink-flowered form now in commercial production.

Cladrastis kentukea flowers

Clerodendrum trichotomum

Harlequin Glorybower

I was never particularly enamored with Harlequin Glorybower until I observed the excellent flower and fruit set, which has provided cause for reassessment. The habit is rounded and shrubby, but some plants, particularly those located farther south, develop into small trees. In the North, plants should be treated as partial dieback shrubs. *Clerodendrum trichotomum* flowers on new growth, so the principal ornamental characteristics are not lost. The fragrant, white flowers occur in long-stalked, 6- to 9-in.-wide cymes during July and August. Each 1- to $1\frac{1}{2}$-in.-wide flower has a tubular base and five spreading lobes. The pea-shaped, $\frac{1}{4}$- to $\frac{3}{8}$-in.-diameter, bright blue drupe is subtended by a leathery, reddish calyx, $\frac{1}{2}$ to $\frac{3}{4}$ in. wide, five angled, and five lobed. Fruit and flowers are often present at the same time. The 4- to 9-in.-long, 2- to 5-in.-wide, dark green leaves develop no fall color. Provide moist, organic-laden, acid, well-drained soils, in sun or partial shade. Wilting occurs in extremely dry soils. Makes a good filler in a border. Grows 10 to 15 ft. high and wide. Zones (6)7 to 9. Eastern China, Japan.

Cladrastis kentukea, American Yellowwood

Cladrastis kentukea fall color

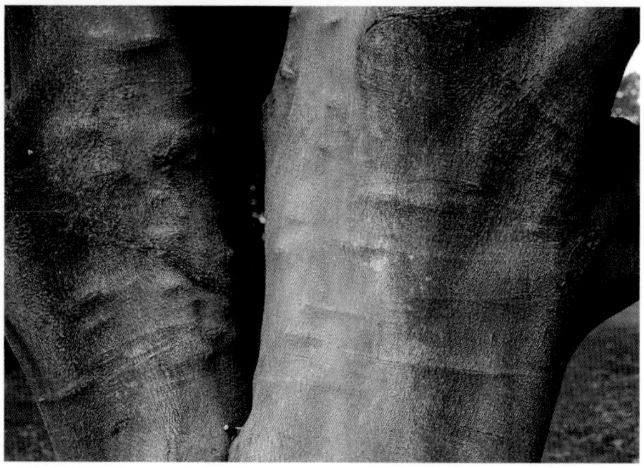

Cladrastis kentukea bark

Clerodendrum trichotomum, Harlequin Glorybower

Clerodendrum trichotomum flowers

Clerodendrum trichotomum fruit

Clethra acuminata, Cinnamon Clethra

Clethra acuminata
Cinnamon Clethra

Arguably, this species is so specialized that it may belong in a more ethereal reference. Although Cinnamon Clethra is hard to come by in the commercial trade, work at the North Carolina State University Mountain Home Station in Fletcher has provided some keys to successful commercial culture, and the species is becoming more widely available. I have observed *Clethra acuminata* on the tallest mountain in Georgia and marveled at the rich cinnamon-brown, flaky bark. Bark color varies from almost purplish or bluish to flat brown. The species develops a suckering habit and tends to slowly colonize. In the North, it grows much more shrublike and is more slow growing. The 3- to 6- (to 8-) in.-long, dark green leaves develop yellow fall color. White flowers occur in 3- to 8-in.-long terminal racemes in July and August. Although often listed as fragrant, the odor is rather faint; in repeated nose-to-flower confrontations, I could not detect much odor. Appears to prosper under less-than-ideal conditions; in the wild, it is commonly found in dry, rocky terrain. In the Dirr garden (Zone 7), the species has succumbed to heat and drought. Good plant for a semishaded garden nook. Grows 8 to 12 ft. high, wider at maturity. Zones 5 to 7(8). Mountains from Virginia to West Virginia, south to Georgia and Alabama.

Clethra acuminata bark

Clethra acuminata fall color

Clethra alnifolia
Summersweet Clethra

During July and August, the sweet floral fragrance of summersweet can permeate an entire garden. The habit is densely rounded and often suckering, resulting in large colonies. The 1½- to 4-in.-long, sharply serrated, lustrous dark green leaves turn pale yellow to rich golden yellow in fall. Fragrant, white flowers occur in 2- to 6-in.-long, ¾-in.-wide racemes and are effective for four to six weeks. Provide acid, moist, well-drained soils, in full sun to relatively heavy shade. It has proven more heat and drought tolerant than *Clethra acuminata*. An amazingly adaptable plant. Great choice in a shrub border, along streams and ponds, or in large masses by the edge of woodlands. Grows 3 to 8 ft. high, variable spread. Zones 4 to 9. Maine to Florida.

Clethra alnifolia fall color

Cultivars and Varieties. Several compact forms, including 'Compacta' and 'Hummingbird', are available. They grow 2½ to 3½ ft. high. 'Hummingbird' forms large colonies, whereas 'Compacta' is more shrubby.

'Pink Spires' and 'Rosea' offer pink buds and pink (or light pink) flowers as fragrant as those of the white form. Habit is like that of the species.

'Ruby Spice' is a new (1995) introduction with deep rose-colored, non-fading, fragrant flowers. Grows 6 to 8 ft. high. An outstanding selection.

Clethra alnifolia 'Hummingbird' flowers

Clethra alnifolia, Summersweet Clethra

Clethra alnifolia 'Pink Spires' flowers

Clethra alnifolia 'Ruby Spice' flowers

Colutea arborescens
Common Bladder-Senna

An essentially unknown shrub in American gardens and, to my knowledge, not particularly prized in any country. The sum of its ornamental parts, however, makes it worth considering. It is a large, rounded, sometimes scruffy shrub that may require pruning to keep it tidy. The bright green, compound pinnate leaves are composed of 9 to 13 leaflets, each ½ to 1 in. long. The foliage color is distinct from that of many other shrubs, and it seems to jump out and identify the plant. The ¾-in.-long, pea-shaped flowers are yellow with red markings and appear in six- to eight-flowered racemes from May to July. The flowers do not overwhelm, but they are curiously pretty—with the right amount of imagination they conjure visions of "Yosemite Sam." The inflated, pealike fruit, 3 in. long and 1½ in. wide, range in color from green to reddish to brown at maturity. Transplant from a container into any soil short of permanently wet. Use the species on hot, dry sites; it might be a decent choice for highway right-of-ways. Grows 6 to 8 ft. high and wide. Zones 5 to 7. Mediterranean region, southeastern Europe.

Colutea arborescens, Common Bladder-Senna

Colutea arborescens fruit

Colutea arborescens flowers

Comptonia peregrina
Sweetfern

I have loved this denizen of sandy, acid soil since my days as a graduate student at the University of Massachusetts, where the nearby highway verges were covered with the shrub. Small, dainty, wispy, spreading, and colonizing, it forms broad, flat-topped colonies. The 2- to 4½-in.-long, dark green, deeply incised leaves give the plant a woodsy appearance. Transplant only as a container specimen. Thrives in low-fertility soils, in sun or light shade. Good "no maintenance" groundcover for naturalistic plantings. Grows 2 to 4 ft. high, 4 to 8 ft. wide or more. Zones 2 to 6. Nova Scotia to Manitoba, south to North Carolina.

Comptonia peregrina, Sweetfern

Comptonia peregrina foliage

Comptonia peregrina fruit

Cornus alba
Tatarian Dogwood

I had forgotten how spectacular this species can be, but a most magnificent planting of *Cornus alba* 'Sibirica' and *C. sericea* 'Flaviramea' at the John F. Kennedy Arboretum in Ireland (seen during a January 1991 visit) ignited the passion. The bright red and yellow stems set against a steel-gray winter sky provides a tremendous psychological lift. The habit is distinctly upright, with many slender branches arching to form a rounded outline. In leaf, the plant looks like every other deciduous shrub. The typical dogwood leaves, 2 to 4½ in. long, may turn reddish purple in autumn. White flowers occur in 1½- to 2-in.-diameter, flat-topped inflorescences in May and June and are followed by whitish or slightly blue-tinted, ⅜-in.-diameter, rounded fruit in summer. The species will grow in acid or alkaline, dry or wet soils, in full sun or heavy shade. Canker can be a problem, especially in Zones 7 and 8. Use in mass plantings where the winter stem color will be effective. Young stems have the most intense coloration. To foster maximum stem color, remove one-third of the oldest canes each year or cut the plants to the ground in late winter. Grows 8 to 10 ft. high, 5 to 10 ft. wide. Zones 2 to 6(7). Eastern Russia to northeast China and North Korea.

Cultivars and Varieties. 'Argenteo-marginata' ('Elegantissima') has leaves with an irregular, creamy white border and a subdued grayish green center. Stems are red in winter. This is a fine plant for brightening shady areas of the garden. A form with crisp, white margins and a green middle is occasionally available.

'Aurea' offers uniform, soft yellow leaves during the growing season that turn birch-yellow in autumn. Reports indicate it is resistant to sun scorch.

'Sibirica' is genuinely confused in the trade, and what I perceive as the true selection may or may not be so. 'Sibirica' is smaller in stature than the species and has bright coral-red stem color.

'Spaethii' has golden-edged leaves that do not scorch. Several clones of 'Spaethii' are flashing around in commerce. The real entity is quite colorful.

Cornus alba, Tatarian Dogwood, grown as a hedge

Cornus alba 'Argenteo-marginata'

Cornus alba flowers

Cornus alba fruit

Cornus alternifolia
Pagoda Dogwood

Cornus alba 'Aurea' foliage

In most situations, this species develops into a large, multistemmed shrub, although single-stemmed tree specimens are common. Pagoda Dogwood has a spreading habit, with horizontal branches that create a layered look. Young stems are deep purplish brown; older stems and the trunk turn gray. The 2- to 5-in.-long, dark green leaves may turn reddish purple in fall, but fall color is seldom spectacular. White flowers are borne in 1½- to 2½-in.-wide clusters above the foliage during May and June. The ¼- to ⅓-in.-wide, rounded, purplish black fruit ripen in July. The fruit stalks are rich pinkish red and more ornamental than the fruit. In theory, the species is more stress tolerant than *Cornus florida*, Flowering Dogwood, but in actual landscape practice, few trees withstand the test. Moist, acid, well-drained soils and partial shade are ideal. Use the strong horizontal lines to soften sharp architectural features. Grows 15 to 25 ft. high, ⅔ to equal in spread. Zones 3 to 7. New Brunswick to Minnesota, south to Georgia and Alabama.

Cornus controversa, Giant Dogwood, is similar to *C. alternifolia*, only slightly larger in all its parts. Although promoted as stress adaptable, it has not lived up to the press clippings.

Cultivars and Varieties. 'Variegata', with creamy margined leaves, occurs in both species. *Cornus controversa* 'Variegata' is the stronger grower.

Cornus alba 'Sibirica' in winter

Cornus alternifolia flowers

Cornus alternifolia fruit

Cornus alternifolia, Pagoda Dogwood

Cornus amomum
Silky Dogwood

This rather pleasant species takes a commercial backseat to the red-stemmed species. In fact, I doubt if it could be purchased from more than five nurseries in the United States. At its best, a large, robust, rounded shrub. The medium to dark green, 2- to 4-in.-long leaves may turn reddish purple in fall. The creamy flowers occur in flat-topped, 1½- to 2½-in.-diameter cymes in June, seldom raising an eyebrow. Fruit, on close inspection, are spectacular shades of blue with white blotches, almost porcelain-blue. Birds are attracted to the fruit and can empty a shrub in a short time. It is adaptable to extremes of soil, in sun or shade. Great for the shrub border or for massing and naturalizing. Grows 6 to 10 ft. high and wide. Zones 6 to 8. Massachusetts to New York, south to Georgia and Tennessee.

Cornus amomum, Silky Dogwood

Cornus amomum flowers

Cornus amomum fruit

Cornus florida
Flowering Dogwood

Many gardeners consider this species the aristocrat of small flowering trees, and this claim is not unjustified. Normally a low-branched tree with a rounded to flat-topped crown and strong horizontal or tiered branching. The dark green, 3- to 6-in.-long leaves provide excellent red to reddish purple fall color. The handsome 3- to 4-in.-diameter, white flowers open in April and May, usually before the leaves, and are the envy of every landscape plant. Glistening red fruit ripen in late September and October. Bark on older branches develops an alligator-hide appearance, which is particularly distinctive and attractive in the winter landscape. *Cornus florida* has suffered over the past 15 years in the Midwest, East, and South from cold and drought cycles, which predisposed plants to insects and diseases. If provided evenly moist, acid, well-drained soils and partial shade, it should prove a long-lived plant. Unfortunately, it is often placed in the most inhospitable situations imaginable, without the necessary drainage, moisture, or shade. When grown in full sun, the species tends to be denser and loses a measure of the character that is evident on specimens grown in shadier sites. A superb landscape tree that will never go out of style. Grows 20 ft. high and wide; can reach 30 to 40 ft. high. Zones 5 to 9. Massachusetts to Florida, west to Ontario, Texas, and Mexico.

Cultivars and Varieties. 'Cherokee Chief' is a garden-tested, deep red-bracted form.

'Cherokee Princess' sets numerous buds at an early age that expand to large white-bracted flowers.

'Cloud Nine' offers good hardiness, and it flowers profusely at a young age.

'First Lady' has variegated yellow-green foliage and white flowers.

'Pluribracteata' has double white flowers that last longer and open later than those of the species.

'Rubra' produces pink flowers.

Cornus florida, Flowering Dogwood

Cornus florida fall color

Cornus florida bark

Cornus florida flowers

Cornus florida 'Pluribracteata' flowers

Cornus kousa
Kousa Dogwood

A most elegant dogwood, but often lost in the landscape shadow of *Cornus florida*. For many parts of the country, however, *C. kousa* is probably a better choice. In youth the habit is stiffly upright, almost vase-shaped, but with age it becomes rounded to broad-spreading, with distinct horizontal branches. Multicolored mosaics of gray, tan, and rich brown develop on older trunks, and the jigsaw puzzle–like pattern becomes graphically evident when the bark is wet. The dark green, 2- to 4-in.-long leaves are slightly smaller than those of *C. florida* and may develop respectable deep red fall color. The creamy white, 2- to 4-in.-wide flowers, which are composed of four long-pointed bracts, open two to three weeks later than those of *C. florida*. Raspberry-shaped, ½- to 1-in.-diameter, red fruit appear in September and October. Prefers moist, acid, well-drained soils, in sun or partial shade, although it is probably more adaptable to extremes of soil than *C. florida*. Makes a choice specimen plant and can be incorporated into borders or used in groupings. Resistant to *Discula* spp., the organism that causes dogwood anthracnose. Grows 20 to 30 ft. high and wide. Zones 5 to 8. Japan, Korea, China.

Cornus kousa in winter

Cultivars and Varieties. Many have been selected but are seldom available in commerce. Be leery when buying the old cultivar 'Milky Way', for it is seed produced and generally does not deliver on its promises.

Rutger's Hybrids (*Cornus kousa* × *C. florida*), developed by Elwin Orton of Rutgers University, include Aurora®, Celestial®, Constellation®, Ruth Ellen®, Star Dust®, and Stellar Pink®. They exhibit characteristics intermediate between those of the parents and are resistant to dogwood anthracnose.

Cornus kousa, Kousa Dogwood

Cornus kousa flower

Cornus Aurora® flower

Cornus Constellation® flower

Cornus Stellar Pink® flow

Cornus mas
Corneliancherry Dogwood

Cornus kousa foliage

Cornus kousa fall color

Cornus mas flowers

Cornus mas bark

Few dogwoods are as durable as this underutilized yellow-flowered, red-fruited species. In the Midwest, it is the longest lived of all *Cornus* species. The habit is oval-rounded to rounded, with a dense network of rather fine stems. Used as a hedge, the branches grow so close-knit as to be impenetrable. The 2- to 4-in.-long, lustrous dark green leaves hold late into fall and may develop a semblance of purple-red fall color. Bright yellow flowers open on naked branches in March and are the only show in town. The ⅝-in.-long, ovoid, bright cherry-red fruit ripen in June and July. They serve as snacks for the birds or can be used for preserves and syrup. The species tolerates acid and high pH, as well as heavy clay soils, better than any dogwood. It usually suckers and develops large colonies, although some plants do not show this tendency. Great in groupings or for screens, hedges, or the border. Grows 20 to 25 ft. high, 15 to 20 ft. wide. Zones 4 to 8. Central and southern Europe, western Asia.

Cultivars and Varieties. 'Aurea' (yellow), 'Elegantissima' (green center, yellow border; pink shading on young leaves), and 'Variegata' (green center, white border) are the best available cultivars for colorful foliage.

'Golden Glory' is an upright form with abundant flowers, and it has proven its mettle in the Midwest, particularly in the Chicago area.

Cornus mas, Corneliancherry Dogwood

MORE ➤

Cornus mas continued

Cornus mas fruit

Cornus mas 'Aurea' foliage

Cornus mas 'Elegantissima' foliage

Cornus officinalis

Japanese Cornel Dogwood

Many gardeners who have seen the true species develop a lifelong passion to procure the plant. Unfortunately, the true species is difficult to locate in commerce. In many respects, *Cornus officinalis* is similar to *C. mas*, although it flowers earlier (the species will overlap) and the fruit ripen later. Other primary differences are the tufts of brownish hairs in the leaf axils (although this trait is variable) and the exquisite gray, orange, and brown bark, which exfoliates in large scales and plates. Landscape uses and culture are similar to that of *C. mas*. The size also approximates *C. mas*, but a 46-year-old tree at the Secrest Arboretum in Wooster, Ohio, grew 22 ft. high and 35 ft. wide. Zones (4)5 to 7(8). Japan, Korea.

Cornus officinalis, Japanese Cornel Dogwood

Cornus officinalis flowers

Cornus officinalis bark

Cornus racemosa
Gray Dogwood

Like *Cornus amomum*, Silky Dogwood, this is a sleeping giant in the world of deciduous shrubs, and one day it will emerge with a vengeance. A pleasant shrub with excellent blue-green foliage, creamy white flowers, and whitish fruit, it prospers in sun or shade and under varied cultural conditions. Use as a filler in the shrub border or in a naturalized situation. Can become a massive suckering shrub that will easily overgrow its boundaries. Grows 10 to 15 ft. high and wide. Zones 4 to 8. Maine to Ontario and Minnesota, south to Georgia and Nebraska.

Cornus racemosa, Gray Dogwood

Cornus racemosa fruit and fall color

Cornus sanguinea flowers

Cornus sanguinea fruit

Cornus sanguinea
Bloodtwig Dogwood

Like the previous two species, the Bloodtwig Dogwood labors in landscape obscurity. In general, it serves similar landscape purposes as the other two. Its large, round-topped, spreading outline is sloppy and unkempt, and the few specimens I have seen always left me cold. The 1½- to 3-in.-long, dark green leaves seldom develop respectable fall color, although blood-red is described. The young stems are blood-red where exposed to the sun; older branches are greenish gray. For winter stem color, cut to the ground in late winter to foster long shoot extensions. Quite adaptable and may be worthy for difficult sites. Grows 6 to 15 ft. high and wide. Zones 4 to 7. Europe.

Cultivars and Varieties. 'Viridissima' is a rather attractive selection with yellowish green winter stems.

'Winter Flame' produces yellow-orange winter stems.

Cornus sanguinea, Bloodtwig Dogwood

Cornus sanguinea 'Viridissima' in winter

Cornus sericea (C. stolonifera)

Redosier Dogwood

In most respects quite similar to *Cornus alba*, although this species is more suckering, stoloniferous, and colonizing. Even the seasoned pro has difficulty separating the two. This species may be more tolerant of wet soils. Grows 7 to 9 ft. high, 10 ft. wide or more. Zones 2 to 7. Newfoundland to Manitoba, south to Virginia and Nebraska.

Cultivars and Varieties. 'Flaviramea' has forever graced midwestern and northeastern gardens. Yellow stems with a hint of green brighten the winter landscape.

'Kelseyi' is a neat, compact, mounded form, 2 to 2½ ft. high and wide. Frequently encountered in the Midwest. It is quite susceptible to leaf spot.

'Silver and Gold' has cream-margined leaves and yellow stems.

Cornus sericea 'Flaviramea'

Cornus sericea, Redosier Dogwood

Cornus sericea 'Silver and Gold'

Cornus sericea in winter

Cornus sericea stems

Corylopsis, Winterhazel

The winterhazels are quite confused taxonomically. To provide some concept of the potential for confusion, an article in the Journal of the Arnold Arboretum *in 1977 reduced the then-described 33 species to 7.* Corylopsis *species prefer organic, acid, well-drained soils, in partial shade. Plants appear to prosper in full sun, however, and in less-than-ideal sites. They are excellent plants for the shrub border or in mass plantings.*

Corylopsis glabrescens
Fragrant Winterhazel

Fragrant Winterhazel can be spectacular in flower, although it tends to become a massive, wide-spreading, dense shrub. It is somewhat flat-topped to rounded in outline and multi-stemmed. The dark green, 2- to 4- (to 5-) in.-long leaves may turn yellow in fall. Fragrant, pale yellow flowers occur in 1- to 1½-in.-long, pendulous racemes in April, before the leaves. Same requirements as *Corylopsis spicata*, Spike Winterhazel. Grows 8 to 15 ft. high and wide. Zones 5 to 8. Japan.

Corylopsis glabrescens, Fragrant Winterhazel

Corylopsis glabrescens foliage

Corylopsis gotoana

Corylopsis gotoana is becoming more common in commerce. It is considered superior to *C. glabrescens* for general landscape use, although the individual flowers are smaller. The true botanical differences are trivial, and some sources consider them the same species. *Corylopsis glabrescens* is considered the more cold-hardy species. Grows 8 to 15 ft. high and wide. Zones 5 to 8. Japan.

Corylopsis gotoana

Corylopsis gotoana flowers

Corylopsis pauciflora
Buttercup Winterhazel

Gardeners will argue the merits of this species over the rest because of its small size, spreading habit, fragrant primrose-yellow flowers, and overall neatness. Like *Corylopsis spicata*, this is a great plant for the woodland garden. Protect from incessant wind and sun. Grows 4 to 6 ft. high and wide. Zones 6 to 8. Japan, Taiwan.

Corylopsis platypetala

The garden version of *Corylopsis platypetala* is the largest of the cultivated winterhazel species. It forms a multistemmed, rounded shrub. The 2- to 4- (to 5-) in.-long, blue-green leaves die off green or brown in fall. Bright yellow flowers occur in 1- to 2-in.-long racemes in April. Combine with dwarf conifers and broadleaf evergreens for maximum effect. Grows 10 to 15 ft. high and wide. Zones 6 to 8. China.

Corylopsis pauciflora, Buttercup Winterhazel

Corylopsis platypetala

Corylopsis pauciflora flowers

Corylopsis platypetala flowers

Corylopsis spicata
Spike Winterhazel

In my April forays through the Arnold Arboretum, I found that Spike Winterhazel appeared to be the best behaved and most floriferous of the winterhazels. The delicate flowers hang like yellow tassels from the naked branches and shift with every breath of the wind. New foliage emerges rich, vinous purple, eventually changing to blue-green. The 2- to 4-in.-long, strongly serrated leaves tend to hold late and are rendered brown by fall freezes. Becomes a mass of crooked, flexible, wide-spreading branches at maturity. A great plant for the shrub border or in mass plantings. Flowers about the same time as Korean Rhododendron *(Rhododendron mucronulatum)*. Grows 4 to 6 (to 10) ft. high. Zones 5 to 8. Japan.

Corylopsis spicata, Spike Winterhazel

Corylus americana
American Filbert

American Filbert is a fine plant for naturalizing, yet it is scarce in commerce. Although no single feature attracts attention, the dark green leaves, yellowish brown catkins, and interesting fruit provide multiseason interest. Prospers in shade or sun and in moist or dry, acid or high pH soils. Although often listed as a smallish shrub, it can easily grow larger, devouring large tracts of garden real estate. Use with discretion and the knowledge that it will outgrow the space. Grows 8 to 10 ft. high and wide; often grows 15 to 18 ft. high and wide. Zones 4 to 9. New England to Saskatchewan, south to Florida.

Corylus americana foliage

Corylus americana, American Filbert

Corylopsis spicata foliage

Corylopsis spicata flowers

Corylus americana catkins

Corylus avellana
European Filbert

An immense shrub or small tree often cultivated for its nuts. The species is seldom planted, and the cultivars represent the species in garden cultivation. Grows 12 to 20 ft. high and wide. Zones 4 to 8. Europe, western Asia, northern Africa.

Cultivars and Varieties. 'Aurea' is a slow-growing form, with yellow leaves that become green with the heat of summer.

'Contorta' is the most popular cultivar. It has artistically contorted stems that provide great interest in the winter garden. Leaves are also slightly twisted. Numerous male catkins are present during fall and winter. I have never observed fruit production in this cultivar. Often grafted, and the understock will sucker. Buy plants that are on their own roots. Grows 8 to 10 ft. high and wide, although plants to 20 ft. are known.

'Pendula' has distinctly weeping branches and forms a large, cascading, arching shrub. Could be grafted onto *Corylus colurna*, Turkish Filbert, to form a small weeping tree.

Corylus avellana, European Filbert

Corylus avellana catkins

Corylus avellana 'Contorta' stems

Corylus avellana 'Aurea' foliage

Corylus colurna
Turkish Filbert

A notably underutilized species in northern landscapes, although such neglect is not justified. *Corylus colurna* is densely pyramidal in youth, pyramidal-oval to almost rounded at maturity. The brown bark exfoliates in small, scaly plates. The best forms offer lustrous dark green, 2½- to 6-in.-long leaves that are resistant to insects and diseases. No appreciable fall color develops. In March, the male flowers appear in 2- to 3-in.-long, brownish catkins, hinting that spring is just around the corner. Nuts develop inside a rather unusual deeply divided bract (modified leaf). Turkish Filbert will grow in a variety of soils and, once established, displays excellent drought tolerance. Superb as a single specimen or in groupings; use along streets, in parks, on golf courses, and on campuses. Grows 40 to 50 ft. high, 15 to 35 ft. wide. Zones 4 to 7. Southeastern Europe, western Asia.

Corylus colurna foliage

Corylus colurna, Turkish Filbert

Corylus colurna fruit

Corylus colurna bark

Corylus maxima var. *purpurea*
Purple Giant Filbert

To my knowledge, the species is seldom grown in the United States, but the variety *purpurea* is relatively common. For rich color in the spring garden, in sun or shade, this is a great choice. The 2- to 5-in.-long, strongly toothed to incised leaves emerge a rich maroon-purple, but the bright color is lost in the heat of summer. Even in late summer and fall, the male catkins and fruit have a purplish tint. Like the previous species, it is adaptable to many soils and climates. Grows 15 to 20 ft. high and wide. Zones 4 to 8. Southern Europe.

Corylus maxima var. *purpurea*, Purple Giant Filbert

Corylus maxima var. *purpurea* foliage

Corylus maxima var. *purpurea* fruit

Cotinus coggygria
Common Smoketree, Smokebush

One of the more common shrubs in the Midwest and East. This species has tremendous visual appeal in May and June (and sometimes July) when the plumy, pink, smokelike panicles are at their peak. The "smoke" effect is provided by the silklike hairs that develop on the inflorescences. Actual flowers are 1/3 in. in diameter, yellowish green, and five petaled. The bluish green leaves, 1½ to 3½ in. long and wide, turn rich yellows, reds, and purples in autumn. The habit of this immense, rounded shrub is often unkempt, and pruning it results in long, buggy-whip branch extensions. Several major gardens cut the plants, particularly the purple-leaf cultivars, to within 6 to 12 in. of the ground to promote colorful, long shoot extensions. *Cotinus coggygria* grows in anything but wet soils. Plant in full sun. Use in borders or groupings. Grows 10 to 15 ft. high and wide. Zones 4 to 8. Southern Europe to central China and the Himalayas.

Cultivars and Varieties. 'Daydream' produces an abundance of dense, ovoid, fluffy inflorescences that mature rich brownish pink. Bears green leaves and has a smaller stature, possibly 10 to 12 ft. high.

'Nordine', 'Notcutt's Variety', 'Royal Purple', and 'Velvet Cloak' are cultivars with maroon to reddish purple leaves. 'Royal Purple' and 'Velvet Cloak' may be the same plant masquerading under two names.

Cotinus coggygria, Common Smoketree

Cotinus obovatus (C. americanus)
American Smoketree

A choice native species that occurs in limestone soils. In the wild, it is often a large shrub rather than a tree, but most cultivated specimens are small trees. The habit is oval to rounded, with a dense crown. The gray-black bark develops a fish-scale constitution that is particularly noticeable in the winter landscape. The rich blue-green, 1½- to 3½-in.-long, oval leaves turn magnificent yellow, orange, red, and reddish purple in fall, with no two trees exactly alike. In fact, a single tree may display all these colors. Makes an excellent small lawn tree and offers possibilities for street and urban planting in dry soils. No serious insect or disease problems. Should become more commonly used in gardens as people discover its many virtues. Grows 20 to 30 ft. high, variable spread. Zones 4 to 8. Tennessee to Alabama, west to the Edwards Plateau of Texas.

Cotinus coggygria inflorescence

Cotinus coggygria 'Daydream' inflorescence

Cotinus coggygria 'Royal Purple'

Cotinus obovatus, American Smoketree

Cotinus obovatus fall color

Cotinus obovatus bark

Cotoneaster adpressus
Creeping Cotoneaster

This species and *Cotoneaster apiculatus*, Cranberry Cotoneaster, are among the most popular of all groundcover and massing cotoneasters because of their handsome dark green foliage and large, lustrous red fruit. The habit is low-spreading, compact, and rigidly branched. The ¼- to ⅝-in.-long leaves turn reddish purple in fall. The pinkish flowers are rather inconspicuous, but the ¼-in.-diameter, dark red fruit persist into winter. Transplant as a container-grown plant into any well-drained soil. Quite tolerant of high pH soils. Makes a great groundcover or mass planting, in full sun to partial shade. Grows 1 to 1½ ft. high, 4 to 6 ft. wide. Zones 4 to 6. Western China.

Cultivars and Varieties. var. *praecox* is larger than the species in all its parts and offers better fruit display.

Cotoneaster adpressus, Creeping Cotoneaster

Cotoneaster apiculatus
Cranberry Cotoneaster

Much like the previous species, but more common in cultivation. Tends toward a stiffer habit, with the branches forming impenetrable tangles. The ¼- to ⅓-in.-diameter, cranberry-red fruit are often spectacular, and they persist into November. The lustrous dark green, ¼- to ¾-in.-long and wide leaves have wavy margins. Habit is perhaps more shrubby than that of *Cotoneaster adpressus*. Grows 3 ft. high, 3 to 6 ft. wide. Zones 4 to 7. Western China.

Cotoneaster apiculatus, Cranberry Cotoneaster

Cotoneaster apiculatus flowers

Cotoneaster apiculatus fruit

Cotoneaster dammeri
Bearberry Cotoneaster

Bearberry Cotoneaster has achieved celebrity status in landscapes in recent decades. In northern gardens, the leaves are usually persistent, unless winter temperatures drop below –10°F. The initial growth habit is relatively prostrate; branches build up, however, layer upon layer, resulting in a sizable plant. The ¾- to 1¼-in.-long leaves are lustrous dark green, turning reddish purple with the coming of cold weather. The ⅓- to ½-in.-diameter, five-petaled, white flowers appear in profusion during May, followed by globose to top-shaped, ¼-in.-diameter, red fruit. Fruit set is often sparse. Adaptable and extremely fast growing, it is a popular choice for quick cover. Tends to become ratty with time and requires pruning to maintain neatness. Fireblight, a bacterial disease, and lace bug, which causes a yellowing of the leaves, may be problematic. Grows 1 to 1½ ft. high, 6 ft. wide or more. Zones 5 to 8. Central China.

Cultivars and Varieties. 'Royal Beauty' ('Coral Beauty') is described as a free-fruiting clone, but for all intents it is not much different than 'Skogholm'. It sets reasonable quantities of red fruit. Grows 2 to 2½ ft. high.

'Skogholm' is a most vigorous, wide-spreading form that covers the ground as fast as any cotoneaster. Grows 1½ to 3 ft. high.

'Streib's Findling' is a small-leaved form of prostrate habit that sets heavy crops of bright red fruit.

Cotoneaster dammeri 'Royal Beauty' flowers

Cotoneaster dammeri 'Royal Beauty' fruit

Cotoneaster dammeri, Bearberry Cotoneaster

Cotoneaster divaricatus

Spreading Cotoneaster

Spreading Cotoneaster is an extremely vigorous, upright-spreading form that eventually develops into a rather refined shrub. The ⅓- to 1-in.-long, lustrous dark green leaves may turn rich, almost fluorescent reddish purple in autumn. The fall color can persist for as long as four to six weeks. Small, rose-colored flowers produce handsome red to dark red fruit, ⅓ in. long and ¼ in. wide, that persist into November. Like the previous species, it is tremendously adaptable. Makes a serviceable screen, mass, grouping, or hedge. In fact, I have observed numerous *Cotoneaster divaricatus* hedges that out perform the ubiquitous privet *(Ligustrum)*. Grows 5 to 6 ft. high, 6 to 8 ft. wide. Zones 4 to 7. Central and western China.

Cotoneaster divaricatus, Spreading Cotoneaster

Cotoneaster divaricatus fall color

Cotoneaster divaricatus fruit

Cotoneaster divaricatus flowers

Cotoneaster horizontalis
Rockspray Cotoneaster

This is a plant of great beauty, and it is used as a groundcover and espalier plant in great gardens the world over. The flat, fanlike, herringbone branching pattern distinguishes this species from the others. The ⅓- to ½- (to ¾-) in.-long, rounded, flattish leaves are lustrous dark green and often turn excellent reddish purple in fall, holding into November. The branches mound upon one another, forming a horizontal, tiered effect. Rose-colored flowers in May and June are followed by abundant red fruit that often persist into winter. May be slightly more susceptible to fireblight than *Cotoneaster adpressus* or *C. apiculatus*. Grows 2 to 3 ft. high, 5 to 8 ft. wide. Zones (4)5 to 7. Western China.

Cultivars and Varieties. 'Hessei' is purportedly a hybrid between *Cotoneaster horizontalis* and *C. adpressus* var. *praecox*. It has ¼- to ⅗-in.- long and wide leaves, pinkish red flowers, and ¼-in.-diameter, globose, red fruit.

'Tom Thumb' is a dense, closely branched, broad-spreading mound. Makes a handsome rock garden plant. Taxonomy is confused, and it might be placed under *Cotoneaster adpressus*.

'Variegatus' has leaves edged with cream and is one of the daintiest of variegated shrubs. The leaves turn lovely rose-red in fall.

Cotoneaster horizontalis, Rockspray Cotoneaster

Cotoneaster horizontalis 'Tom Thumb'

Cotoneaster horizontalis fall color

Cotoneaster horizontalis 'Variegatus' flowers and foliage

Cotoneaster lucidus

Hedge Cotoneaster

Unfortunately, Hedge Cotoneaster is often totally confused with *Cotoneaster acutifolius*, Peking Cotoneaster, in the trade, but it is easily distinguished by its glossy dark green leaves, as compared to the dull green of the latter species. This large, rounded shrub is ideal for pruning and manipulating into geometric shapes—the common name was derived quite honestly. The leaves, ¾ to 2 in. long, turn yellow to red in fall. Pinkish white flowers appear in May and are followed by rounded, ⅖-in.-diameter, black fruit; neither are showy. Easily grown, it is frequently encountered on college campuses in the Midwest as a hedge. Many plants are better for hedging, and this species is actually more aesthetic when left unpruned. Grows 6 to 10 ft. high and wide. Zones 3 to 7. Siberia, northern Asia.

Cotoneaster lucidus, Hedge Cotoneaster

Cotoneaster multiflorus

Manyflowered Cotoneaster

In flower, *Cotoneaster multiflorus* is reminiscent of a white froth, but unfortunately, the flowers are malodorous. Locate the plant at a safe distance from trafficked areas. A massive shrub with upright-arching branches, it requires ample space. The blue-green, ¾- to 2½-in.-long leaves develop before the flowers and provide a rather handsome foil for the five-petaled, ½-in.-diameter, white flowers that appear in May. The ⅓-in.-diameter, rounded, red fruit ripen in late August and persist into October. It thrives in heavy clay soils and full sun. Excellent for massing or large-area use. Grows 8 to 12 ft. high, 12 to 15 ft. wide. Zones 3 to 7. Western China.

Cotoneaster multiflorus, Manyflowered Cotoneaster

Cotoneaster lucidus foliage

Cotoneaster multiflorus flowers

Cotoneaster multiflorus fruit

Cotoneaster salicifolius
Willowleaf Cotoneaster

Somewhat of an enigma in American gardening, Willowleaf Cotoneaster is principally represented by the smaller hybrids and cultivars. The species is a broadleaf evergreen shrub of spreading, arching habit. The 1½- to 3½-in.-long, leathery, lustrous dark green leaves are pubescent on their undersides. White flowers occur in 2-in.-diameter, flat-topped inflorescences in May and June and are followed by ¼-in.-diameter, bright red fruit. Same cultural requirements as for the other cotoneasters. Use in a shrub border for winter foliage and fruit effect. Grows 10 to 15 ft. high, slightly less in spread. Zones 6 to 8. Western China.

Cultivars and Varieties. Many low-growing, 1- to 2½-ft.-high types appear to be hybrids between this species and *Cotoneaster dammeri*, Bearberry Cotoneaster. Among these are 'Autumn Fire', 'Gnom' ('Gnome'), 'Repens' ('Repandens'), and 'Scarlet Leader'. 'Repens' has 1- to 1½-in.-long, lustrous dark green leaves that turn reddish purple in winter. It is the most common selection in American gardens.

Cotoneaster salicifolius, Willowleaf Cotoneaster

Cotoneaster salicifolius 'Gnom' fruit and foliage

Cotoneaster salicifolius 'Repens'

Crataegus crusgalli
Cockspur Hawthorn

One of the most popular species in the Midwest because of its legendary tolerance to hot, dry conditions. Forms a low-branched tree, with wide-spreading, horizontal branches that are armed with 1½- to 3-in.-long thorns. The lustrous dark green, 1- to 4-in.-long leaves have variable bronze-red to purplish red fall color. White, disagreeably scented flowers occur in 2- to 3-in.-diameter clusters (corymbs) in May. The ½-in.-diameter, rounded, deep red fruit ripen in late September and October and persist into winter. Cedar hawthorn rust can disfigure leaves and fruit. No special soil requirements, although the tree prefers well-drained, slightly acid soils and full sun. Excellent plant to use in mass plantings, screens, groupings, or as a general barrier. The thorns do present problems where there is much pedestrian traffic or where children play. Grows 20 to 30 ft. high, 20 to 35 ft. wide. Zones 3 to 7. Quebec to North Carolina, west to Kansas.

Cultivars and Varieties. var. *inermis* ('Crusader') is a thornless form with the same high-quality ornamental attributes as the species.

Crataegus crusgalli, Cockspur Hawthorn, in winter

Crataegus crusgalli fall color

Crataegus crusgalli fruit

Crataegus laevigata
English Hawthorn

A very beautiful species commonly found in English and continental European landscapes. It is common in hedgerows throughout Great Britain and can be observed in open pastures, on rocky mountain slopes, and in waste areas. In this country, however, English Hawthorn is not without its problems. The species and several cultivars are affected by leaf spot (caused by a blight), which may defoliate the tree by July or August. The habit is low branching and round topped, with a close, dense head of ascending branches. The stiff, zig-zag branches are well armed with thorns to 1 in. in length. The lustrous dark green, three- to five-lobed leaves, ½ to 2½ in. long, develop no appreciable fall color. White flowers emerge with the leaves in May and turn the plant into a cloud of snow. The small, red fruit ripen in September and October but are not as showy as those of the American species, *Crataegus crusgalli*. Same soil requirements as *C. crusgalli*. Grows 15 to 20 ft. high and wide. Zones 4 to 7. Europe, northern Africa.

Cultivars and Varieties. 'Crimson Cloud' offers single red flowers with a white, star-shaped center. It is resistant to leaf blight.

'Paul's Scarlet' ('Paulii') displays beautiful double, rose-red flowers, but unfortunately, it is tremendously susceptible to blight.

Crataegus laevigata 'Crimson Cloud' flowers

Crataegus laevigata fruit

Crataegus laevigata, English Hawthorn

Crataegus ×lavallei
Lavalle Hawthorn

This hybrid between *Crataegus crusgalli* and an unknown species has an oval-rounded habit, rich silver-gray branches, and minimal thorns. The 2- to 4-in.-long leaves are lustrous dark green in summer, followed by bronzy or coppery red colors in fall. White flowers occur in 3-in.-diameter clusters in May. The ½- to ¾-in.-diameter, brick-red to orange-red fruit persist into winter. As with *C. crusgalli*, this species prefers well-drained, slightly acid soils. It is more resistant to hawthorn leaf rusts than the parent species. Grows 15 to 30 ft. high, variable spread. Zones 4 to 8.

Crataegus ×lavallei, Lavalle Hawthorn

Crataegus ×lavallei fruit

Crataegus ×lavallei flowers

Crataegus ×*mordenensis*

This complex hybrid resulted from crosses between *Crataegus laevigata* 'Paul's Scarlet' and *C. succulenta*, Fleshy Hawthorn. Two commercial introductions are 'Toba' and 'Snowbird', and they are discussed below. I have not seen a quality specimen of either, but perhaps in the northern part of the range the trees are less afflicted by the leaf blight that is so troublesome to *C. laevigata*. Grows 20 ft. high and wide. Zones 4 to 6.

Cultivars and Varieties. 'Snowbird' is a double white form that originated as an open-pollinated seedling of 'Toba'.

'Toba' has fragrant, white, double flowers that age to pink, and its two- to four-lobed leaves are larger and darker green than those of typical *Crataegus laevigata*.

Crataegus ×*mordenensis* 'Toba'

Crataegus nitida fruit and fall color

Crataegus nitida
Glossy Hawthorn

In the Midwest and East, this species is often spectacular in flower, fruit, and foliage, but it is never common in commerce. Its wide-spreading branches form a broad, dome-shaped outline. The extremely lustrous, 1- to 3-in.-long, dark green leaves turn orangish to red in fall. Small, white flowers appear in 1- to 2-in.-diameter clusters in May and are followed by ½-in.-diameter, dull red fruit, which persist into winter. The rich orange-brown bark is somewhat exfoliating and quite attractive. Relatively free of diseases, this might be a good choice in lieu of the more susceptible types. Grows 20 to 30 ft. high and wide. Zones 4 to 7. Illinois to Missouri and Arkansas.

Crataegus nitida, Glossy Hawthorn

Crataegus nitida flowers

Crataegus nitida bark

Crataegus phaenopyrum
Washington Hawthorn

The most popular landscape hawthorn species because of its adaptability, its clean foliage, and its persistent, brilliant red fruit. The habit is broadly oval to rounded, and the tree is densely thorny, bearing 1- to 3-in.-long spines. The three- to five-lobed, 1- to 3-in.-long, lustrous dark green leaves color orange and scarlet to purplish in fall. Creamy white flowers appear in May and early June and are followed in September and October by the ¼-in.-diameter, glossy red fruit, which persist all winter. One of the most adaptable hawthorns, more comfortable in the heat of the South than any of the other commonly cultivated species. Grows 25 to 30 ft. high, 20 to 25 ft. wide. Zones (3)4 to 8. Virginia to Alabama, west to Missouri.

Crataegus phaenopyrum leaf

Crataegus phaenopyrum, Washington Hawthorn

Crataegus phaenopyrum fruit

Crataegus punctata
Thicket Hawthorn

A rather innocuous species that has yielded a fine cultivar, 'Ohio Pioneer', an essentially thornless type with good vigor, growth, and fruiting characteristics. Abundant white flowers are followed by dark red fruit. Grows 20 to 30 ft. high. Zones 4 to 7. Quebec to Georgia, west to Ontario and Illinois.

Crataegus punctata 'Ohio Pioneer'

Crataegus punctata 'Ohio Pioneer' flowers

Crataegus viridis 'Winter King'
Winter King Green Hawthorn

No other hawthorn selection has received as much attention as 'Winter King'. The lovely rounded habit, almost vase-shaped branching structure, and distinct gray-green stems provide ideal architecture. The lustrous dark green foliage, white flowers, and 3/8-in.-diameter, red fruit are outstanding. Has become extremely popular in the Midwest and East. Will contract some rust in wet weather, and leaves and fruit can be infected. Excellent choice as a small ornamental tree or for use against an evergreen background, where the gray stems and persistent red fruit are more prominent. Bark on older stems exfoliates and exposes grays, greens, and orangish browns. 'Winter King' was selected by Robert Simpson, of Vincennes, Indiana, in 1955. Grows 20 to 25 ft. high, 20 to 30 ft. wide. Zones 4 to 7. Maryland to Florida, west to Iowa and Texas.

Crataegus viridis 'Winter King', Winter King Green Hawthorn

Crataegus viridis 'Winter King' flowers

Crataegus viridis 'Winter King' continued

Crataegus viridis 'Winter King' fruit

Crataegus viridis 'Winter King' fall color

Crataegus viridis 'Winter King' bark

Cryptomeria japonica foliage

Cryptomeria japonica

Japanese Cryptomeria

Possibly the finest planting of this species in the country is housed at the National Arboretum in Washington, DC, framing the entrance to the bonsai collection. A tall, lofty, pyramidal or conical tree with a stout trunk, it makes an effective screen or grouping. The rich blue-green, ¼- to ¾-in.-long needles point toward the ends of the stems, clothing the branches in a foxtail effect. Needles tend to develop a bronzy or purple-bronze color in cold climates. The rich reddish brown bark peels off in shreds and strips. Provide moist, well-drained, acid soils, in full sun to partial shade. Certainly a beautiful evergreen and worth considering as an alternative to pines, spruces, and firs. Grows 50 to 60 ft. high, 20 to 30 ft. wide. Zones (5)6 to 8(9). China, Japan.

Cultivars and Varieties. 'Lobbii' is an upright, pyramidal-columnar form, with denser and less-pendulous branching than the species. The needles are deeper green and will bronze in cold weather.

'Yoshino' is a handsome blue-green form, with foliage turning slightly bronze-green in cold weather. Growth rate is fast (2 to 3 ft. per year), and the plant becomes quite dense without extensive pruning.

Cryptomeria japonica, Japanese Cryptomeria

×*Cupressocyparis leylandii*
Leyland Cypress

Cryptomeria japonica 'Yoshino'

This species has become popular as a Christmas tree in the South and is used for screening and hedges from coastal Massachusetts to Florida. The habit is tightly columnar, with feathery, blue-green foliage sprays. Without extensive pruning, Leyland Cypress makes a very dense plant and it should be restrained at an early age before pruning becomes impossible. Transplant from a container or as a small, balled and burlapped specimen. Expect 3 ft. of vertical growth per year if soils are moist and fertile. Displays excellent salt tolerance and is a choice evergreen for protecting the garden from salt spray. Bagworms and canker can prove troublesome. Grows 60 to 70 ft. high, 6 to 12 ft. wide; can reach 70 to 100 ft. high. Zones 6 to 9.

Cultivars and Varieties. The cultivars of Leyland Cypress are numerous and somewhat confused taxonomically.

'Castlewellan' is a form with soft, golden foliage and excellent vigor. In the heat of summer, the foliage is green; golden coloration intensifies with the coming of cold weather. Excellent, tight habit and fast growth rate.

'Green Spire' is densely narrow-columnar in habit and has rich green foliage.

'Haggerston Grey' has a more open habit (still dense and columnar), with bluish green (to gray-green) foliage.

'Leighton Green' is a tall, columnar form with a central leader and rich green foliage.

'Naylor's Blue' is the most open, loosely branched form. It has distinct glaucous blue-green foliage.

'Silver Dust' offers cream-splotched and -streaked foliage. It is considered a branch sport of 'Leighton Green'.

MORE ➤

×*Cupressocyparis leylandii*, Leyland Cypress

×*Cupressocyparis leylandii* cones

×*Cupressocyparis leylandii* 'Silver Dust' foliage

×*Cupressocyparis leylandii* 'Castlewellan'

×*Cupressocyparis leylandii* 'Naylor's Blue'

Cytisus scoparius
Scotch Broom

Numerous species of *Cytisus* are known, but few are prominent in modern gardens. In Europe, the Scotch Broom, with its bright yellow flowers, is abundant along roadsides and in waste areas. The habit is rounded-mounded, with erect, slender, grass-green stems. The species becomes unkempt with age and requires renewal pruning. Leaves are much reduced, about ¼ to ⅝ in. long, and sparingly evident. The stems function as the principal photosynthesizing organ. Flowers are magnificent and range in color from white to shades of yellow, orange, and red, and bicolors. The entire shrub truly lights up in May and June—one must wonder why the species is not more commonly planted. Unfortunately, the species and cultivars are not persistent and simply die out over time. Many times new seedlings will appear, but they are generally inferior to the parent plant. Broom seems to thrive with neglect, and sandy, infertile soils are most suitable. Transplant from a container. Use along highways, in mass plantings, or in a shrub border. Some of the smaller types may be suitable for pockets in perennial or rock gardens. Grows 5 to 6 ft. high and wide. Zones 5 to 8. Europe.

Cultivars and Varieties. Hundreds of cultivars are known, the greatest concentration originating in the Netherlands. The following are a few of the most common and/or ones that I have observed in my travels.

'Allgold' is a form of *Cytisus* ×*praecox (C. multiflorus* × *C. purgans)* with dark yellow flowers. It is a relatively compact, 3- to 4-ft.-high shrub. Also considered quite cold hardy.

'Burkwoodii' is a vigorous, bushy form with garnet-red flowers. The standard of the blossom is red-carmine and the wings are red-brown with a narrow gold border.

'Hollandia' is a standard rose-pink form. Grows 5 to 8 ft. high.

'Lena' is a compact, comparatively dwarf form, 3 to 4 ft. high. Its flowers have ruby-red standards and wings and pale yellow keels.

Cytisus scoparius, Scotch Broom

Cytisus scoparius in flower

Cytisus scoparius 'Burkwoodii'

Cytisus scoparius flowers

Daphne

The daphnes are great garden plants, and several species offer the sweetest fragrance. They are fickle, however, and many turn up their root tips and die for no explicable reason (although it is often attributed to a virus). Daphne *culture is akin to voodoo medicine, and many different recommendations are given. From my experience, it is best to provide well-drained soils with adequate organic matter and moisture, in shade or sun. A pH range of 6 to 7 is recommended, but daphnes will grow in soils with pH of 4.5. Once planted, do not move, prune, or abuse in any way.*

Daphne ×burkwoodii 'Carol Mackie' foliage

Daphne ×burkwoodii

Burkwood Daphne

This rather dapper, densely branched, compact-rounded form might be the toughest of all the daphnes. The narrow, 1- to 1½-in.-long, blue-green leaves persist into November and December (at least in Boston). Pink-budded flowers open pinkish white to white and are borne in 2-in.-diameter umbels in May. The flowers nestle in the foliage and are lovely on close inspection. The sweet fragrance is fantastic and this alone makes the plant a candidate for virtually any garden (although the finicky requirements of daphnes may preclude use in certain environments). Makes a great filler in any border or rock garden, particularly where people walk. Grows 3 to 4 ft. high and wide. Zones 4 to 8.

Cultivars and Varieties. 'Carol Mackie' has delicate cream edges on the leaves and fragrant flowers, light pink maturing to white. It grows about the same as the species, possibly broader, and shows the same adaptability. Excellent for a touch of color in a shady niche of the garden.

'Somerset' is probably the most common form of *Daphne ×burkwoodii* in cultivation. Two seedlings resulted from the original cross, and this form is the one described above.

Daphne ×burkwoodii flowers

Daphne ×burkwoodii, Burkwood Daphne

Daphne ×burkwoodii fruit

Daphne caucasica
Caucasian Daphne

This species is all the rage in the Mid-Atlantic and New England states. It flowers sporadically throughout the summer and provides a sweet, delicate perfume. Habit is rounded and reasonably dense, with 1- to 1¾-in.-long, glaucous blue-green leaves. Foliage does not develop fall color. Four-sepaled, fragrant, white flowers occur in groups of 4 to 20 in small inflorescences in May and June, and sporadically thereafter. Prefers well-drained soils and partial shade. Observed in Bangor, Maine, in early September, and appears more cold hardy than would be expected. Grows 4 to 5 ft. high and wide. Zones (4)5 to 8. Caucasus.

Daphne caucasica flowers

Daphne caucasica, Caucasian Daphne

Daphne cneorum
Rose Daphne

My own attempts to grow this species have been unsuccessful, but on occasion handsome plantings have crossed my path. *Daphne cneorum* has a groundcoverlike habit, with trailing and ascending branches forming low, loose masses of evergreen foliage. Bright rose-pink, fragrant flowers smother the dark green foliage during May. Overall, the flowering habit reminds one of candytuft. Culture is similar to that of *D.* ×*burkwoodii*, although this species may be more sensitive to inadequate drainage. The best specimens usually develop in rock, scree, or wall gardens. Grows ½ to 1 ft. high, 2 ft. wide or more. Zones 4 to 7. Europe.

Daphne cneorum, Rose Daphne, flowers

Daphne mezereum
February Daphne

During a late-January trip to Ireland, I observed the naked stems of *Daphne mezereum* adorned with vivid rose-purple, fragrant flowers. In Boston, the plant flowered in late March—so the common name doesn't always fit the flowering response. February Daphne lacks the grace of the previous species because of its size, its leggy, upright growth habit, and its large, dark blue-green leaves ($1\frac{1}{2}$ to $3\frac{1}{2}$ in. long). Fruit are bright red, $\frac{1}{2}$-in.-long drupes. Utilize in a shrub border. Possibly a good plant for cut-branch production because of its early flowering date. Grows 3 to 5 ft. high and wide. Zones 4 to 6. Europe, Siberia.

Cultivars and Varieties. var. *alba* offers dull white flowers and yellowish white fruit. In addition to this variety, several other white-flowered forms have been described.

Daphne mezereum, February Daphne

Daphne mezereum foliage and fruit

Daphne mezereum flowers

Davidia involucrata

Dove Tree

One of the most fabled of all garden plants because of the heroic collecting efforts of Ernest H. Wilson in the late 1800s and early 1900s. Wilson eventually collected numerous fruit and sent them to England. Dove Tree is distinctly pyramidal in youth; with age it is pyramidal-oval, although certain trees become rounded. The deep green, 2- to 5½-in.-long, strongly serrated leaves do not color in fall. The most famous characteristic of the species is the two large, creamy white bracts, which subtend the true flower and give the appearance of white dove tails or handkerchiefs fluttering in the breeze. The flowering may not be prolific every year, but a tree in full flower is a spectacle that will be carried through a lifetime of memories. Even the orange-brown bark is attractive, developing a handsome scaly, exfoliating character. Prefers moist, well-drained soils, in full sun or partial shade. A splendid specimen tree worthy of greater use in American gardens. Grows 20 to 40 ft. high, variable spread. Zones (5)6 to 7. China.

Davidia involucrata, Dove Tree

Davidia involucrata bark

Davidia involucrata foliage and white bracts

Deutzia

Perhaps because deutzias were as common as mud in the Midwest landscape, I never afforded them the respect they deserve. On too many occasions, the massive Deutzia scabra, *Fuzzy Deutzia, and* D. ×magnifica *lumbered across even the smallest of landscapes and offered floral interest only in May and June—a pile of leaves and brush the rest of the year. My opinions have changed, however, and some of the smaller types, like* D. gracilis, *are certainly garden worthy. Deutzias across the board thrive with neglect, but they require full sun for maximum flowering. Occasional renewal pruning or selective branch removal are necessary to keep the plants presentable.*

Deutzia gracilis, Slender Deutzia

Deutzia gracilis

Slender Deutzia

This lovely species develops into a low, graceful, free-flowering, broad-mounded shrub with slender, ascending branches. The 1- to 3-in.-long, flat, deep green leaves may develop a hint of maroon in fall. The real show is on in May when the pure white, ½- to ¾-in.-wide flowers smother the plant in a billowy white foam. For floral effect, it is a great overachiever. Use Slender Deutzia as a filler in rock gardens, in perennial and shrub borders, and for mass plantings. Grows 2 to 4 ft. high, 3 to 4 ft. wide. Zones 4 to 8. Japan.

Deutzia gracilis flowers

Cultivars and Varieties. 'Nikko' (var. *nakaiana*) is a graceful, compact, small-leaved shrub. It offers good white flowers, dark blue-green foliage, and deep burgundy fall color. Almost a groundcover. Grows 1½ ft. high, 5 ft. wide.

Deutzia ×kalmiiflora

On first inspection, it is difficult to recognize the flower of this hybrid as that of a *Deutzia*. The good pink (or darker), five-petaled flowers are more open and saucer-shaped than those of other deutzia species, occurring in loose inflorescences of 5 to 12 blossoms. Foliage is light green. Grows 4 to 5 ft. high and wide. Zones 5 to 8.

Cultivars and Varieties. Selected cultivars include 'Contraste', 'Magician', 'Mont Rose', 'Perle Rose', and 'Pink Pompon', all in shades of pink to fuchsia-purple.

Deutzia ×kalmiiflora

Deutzia ×*lemoinei*

Lemoine Deutzia

The great French nurseryman Lemoine produced many hybrids between *Deutzia gracilis* and *D. parviflora*. Most of these produce abundant white flowers on 1- to 3-in.-long, pyramidal corymbs. The habit is typically quite twiggy, dense, erect-branched, and ultimately rounded in outline. Considered one of the hardiest deutzias, able to survive –30°F. Grows 5 to 7 ft. high and wide. Zones 4 to 7.

Deutzia ×*lemoinei*, Lemoine Deutzia

Deutzia ×*lemoinei* flowers

Deutzia scabra

Fuzzy Deutzia

Essentially a dinosaur in modern landscapes, but very much a part of older gardens. *Deutzia scabra* forms an oval or obovate, round-topped shrub, taller than broad, with spreading, somewhat arching branches and brown, peeling bark. The dull green leaves are 1 to 4 in. long and have a sandpapery texture on the upper surface. The white flowers, often tinged with pink, are the only salvation of this shrub. The flowers, each about ½ to ¾ in. long and wide, occur in 3- to 6-in.-long panicles in May and June. Easy to grow. Grows 6 to 10 ft. high, 4 to 8 ft. wide. Zones 5 to 7. Japan, China.

Cultivars and Varieties. 'Plena' is a form with double, pure white flowers.

'Pride of Rochester' has double flowers that are tinged with pink.

Deutzia scabra, Fuzzy Deutzia

Deutzia scabra 'Pride of Rochester' flowers

Deutzia scabra leaf

Diervilla sessilifolia
Southern Bush-Honeysuckle

This species will doubtfully make anyone's list of the top 50 flowering shrubs, but it can be a serviceable filler in sun or shade and in inhospitable soils. Forms a low-growing, wide-spreading, flat-topped shrub. The 2- to 6-in.-long leaves emerge bronze-purple in spring, change to lustrous dark green, and may develop tints of red-purple in autumn. Sulfur-yellow flowers appear at the ends of the shoots in June through August. The floral display is not potent and is really only noticeable if one stumbles into the shrub. An extremely adaptable and versatile plant. Could be used for large-area coverage on banks. Grows 3 to 5 ft. high and wide. Zones 4 to 8. North Carolina to Georgia and Alabama.

Diervilla sessilifolia, Southern Bush-Honeysuckle

Diervilla sessilifolia flowers

Diervilla sessilifolia fall color

Diospyros virginiana
Common Persimmon

This native species will never win a landscape beauty contest, but it possesses an inherent toughness that assures survival under difficult conditions. Common Persimmon is seldom available in commerce, so gardeners must be satisfied with transplanting seedlings from the wild. Pyramidal to oval-rounded in outline, with dark green, 2- to 5½-in.-long leaves, yellow to reddish purple fall color, and squarish, blocky, gray-black bark. The foliage may contract a disfiguring blackish leaf spot. Fragrant, white, blueberry-shaped flowers occur in May and June, with male and female on separate trees. The 1- to 1½-in.-diameter, yellowish red to pale orange, edible berries ripen in fall. The species is adaptable to extremely dry soils. Superior selections of male (i.e., nonfruiting) trees might be utilized for urban plantings. Grows 35 to 60 ft. high, 20 to 35 (to 50) ft. wide. Zones 4 to 9. Connecticut to Florida, west to Kansas and Texas.

Diospyros virginiana, Common Persimmon

Dirca palustris
Leatherwood

Diospyros virginiana flowers

A great, dapper, shade-loving native shrub that simply cannot find its way out of the shadows into commerce. This is a choice plant for those impossible shady garden areas; in fact, it performs more admirably in shade than in full sun, where the leaves bleach. The habit is oval to rounded, with light brown stems that are almost leathery. The egg-shaped, 1- to 3-in.-long, light green leaves are among the first to emerge in spring. In fall, they turn clear yellow. Pale to bright yellow flowers occur on leafless stems in March and April and provide a barometer for spring. Fruit are ⅓-in.-long, oval, (reddish) green drupes that ripen in June and July. Provide organic-laden, moist, acid soils. Use in a woodland garden, in a naturalized situation, or in combination with ericaceous plants. Grows 3 to 6 ft. high and wide. Zones 4 to 9. New Brunswick to Ontario, south to Florida and Missouri.

Diospyros virginiana fruit

Dirca palustris, Leatherwood

Dirca palustris in fall

Dirca palustris flowers

Disanthus cercidifolius
Disanthus

Virtually unknown in American gardens, this shrub is worthy of use because of its excellent wine-red fall color. The few specimens I have encountered invariably were located at botanic gardens and arboreta. Disanthus forms a broad, spreading shrub with slender branches, and it requires room to develop. The lustrous, dark bluish green, 2- to 4½-in.-long leaves are heart-shaped, like those of redbud *(Cercis)*. In fall, the foliage turns combinations of claret-red and purple, often suffused with orange. Dark purple flowers occur in October and are, at best, curiously interesting. Provide moist, acid, organic, well-drained soils. Light shade is preferable, although I have observed plants that were prosperous in full sun. Grows 6 to 10 (to 15) ft. high and wide. Zones 4 to 7. Japan.

Disanthus cercidifolius, Disanthus

Disanthus cercidifolius fall color

Elaeagnus angustifolia
Russian-Olive

An excellent plant for its silvery gray foliage effect, as well as its salt tolerance. It is used in abundance along highways in the Midwest, where de-icing salts are common. The habit is quite loose, of light texture, and generally rounded in outline. The elliptical, 1- to 3-in.-long, silvery leaves hold late in fall and do not color. The silvery white to yellowish flowers and the silver-scaled fruit, which eventually turn reddish, are lost among the foliage. Tolerates acid, high pH, saline, and dry soils; also fixes atmospheric nitrogen. Unfortunately, *Verticillium* wilt can severely injure the tree. A respectable plant for difficult sites or where a change in foliage color is warranted. Grows 12 to 15 (to 20) ft. high and wide; can grow 30 to 40 ft. Zones 2 to 7. Southern Europe, Asia.

Elaeagnus angustifolia fruit and foliage

Elaeagnus angustifolia flowers

Elaeagnus multiflora
Cherry Elaeagnus

Many gardeners are wary of *Elaeagnus* species because of the weedy nature of *E. umbellata*, Autumn-Olive. *Elaeagnus multiflora* makes a rather handsome rounded shrub, however, and it does not produce the stray seedlings like *E. umbellata*. The 1½- to 2½-in.-long leaves are dark green above and silvery brown below. Dirty white or silvery brown, tubular, fragrant flowers occur from the leaf axils in April and May. The scaly, ovoid, ½-in.-long, red fruit ripen in June and July. Adaptable to infertile soils, in full sun to half shade. Good plant to use for screening or massing. Definitely not for the small garden. Grows 6 to 10 ft. high and wide. Zones 5 to 7. China, Japan.

Elaeagnus angustifolia, Russian-Olive

Elaeagnus multiflora fruit

Elaeagnus multiflora, Cherry Elaeagnus

Elaeagnus umbellata
Autumn-Olive

Elaeagnus umbellata, Autumn-Olive

This introduced species has become a pernicious pest of woodlands on the southeast and east coasts. It has crowded out many of the better native understory species because of its tolerance of shade and infertile, dry soils. By no means a wee lad, Autumn-Olive becomes a massive shrub or small tree. The 2- to 4-in.-long leaves are bright green above, silver-white beneath. Fragrant, silvery white, ½-in.-long, funnel-shaped flowers occur in May and June, after the leaves have emerged. Numerous globose, ⅓-in.-diameter, red fruit develop in September and October. Birds are the great disseminators of the species, and stray seedlings are evident everywhere. Use only with the knowledge that it can become an ineradicable liability. Grows 12 to 18 ft. high and wide. Zones 3 to 8. China, Korea, Japan.

Cultivars and Varieties. 'Titan' is a new introduction that grows 12 ft. high, 6 ft. wide.

Elaeagnus umbellata flowers

Elaeagnus umbellata fruit

Elsholtzia stauntonii
Staunton Elsholtzia

One can debate its relative garden merits, but this shrubby member of the mint family offers fragrant foliage and purplish pink flowers on terminal panicles in September and October, when precious few shrubs are anything but green. The strongly toothed, 2- to 6-in.-long leaves are bright green in summer. Provide loamy, well-drained soils, in full sun. Cut back old branches in late winter, since flowers occur on new growth of the season. Use in a perennial or shrub border for late-season color. Grows 3 to 5 ft. high and wide. Zones 4 to 8. Northern China.

Elsholtzia stauntonii, Staunton Elsholtzia

Elsholtzia stauntonii flowers

Enkianthus campanulatus

Redvein Enkianthus

For some reason, I have had limited success with *Enkianthus* species. They sit in the garden and look at me, never growing or prospering. Mature specimens, however, are superb, particularly in fall color. Redvein Enkianthus is the most popular and the easiest member of the genus to cultivate, and it is also the most commonly available in commerce. The habit is upright in youth, becoming more open and layered (stratified) with age. The 1- to 3-in.-long, sharply serrated, blue-green leaves may turn brilliant yellow to orange and red in fall. The ⅓- to ½-in.-long, bell-shaped flowers are creamy yellow or light orange, veined with red. Flowers open in May and June and have a curious, rather unpleasant odor. Provide acid, organic, moist, well-drained soils, in partial shade or sun. Excellent choice for flower and fall color. Combines well with other ericaceous plants, such as rhododendrons and azaleas. Several excellent cultivars, ranging in flower color from white to deep rose or maroon, are available. Grows 6 to 8 ft. high in the Midwest; 12 to 15 ft. high in the Northeast. Zones 4 to 7. Japan.

Enkianthus campanulatus, Redvein Enkianthus

Enkianthus campanulatus flowers

Enkianthus campanulatus fall color

Enkianthus cernuus

Although not as robust as *Enkianthus campanulatus*, *E. cernuus* bears ¼-in.-long, white flowers in 10- to 12-flowered racemes, providing a lovely accent in May. Generally smaller in all its parts than *E. campanulatus*. Similar cultural requirements. Grows 5 to 10 ft. high. Zones 5 to 7. Japan.

Cultivars and Varieties. var. *rubens* has deep red flowers.

Enkianthus cernuus var. *rubens*

Enkianthus perulatus
White Enkianthus

Possibly the most refined and elegant enkianthus, but nowhere common in gardens. The bright green leaves, the fine-textured, slender stems, and the dainty rounded habit contribute to its garden worthiness. Urn-shaped, 1⁄3-in.-long, white flowers open with or before the 1- to 2-in.-long leaves in May. As with the other *Enkianthus* species, the flowers are somewhat ill-scented. Fall color is often brilliant scarlet. Use as an accent plant in a border or rock garden, or in a prominent position. Grows 6 ft. high and wide. Zones 5 to 7. Japan.

Enkianthus perulatus in fall

Enkianthus perulatus flowers

Enkianthus perulatus, White Enkianthus

Erica carnea
Spring Heath

The heaths are a most difficult group to discuss since some 500 species are known, and most of these are not cold hardy. Spring Heath makes a fine evergreen groundcover in well-drained, acid soils and a sunny exposure. The ½-in.-long, lustrous green, needlelike leaves provide a delicate texture. Urn-shaped, ¼-in.-long flowers, which appear from January through March, are constricted at the end of the lobe. The principal flower colors are white to rose-pink to rose-fuchsia. Remove spent inflorescences. Plant in sandy, acid, loamy soils. Does not appear as sensitive to high pH soils as other ericaceous genera. Lovely for color in the winter garden. Grows 1 ft. high, variable spread. Zone 5 to 7. Europe.

Erica carnea, Spring Heath

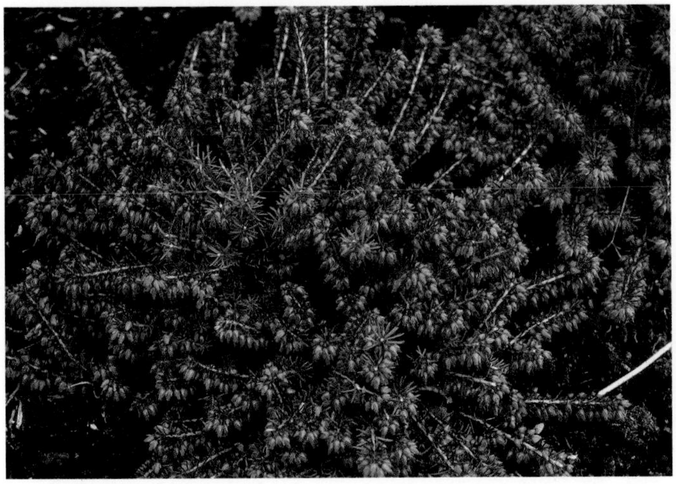

Erica carnea flowers

Eucommia ulmoides
Hardy Rubber Tree

A most unusual tree because of the high latex content (3%) in the leaves and stems; strands of latex are evident when a leaf is torn apart. A rounded to broad-spreading tree of rather uniform outline at maturity. The 3- to 6-in.-long, lustrous dark green leaves do not color in fall. Tolerant of a wide range of soils and pH. At one time considered a possibility for street and urban use, but this tree never jumped the hurdle. Nice for lawns, parks, golf courses, or commercial grounds. Grows 40 to 60 ft. high and wide. Zones 4 to 7. China.

Eucommia ulmoides, Hardy Rubber Tree

Eucommia ulmoides foliage

Eucommia ulmoides male flowers

Euonymus alatus
Winged Euonymus

Truly one of the great aesthetic and functional shrubs available for American gardens. Too often, it is pruned into oblivion; an open-grown specimen is much more appealing and retains an aura of elegance. The medium green, 1- to 3-in.-long leaves, finely and sharply serrated, become fluorescent pinkish red to vibrant red in fall. Coloration is as intense and consistent as that provided by any shrub. Flowers are a rather insignificant greenish yellow. Fruit are reddish with an orange-red seed. The large, corky wings are arranged at 90° separations around the stem. The wings range from ¼ to ½ in. wide, and if plants are severely pruned, the wings on the new growth extensions may average ¾ in. or greater. Easily transplanted and culturally adaptable. Develops premature fall color if summer or early-fall drought occurs. Great plant for massing or grouping. Ideally do not prune. I have observed tree-form specimens in New England and the Midwest. Grows 15 to 20 ft. high and wide. Zones 4 to 8. Northeastern Asia to central China.

Cultivars and Varieties. 'Compactus' lacks the prominent corky wings of the species. It is used for hedging, grouping, or massing. Beautiful red fall color. Grows 5 to 10 ft. high and wide.

'Rudy Haag' is more compact than 'Compactus', growing about 5 ft. high and wide in 15 years. The fall color is more pinkish red.

Euonymus alatus, Winged Euonymus, in fall

Euonymus alatus fruit

Euonymus alatus fall color

Euonymus alatus 'Rudy Haag'

Euonymus alatus 'Compactus' in fall

Euonymus alatus winter stems

Euonymus bungeanus
Winterberry Euonymus

Although not common in landscapes, the tree-type *Euonymus*, including this species, can be spectacular for fruit display. Unfortunately, all tree-type *Euonymus* are horrendously susceptible to scale, so one that appears healthy one year may be dead the next. The gardener is largely powerless to stop scale infestations. Weigh the ornamental features against this admonition. The habit is distinctly rounded with fine-textured, almost pendulous branches. The light green, 2- to 4-in.-long leaves seldom color yellowish in fall. The yellowish green flowers are inconspicuous, but in fall, the pinkish fruit capsules open to expose showy orange seeds—this is possibly the only reason to grow the species. Tolerant of most soils and hot, dry, windy exposures. Grows 18 to 24 ft. high and wide. Zones 4 to 8. Northern and northeastern China.

Euonymus bungeanus, Winterberry Euonymus

Euonymus bungeanus fruit

Euonymus europaeus
European Euonymus

Not unlike the previous species in susceptibility to scale, but with prettier fruit, which range in color from pink to red and have orange seeds. Grows 12 to 30 ft. high, 10 to 25 ft. wide. Zones 3 to 7. Europe, western Asia.

Cultivars and Varieties. 'Red Cascade' has proven an excellent cultivar in the Midwest, with its abundant rosy red capsules and orange seeds.

Euonymus europaeus, European Euonymus

Euonymus europaeus fruit

Euonymus fortunei
Wintercreeper Euonymus

The species is seldom grown, and the many cultivars provide the major representation in cultivation. Habit varies from an evergreen groundcover to a 3- to 4-ft.-high and wide shrub. The 1- to 2-in.-long leaves are dark green with lighter colored veins. Greenish white flowers appear in June and July, followed by pinkish to reddish capsules that dehisce to expose the orange-red seeds. Prefers moist, loamy soils, in sun or shade. Scale can be devastating. Use for foliage color; see cultivars below. A good choice in borders, use with junipers to provide color and texture. Zones 5 to 8(9). China.

Cultivars and Varieties. var. *coloratus* ('Coloratus') is possibly the most common form and is used for groundcover purposes. In winter, the glossy deep green leaves turn a lurid plum-purple. This variety has the advantage of being very tolerant of sun and shade. Grows ¾ to 1 ft. high, spreads indefinitely.

'Emerald Gaiety' is a shrubby form that develops into a large mound of silver-edged leaves. Leaves average ¾ to 1¾ in. long and almost as wide. Grows 4 to 5 ft. high, slightly greater in spread.

'Emerald 'n' Gold' offers 1- to 1½-in.-long, glossy dark green leaves with yellow margins. Although often listed as smaller than 'Emerald Gaiety', it will grow as large.

'Kewensis' has ¼- to ⅝-in.-long leaves and makes an excellent, dainty groundcover.

'Vegetus' is a robust shrub form that has been used extensively in the Midwest. The 1- to 2-in.-long, dull green leaves are almost rounded. It is a free-fruiting clone. More susceptible to scale than other clones. Grows 4 to 5 ft. high and wide.

Euonymus fortunei, Wintercreeper Euonymus, climbing a tree trunk

Euonymus fortunei fruit

Euonymus fortunei var. *coloratus*

MORE ➤

Euonymus fortunei 'Emerald 'n' Gold'

Euonymus fortunei 'Kewensis'

Euonymus fortunei 'Vegetus'

Euonymus kiautschovicus
Spreading Euonymus

In the past, this species was about as common as soil in many northern gardens, but it has lost favor in recent years. It is rounded in habit and has semievergreen (evergreen in the South), 2- to 3-in.-long, lustrous dark green leaves. Flowers and fruit are somewhat similar to those of *Euonymus fortunei*. Adaptable to virtually any soil, in sun or shade. Susceptible to scale. Use for hedges, screens, or masses. Grows 8 to 10 ft. high and wide. Zones 5 to 8. Eastern and central China.

Cultivars and Varieties. 'Manhattan' is the most common cultivar. It has more rounded foliage and is smaller in stature than the species. Probably not as cold hardy; –15°F temperatures will likely reduce it to rubble. Grows 4 to 6 ft. high and wide; I have seen plants 8 ft. high, 12 ft. wide.

Euonymus kiautschovicus, Spreading Euonymus

Euonymus kiautschovicus fruit

Evodia daniellii
Korean Evodia

Euonymus kiautschovicus 'Manhattan'

In its finest form, a uniform, round-headed tree with lustrous dark green, compound pinnate foliage. The leaves are composed of five to eleven 2- to 5-in.-long leaflets. It has never become popular in American gardens, but numerous assets make it worthy of consideration. Creamy white flowers are borne in 4- to 6-in.-wide, flattish corymbs in July and provide excellent bee pasture. The fruit capsule changes from red to black and splits to expose shiny, brownish black seeds. Even the bark is handsome, becoming smooth and gray with maturity. This species and the closely related *Evodia hupehensis* have no serious flaws. Not finicky as to soil types, it makes a good choice for difficult sites. Grows 25 to 30 (to 50) ft. high and wide. Zones 4 to 8. Northern China, Korea.

Euonymus kiautschovicus 'Manhattan' flowers

Evodia daniellii fruit in August

Evodia daniellii fruit in October, changing to black

Evodia daniellii, Korean Evodia

Evodia daniellii bark

Exochorda racemosa
Common Pearlbush

To see one pearlbush species is to see them all. Common Pearlbush is a large, irregular shrub that becomes floppy and often unkempt with age. White, 1½-in.-diameter flowers occur in 3- to 5-in.-long racemes before the leaves in April. The expanding buds appear as small pearls—hence, the common name. The 1- to 3-in.-long, medium green leaves are not troubled by insects or diseases. The gray to orange-brown bark on older branches develops a scaly constitution. Adaptable and easy to grow. Once established, it tolerates drought. Excellent for flower effect, and best reserved for the shrub borders. Grows 10 to 15 ft. high and wide. Zones 4 to 8. Eastern China.

Cultivars and Varieties. 'The Bride' is a hybrid between *Exochorda racemosa* and *E. korolkowii*. It has a delicate, arching branch structure and broad-rounded habit. The 1¼-in.-diameter flowers occur in 3- to 4-in.-long racemes of six to ten flowers. Grows 3 to 4 ft. high, slightly wider.

Exochorda racemosa, Common Pearlbush

Exochorda racemosa foliage

Exochorda racemosa flowers

Fagus grandifolia
American Beech

Described by Florence Bell Robinson as "'The Beau Brummel' of trees but clannish and fastidious as to soil and atmosphere, magnificent specimen, casting shade which does not permit undergrowth." The accolades continue: "If the word noble had to be applied to only one kind of tree, the honor would probably go to the beech," says James U. Crockett; "A sturdy, imposing tree often with a short trunk and wide-spreading crown, a picture of character" (from the description in my *Manual of Woody Landscape Plants*). A beech forest is perhaps the most awe-inspiring sight in the natural world, especially when the shimmering green leaves emerge in spring and again in fall when the leafy mantle assumes a rich golden hue. The 2- to 5-in.-long, coarsely serrated, lustrous dark green leaves turn yellow to golden brown to brown in fall and persist on the tree's lower extremities into winter. In winter, the silver-gray trunks and branches are outstanding. Unfortunately, the American Beech is seldom available in the garden center and nursery trades. Difficult to transplant, but as a small, container or balled and burlapped tree it will move successfully. It prefers well-drained, acid, moist soils but is amazingly tolerant to a variety of soil conditions, and in the wild across its native range, it is found in soils from acid to calcareous, wet to dry. Will grow in sun or shade. Grows 50 to 70 ft. high, equal or slightly less in spread. Zones 4 to 9. New Brunswick to Ontario, south to Florida and Texas.

Fagus grandifolia, American Beech

Fagus grandifolia fruit

Fagus grandifolia fall color

Fagus sylvatica
European Beech

Considerably more amenable to garden culture than *Fagus grandifolia*, *F. sylvatica* has been widely planted in Europe and North America for centuries. Numerous cultivars have gained greater popularity than the species. The species is a star in its own right, with a densely pyramidal to oval outline in youth, branching to the ground. It becomes more rounded in age but never loses the stately elegance. The lustrous dark green, 2- to 4- (to 5-) in.-long leaves hold late in fall before developing the rich russet and golden brown colors. The smooth, gray, elephant hide–like bark is absolutely stunning in the winter landscape. This species should be reserved for large-area planting because of its massive mature size. Possibly more tolerant than *F. grandifolia* to extremes of soil, and easier to transplant. Grows 50 to 60 ft. high, 35 to 45 (to 60) ft. wide; often larger. Zones (4)5 to 7. Europe.

Fagus sylvatica, European Beech

Cultivars and Varieties. 'Asplenifolia' is a delicate, fine-textured form, with gracefully cut (dissected) leaves that impart a fernlike texture. Makes a soft, billowy impression in the landscape. Will mature into a large tree.

'Atropunicea' is a catchall term for the purple-leaf forms. On many of these, new leaves emerge coppery purple and mature to dark purple-maroon. The foliage fades in the heat of summer to green with tinges of the original purplish pigmentation. The best forms are possibly 'Spaethiana' and 'Riversii', although others exist.

'Fastigiata' is an elegant, upright, columnar to slightly columnar-oval form. In a landscape setting, the tree makes a strong vertical element. Fastigiate forms with yellow foliage ('Dawyck Gold') and purple foliage ('Dawyck Purple') are available.

'Pendula' has a personality all its own: most are certainly weeping, but also dipping, diving, arching, and permutating in all directions. No two are alike. Several purple weeping types and a golden weeping form ('Aurea Pendula') are available.

'Rotundifolia' is a most beautiful form, with ½- to 1½-in.-diameter, rounded, black-green leaves. It leafs out about two weeks later than the species and is also more tightly branched.

Fagus sylvatica bark

Fagus sylvatica 'Asplenifolia' foliage

Fagus sylvatica 'Fastigiata'

Fagus sylvatica 'Pendula'

Forsythia

Several cold-hardy Forsythia *cultivars have been introduced, with buds hardy to at least –20°F. None measure up to the* Forsythia ×intermedia *types for floral quality, but where temperatures drop below –15°F, their use is justified. After a –20°F Illinois winter,* F. ×intermedia *types flowered only below the snowline; the cultivar 'Meadowlark' (a cross between* F. ovata *and* F. europaea*), however, flowered to the tips of the branches. The new cold-hardy selections may be somewhat difficult to locate. Try northern-based, specialty mail-order firms. Ask for 'Happy Centennial', 'Meadowlark', 'New Hampshire Gold', 'Northern Sun', 'Sunrise', and 'Vermont Sun'.*

Forsythia 'Arnold Dwarf'

Forsythia 'Arnold Dwarf'

This hybrid cultivar (*Forsythia ×intermedia × F. japonica* var. *saxatilis*) can be used effectively for mass or groundcover. I have even seen 'Arnold Dwarf' covering 45° banks. Habit is mounded with long, trailing branches. Flowers are somewhat greenish yellow and sparingly produced, although older specimens flower quite abundantly. Grows 3 (to 6) ft. high, 7 ft. wide. Zones 5 to 8.

Forsythia 'Arnold Dwarf' flowers

Forsythia ×intermedia

Border Forsythia

My horticultural development was hampered by this species, since it seemed to be the only flowering shrub on the planet. Widely planted because of its vivid golden yellow flowers, Border Forsythia is truly a harbinger of the spring season. A large, at times wild and woolly shrub with intricate tangles of branches, it forms a broad-rounded outline. The 3- to 5-in.-long, sharply serrated, medium to dark green leaves die off green or with a hint of burgundy. Four-petaled, yellow flowers, 1¼ to 1½ in. long and often as wide, open on naked branches in April. The flower effect is spectacular, making this the most recognized and beloved of garden shrubs. It offers ironclad adaptability to soils and climates. Prune after flowering, or remove the largest canes each year. Use in mass plantings, shrub borders, parking lot islands, and other inhospitable places. Grows 8 to 10 ft. high, 10 to 12 ft. wide. Zones 5 to 8.

Cultivars and Varieties. 'Beatrix Farrand' offers 1½- to 2-in.-diameter, vivid golden yellow flowers on a robust, 8- to 10-ft.-high shrub. Petals are thick-textured, waxy, and overlapping.

'Karl Sax' is bushier in habit and not as tall as 'Beatrix Farrand'. It bears golden yellow flowers and the buds are considered slightly more cold hardy.

'Lynwood' has lighter yellow flowers, more open and better distributed along the stem. Petals are strap-shaped and do not overlap like those of 'Beatrix Farrand'.

'Spring Glory' offers abundant soft yellow flowers on a robust shrub. The color is lighter than that of 'Lynwood' and not as harsh and obtrusive as that of 'Beatrix Farrand'. 'Primulina' is similar. Grows 10 ft. high, 12 ft. wide.

Forsythia ×intermedia, Border Forsythia

Forsythia ×intermedia 'Karl Sax' flowers

Forsythia ×intermedia 'Lynwood' flowers

Forsythia ×intermedia fall color

Forsythia suspensa var. *sieboldii*
Weeping Forsythia

This pretty, gracefully arching shrub can be used creatively on banks, walls, or any place the long, trailing branches are able to stretch and arch. Unfortunately, the golden yellow flowers are smaller, 1 to 1¼ in. across, and not as profuse as those of many of the *Forsythia* ×*intermedia* types. Leaves vary from simple to three-parted or trifoliated, a trait that further permits separation from *F.* ×*intermedia*. Forms a large, upright-spreading, almost fountainlike shrub. Grows 8 to 10 ft. high, 10 to 15 ft. wide. Zones 5 to 8. China.

Forsythia suspensa var. *sieboldii*, Weeping Forsythia

Forsythia suspensa var. *sieboldii* foliage

Forsythia suspensa var. *sieboldii* flowers

Forsythia viridissima 'Bronxensis'
Bronx Greenstem Forsythia

The species is seldom used, but 'Bronxensis', a compact, flat-topped, spreading form, is quite common in northern gardens. The bright green, ¾- to 1½-in.-long leaves are sharply serrated and are handsome through the growing season. Primrose-yellow flowers appear in late March or early April and are effective, but not to the degree of those of *Forsythia* ×*intermedia* types. Use as a groundcover or in mass plantings, rock gardens, and borders. Grows 1 ft. high, 2 to 3 ft. wide. Zones 4 to 8.

Forsythia viridissima 'Bronxensis', Bronx Greenstem Forsythia

Fothergilla gardenii

Dwarf Fothergilla

A magnificent shrub that offers superb flowers and foliage, in both summer and fall, as well as sun and shade tolerance. Fothergillas are just now becoming more available and in the future will assume a rightful place in American gardens. The habit of Dwarf Fothergilla is significantly variable, from a small, finely twiggy, rounded shrub to a more open, suckering, colonizing form. The 1- to 2½-in.-long, dark blue-green leaves turn shades of fluorescent yellow, orange, and red in fall, with all colors present in the same leaf. The leaves hold late, and fall color is expressed over a long period. White, fragrant flowers occur in 1- to 2-in.-long, bottlebrushlike inflorescences in April and May, before or as the leaves develop. The flowers appear about the same time as those of Kurume azaleas and make a handsome complement to the often loud-colored azaleas. Much has been written about *Fothergilla* adaptability, but the greatest success is guaranteed with acid, moist, organic-laden, well-drained soils. Plants flower and color best in full sun but respond quite nicely to half shade. Use in shrub borders, perennial borders, groupings, or foundation plantings. Fothergillas do not have a bad season. Grows 2 to 3 ft. high and wide; 5- to 6-ft.-high plants are not uncommon. Zones (4)5 to 9. Southeastern United States.

Cultivars and Varieties. 'Blue Mist' has rich, glaucous blue foliage and somewhat disappointing yellow or bronze fall color. Flowers are slightly smaller than typical. It is a rather wispy grower, probably maturing about 3 ft. high.

Fothergilla gardenii, Dwarf Fothergilla

Fothergilla gardenii flowers

Fothergilla gardenii fall color

Fothergilla gardenii 'Blue Mist'

Fothergilla major
Large Fothergilla

Virtually everything mentioned under *Fothergilla gardenii* can be applied to this species, with the exception that it is larger in all its parts. Grows 6 to 10 ft. high and wide; 15-ft.-high specimens are known. Zones 4 to 8. Mountains of southeastern United States.

Cultivars and Varieties. 'Mount Airy' is a vigorous selection with large flowers (2 in. long by 1¾ in. wide) and consistent yellow, orange, and red fall color, even under mediocre environmental conditions. Heavy textured, rich blue-green leaves with whitish undersides make this a superb selection. Grows 5 to 6 ft. high and wide.

Fothergilla major, Large Fothergilla

Fothergilla major fall color

Fothergilla major flowers

Fothergilla major 'Mount Airy'

Fothergilla major 'Mount Airy' in fall

Franklinia alatamaha

Franklinia, Franklin Tree

Originally found by John Bartram along the banks of the Altamaha River in Georgia in 1770 and last sighted in the wild in about 1790, *Franklinia* has perhaps engendered more folklore than any shrub or small tree. Bartram's foresight resulted in a most handsome and somewhat persnickety landscape plant. Franklinia has upright-spreading branches, giving the plant an open, airy appearance. The smooth gray bark is broken by irregular vertical fissures. The 5- to 6-in.-long, lustrous dark green leaves turn orange and red in fall. Five-petaled, fragrant, white flowers, 3 in. in diameter, open from late July into August, with a smattering in September. Transplant from a container into acid, organic-laden, moist, well-drained soils. Poorly drained soils generally prove lethal. Use as an accent or specimen, or incorporate into borders. Grows 10 to 20 (to 30) ft. high, 6 to 15 ft. wide. Zones 5 to 8. Georgia.

Franklinia alatamaha, Franklinia

Franklinia alatamaha flower

Franklinia alatamaha fall color

Franklinia alatamaha bark

Fraxinus americana
White Ash

This wide-ranging, eastern North American species appears to reach its greatest development in fertile midwestern soils, but it is also likely to occur on a rocky slope in Connecticut or in an overgrown field in Georgia. Young trees are irregularly pyramidal to upright-oval, and with maturity become rounded. The compound pinnate leaves contain five to nine dark green, 2- to 6-in.-long, ovate leaflets. In fall, the leaves turn rich shades of yellow to reddish purple and almost maroon. The pattern of fall coloration is fascinating: at the extremities of the canopy the color is often reddish purple, and it grades to yellow toward the center. The grayish brown bark is ridged and furrowed into close, diamond-shaped patterns. Performs best in deep, moist, well-drained soils of varying pH. Scale and borer can be problems. A splendid large shade tree. Give ample room to develop. Grows 50 to 80 ft. high, similar spread. Zones 3 to 9. Nova Scotia to Minnesota, south to Florida and Texas.

Cultivars and Varieties. 'Autumn Purple' has beautiful, lustrous dark green foliage that turns red to reddish purple in the fall. Environment plays a significant role in the expression of fall color: in Maine, it is knockout red; in Athens, Georgia, it is significantly less intense.

Fraxinus americana, White Ash, in fall

Fraxinus americana bark

Fraxinus americana foliage

Fraxinus americana 'Autumn Purple' fall color, in Maine

Fraxinus pennsylvanica
Green Ash

Landscapes in the West, Midwest, and East cannot escape the clutches of this everyman's tree. Its tolerance of hot, dry, sweeping winds, wet and dry soils, and high pH environments makes it universally functional. As a young tree, the habit is irregularly pyramidal; with age it becomes upright-spreading, with several large main branches and many coarse, twiggy branchlets, which bend down and then up at the ends. More or less oval to rounded in outline at maturity. Summer leaf color is variable, from medium to dark green. Respectable to superb yellow fall color. Each leaf is composed of five to nine lustrous, 2- to 5-in.-long leaflets. Trees grown from seedlings often bear 1- to 2-in.-long, ¼-in.-wide fruit (samaras), which can become a nuisance. Use as a street tree or in lawns, parks, commercial plantings, or planters. Displays excellent heat and cold tolerance, but plants can contract borer and scale. Grows 50 to 60 ft. high, variable spread. Zones 3 to 9. Nova Scotia to Manitoba, south to northern Florida and Texas.

Cultivars and Varieties. 'Marshall's Seedless' is a male form with glossy dark green foliage, good yellow fall color, and no fruit.

'Patmore' is a newer, hardier male selection, with upright branching and a more uniform outline than 'Marshall's Seedless'.

'Summit' produces a central leader, displays better growth habit than 'Marshall's Seedless', and has good yellow fall color and no fruit.

Fraxinus pennsylvanica bark

Fraxinus pennsylvanica, Green Ash

Fraxinus pennsylvanica 'Marshall's Seedless'

Gaylussacia brachycera
Box Huckleberry

An unknown treasure among the broadleaf evergreens, Box Huckleberry offers lustrous dark green foliage that turns deep bronze to reddish purple in winter. The habit is low, mounded, almost suckering, and with time, large colonies are formed. One stand in Pennsylvania covers 300 acres and is estimated to be over 12,000 years old. Urn-shaped, white to pink, ¼-in.-long flowers open in May and June. Leaves are ⅓ to 1 in. long. Provide acid, organic-laden, well-drained soils and partial shade. Plants will grow in full sun. Use in combination with other ericaceous plants. Grows ½ to 1½ ft. high, spreads indefinitely. Zones 5 to 7. Pennsylvania to Virginia, Kentucky, and Tennessee.

Gaylussacia brachycera, Box Huckleberry, flowers

Gaylussacia brachycera foliage in winter

Genista lydia

This low-growing groundcover species has become quite popular in recent years, particularly in the West and Northeast. It forms a prostrate, small-leaved (⅜ in. long), dark olive-green carpet. The stems are four- to five-angled. In May and June, bright yellow flowers explode from each node to form a sea of gold. A great plant for rock walls and dry, sandy pockets. Requires full sun for best flowers. Grows ½ to 1 ft. high. Zones 6 to 8(9). Southeastern Europe, western Asia.

Genista lydia

Genista pilosa
Silkyleaf Woadwaxen

Silkyleaf Woadwaxen offers grayish green leaves and bright yellow flowers that appear in 2- to 6-in.-long racemes. Reports indicate that this species is more reliable than *Genista lydia*. Grows 1 to 1½ ft. high. Zones 5 to 7(8). Europe.

Cultivars and Varieties. 'Vancouver Gold' is a heavy flowering, golden yellow form. Grows 1 ft. high, 3 ft. wide.

Genista pilosa, Silkyleaf Woadwaxen

Genista pilosa in flower

Genista tinctoria
Dyer's Greenwood

When adorned with bright yellow flowers in summer, *Genista tinctoria* stirs the soul and landscape imagination. During the rest of the year, the plant blends in with the woodwork. Develops into a wispy, rounded shrub with slender, almost vertical, green stems and limited branching. The bright green, ½- to 1-in.-long leaves are sharp pointed. Yellow, ½- to ¾-in.-long flowers occur in erect, 1- to 3-in.-long racemes in June and sporadically thereafter. Remove spent flowers to allow new flowers to develop on the new growth. Considered difficult to transplant; it should be container grown and then transplanted to a permanent location. Performs best in dryish, well-drained soils and in full sun. Use where few other plants will provide summer color. Grows 2 to 3 ft. high and wide. Zones (4)5 to 7. Europe, western Asia.

Genista tinctoria flowers

Genista tinctoria, Dyer's Greenwood

Ginkgo biloba, Ginkgo

Ginkgo biloba
Ginkgo

The Ginkgo has existed, unchanged, for some 150 million years on the planet earth. This long history and the plant's unique fan-shaped leaf make it perhaps the most widely recognized of all shade and ornamental trees. Every child who has ever made a leaf collection probably included a leaf from a *Ginkgo*. In addition to its history, *Ginkgo biloba* has much to offer as an ornamental plant. In youth the habit is somewhat gaunt and open; with age it becomes full and dense, an imposing, beautiful specimen. Male and female flowers are borne on separate trees, and it often takes 20 years or more before flowers develop. Purchase male trees whenever possible; female trees can be quite objectionable—the orangish, 1- to 1½-in.-long, plumlike seeds drop to the ground and, when the outer flesh decomposes, provide a rancid butter odor that is the scourge of the neighborhood. The bright green, fan-shaped leaves, 2 to 3 in. long and wide, turn brilliant yellow in fall. If faced with a hard freeze, virtually all the leaves will cascade to the ground in a single day. Tolerates extremes of soil, except permanently wet. Great park or large-area tree. I have observed this tree from Minnesota to Florida and from Massachusetts to California, which provides some idea of its adaptability. Grows 50 to 80 ft. high, variable spread. Zones 4 to 9. China.

Cultivars and Varieties. 'Autumn Gold' is a handsome male form, broad-spreading in habit.

'Fastigiata' is an upright, columnar form, of which 'Princeton Sentry' is a male selection.

Ginkgo biloba fall color

Ginkgo biloba seeds

Gleditsia triacanthos var. *inermis*

Thornless Common Honeylocust

A popular lawn and street tree in the Midwest and East, it offers a graceful habit and fine-textured leaves. Can be spectacular in fall when the ½-in.-long leaflets turn rich golden yellow. Usually develops a short trunk and an open, spreading crown with a delicate and sophisticated silhouette. The light shade it casts permits grass to grow next to the trunk. The bright green summer foliage is quite handsome, and in autumn the fallen leaflets sift their way through the grass and understory litter, requiring little raking. Most trees, however, produce brownish, 7- to 8-in.-long pods, which drop off in fall and winter and create a mess. The cultivars do not produce as much fruit as the species form. In the Midwest, webworm, mites, galls, and various cankers have wreaked havoc on a number of plantings. Many trees planted in the 1950s were removed in the 1980s because of these problems. Very adaptable to soils, and displays excellent salt tolerance. Grows 30 to 70 ft. high and wide. Zones 4 to 9. Pennsylvania to Nebraska, south to Mississippi and Texas.

Cultivars and Varieties. 'Majestic', 'Moraine', 'Shademaster', and 'Skyline' are superior to the species.

'Sunburst' offers golden yellow new foliage, which eventually matures to bright green.

Gleditsia triacanthos var. *inermis*, Thornless Common Honeylocust

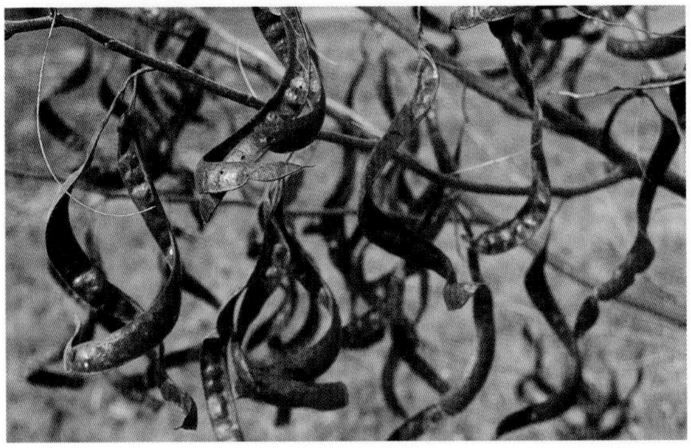

Gleditsia triacanthos var. *inermis* fruit

Gleditsia triacanthos var. *inermis* 'Sunburst' foliage

Gleditsia triacanthos var. *inermis* 'Moraine'

Gymnocladus dioica
Kentucky Coffeetree

To know her is to love her. A wonderful native species that tolerates the worst stresses nature and humanity can impose, yet it is nowhere very common in the landscape. As a young tree, the shape is irregular and the texture is coarse, especially in the winter months. The rich bluish green, bipinnate compound leaves, composed of 1½- to 3-in.-long leaflets, soon cover the blemishes of winter, however. With age the habit becomes more uniform, producing a picturesque, obovate crown of rugged branches. Scaly, recurving ridges develop on the gray-brown bark and provide additional seasonal interest. Male and female flowers appear on separate trees. The females produce 5- to 10-in.-long, leathery, brownish black pods. The fruitless male trees, such as 'Espresso' and 'Stately Manor', are preferable, and they can be grown from root cuttings or produced through micropropagation (tissue culture). Kentucky Coffeetree tolerates drought, city conditions, and a wide range of soils. A superb tree for large-area use. Grows 60 to 75 ft. high, 40 to 50 ft. wide. Zones 4 to 8. New York to Minnesota, south to Tennessee and Oklahoma.

Gymnocladus dioica, Kentucky Coffeetree

Gymnocladus dioica foliage

Gymnocladus dioica fruit

Gymnocladus dioica bark in winter

Gymnocladus dioica flowers

Halesia diptera
Two-Wing Silverbell

A round-headed small tree, *Halesia diptera* bears white flowers with four deeply cut lobes and two-winged fruit. Similar to *H. tetraptera*, Carolina Silverbell, in its other traits. Very delicate in flower and certainly worth considering when available. Grows 20 to 30 ft. high; 50-ft.-high specimens are known. Zones 5 to 9. South Carolina and Tennessee to Florida and Texas.

Cultivars and Varieties. The variety *magniflora* produces more abundant and larger flowers than the species.

Halesia diptera flowers

Halesia diptera, Two-Wing Silverbell

Halesia diptera fruit

Halesia monticola
Mountain Silverbell

Halesia monticola is an old name that has been merged with *H. tetraptera*, although it is sometimes listed separately in nursery catalogs. Trees labeled as Mountain Silverbell are larger in habit, leaf, flower, and fruit than typical *H. tetraptera*.

Halesia tetraptera (H. carolina, H. monticola)
Carolina Silverbell

A great tree for understory planting along stream banks, in the back of the shrub border, against a background of large conifers, or as a single specimen, yet not common anywhere in American gardens. The species develops a low-branched profile, often with several trunks, and forms a rounded crown. Single-trunked specimens are more pyramidal to oval in outline. The bark on young stems is brown and stringy, becoming gray with darker striations, and finally developing flattened, scaly ridges of gray, brown, and black colors. The dark yellowish green, 2- to 5-in.-long leaves seldom color in fall, at best showing glimpses of muted yellow. In April and May, slightly before or with the leaves, ½- to 1-in.-long, white, bell-shaped flowers appear in clusters from the axils of the branches. The flowers, in a subtle, not boisterous way, are among the most beautiful of all flowering trees. The 1- to 1½-in.-long, ovoid fruit, with four distinct wings, ripen in September and October. Prefers cool, moist, acid, well-drained soils, in shade or sun. Will develop chlorosis in extremely high pH soils. Found along streams, on the banks above watercourses, and in sheltered coves throughout its native range. Grows 30 to 40 ft. high, 20 to 35 ft. wide. Zones 5 to 8(9). West Virginia to Florida, west to eastern Texas.

Cultivars and Varieties. 'Rosea' (var. *rosea*) is a pink-flowered form of great beauty. The pink forms may crop up in seedling populations. Look at the flowers before buying, because the pinkness can vary from near white to almost rose.

Halesia tetraptera, Carolina Silverbell

Halesia tetraptera flowers

Halesia tetraptera fruit

Halesia tetraptera bark

Hamamelis ×*intermedia*

With such an excellent pedigree—this is a hybrid between *Hamamelis japonica* and *H. mollis*—it is obvious why the offspring are so handsome. For color in the winter garden, this group of hybrids ranks among the best shrubs. The soft yellow to bronzy red flowers occur in clusters of two to four, each bud opening to expose four strap-shaped, often slightly twisted petals from January to March, depending on the cultivar. Flowers persist for as long as one month and resist the vagaries of the winter weather. Most are wonderfully fragrant, an attribute that makes them useful near trafficked areas. The 2- to 4-in.-long, dark green to blue-green leaves are intermediate between those of the parents. In fall, the foliage develops gorgeous yellow to deep red tints. Transplant container- or field-grown plants into organic-laden, moist, well-drained soils. Appears quite pH adaptable. Maximum flowering is achieved in full sun, but will produce a reliable show in partial shade. Plants are much slower growing in hot, dry, exposed locations. Great element for the shrub border, or as an artistic specimen, combined with a dark green groundcover like *Pachysandra*. Grows 10 to 20 ft. high. Zones 5 to 8.

Cultivars and Varieties. Cultivars are variable in habit, ranging from broad-spreading to upright vase-shaped. Most cultivars are grafted, and the understock, usually *Hamamelis vernalis* or *H. virginiana*, will often sucker and overgrow the scion.

'Arnold Promise' is one of the oldest and most popular cultivars. Its bright yellow, fragrant flowers, which have a reddish calyx cup, appear in February and March. Fall color is a rich yellow to orange-apricot. Grows over 20 ft. high. One of the best. Introduced by the Arnold Arboretum.

'Diane' is red, actually deep bronzy red, with faint fragrance. Habit is medium-spreading. Old leaves may persist and require removal to maximize flower effect.

'Jelena' is a great favorite of mine because of its strong horizontal habit and coppery colored, fragrant flowers. Excellent orange-red fall color.

'Pallida' is an early flowering form with soft sulfur-yellow, highly fragrant flowers. Probably not as large as 'Arnold Promise' at maturity, and better suited to smaller gardens.

'Ruby Glow' has bronze-red flowers on a robust, upright-spreading shrub.

Hamamelis ×intermedia 'Arnold Promise' flowers

Hamamelis ×intermedia 'Diane' flowers

Hamamelis ×intermedia 'Arnold Promise' fall color

Hamamelis ×intermedia 'Diane' fall color

Hamamelis ×intermedia 'Jelena' flowering in January

Hamamelis ×intermedia 'Pallida' flowers

Hamamelis ×intermedia 'Ruby Glow' flowers

Hamamelis japonica
Japanese Witchhazel

I have seen this shrub in European gardens, but only sporadically in America. *Hamamelis japonica* is a large, spreading shrub with criss-crossing, architecturally sculptured branches. It is much wider spreading than *H. mollis* or *H. ×intermedia* and requires ample room. The flowers have thin, wrinkled-crinkled petals and appear in February and March. Color ranges from yellow to coppery red, with a deep purple calyx cup. Fragrance is generally not as potent as that of *H. mollis* or the better *H. ×intermedia* forms. This species is probably too large and too florally inferior to compete with the other types for average landscape use, but a large specimen in full flower is a sight to appreciate. Grows 10 to 15 ft. high and wide. Zones 5 to 8. Japan.

Hamamelis japonica, Japanese Witchhazel

Hamamelis japonica flowers

Hamamelis mollis
Chinese Witchhazel

In late January, this is often the first Asian witchhazel to spread its petals. It is a robust, rounded, densely branched shrub, with dull dark green, roundish leaves that are covered with grayish, woolly pubescence on their undersides. (The other species included here are sparingly pubescent.) Fall color is vivid yellow to almost orange-yellow. Flowers are yellow with a reddish brown calyx cup and extremely fragrant. Culture is the same as that of *Hamamelis ×intermedia*. Grows 10 to 15 (to 20) ft. high and wide. Zones 5 to 8. Central China.

Hamamelis mollis fall color

Hamamelis mollis, Chinese Witchhazel

Hamamelis mollis flowers

Hamamelis vernalis flowers

Hamamelis vernalis
Vernal Witchhazel

This fine native shrub pales by floral comparison with the previous species, but it offers several desirable ornamental traits. The habit is mounded-rounded, often suckering and colonizing. The 2- to 5-in.-long, dark green leaves turn rich butter-yellow to golden yellow in autumn. The pungently fragrant flowers, each petal about ½ in. long, are the smallest of the species discussed here. Color varies from yellow and orange to red, and the flowers open in January and February. A great plant for massing, naturalizing, or grouping, in quite moist or dry soils. A tough plant with an alley-cat tenacity. Grows 6 to 10 ft. high, generally wider at maturity. Zones 4 to 8. Missouri to Louisiana and Oklahoma.

Hamamelis vernalis, Vernal Witchhazel, in fall

Hamamelis virginiana

Common Witchhazel

Another wonderful native plant that displays excellent climatic and cultural adaptability. In the wild, *Hamamelis virginiana* is often found as an understory plant in moist soils along stream banks, but I have also found it on drier hillsides. Forms a large, multistemmed shrub or a small tree, with several crooked, spreading, gray-brown branches. The 3- to 6-in.-long, medium to dark green leaves turn handsome yellow in autumn. Yellow, fragrant flowers appear from October to as late as December. Unfortunately, fall foliage color develops as the flowers open, and much of the floral effect is lost. Use like the previous species, although this shrub is much more massive than *H. vernalis*. Grows 15 to 20 (to 30) ft. high and wide. Zones 3 to 8(9). Canada to Georgia, west to Nebraska and Arkansas.

Hamamelis virginiana, Common Witchhazel

Hamamelis virginiana leaf

Hamamelis virginiana flowers

Hamamelis virginiana fall color

Hedera helix
English Ivy

Without equivocation, English Ivy is one of the dominant groundcovers, but it also produces a viny green mantle on trees and structures. It will climb trees to great heights but does not grow over and shade the foliage like Kudzu. The three- to five-lobed, $1\frac{1}{2}$- to 4-in.-long, maplelike evergreen leaves are lustrous dark green with lighter colored veins. As the plant ascends trees and buildings, the leaves mature and lose the distinct lobing and the veinal mosaic pattern. In this adult stage, greenish white flowers develop in September and October, followed by $\frac{1}{4}$-in.-diameter, blackish fruit. English Ivy prefers shade and moist, well-drained soils, but it is remarkably adaptable. The plant faces no serious problems, although mites and bacterial leaf spot crop up occasionally. Can climb as high as 90 ft. Zones 5 to 9. Caucasian Mountains.

Cultivars and Varieties. Numerous cultivars are available. Check with a local nursery for those best adapted in a given area. 'Baltica', 'Bulgaria', 'Thorndale', and 'Wilson' are good cold-hardy selections.

Hedera helix, English Ivy

Hedera helix foliage

Hedera helix bark, displayed climbing a tree trunk

Hedera helix fruit

Heptacodium miconioides
Seven-Son Flower

A new garden species, introduced from China by the Sino-American Botanical Expedition in 1980, this shrub has become the horticultural rage in the Northeast, and the Arnold Arboretum has done more than any other agency to popularize the species. It is a rather handsome plant, but one that I initially was not enamored with. After observing it over several years, however, I planted one in my own garden. The habit is multistemmed and upright-spreading with a cloudlike canopy. The 3- to 4-in.-long, dark green leaves emerge early in spring, around mid- to late April, and persist into November, but they do not develop appreciable fall color. The bark exfoliates to expose a light brown underbark. Pale, creamy white, fragrant flowers are borne on seven-tiered panicles from August into October. The real show occurs in October and November when the calyces (sepals) turn reddish—the effect is spectacular and long lasting. Best growth occurs in moist soils and full sun, but the species is adaptable to dry, acid soils and at least semishade. Use as an accent, in shrub borders, or in groupings. Grows 10 to 20 ft. high, slightly less in spread. Zones (4)5 to 8. China.

Heptacodium miconioides, Seven-Son Flower

Heptacodium miconioides foliage and flowers

Heptacodium miconioides showing its reddish calyces in October

Heptacodium miconioides winter stems

Hibiscus syriacus
Rose-of-Sharon, Shrub Althea

Antique nursery catalogs listed numerous cultivars of this species. Unfortunately (perhaps fortunately, to some gardeners), most have disappeared from cultivation. The shrub is often found at older residences, but it has fallen from favor in recent years. The habit is stiffly upright and strongly multistemmed. The three-lobed, medium green, 2- to 4-in.-long leaves do not color appreciably in fall. The flowers range in colors from white, pink, red, and purple to almost blue, and come in singles and doubles. Flowers appear from July into September on new growth of the season, and so it is prudent to remove old branches in late winter to encourage best flowering. Grows in any soil, except those that are extremely dry or wet. Quite pH adaptable. Use in the border, in groupings, or perhaps as an accent in the summer garden. The plant essentially fruits itself out of flower; several of the new sterile types (which are triploids) are everblooming. Grows 8 to 12 ft. high, 6 to 10 ft. wide. Zones 5 to 8(9). China, India.

Cultivars and Varieties. 'Aphrodite' (dark pink with prominent dark red eye), 'Diana' (pure white and large), 'Helene' (white with maroon eye), and 'Minerva' (lavender-pink with prominent dark red eye) were bred by Don Egolf, U.S. National Arboretum, for floral quality and nonstop flowering. These new cultivars are now in production and should be given first consideration.

'Blue Bird' is an older introduction (1958) with single, lilac-blue flowers and a small red center. Flowers average 4 to 5 in. across. It is a vigorous grower. Flowers close in rainy weather.

Hibiscus syriacus, Rose-of-Sharon

Hibiscus syriacus 'Blue Bird' flower

Hibiscus syriacus 'Diana'

Hibiscus syriacus 'Helene' flowers

Hippophae rhamnoides
Seabuckthorn

Although seldom available in the United States, this species has potential for use in sandy soils where oceanic salts are prevalent. It is an extremely irregular, multistemmed, rounded small tree or shrub with 1- to 3-in.-long leaves. The grayish foliage, like that of *Elaeagnus angustifolia*, Russian-Olive, is rather attractive and serves as a pleasant diversion from the typical shades of green. The yellowish flowers, which open before the leaves in March and April, are not particularly showy. The ¼- to ⅓-in.-long, orange fruit ripen in September and persist into fall and winter. The species languishes under high fertility and should only be used in infertile soils. I have tried to grow the species on several occasions without any success. In Europe, particularly the Netherlands and Germany, Seabuckthorn is used in highway plantings. Grows 8 to 30 ft. high, 10 to 40 ft. wide. Zones 4 to 7. Europe, China, Himalayas.

Hippophae rhamnoides, Seabuckthorn

Hippophae rhamnoides foliage

Hippophae rhamnoides fruit

Hovenia dulcis
Japanese Raisin Tree

A little-known tree with several outstanding attributes, including lustrous green, pest-free foliage, greenish white flowers in June and July, and edible fruiting structures in September and October. The reddish, fleshy fruiting branches have a pleasant sweet taste. The habit is oval to rounded, with uniform, ascending main branches and a paucity of lateral branches. Leaves are 4 to 6 in. long and 3 to 5 in. wide. The gray to gray-brown bark develops wide, flat ridges and shallow, darker furrows. Adaptable to varied soils and presents no cultural problems. Grows 30 ft. high under cultivation; 40- to 45-ft.-tall specimens are occasionally seen. Zones (5)6 to 7(8); severe damage was evident after exposure to –22°F. Japan.

Hovenia dulcis, Japanese Raisin Tree

Hovenia dulcis foliage and flowers

Hovenia dulcis fruiting branches

Hovenia dulcis bark

Hydrangea anomala subsp. *petiolaris*
Climbing Hydrangea

Considered the supreme flowering vine because of its beautiful foliage, flowers, and habit. The lustrous dark green leaves, 2 to 4 in. long and almost as wide, serve as a background for the 6- to 10-in.-diameter corymbs of fragrant, white flowers, which open in June and July. The inflorescence is composed of showy white, sterile outer sepals that surround the dull white, fertile inner flowers. Flowers persist for four to six weeks, the sepals aging from white to green to brown. Climbing Hydrangea is a true clinging vine, cementing itself to any structure. With time, the vine becomes woody, and the cinnamon-brown bark exfoliates. Tolerates shade or sun and is adaptable to a variety of soils. Somewhat slow in the early years of establishment. It is a long-lived and almost trouble-free vine. Use on walls, trees, fences, or over rocks; it has also been used as a groundcover. Almost unlimited in its ability to climb tall trees. Grows 60 to 80 ft. high; can be maintained to attain lesser size. Zones 4 to 8. Japan, China.

Hydrangea anomala subsp. *petiolaris*, Climbing Hydrangea

Hydrangea anomala subsp. *petiolaris* flowers

Hydrangea anomala subsp. *petiolaris* bark

Hydrangea anomala subsp. *petiolaris*, grown to offer a shrubbier habit

Hydrangea arborescens
Smooth Hydrangea

To witness this species in the wild makes one wonder how it could ever be a popular garden plant. When brought from the shady nooks and crannies of the wild to a relatively fertile garden setting, the transformation brings to mind the story of the beauty and the beast. Plants in the wild are often loose and open in habit, but when provided with moisture and moderate fertility, plants become impressive dense, mounded specimens. In cultivation, it forms a clumpy, rounded mound, often broader than high at maturity. The 2- to 8-in.-long, strongly serrated, dark green leaves seldom develop appreciable fall color, except in more southerly locales, where they turn almost lemon-yellow in November. The flowers are not overwhelming, often consisting of nonshowy creamy, fertile flowers with an outer whorl of showy white sepals. Flowers appear in June and are at their showiest for three to four weeks when they pass from apple-green to white to brown. If spent flowers are removed, the new growth will produce a second flush of flowers, generally in August. Provide moist, organic-laden, well-drained, acid or higher pH soils. The plant is well adapted to full sun or shade. Cut to within 6 in. of the ground in late winter and fertilize. Use in masses or groupings. Combine with cultivars of *Spiraea japonica*, Japanese Spirea, or *S.* ×*bumalda*, Bumald Spirea, for a real summer show. Grows 3 to 5 ft. high and wide. Zones 3 to 8(9). New York to Iowa, south to Florida and Louisiana.

Cultivars and Varieties. 'Annabelle' is a superb selection with large, broad-rounded inflorescences. The individual inflorescences, up to 12 in. in diameter, are more uniformly symmetrical than those of 'Grandiflora'.

'Grandiflora' is the standard large-flowered form, with rather lumpy, 6- to 8-in.-diameter clusters of white flowers.

Hydrangea arborescens flowers

Hydrangea arborescens, Smooth Hydrangea

Hydrangea arborescens 'Annabelle'

Hydrangea arborescens 'Grandiflora'

Hydrangea macrophylla
Bigleaf Hydrangea

Perhaps no flowering plant commands greater attention than Bigleaf Hydrangea, particularly in July and August when the hortensia types, with their pink to blue snowballs, all but tackle passersby. The habit is rounded-mounded. The waxy, thickish, 4- to 8-in.-long leaves are lustrous medium to dark green. Flowers are displayed in two forms: the *lacecaps*, with showy sterile outer sepals and fertile inner flowers (often sepals mixed with fertile flowers); and the *hortensias*, with mostly showy sepals in rounded to broad-rounded inflorescences. Depending on temperatures, flowers last for four weeks or longer, generally metamorphosing through several colors. The flowers occur primarily on old wood, so do not prune until after flowering. Provide either sun or partial shade, in deep, moist, organic-laden, well-drained soils. Plants require abundant moisture. For some types, flowers are blue in acid soils, pink in high pH soils. Withstands salt spray and is a good seashore garden plant—the abundance of plants from Cape Cod, Massachusetts, south to Cape May, New Jersey, provides proof of its salt tolerance. Over 500 cultivars have been named, and it is difficult to buy true-to-name selections in the everyday nursery trade; it is best to purchase these plants from a specialty nursery. Grows 3 to 6 (to 10) ft. high, wider at maturity. Zones 6 to 8(9). Japan.

Cultivars and Varieties.

Hortensia. 'All Summer Beauty' has rich blue flowers in acid soils and pinkish blue flowers in near neutral conditions. Flowers occur on new growth. Grows 3 to 4 ft. high.

'Alpengluhen' has robust, lustrous dark green foliage and blue flowers. The old flowers are hidden by the new shoots produced later in the season.

'Forever Pink' is a compact form with 4-in.-diameter, pink flowers (rose-red in cool weather). Flowers earlier than the species, and maintains good foliage color until frost. Grows 3 ft. high.

'Nikko Blue', possibly the most common form, has rounded, deep blue inflorescences on a 6-ft.-high or larger plant.

'Pia' is a compact, pink-flowered form that grows 2½ ft. high.

Lacecap. 'Blue Billows' was introduced from Korea by Richard Lighty, and it has proved more cold hardy than the typical species. Flowers are intense blue.

'Mariesii' is a common form. Sepals are showy pink or mauve-pink in near neutral soils, pale blue in very acid ones. Grows 4 to 5 ft. high.

'Variegata' has leaves edged with creamy white. Flowers as described for 'Mariesii'. Makes a good color accent in shady nooks. Considerable variation in degree of variegation, so look before buying.

Hydrangea macrophylla 'Mariesii' lacecap inflorescence

Hydrangea macrophylla 'Nikko Blue' hortensia inflorescence

Hydrangea macrophylla 'Pia' hortensia inflorescence

Hydrangea macrophylla, Bigleaf Hydrangea

Hydrangea macrophylla lacecap inflorescence

Hydrangea paniculata 'Grandiflora'
Peegee Hydrangea

The species form of Panicle Hydrangea is seldom planted, but the cultivar 'Grandiflora', Peegee Hydrangea, is common throughout the northern states. It forms a coarsely spreading, low-branched large shrub or small tree. The 3- to 6-in.-long, dark green leaves show hints of yellow to reddish purple fall color. The flowers of 'Grandiflora', almost all of which are sterile, average 6 to 8 in. long, although flower panicles on vigorous shoots may reach 12 to 18 in. long and 6 to 12 in. wide. Flowers open white in late July to August, aging to a blushed purplish pink. Flowers occur on new growth of the season, so prune in late winter. Probably the most culturally adaptable of the hydrangeas. Tolerates any soil condition, except wet. I have never been enamored with this species and find it hard to blend into any landscape, although it is certainly showy in flower. A shrub border is probably the most logical usage for this species. Grows 15 to 25 ft. high, 10 to 20 ft. wide. Zones 3 to 8. Japan, Sakhalin Island, eastern and southern China.

Cultivars and Varieties. 'Praecox' has a mixture of sterile and fertile flowers that open three to six weeks earlier than those of 'Grandiflora'.

'Tardiva' provides a mixture of sterile and fertile flowers that open in September.

Hydrangea paniculata 'Praecox' flowers

Hydrangea paniculata 'Grandiflora', Peegee Hydrangea

Hydrangea paniculata 'Tardiva' flowers

Hydrangea quercifolia
Oakleaf Hydrangea

This is one of the most handsome plants that landscape designers have at their disposal, but it is not utilized to its fullest potential in American gardens. The full, rounded-mounded outline, lobed leaves, and magnificent white flowers provide full measure for the landscape dollar. The dark green, three- to seven-lobed leaves, 3 to 8 in. long and wide, turn rich burgundy in fall and may persist into December. The 4- to 12-in.-long, paniculate inflorescences are composed of 1- to 1½-in.-diameter, showy sepals interspersed with fertile flowers. The flowers open in June and last for three to four weeks, often developing purplish pink coloration with age. The bark peels off in papery, light brown to cinnamon-brown strips. Provide moist, acid, organic-laden, well-drained soils, in full sun to partial shade. Easily transplanted from a container or the field. Grows rapidly if ample moisture and fertilizer are provided. Use in mass plantings, groupings, or the border. One of the best landscape plants for use at the edge of woodlands. Grows 4 to 6 (to 8) ft. high, equal or greater in spread. Zones 5 to 9. Georgia to Florida and Mississippi.

Cultivars and Varieties. 'Alice' produces 10- to 14-in.-long inflorescences composed of half-dollar-sized sepals that age to rosy pink. Grows 12 ft. high and wide.

'Alison' is a large, robust, mounded form with large, leathery leaves and 10- to 12-in.-long inflorescences. Develops superior brilliant red to reddish purple fall color. Grows 8 to 10 ft. high, 10 to 14 ft. wide.

'Harmony' and 'Roanoke' have large, mostly sterile inflorescences, up to 12 in. long, so heavy as to cause the branches to arch.

'Pee Wee' is a dwarfish, broad-mounded form, with leaves and flowers about half the size of those of the species.

'Snowflake', always a favorite, has multiple sepals emerging on top of the older ones, creating a double-flowered appearance. The large, 12- to 15-in.-long inflorescences may cause the branches to arch, although usually not to the degree of 'Harmony' and 'Roanoke'.

'Snow Queen' was only a photograph in a nursery catalog to me until the real thing flowered at the local botanical garden. What a beauty. Large, showy white sepals cover the fertile flowers, producing an 8-in.-long cone of white. The inflorescences are not as large as those of the previous cultivars and they remain upright. Fall color is potent red with a hint of burgundy. May prove more compact in habit than the others.

Hydrangea quercifolia, Oakleaf Hydrangea

MORE ➤

Hydrangea quercifolia continued

Hydrangea quercifolia fall color

Hydrangea quercifolia 'Alice' flowers

Hydrangea quercifolia 'Alison' fall color

Hydrangea quercifolia 'Roanoke' flowers

Hydrangea quercifolia 'Snowflake' flowers

Hydrangea quercifolia 'Snow Queen'

Hypericum, St. Johnswort

St. Johnswort is hardly a household word in American gardens, though Hypericum *'Hidcote' and* H. calycinum, *Aaronsbeard St. Johnswort, do enjoy some popularity. With about 300 species of* Hypericum *worldwide, the choices are nearly infinite.*

Hypericum frondosum
Golden St. Johnswort

This species is a rounded-mounded shrub with reddish brown exfoliating branches and distinct, glaucous bluish green leaves. The 1- to 2-in.-diameter, five-petaled, bright yellow flowers have a dense, brushy, ¾-in.-diameter mass of stamens in the center. Prefers well-drained soils and full sun. Great plant for grouping or for a spot of color in the border. Grows 3 to 4 ft. high and wide. Zones 5 to 8. South Carolina and Tennessee to Georgia, west to Texas.

Cultivars and Varieties. 'Sunburst' is lower growing than the species and has more-glaucous blue foliage and larger (3 in. in diameter) flowers. A fine performer in tests at the University of Illinois, Urbana (Zone 5). Grows 3 ft. high.

Hypericum frondosum 'Sunburst'

Hypericum frondosum 'Sunburst' flower

Hypericum 'Hidcote'

'Hidcote' is a hybrid cultivar of confusing parentage, but at its best, it is the benchmark for the other landscape hypericums. It forms a mounded, arching framework of rich blue-green leaves, which are followed by 2½- to 3-in.-diameter, golden yellow flowers from June and, sporadically, into fall. Unfortunately, the petals brown with age and become unsightly. Flowering occurs on new growth of the season, so treat the plant as a herbaceous perennial and cut back in winter. Provide well-drained soils, in sun or partial shade. Use as a mass or grouping. In my Georgia garden, every 'Hidcote' plant succumbed to a wilt-type phenomenon. Grows 3 ft. or more high and wide. Zones (5)6 to 9.

Hypericum 'Hidcote'

Hypericum 'Hidcote' flowers

Hypericum prolificum
Shrubby St. Johnswort

Seldom seen in contemporary landscaping, but this species offers ¾- to 1-in.-diameter, bright yellow flowers in June, July, and August. It develops into a dense little shrub with stout, stiff, erect stems. Provide well-drained soils, in sun or partial shade. Useful in the shrub border. Grows 1 to 4 ft. high and wide. Zones 3 to 8. New Jersey to Iowa, south to Georgia.

Hypericum prolificum, Shrubby St. Johnswort

Hypericum prolificum flowers

Ilex ×aquipernyi 'San Jose' foliage

Ilex ×aquipernyi

This grex includes crosses between *Ilex aquifolium* and *I. pernyi*. Habit is distinctly pyramidal-conical. Plants respond well to pruning. Use for a handsome hedge or screen. Grows 20 to 30 ft. high. Zones 6 to 8.

Cultivars and Varieties. 'Aquipern' is a male clone; 'Brilliant' a female, berried form.

'San Jose' is the best form. It has lustrous dark green foliage and ⅜-in.-diameter, bright red fruit, which are borne in abundance even on young plants.

Ilex ×aquipernyi

Ilex ×*attenuata*

This group of hybrids between *Ilex cassine* and *I. opaca* has produced many superior broadleaf evergreens for contemporary landscape use. Since no single type is representative of the grex, only the cultivars are discussed. Zones 6 to 9.

Cultivars and Varieties. 'Foster's #2', the most cold hardy of the group, has survived –20°F. The 1½- to 3-in.-long, lustrous dark green leaves may be entire or they may possess one to four spiny teeth on each side. Brilliant, almost fluorescent red fruit, ¼ in. in diameter, are borne in abundance and persist into winter. Habit is conical-pyramidal. Good in groupings, against walls in narrow planting areas where other hollies would grow too wide. Grows 20 to 30 ft. high.

'East Palatka', 'Hume #2', and 'Savannah' are less cold hardy and are more popular in the South. They may be hardy into Zone 6.

Ilex ×*attenuata*

Ilex ×*attenuata* 'Foster's #2'

Ilex ×*attenuata* 'Foster's #2' foliage

Ilex ×*attenuata* 'East Palatka' foliage

Ilex crenata
Japanese Holly

At its best, a functional broadleaf evergreen shrub that has been widely used for massing and hedges. The habit is extremely variable, ranging from a dense, many-branched shrub to a small, upright tree; most of the cultivars are densely shrubby. The dark green leaves range from ½ to 1¼ in. in length and have small, blackish glands on the undersides. Leaves may be either flat or cupped (convex). The ¼-in.-diameter, blackish fruit occur under the foliage, hidden to all but the most observant. Easy to transplant and grow. Provide well-drained soils. As with most hollies, full sun is ideal, though *Ilex crenata* performs quite well in half shade. Susceptible to black knot *(Thielaviopsis)* fungus and nematodes. Grows 5 to 10 ft. high and wide; can reach 20 ft. high. Zones 5 to 8. Japan, Korea.

Cultivars and Varieties. 'Beehive' is a dense, compact-mounded form with medium green, ½-in.-long and ¼-in.-wide leaves. Originated as a cross of 'Convexa' × 'Stokes'. Possibly the most cold hardy of the *Ilex crenata* cultivars.

'Compacta', a globose form, has obovate, flat, ¾-in.-long, lustrous dark green leaves. Young stems are purple. Unfortunately, many different forms of 'Compacta' are in the trade, so you cannot always be sure of what you will get. Grows 6 ft. high.

'Convexa' is an old standby, with ½-in.-long, lustrous dark green, convex leaves. Although considered compact, plants can become quite large if not pruned. This is a female form that produces abundant black fruit. One of the more cold-hardy cultivars. Grows 3 to 5 ft. high, slightly greater in spread.

'Glory' is among the most cold hardy of all *Ilex crenata* cultivars, and has survived –23°F with minimal injury. The flat, lustrous dark green leaves are ¼ to 1 in. long and ⅛ to ⅜ in. wide. Grows 5 ft. high and 8 ft. wide after 12 growing seasons.

'Green Luster' has flat, lustrous dark green leaves. It grows about twice as wide as it does tall. An 11-year-old plant measures 3 ft. high by 6 ft. wide.

'Helleri' is a dwarf, broad-mounded, compact form with flat, dark green, ½-in.-long leaves. A 26-year-old plant is 4 ft. high by 5 ft. wide.

'Hetzii' is a large, robust shrub with ½- to 1-in.-long, lustrous dark green, cupped leaves. It is a female, and not as cold hardy as 'Convexa'. Grows 6 to 8 ft. high and wide.

'Rotundifolia' is a larger-leaved form, but it is somewhat confused in commerce. Not as cold hardy as some cultivars; –18°F caused complete defoliation. Grows 8 to 12 ft. high and wide.

'Stokes' is an old cultivar with a rounded-mounded habit and flat, lustrous dark green leaves. Somewhat similar to 'Helleri'. Withstood –18°F without injury.

Ilex crenata, Japanese Holly

Ilex crenata 'Compacta'

Ilex crenata 'Glory'

Ilex crenata fruit

Ilex crenata 'Helleri'

Ilex decidua
Possumhaw

At one time, I thought this species would become a popular landscape plant because of its showy red fruit, rich silver-gray stems, and tolerance to dry, alkaline soils. Unfortunately, the lack of hardiness to extreme cold and the fact that the fruit may drop or discolor, plus the immense size and suckering habit of the plant, limit landscape uses. The large specimens that I have observed in Oklahoma, Missouri, Georgia, and Washington, DC—all 20 to 30 ft. high and wide, strongly suckering, and untidy—are what stick in my mind for this species. The ¼- to ⅓-in.-diameter, rounded, red fruit, which color while the leaves are still green, ripen in September and persist until the following April, although they may look ragged. The 1½- to 3-in.-long, lustrous dark green leaves hold late, into November, and often mask the fruit effect. Possumhaw withstands dry, alkaline, as well as moist, soils. Requires full sun for best fruit set. Use only in large areas. Might be a good plant for naturalizing or for use along highways. Grows 7 to 15 ft. high, 5 to 10 ft. wide in cultivation. Zones (5)6 to 9. Virginia to Florida, west to Texas.

Cultivars and Varieties. 'Warren's Red' is possibly the best-known cultivar. It has glossy dark green foliage and ¼-in.-diameter, glossy, bright red fruit. May grow 25 ft. high, 20 ft. wide. Possibly a zone hardier than the other cultivars.

Many other selections are becoming available, including 'Byers Golden' (yellow fruit), 'Council Fire' (persistent, orange fruit), 'Pocahontas' (red fruit), and 'Sundance' (orange-red fruit).

Ilex decidua 'Byers Golden' fruit

Ilex decidua 'Warren's Red' fruit

Ilex decidua, Possumhaw

Ilex decidua 'Warren's Red' foliage

Ilex glabra
Inkberry

Horticulturists have spent so much time making selections of *Ilex crenata* that they forgot to assess the landscape worth of *I. glabra*, a most aesthetic native species. *Ilex glabra*, in its wildest form, is a spreading, suckering, colonizing broadleaf evergreen shrub of rather billowy constitution. The flat, ¾- to 2-in.-long, lustrous dark green leaves may assume a bronzy purple cast in cold climates. Fruit are normally black, but several white-fruited forms are known. Inkberry grows in wet or drier soils, under acid or higher pH conditions, in full sun to moderate shade. One of the great plants for massing—trouble-free and beautiful. Certainly not used enough in modern landscaping, but many of the newer cultivars offer great promise. Grows 6 to 8 ft. high, 8 to 10 ft. wide. Zones 4 to 9. Nova Scotia to Florida, west to Mississippi.

Cultivars and Varieties. 'Compacta' is a somewhat oval-rounded, densely branched female form. It is a fine plant, but it tends to drop its lower foliage and becomes leggy at the base. Grows 4 to 6 (to 10) ft. high.

'Nigra' offers thick-textured, lustrous dark green leaves. Four-year-old plants are 2½ ft. high and 3 ft. wide, and leaves are retained on the lower branches. It is a female and produces lustrous black fruit.

'Nordic' is a compact, more rounded form, and it, too, will drop its lower leaves. Grows 3 to 4 ft. high and wide.

'Shamrock' has lustrous dark green leaves and is denser in habit than 'Compacta' and 'Nordic'. Older plants exhibit a degree of legginess. Grows 5 ft. high and more.

Ilex glabra, Inkberry

Ilex glabra 'Compacta'

Ilex glabra fruit

Ilex glabra 'Nigra' foliage

MORE ➤

Ilex glabra continued

Ilex glabra 'Shamrock'

Ilex ×*meserveae*

Meserve Hybrid Hollies

This group of broadleaf evergreen hybrids has provided excellent choices for northern gardens. The Blue Series cultivars, hybrids of *Ilex aquifolium* × *I. rugosa*, are shrubby in habit and offer leathery, lustrous dark green, almost blue-green leaves and excellent red fruit on the female forms. Grows 10 to 15 ft. high; can be pruned to maintain desired size and shape.

Several hybrids with *Ilex cornuta* × *I. rugosa* parentage have been introduced, and they are also quite worthy plants for northern gardens. These hybrids are more rounded, and the fruit can be spectacular. Several of these cultivars display greater heat tolerance than the Blue Series cultivars. Grows 10 ft. high and wide; can be pruned to maintain any height. Zones (4)5 to 7.

Cultivars and Varieties. 'Blue Girl' and 'Blue Princess' are the best females of the Blue Series; 'Blue Boy' and 'Blue Prince', the best males. Hardy to –10 to –20°F, even lower with protection.

'China Boy' and 'China Girl', introduced in 1979, are *Ilex cornuta* × *I. rugosa* hybrids. The ⅓-in.-diameter, red fruit of 'China Girl' are outstanding. Hardy to about –20°F.

'Golden Girl', a golden-fruited form with *Ilex cornuta* × *I. rugosa* parentage, was introduced in 1989.

Ilex ×*meserveae*, Meserve Hybrid Holly

Ilex ×meserveae 'Blue Princess'

Ilex ×meserveae 'Blue Girl' fruit

Ilex ×meserveae 'China Boy' foliage

Ilex ×meserveae 'China Girl' fruit and foliage

Ilex opaca
American Holly

Considered by many gardeners the finest tree-type evergreen holly. Over the years, more than 1000 cultivars have been named. The best forms have a densely pyramidal growth habit, dark green foliage, and abundant red fruit. Leaves vary from 1½ to 3½ in. in length, with widely spaced, spine-tipped teeth. Leaf miner, which causes serpentine tunnels, can be a problem. The dull red, ⅓-in.-diameter fruit ripen in October and persist into winter. For optimal growth, provide moist, organic-laden, acid, well-drained soils, in sun or partial shade. Protect plants from desiccating winter sun and winds. Unfortunately for the grower, American Holly is slow growing; work in Ohio with 48 cultivars showed average growth of 6 in. per year. Use as a specimen or in groupings. Grows 40 to 50 ft. high, 18 to 40 ft. wide. Zones 5 to 9. Massachusetts to Florida, west to Missouri and Texas.

Cultivars and Varieties. Cultivars are somewhat region-specific. 'Carolina #2', 'Croonenburg', 'Dan Fenton', 'Jersey Princess', 'Judy Evans', and 'Miss Helen' are worth considering for northern gardens.

Ilex opaca, American Holly

Ilex opaca 'Carolina #2'

Ilex opaca fruit and foliage

Ilex opaca 'Dan Fenton' foliage

Ilex pedunculosa
Longstalk Holly

An evergreen holly that looks like Mountain-laurel *(Kalmia)*, with long-stalked, bright red fruit and excellent cold hardiness—should be a sure thing in commerce, right? Wrong! Very few gardeners have heard of this plant. In its finest form, *Ilex pedunculosa* develops into a broad shrub or small tree, with 1- to 3-in.-long, lustrous dark green, entire-margined leaves. The ¼-in.-diameter fruit occur on 1- to 2-in.-long stalks in October and November. Appears to be more tolerant of adverse conditions, particularly wind and cold, than many other hollies. Use in groupings, in borders, or as a specimen. Grows 20 to 30 ft. high, slightly less in spread. Zones 5 to 7. Japan, China.

Ilex pedunculosa, Longstalk Holly

Ilex pedunculosa fruit

Ilex serrata
Finetooth Holly

Finetooth Holly, a broad-rounded, finely branched shrub, plays second fiddle to the showier native *Ilex verticillata*, Common Winterberry. The 2- to 3-in.-long leaves emerge reddish purple and mature to dull dark green. The ¼-in.-diameter, red fruit are smaller than and not as persistent as those of *I. verticillata*, and they will bleach (sunscald) on the side exposed to full sun. Fruit occur in great numbers. I have observed many beautiful fruiting specimens and believe the species is worthy of consideration. It is one of the parents of the newer holly hybrids *(I. serrata × I. verticillata)*. Grows 4 to 8 ft. high and wide; can reach 12 to 15 ft. Zones 5 to 8. Japan, China.

Cultivars and Varieties. 'Leucocarpa' has creamy white fruit that are produced in great numbers.

Ilex serrata, Finetooth Holly

Ilex serrata 'Leucocarpa' fruit

Ilex serrata × *I. verticillata* Hybrids

Another popular group of deciduous hollies. The red fruit of these hybrids are larger than those of *Ilex serrata*, which discolor earlier and are less persistent. New growth of the hybrids displays the rich plum-purple color found on *I. serrata*. Zones 5 to 8. Japan, China.

Cultivars and Varieties. 'Autumn Glow', 'Bonfire', 'Harvest Red', and 'Sparkleberry' are the most common female forms, 'Harvest Red' and 'Bonfire' being the best of the bunch. The fruit of these cultivars color early and may bleach on the side facing the sun. These are vigorous, large shrubs in the 10-ft. range. 'Apollo' is a male for 'Sparkleberry'; 'Raritan Chief' is a male for 'Autumn Glow' and 'Harvest Red'.

Ilex serrata × *I. verticillata* hybrid

Ilex 'Bonfire' fruit

Ilex 'Harvest Red'

Ilex verticillata
Common Winterberry

Like *Ilex decidua*, this is a deciduous species with bright red fruit, but it has a more compact habit and is better adapted to contemporary landscapes. The habit is distinctly oval to rounded, with a dense complement of fine, twiggy branches. Mature stems are dark gray to brown. The 1½- to 3-in.-long, dark green leaves may develop yellow- to purple-tinged fall color. The ¼-in.-diameter, rounded, bright red fruit ripen in September and persist into December and January. A few cultivars, like 'Winter Red', may hold the fruit into March and April. For best landscape performance, site in full sun and provide moist, acid, reasonably fertile, well-drained soils. In the wild, it often grows in moist to wet soils. Great plant for color in the winter landscape. Use in groupings or masses for maximum effect. Needs a male for pollination. Grows 6 to 10 ft. high and wide. Zones 3 to 9. Eastern North America.

Cultivars and Varieties. 'Cacapon' is a compact, upright-rounded form with large, true red fruit and glossy dark green, crinkled leaves. Grows 6 to 8 ft. high.

'Red Sprite' has lustrous dark green leaves and large, ⅜-in.-diameter fruit. Possibly the best choice for smaller landscapes. Grows 3 to 5 ft. high and wide.

'Winter Red' is the best form of *Ilex verticillata* for quantity and quality of bright red fruit. Fruit average ⅜ in. in diameter, and they do not discolor to the degree of other cultivars. Foliage is leathery, lustrous dark green. Grows 9 ft. high, 8 ft. wide after 30 years.

Ilex verticillata, Common Winterberry

Ilex verticillata fruit

Ilex verticillata 'Cacapon' fruit and foliage

Ilex verticillata 'Winter Red' fruit

Indigofera kirilowii
Kirilow Indigo

A little-known but rather pretty shrub, this species forms great swaths of bright green summer foliage, followed in June and July by rose-colored flowers borne in 4- to 5-in.-long, erect inflorescences. The bright green leaves are composed of seven to eleven leaflets, each leaflet ½ to 1½ in. long. Extremely adaptable, well suited to acid and calcareous soils. Requires full sun for best growth. The plant may respond like a herbaceous perennial in extremely cold climates, but it comes back to normal by the summer. Use as a large groundcover on banks, parking lot islands, and other dry sites. Forms colonies 3 to 6 ft. high and wide. Zones 4 to 7(8). China, Korea, southern Japan.

Cultivars and Varieties. var. *alba*, a white-flowered form, has lighter green foliage.

Indigofera kirilowii, Kirilow Indigo

Indigofera kirilowii flowers

Itea virginica
Virginia Sweetspire

Not long ago, if you had asked American gardeners if they ever heard of *Itea*, most would have probably answered "no." With the selection of several new forms, however, the species is becoming more popular. *Itea virginica* is found along shady stream banks throughout its native range. The roots dip their apices into the water, and the long, arching shoots playfully tickle the water's surface. The habit is strongly suckering and multistemmed, forming a rounded-mounded colony. The lustrous rich to dark green, 1½- to 4-in.-long leaves turn shades of reddish purple, scarlet, and crimson in fall. In mild winters, the leaves persist into December and beyond. Fragrant white flowers occur in 2- to 6-in.-long, ⅝-in.-wide racemes in June and July, and they are borne in sufficient numbers to be quite effective. One of the easiest shrubs to grow. It withstands heavy shade and full sun, in wet or dry soils. Great plant for massing, along waterways, on banks, or in a border. One of this author's favorite shrubs. Grows 3 to 5 ft. high, generally greater in spread. Zones 5 to 9. New Jersey to Florida, west to Missouri and Louisiana.

Cultivars and Varieties. 'Henry's Garnet' is a choice selection from the campus of Swarthmore College in Pennsylvania. It bears inflorescences up to 6 in. long and has consistent, brilliant reddish purple fall color. Grows 4 to 5 ft. high, about 6 ft. wide.

Itea virginica flowers

Itea virginica 'Henry's Garnet' fall color

Itea virginica, Virginia Sweetspire

Juglans nigra, Black Walnut

Juglans nigra
Black Walnut

Like the hickories of the genus *Carya*, *Juglans* species are seldom planted in the everyday landscape. If native, however, they are certainly worth saving, and on large properties, a grouping of Black Walnut serves an aesthetically pleasing as well as functional purpose (the nuts are edible). This is a massive, upright-spreading tree that dwarfs the average home. The dark yellow-green, pinnately compound leaves drop sporadically through the growing season, especially on trees stressed by drought. The leaflets average 2 to 5 in. long and are strongly aromatic. The green, 1½- to 2-in.-diameter, rounded fruit cascade to the ground, seemingly continually, in late summer and fall—one needs to wear a hard-hat in the garden. Black Walnut makes its best growth in deep, alluvial, moist, well-drained soils. Certainly not a plant for every landscape. Grows 50 to 75 ft. high. Zones 4 to 9. Massachusetts to Florida, west to Minnesota and Texas.

Cultivars and Varieties. 'Laciniata' has finely divided leaflets that impart a fernlike texture.

Juglans nigra fruit

Juglans regia
Persian or English Walnut

This species produces the thin-shelled nuts that are so common in mixes around the holidays. (Commercial nut production is centered in California.) The habit is distinctly rounded, with large, spreading branches forming a rather open crown. The deep green, compound pinnate leaves are composed of five to nine 2- to 5-in.-long leaflets and do not develop appreciable fall color. Soils should be deep and loamy. Grows 40 to 60 ft. high and wide. Zones 4 to 9. Southeastern Europe to China and the Himalayas.

Juglans regia, Persian Walnut

Juglans regia bark

Juglans regia fruit

Juniperus, Juniper

Without question the most ubiquitous of all needle evergreens for general landscape use. Junipers inhabit the most adverse cultural niches in nature, and they bring this durability to the human-made landscape. Highly variable in habit, junipers exist as 60-ft.-tall trees and sprawling, 2- to 4-in.-high groundcovers. All have small, needle or scalelike foliage ranging in color from green to blue. They are readily transplanted and will prosper in anything but wet soils. Full sun is necessary for maximum growth. Mites, bagworms, and juniper blight (fungus) are the principal problems. Junipers are used for screens, groupings, masses, hedges, single specimens, groundcovers, and topiary. The following species and cultivars represent the more common types available for American landscapes.

Juniperus chinensis, Chinese Juniper, cones and foliage

Juniperus chinensis
Chinese Juniper

The variation in this species has caused many good taxonomists to lose their minds. Some authorities have proposed that the shrubby types be included with *Juniperus* ×*media (J. chinensis* × *J. sabina)*. The species has blue-green, needlelike foliage. The fleshy, rounded cones, which range in size from ⅓ to ½ in. in diameter, are often the largest of the cones of the cultivated junipers. Grows 50 to 60 ft. high. Zones 3 to 9. China, Mongolia, Japan.

Juniperus chinensis 'Hetzii'

Cultivars and Varieties. 'Hetzii' is a large, upright-spreading female form with distinct bluish green needles. Landscape size ranges from 5 to 10 ft. high and wide.

'Hetzii Columnaris' is a good plant for screens or vertical accents because of its uniform, columnar-pyramidal outline. This female cultivar has blue-green needles and sets abundant cones. Grows 15 to 20 ft. high.

'Keteleerii', commonly used in Midwest landscapes, has scalelike, grass-green foliage and a distinct broad-pyramidal outline. Sets abundant crops of silvery cones. Grows 15 to 20 ft. high.

'Pfitzeriana', commonly referred to as Pfitzer, is the granddaddy of juniper cultivars, and still one of the most popular. A male cultivar, it forms a large, 5- to 10-ft.-high shrub. The branches diverge at a 45° angle to the central axis, with the outer tips

Juniperus chinensis 'Hetzii Columnaris'

MORE ➤

Juniperus chinensis **continued**

somewhat pendulous. The foliage is sage-green. Use as a foundation shrub, in masses, on banks, or as an accent. Many cultivars have been selected from branch sports of 'Pfitzeriana', including the next three discussed here.

'Pfitzeriana Aurea' has golden new growth that matures to green.

'Pfitzeriana Compacta' is a compact form, with the typical Pfitzer foliage. Grows 4 ft. high, 4 to 6 ft. wide at maturity.

'Pfitzeriana Glauca' has soft, bluish gray-green foliage and a habit similar to that of 'Pfitzeriana'. More wide spreading than 'Hetzii', although it is often confused with that cultivar.

'Robusta Green' has a certain artistic bent, displaying heavy tufts of gray-green foliage on a rather upright, open framework. Sets abundant cones. Makes a good accent or container plant. I have seen 15-ft.-high plants.

'San Jose' is a popular cultivar for massing or groundcovers. It has sage-green foliage that is both needled and scalelike. Grows 1 to 2 ft. high, 7 to 9 ft. wide.

var. *sargentii* is truly one of the best groundcover types because of its handsome blue-green (more green than blue), scalelike foliage. 'Glauca' is a selection of var. *sargentii* with bluer needle color. Both grow 1½ to 2 ft. high, 6 to 8 ft. wide.

'Sea Green', as it becomes better known, will find increasing use among the gardeners of America. It is a compact spreader with fountain-like, arching branches and rich, dark minty green foliage. Grows 4 to 6 ft. high, 6 to 8 ft. wide.

'Torulosa' is a softly textured, rich green form with tight, bunchy growth. The pyramidal growth habit is artistic and sculptural. Grows 20 ft. high or more.

Juniperus chinensis 'Pfitzeriana'

Juniperus chinensis 'Pfitzeriana Glauca'

Juniperus chinensis var. *sargentii* 'Glauca'

Juniperus communis
Common Juniper

A fantastically varied species. I reflect on abandoned pastures in New England, where this species was dominant and where I found variation from large, columnar tree types to low groundcovers. The spine-tipped, ½- to ¾-in.-long needles are usually dark green to bluish green below with a broad, silvery white band above. *Juniperus communis* prefers colder climates than the *J. chinensis* types. Grows 5 to 10 (to 15) ft. high, 8 to 12 ft. wide; can reach 40 ft. high. Zones 2 to 5(6). Worldwide.

Cultivars and Varieties. 'Depressa' is a low, broad, vase-shaped shrub, rarely growing taller than 4 ft. It spreads to form large circular masses. Many plants in the wild look like this form.

'Depressa Aurea' has strong, yellow-variegated shoots that fade with time.

'Hibernica' is a tall, columnar form with bluish green, prickly needles. It was common in older landscapes but has lost favor and is now seldom available in commerce. Called Irish Juniper. Grows 10 to 15 ft. high or more.

'Sueicica', called the Swedish Juniper, is quite similar to 'Hibernica', except the tips of its branchlets droop.

Juniperus communis, Common Juniper

Juniperus communis 'Depressa Aurea'

Juniperus conferta
Shore Juniper

Truly a superb groundcover for dry, sandy soils and areas where salinity poses a problem. The rich blue-green, prickly, ¼- to ⅝-in.-long needles lose some of their sheen in cold weather. The silvery, ⅓- to ½-in.-diameter cones are attractive throughout the year. Grows 1 to 1½ ft. high, 6 to 9 ft. wide. Zones (5)6 to 9. Japan.

Cultivars and Varieties. 'Blue Pacific' has superseded the species in many areas of the United States because of its more compact habit and superior foliage. The rich, ocean blue-green needles are shorter and more densely borne than those of the species, and they do not discolor in cold weather to the degree of those of the species. Usually grows less than 1 ft. high.

'Emerald Sea' is somewhat similar to 'Blue Pacific', but with looser blue-green foliage and a taller habit. Considered hardier than either the typical species or 'Blue Pacific'.

'Silver Mist' could prove a delightful addition to the stable of *Juniperus conferta* cultivars because of the distinct silvery overcast of its blue-green needles and more compact habit.

Juniperus conferta, Shore Juniper

Juniperus conferta 'Blue Pacific'

Juniperus conferta cones

Juniperus conferta 'Silver Mist'

Juniperus davurica 'Parsoni'
Dahurian Juniper

The characteristics of the species are unknown; the cultivar 'Parsoni' is the major representative of Dahurian Juniper in the trade. 'Parsoni' ('Expansa') has primarily soft-textured, gray-green, scalelike needles, with an occasional shoot of prickly, needle-like foliage. This cultivar is often confused with *Juniperus chinensis* 'San Jose', but it differs in its foliage characteristics and in the presence of cones. Growth habit is a dome-shaped mound. Grows 2 to 3 ft. high, 8 to 9 ft. wide. Zones (5)6 to 9. Japan.

Cultivars and Varieties. 'Expansa Variegata', with creamy white splotches, and 'Expansa Aureospicata', with golden splashes, are among the available cultivars of *Juniperus davurica* with variegated foliage.

Juniperus davurica 'Parsoni', Dahurian Juniper

Juniperus davurica 'Expansa Aureospicata' foliage

Juniperus horizontalis
Creeping Juniper

A true spreading groundcover type with blue-green, plumelike, soft-textured foliage. The cultivars of this species consistently develop mauve to deep purple colors in cold weather, and this is a good way to distinguish Creeping Juniper from the other groundcover junipers. *Phomopsis* blight can be more troublesome on this group. Grows 1 to 4 ft. high, spread is variable. Zones 3 to 9. Nova Scotia to British Columbia, south in the higher elevations.

Cultivars and Varieties. Numerous cultivars have been selected, and some nurseries offer six to ten different forms.

'Bar Harbor' has bluish green summer foliage that turns reddish purple in winter. It is a male. Grows $2/3$ to 1 ft. high, 6 to 8 ft. wide.

'Blue Chip' is a true blue-needled form. Appears better suited to cooler climates. Grows $2/3$ to 1 ft. high, 8 to 10 ft. wide.

'Blue Horizon' is a genuine pancake, never mounding in the center. It has blue-green foliage that turns bronze-green in winter.

'Plumosa' has long been the dominant Creeping Juniper cultivar and can be found in virtually every retail outlet in the United States. Blue-green summer foliage turns a rather ugly purple-bronze in winter. Grows 2 ft. high, up to 10 ft. wide.

Juniperus horizontalis 'Bar Harbor' in winter

MORE ➤

'Plumosa Compacta', a male, tends to be smaller in habit and fuller in the center than the previous type, and its foliage is light purple in winter.

'Wiltonii' ('Blue Rug') is an almost carpetlike form, with rich blue foliage that turns slight mauve in winter. Possibly the most popular groundcover juniper; rarely can a person travel anywhere in the United States without seeing the plant. Female with small silver-blue cones. Grows 1/3 to 1/2 ft. high, 6 to 8 ft. wide.

Juniperus horizontalis 'Blue Chip'

Juniperus horizontalis 'Wiltonii'

Juniperus procumbens

Japanese Garden Juniper

I have always considered this dwarf, procumbent form one of the best groundcover junipers. It has long, wide-spreading, stiff branches and rich, shiny blue-green needles. Grows 2 ft. high, 10 to 12 ft. wide; plants over 3 ft. high and 22 ft. wide are known. Zones 4 to 9. Japan.

Cultivars and Varieties. 'Greenmound' (probably the same as 'Nana Californica') is lower growing and has greener needles. It does not "hump up" in the middle like 'Nana', and forms a soft, flat, ruglike texture. Grows 2/3 ft. high, 4 to 6 ft. wide.

'Nana' is a groundcover juniper that can be used as a great accent or draped over a wall or structure. The needles are smaller and more closely spaced than those of the species. By no means compact, it can grow 2 to 2 1/2 ft. high and 10 to 12 ft. wide.

Juniperus procumbens, Japanese Garden Juniper

Juniperus procumbens 'Nana'

Juniperus sabina, Savin Juniper

Juniperus sabina
Savin Juniper

Another variable species that exists as a groundcover as well as a columnar-pyramidal tree. Chiefly represented by the cultivars. The foliage is soft and scalelike, varying in color from green to blue. Bruised foliage has the strong odor of the oil of juniper, a characteristic that can be used to separate this from other species and cultivars. Zones 3 to 7. Mountains of central and southern Europe, the Caucasus, western Asia, Siberia.

Cultivars and Varieties. 'Broadmoor' is an excellent low-spreading male form with green foliage. Has performed well in the Midwest. Resistant to juniper blight. Grows 2 to 3 ft. high, up to 10 ft. wide.

var. *tamariscifolia* has been around forever. At times it appears world-class and at other times worn-out, tired, and bedraggled. Typical habit is broad-mounded with rich green foliage. Grows 1½ to 2 ft. high, 10 to 15 ft. wide.

Juniperus sabina 'Broadmoor'

Juniperus scopulorum
Rocky Mountain Juniper

This species is the western counterpart to the Eastern Redcedar, *Juniperus virginiana*, and the distinguishing characteristics between the two are minimal. This species is softly pyramidal in habit, with needle color varying from light green or gray-green to dark green, blue-green, and almost silver-blue. Numerous selections have been made, primarily for foliage color. In general, these plants are better suited to the northern states. *Phomopsis* blight, *Seiridium* canker, and cedar apple rust are problematic. Grows 30 to 40 ft. high, 3 to 15 ft. wide. Zones 3 to 7. Western North America.

Cultivars and Varieties. 'Blue Heaven' is a uniform, pyramidal form with striking blue foliage in all seasons. Also bears heavy cone crops.

'Skyrocket' is probably the most narrowly columnar of all junipers, and a 15-ft.-high plant may be only 2 ft. wide at the base. Foliage is primarily needlelike and bluish green. In winter, it often develops a slight purple tinge.

'Tolleson's Weeping' has silver-blue foliage that hangs stringlike from arching branches. Rather interesting accent or container plant. A green-foliaged form, 'Tolleson's Green Weeping', is available.

'Welchii' is another narrow, compact form, with silvery blue new growth that matures to bluish green.

'Wichita Blue' has brilliant, bright blue foliage and a pyramidal habit.

Juniperus scopulorum, Rocky Mountain Juniper

Juniperus scopulorum 'Skyrocket'

Juniperus scopulorum 'Tolleson's Weeping'

Juniperus squamata 'Blue Carpet'

Juniperus squamata 'Blue Star'

Juniperus squamata 'Meyeri' foliage

Juniperus squamata
Single-Seed Juniper

The cultivars are the only representatives of this species in cultivation. Supposedly quite variable in growth habit over its native range. Generally not as adaptable as the other types presented here. Zones 4 to 7. Afghanistan, the Himalayas, western China.

Cultivars and Varieties. 'Blue Carpet' is a handsome groundcover form with rich blue-green foliage. Grows ⅔ to 1 ft. high, 4 to 5 ft. wide.

'Blue Star' is a much-ballyhooed cultivar, with rich silver-blue foliage that assumes a dirty tinge in winter. A low, rounded, squat plant, as broad as it is high. Grows 3 ft. high, 3 to 4 ft. wide.

'Meyeri' is the tried-and-true standard of this group, commonly found in older landscapes in the United States. It has rich silvery blue-green foliage. Called Fish-Tail Juniper because the branches resemble a fish's tail. Can become worn and ragged with age. Grows 5 ft. high, 4 ft. wide; plants to 20 ft. high are known.

Juniperus virginiana
Eastern Redcedar

A tough, irrepressible green soldier that can prosper where few other plants even survive. Found over a wide range in the midwestern and eastern United States, it is a great naturalizing type of plant. Densely columnar to broad-pyramidal in outline, it is great as a screen or in groupings. The rich green summer foliage assumes a ruddy, yellow-green to brown-green color in winter. Male trees produce thousands of tiny brown cones that yield clouds of yellowish pollen in March and April. The female trees are often covered with frosty, rich blue, 1/5-in.-diameter cones that provide good bird browse. Many reliable selections are known and raise the species up to a higher level of landscape suitability. Grows 40 to 50 ft. high, 8 to 20 ft. wide. Zones 2 to 9. Eastern and central North America.

Cultivars and Varieties. 'Burkii' is a cultivar with glaucous gray-green foliage that remains in juvenile form, prickly and needlelike. It develops a light purple cast in cold weather. Develops a pyramidal habit and matures around 20 ft. high.

'Canaertii' is quite common in the Midwest. Its dark green, soft-textured, scalelike foliage appears tufted, particularly at the ends of the branches. Heavily pruned plants can be quite dense, but left unpruned, the plants become open and artistic. This is a female clone that sets large quantities of blue-green cones. Grows 20 to 30 ft. high.

'Grey Owl' is an interesting spreading female form with soft, silvery gray-green foliage. Grows 3 ft. high, 6 ft. wide.

'Silver Spreader' is a wide-spreading, low-growing, silver-gray male form. Its branches arise at a 30° angle to the ground.

Juniperus virginiana, Eastern Redcedar

Juniperus virginiana 'Canaertii' cones

Juniperus virginiana bark

Juniperus virginiana 'Silver Spreader'

Kalmia latifolia
Mountainlaurel

Many gardeners wax poetic over the wonderful floral display of this species. Without question, it is one of the handsomest flowering broadleaf evergreens, surpassing even the rhododendrons in its finest forms. The flowers, each ¾ to 1 in. across, are massed in 4- to 6-in.-diameter inflorescences. The individual flowers offer intricate beauty, opening in May and June to a broad bell shape showing 10 stamens with flexed filaments. The typical species form ranges in color from white to pink, and the great breeding work done by Richard Jaynes of Connecticut and by several West Coast horticulturists has resulted in an even wider range, from pure white to almost red, with intricate banding and flecking of the corolla. The habit of Mountainlaurel is dense and rounded in full sun; more open and artistic when grown in shade. The 2- to 5-in.-long leaves emerge bronze, changing to lustrous dark green at maturity. Easily transplanted from containers or as balled and burlapped specimens. Plants prefer excellent drainage, acid soils, and winter shade, especially in the Midwest. My success with Mountainlaurel has been less than laudatory. As a mass or grouping in a shady border, *Kalmia latifolia* has few equals. Grows 7 to 15 ft. high and wide; newer cultivars may be smaller. Zones 4 to 9. New Brunswick to Florida, west to Ohio and Tennessee.

Cultivars and Varieties. At least 75 cultivars are known, and any attempt to describe them is beyond the scope of this book. (Richard Jaynes's *Kalmia: Mountain Laurel and Related Species* [Portland, OR: Timber Press, 1997] is an excellent resource on the wide variety of available Mountainlaurel cultivars.)

'Ostbo Red', an excellent red-budded form, deserves mention because of its longevity in the trade.

Kalmia latifolia, Mountainlaurel

Kalmia latifolia new foliage

Kalmia latifolia 'Ostbo Red' buds and flowers

Kalmia latifolia flowers

Kalopanax pictus
Castor-Aralia

In July and August, the entire canopy of this tree is covered with a creamy veil of flowers. The flowers are borne in immense, 10- to 14-in.-diameter panicles at the ends of the branches. In youth the habit is upright-oval, coarse, gaunt, and not particularly attractive; with age, rounded, massive, and impressive. The large, clubby, coarse stems are armed with stout, broad-based prickles. Old trunks become gray-black and deeply ridged and furrowed. The five- to seven-lobed, glossy dark green leaves are often 10 to 14 in. long and wide, lending an almost tropical appearance to the landscape. Fall color is sporadic; occasional yellow is about the optimum. Prefers moist, well-drained soils, but is adaptable. An interesting tree for large-scale use because of foliage and floral characteristics. Grows 40 to 60 ft. high and wide. Zones 4 to 7. Japan, Korea, China, Russian Far East.

Kalopanax pictus bark

Kalopanax pictus flowers

Kalopanax pictus, Castor-Aralia

Kerria japonica
Japanese Kerria

This fine heirloom shrub pops up in the most unusual places. Its tenacious constitution allows it to thrive where other plants disappear. The typical form is broad-mounded with a twiggy framework of bright green stems. The bright green, 1½- to 4-in.-long leaves may develop lemon-yellow fall color. Bright yellow, five-petaled flowers, 1¼ to 1¾ in. in diameter, open during April and into May and are effective for two to three weeks. Flowers also develop sporadically through summer. Provide reasonable drainage in virtually any soil, from acid to high pH. For best flower effect, site in partial shade, because the yellow tends to bleach in full sun. Makes a great plant for the shady shrub or perennial border. Also useful in large masses. When the shrub becomes overgrown or unkempt, simply cut it to the ground after flowering. Grows 3 to 6 ft. high, slightly greater in spread. Zones 4 to 9. China.

Cultivars and Varieties. 'Picta' is a dapper selection, smaller in stature, with gray-green leaves edged in white. Flowers are yellow but not as profuse or well-formed as those of the species. Site in some shade.

'Pleniflora' is quite common in southern gardens, less so in northern. It bears double, 1- to 2-in.-diameter, almost ball-shaped, golden yellow flowers. Extremely vigorous and suckers with a vengeance. The looser the soil, the wider its reach. Magnificent in flower. Its bloom coincides with that of Dame's Rocket *(Hesperis)* and Columbine *(Aquilegia)*. Grows 6 to 8 ft. high or more.

Kerria japonica flower

Kerria japonica, Japanese Kerria

Kerria japonica 'Pleniflora'

Kerria japonica 'Picta' foliage

Kerria japonica 'Pleniflora' flower

Koelreuteria paniculata

Panicled Goldenrain Tree

This species never receives its due, but it offers amazing climatic and cultural adaptability as well as stunning flowers and handsome fruit. In youth the habit is irregular, but with age it assumes a uniform, rounded outline. The 7 to 15 leaflets of the rich green, compound pinnate foliage may turn a respectable golden yellow in fall, but more often than not fall color is disappointing. Rich yellow flowers appear at the ends of the branches in June and July. Each flower is only ½ in. wide, but they occur in prodigious quantities, forming 12- to 15-in.- long and wide, airy panicles. The papery, lanternlike, 1½- to 2-in.-long capsules pass from rich green to yellow to brown. The brown fruit persist for a time and become rather ragged. The species withstands drought, heat, and wind and tolerates high pH or acid soils. Extremely fast growing in moist, well-drained soils. Three- to four-year-old trees will flower. Excellent small lawn specimen. Use for shading a patio, as a street tree, in groupings, or in planters. Selections could be made for superior habit, foliage, flower, and fruit. Grows 30 to 40 ft. high and wide. Zones 5 to 8. China, Japan, Korea.

Cultivars and Varieties. 'Fastigiata' is a distinct columnar form that seldom flowers. Older trees are rather ragged and unkempt.

'September' has a broad-rounded habit and produces masses of yellow flowers in late August and September. Slightly less cold tolerant than the species, it is hardy to Zones (5)6 to 8.

Koelreuteria paniculata foliage

Koelreuteria paniculata flowers

Koelreuteria paniculata, Panicled Goldenrain Tree

Koelreuteria paniculata fruit

Kolkwitzia amabilis
Beautybush

I have tried to love this species because it was one of Ernest H. Wilson's favorites, but I still cannot embrace it fully for general garden use. Beautybush bears lovely pinkish flowers in May and June that, at their best, smother the dull, dark blue-green foliage. Unfortunately, the rest of the year it offers little to excite even a passionate gardener. The habit is upright-arching and vase-shaped with a fountainlike outline. Tends toward openness at the base. Easy to grow, and perhaps worthy of inclusion in the shrub border. I have seen too many free-standing specimens that beg for help. Grows 6 to 10 (to 15) ft. high, slightly less in spread. Zones 4 to 8. China.

Cultivars and Varieties. 'Pink Cloud' and 'Rosea' offer flowers of a deeper pink than those of the species.

Kolkwitzia amabilis, Beautybush

Kolkwitzia amabilis flowers

Laburnum ×watereri
Waterer Laburnum, Goldenchain Tree

Golden chains of flowers cascade from the branches in May and June like yellow water over rocks, producing a spectacular landscape effect. Unfortunately, over most of the United States the flowering performance of this hybrid species does not measure up to that of specimens growing in cooler, more even climates, like that of England, where there is greater bud set and flowering. The habit of *Laburnum ×watereri* is stiffly upright-spreading, usually with a flat-topped crown at maturity. The bark on younger branches is a pronounced olive-green. The bright green to almost blue-green, trifoliate foliage does not develop good fall color. Slightly fragrant, yellow, pea-shaped flowers appear in May and June in 6- to 10-in.-long, pendulous racemes. In cool weather, flowers last 10 to 14 days. Tolerant of a variety of soils, but not long lived, particularly in the Midwest. Prefers cooler summer temperatures. Grows 15 to 20 ft. high and wide. Zones 5 to 7.

The parent species of *Laburnum ×watereri*, *L. anagyroides* and *L. alpinum*, each have cultivars named 'Pendulum' that offer slender, weeping branches and reasonable flower production.

Cultivars and Varieties. 'Vossii' is a superior form of Waterer Laburnum, with a denser habit and racemes up to 2 ft. long.

Laburnum ×watereri 'Vossii'

Laburnum ×watereri, Waterer Laburnum

Larix decidua
European Larch

A deciduous conifer seldom seen in modern landscapes and most effectively used on larger properties. Pyramidal in habit, with horizontal branches and drooping branchlets, the tree is slender and supple in youth. Unfortunately, it becomes irregular and lacking in dignity with age, when the cones and dead branchlets persist, giving it a ratty appearance. The scaly, brown bark on larger branches is rather handsome. The bright green, 1-in.-long needles develop yellow to amber-yellow fall color. The cone scales are tightly overlapping, not reflexed like those of *Larix kaempferi*. Tolerant of moist and dry soils as well as windswept locations. In the Northeast, the larch case-bearer eats the interior of the needles, resulting in a brownish cast. Grows 70 to 75 ft. high, 25 to 30 ft. wide. Zones 2 to 6. Northern and central Europe.

Cultivars and Varieties. 'Pendula' is an interesting weeping form with a moplike head of long, trailing branches.

Larix kaempferi
Japanese Larch

In most respects, this species is quite similar to *Larix decidua*, differing primarily in its more open pyramidal habit and its slender, pendulous branchlets. The easiest and perhaps only reliable way to distinguish the two species is by cone structure. The cones of *L. kaempferi* have reflexed scales, which give a rosette appearance, almost like the petals of a hybrid tea rose. Same cultural requirements as *L. decidua*. Grows 50 to 70 ft. high, 25 to 40 ft. wide. Zones 4 to 7. Japan.

Larix decidua cones

Larix decidua, European Larch

Larix decidua in fall

Larix kaempferi, Japanese Larch

Larix kaempferi cones

Larix laricina cones

Larix laricina
Tamarack

A native North American species, Tamarack is lovely in fall when the gold needle color lights up the autumn landscape. Open and pyramidal in habit, with a slender trunk and a narrow crown formed by horizontal branches and drooping branchlets. The rich bluish green, ¾- to 1-in.-long needles turn handsome yellow to gold in October. The ½-in.-long cones are the smallest of the *Larix* species included here. Excellent plant for moist, boggy soils and cold climates; abhors heat. Grows 30 to 50 ft. high. Zones 1 to 4(5). Northern North America.

Larix laricina, Tamarack

Leiophyllum buxifolium
Box Sandmyrtle

This small broadleaf evergreen shrub is seldom available in commerce, but it might be considered for nooks and crannies of the garden. Greatly variable, Box Sandmyrtle can be erect, prostrate, or decumbent, depending on its location. The lustrous dark green leaves range from 1/8 to 1/2 in. long. White flowers nearly cover the foliage in May and June. Requires acid, well-drained soils, in sun or partial shade. Somewhat finicky; requires extra care in the early period of establishment. May be a 5-in. groundcover or a 1 1/2- to 3-ft.-high shrub. Zones 5 to 7. New Jersey to higher elevations of the Southeast.

Leiophyllum buxifolium, Box Sandmyrtle

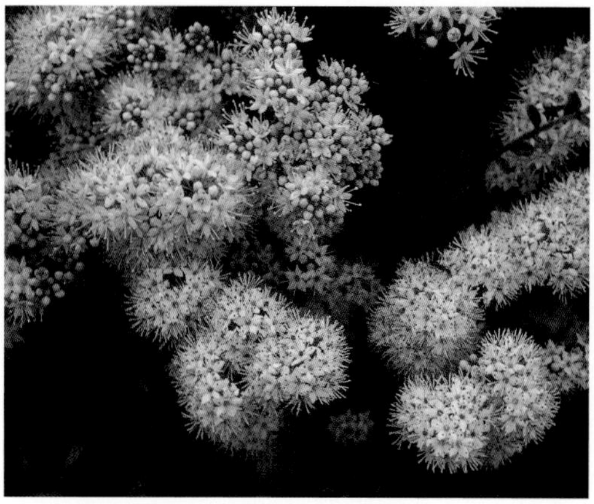

Leiophyllum buxifolium flowers

Leucothoe axillaris, Coastal Leucothoe

Leucothoe axillaris
Coastal Leucothoe

This species is not easily distinguished from *Leucothoe fontanesiana*. It is perhaps slightly smaller in all its parts, but I have been fooled so many times that I hesitate to guess. Supposedly, *L. axillaris* is not as susceptible to leaf spot as *L. fontanesiana*, but my own experience has shown otherwise. Occurs in lowland areas in the wild in its native range. Grows 2 to 4 ft. high, 3 to 6 ft. wide. Zones (5)6 to 9. Virginia to Florida, west to Mississippi.

Leucothoe axillaris foliage and flowers

Leucothoe fontanesiana
Drooping Leucothoe

One of the finest broadleaf evergreens for naturalizing, it develops into a graceful, fountainlike shrub with long, arching branches. However, it is so fragile in exposed sites that extreme caution must be exercised, avoiding drying winds and hot sun. In addition, because of the off scent of the flowers, extreme caution must be exercised in placing plants a safe distance from the nose. *Leucothoe fontanesiana* has leathery, lustrous dark green, 2- to 5-in.-long leaves that often turn bronze to purplish in winter. Urn-shaped, ¼-in.-long, white flowers develop from the leaf axils in 2- to 3-in. long, somewhat pendulous racemes. Their effect is masked by the foliage. Drooping Leucothoe absolutely insists upon moist, acid, well-drained soils in a shady location. Any undue stress predisposes the plant to leaf spot, which disfigures and defoliates the shrub. Use in combination with other ericaceous plants or with other species that require acid soils. Grows 3 to 6 ft. high and wide. Zones 5 to 8. Virginia to Georgia and Tennessee.

Cultivars and Varieties. 'Girard's Rainbow' offers a stunning mixture of white, pink, and copper, in various combinations, on new foliage. Leaf color subsides with maturity to a creamy green variegation. Other characteristics are the same as for the species.

'Nana' is a compact form with slightly smaller, lustrous dark green leaves. Grows 2 ft. high, 6 ft. wide.

'Scarletta' offers glossy scarlet new growth with a hint of purple. Foliage matures to dark green and develops rich burgundy hues in fall.

Leucothoe fontanesiana, Drooping Leucothoe

Leucothoe fontanesiana foliage and flowers

Leucothoe fontanesiana 'Scarletta' winter foliage

Leucothoe fontanesiana 'Girard's Rainbow' foliage

Ligustrum amurense
Amur Privet

In the Midwest, this species is as common as grass. I have seen city blocks where virtually every house had a hedge in front and in back and shared one on either side with the neighbor. Many better plants exist for hedging, but for fast, inexpensive separation, perhaps it has a place. The species develops into a dense, multistemmed shrub with a weak pyramidal outline. The dull medium to dark green foliage shows minimal propensity toward fall color. Creamy white flowers occur in 1- to 2-in.-long, pyramidal panicles in June and July. Their curious fragrance is that mystifying privet odor—heavy and objectionable. Flowers are seldom seen, because the plant is usually pruned to excess. The dusty, gray-black, ¼-in.-long fruit ripen in September and October and often persist. Neither flowers nor fruit overwhelm. All privets thrive with neglect. In dirty, sooty, air-polluted, or salt-laden environments and in impossible soils, the privets will grow. Hedging is the time-honored use. Grows 12 to 15 ft. high, 8 to 10 ft. wide. Zones 3 to 7. China.

Ligustrum amurense, Amur Privet

Ligustrum amurense pruned as a hedge

Ligustrum obtusifolium
Border Privet

As privets go, this may be the best of the lot because of its handsome wide-spreading habit and more refined appearance. The medium to dark green foliage sometimes develops russet to purplish fall color. Flowers and fruit are similar to those of *Ligustrum amurense*. Makes a good screen, background, or hedge plant. Grows 10 to 12 ft. high, 12 to 15 ft. wide. Zones 3 to 7. Japan.

Cultivars and Varieties. var. *regelianum* has horizontally spreading branches. Grows 4 to 5 ft. high.

Ligustrum obtusifolium, Border Privet

Ligustrum ovalifolium
California Privet

Another hedge plant, but a popular choice because its foliage is evergreen in Zones 7 and 8 and semievergreen as far north as Boston (Zone 6), before dropping most of the leaves by spring. The 1- to 2½-in.-long, lustrous dark green leaves of this species are the most attractive of the privets discussed here. The heavy-scented flowers are dull white and occur in 2- to 4-in.- long and wide terminal panicles in June and July. Habit is oval-rounded and strongly multistemmed with erect branches. Without pruning, the species makes a good screen or barrier. Adaptable to extremes of climate. Grows 10 to 15 ft. high. Zones (5)6 to 8(9). Japan.

Cultivars and Varieties. 'Aureum' has leaves that are strongly bordered in golden yellow and have a green spot in the center. This cultivar produces shoots that revert to green and must be removed.

Ligustrum ovalifolium, California Privet, pruned as a hedge

Ligustrum ovalifolium flowers

Ligustrum ×*vicaryi*
Golden Vicary Privet

A hybrid between *Ligustrum ovalifolium* 'Aureum' and *L. vulgare*, this plant develops into a large, oval-rounded shrub. It displays golden yellow leaves for most of the summer. My observations indicate that the cooler the summer weather, the better the color. Use with discretion in any garden situation. Grows 10 to 12 ft. high and wide. Zones 5 to 8.

Ligustrum ×*vicaryi* foliage

Ligustrum ×*vicaryi*, Golden Vicary Privet

Ligustrum vulgare
European Privet

This species has essentially gone the way of the dinosaur. Once a favored privet, now not widely available in commerce here in the United States. It develops into a large, cumbersome, upright-spreading shrub. White flowers occur in 1- to 3-in.-long racemes and are followed by lustrous jet black, ⅓-in.-diameter fruit. The dark green leaves average 1 to 2½ in. long. This species has no advantage over the others, and a twig blight can prove quite troublesome. Grows 12 to 15 ft. high, similar spread. Zones (4)5 to 7. Europe, northern Africa.

Ligustrum vulgare fruit

Ligustrum vulgare, European Privet

Ligustrum vulgare flowers

Lindera benzoin
Spicebush

A most appropriately named shrub, because its bruised stems emit a potent, spicy-sweet odor. Imagine an early April day in the North after a particularly difficult winter, the branches of Spicebush studded with small, greenish yellow flowers—a harbinger that all will be well in the world. To my mind, the species has never been utilized enough in American gardens. It develops into a large, multistemmed, rounded shrub, growing dense in sun, rather artistically open in shade. The 3- to 5-in.-long, bright green leaves turn a respectable to outstanding shade of yellow in fall. The oval, ⅓- to ½-in.-long, bright red fruit ripen in September and October. The species is dioecious—fruit occur only on female plants. Provide acid, moist soils, in full sun to partial shade. Plants appear ragged in extremely dry soils. Fine choice for naturalizing, but unfortunately, it has never found its way into commerce. Grows 6 to 12 ft. high and wide. Zones 4 to 9. Maine to Ontario and Kansas, south to Florida and Texas.

Lindera benzoin flowers

Lindera benzoin, Spicebush

Lindera benzoin in fall

Lindera benzoin fruit

Liquidambar styraciflua
Sweetgum

This lovely tree would be on every gardener's wishlist were it not for the woody, spiny, capsular, 1- to 1½-in.-diameter fruit, which abscise through fall and winter. Nevertheless, Sweetgum is still widely planted throughout the East, Midwest, and South for its excellent fall color. The star-shaped, five- to seven-lobed, 4- to 7½-in.-diameter, lustrous dark green leaves turn gorgeous shades of yellow, orange, red, and purple and persist late into fall. Decidedly pyramidal habit in youth, the tree develops an oblong to rounded crown at maturity. Excellent plant for moist soil areas along streams and watercourses; it also performs well in drier soils. Can develop chlorosis in high pH soils. Grows 60 to 75 ft. high, 40 to 50 ft. wide. Zones 5 to 9. New York to Illinois, south to Florida, Texas, and Mexico.

Cultivars and Varieties. 'Burgundy', 'Festival', and 'Palo Alto' were selected in California for good fall color.

'Moraine' offers excellent glossy dark green foliage, burgundy-red fall color, and better cold hardiness.

'Rotundiloba' has rounded lobes and displays deep reddish purple to burgundy fall color. It is also fruitless.

'Variegata' has leaves blotched and streaked with yellow.

Liquidambar styraciflua, Sweetgum, in fall

Liriodendron tulipifera
Tulip Tree

Easily recognized because of its unique leaf, this native species enjoys near cosmopolitan distribution. It is hard not to bump into a Tulip Tree in the course of one's horticultural travels. The tree is found in many of the great gardens of the world. Vanderbilt used it to frame his Biltmore house in Asheville, North Carolina, as Jefferson had done at Monticello. The only significant drawbacks of this tree are its behemoth size and susceptibility to drought. Under severe drought, the interior leaves turn color prematurely and abscise as early as July or August, with only the outer leaves remaining. These minor flaws, however, do not diminish the plant's numerous landscape assets. Even in youth, when the habit is pyramidal, the uniformly spaced branches make the tree appear full and dense. With age the outline becomes oval-rounded, with several large, sinuous branches constituting the framework around an unusually long, slender bole. It is a magnificent and grand tree in its sunset years. The glossy bright green, 3- to 8-in.- long and wide leaves turn golden yellow in fall. The interesting tulip-shaped flowers of yellow, orange, and green, 2 to 3 in. high and wide, appear after the leaves in May and June. Borne high on the

Liquidambar styraciflua fruit

Liquidambar styraciflua 'Rotundiloba' foliage

tree, the flowers are often missed by the unsuspecting. The conelike fruit provide winter interest and a good identifying characteristic. Splendid for large-area use. Provide deep, moist soils or supplemental water in drought periods, if possible. Grows 70 to 90 ft. high, 35 to 50 ft. wide. Zones 4 to 9. Massachusetts to Wisconsin, south to Florida and Mississippi.

Cultivars and Varieties. 'Aureo-marginatum' has leaves margined with yellow or greenish yellow. The effect is quite striking.

'Fastigiatum' ('Arnold') is an upright form not unlike *Populus nigra* 'Italica', the Lombardy Poplar, but wider at maturity. It makes a good screen, or it can be used in groupings for a strong vertical accent.

Liriodendron tulipifera in fall

Liriodendron tulipifera, Tulip Tree

Liriodendron tulipifera flower

Liriodendron tulipifera stem and fruit

Liriodendron tulipifera 'Aureo-marginatum' foliage

Lonicera, Honeysuckle

Honeysuckles are like sheep: there are too many of them, they all look alike, and they are rather pedestrian. People may argue the validity of this statement, and to be sure, honeysuckles are durable, adaptable, and quite serviceable shrubs. But like privet, they offer a sameness that does not inspire.

Lonicera alpigena, Alps Honeysuckle

Lonicera alpigena
Alps Honeysuckle

This species is an oval-rounded shrub with yellow-green flowers and dull red fruit. The 2- to 4-in.-long leaves are dark green and somewhat leathery. Withstands high-stress conditions. Might be used for groupings, in rock gardens, and as a facer plant. Grows 4 to 8 ft. high. Zones 5 to 7. Mountains of central and southern Europe.

Cultivars and Varieties. 'Nana' is a slow-growing form with large leaves and a dense, rounded-mounded outline. Grows 3 ft. high.

Lonicera alpigena 'Nana'

Lonicera alpigena 'Nana' flowers

Lonicera alpigena 'Nana' fruit

Lonicera ×*brownii*
Brown's Honeysuckle

This hybrid species is a cross between *Lonicera sempervirens*, Trumpet Honeysuckle, and *L. hirsuta*. In general characteristics, Brown's Honeysuckle resembles *L. sempervirens*, and it also displays that species' susceptibility to aphids.

Cultivars and Varieties. 'Dropmore Scarlet' is a red-flowered, cold-hardy form, and 'Fuchsioides' has orange-red flowers. Neither measure up to *Lonicera sempervirens*, however.

Lonicera ×brownii 'Dropmore Scarlet' flowers

Lonicera ×brownii 'Dropmore Scarlet'

Lonicera fragrantissima
Winter Honeysuckle

The small, cream-colored flowers of Winter Honeysuckle seldom attract attention, but their powerful fragrance perfumes an entire garden. Truly one of the best plants for late-winter and early-spring fragrance. The species develops a wide-spreading, irregularly rounded outline and consumes extensive real estate. The dull blue-green to dark green leaves, 1 to 3 in. long and almost as wide, are leathery textured for a honeysuckle. The sweet, lemon-fragrant flowers open in March and April over a three- to four-week period. Dark red berries (two ovaries fused) develop under the foliage and are seldom noticed. Extremely tough and adaptable, this species survives sand, clay, and high pH soils, in sun or shade. Its large size restricts use to borders, groupings, or masses. Grows 6 to 10 (to 15) ft. high and wide. Zones 4 to 8(9). China.

Lonicera fragrantissima, Winter Honeysuckle

Lonicera ×heckrottii
Goldflame Honeysuckle

This is the most common vining honeysuckle in the American commercial market. In most respects, it resembles *Lonicera sempervirens*, one of its parents (the other is *L. ×americana*), but it differs in its waxier blue-green foliage and the carmine flowers with yellowish interiors. Additionally, the flowers are fragrant. I have used the species to cover an old stump, where it flowers heavily in April and May and then sporadically into fall. Leaves are extremely frost tolerant and will survive 15 to 20°F. Grows 10 to 20 ft. high. Zones (4)5 to 8.

Lonicera ×heckrottii, Goldflame Honeysuckle, flowers

Lonicera ×heckrottii and *Lonicera japonica*

Lonicera japonica
Japanese Honeysuckle

This Asian species has become a pernicious pest throughout the eastern United States. In many places, it dominates the understory, outcompeting native wildflowers. The 1- to 3-in.-long, dark green leaves are evergreen, semievergreen, or deciduous, depending on winter temperatures. The 1½-in.-long, white flowers, which age to yellow, open from May to frost. Their fragrance is exceptional, and the air on a warm spring or summer day is heavy with the sweet scent. The ¼-in.-diameter, black berries ripen in August through October and are disseminated by birds. In landscape situations, it should only be used for inhospitable sites and unmanageable areas. Grows 15 to 30 ft. high if provided a structure; 1 to 2 ft. high if used as a groundcover. Zones 4 to 9. Japan, China, Korea.

Cultivars and Varieties. 'Aureo-reticulata' has leaves with a yellow-netted veinal pattern. This is not a plant for the weak at heart.

var. *chinensis* is less rampant than the species form of *Lonicera japonica* and has pretty reddish purple–tinged flowers and similar coloration on new leaves and stems. It makes a better garden plant than the species.

Lonicera japonica, Japanese Honeysuckle

Lonicera korolkowii
Blueleaf Honeysuckle

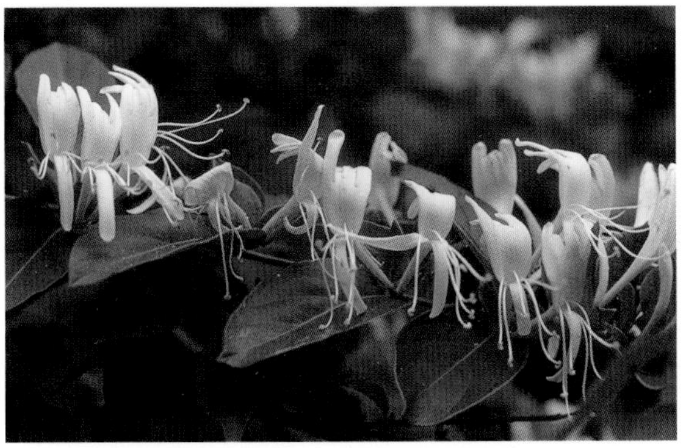
Lonicera japonica flowers

Lonicera japonica 'Aureo-reticulata' foliage

Lonicera japonica var. *chinensis* flowers

This is actually one of the prettiest shrub honeysuckles, but it is either often misidentified or just not very available because it can be difficult to come by in the trade. Blueleaf Honeysuckle forms a billowy, arching mound of blue-green leaves on rather willowy stems. From a textural perspective, it is possibly the finest of the shrubby honeysuckles. The ¾- to 1¼-in.-long leaves are pale bluish green. Rose-colored flowers, about ⅔ in. long, occur in May. The flowers are not overwhelming but are attractive on close inspection. The fruit is a bright red berry that matures in July and August. I have seen the true species only a few times; it was growing in partial shade and appeared quite prosperous. Plants grew 6 ft. high and wide, nowhere close to the 12- to 15-ft. height mentioned in the literature. Zones 4 to 7. Southern Russia to south central Asia.

Lonicera korolkowii, Blueleaf Honeysuckle

Lonicera korolkowii foliage and flower buds

Lonicera maackii
Amur Honeysuckle

A monstrous honeysuckle with few redeeming characteristics, this species has a minimal place in modern landscapes. It is a weedy species, like *Lonicera tatarica*, and will seed into a woodland area and outcompete the native material. Habit is upright-spreading and arching, becoming leggy at the base. Bark becomes ridged and furrowed and develops a pleasing gray-brown color. The 2- to 3-in.-long, dark green leaves hold late in fall. White, 1-in.-long flowers open in May and June and offer minimal to no fragrance. The ¼-in.-diameter, bright red fruit are rather pretty and provide food for the birds. Unfortunately, Amur Honeysuckle is so adaptable that it has become a weed. Think twice before using this species. Grows 12 to 15 ft. high and wide. Zones 2 to 8. Northeastern China, Korea.

Lonicera maackii fruit

Lonicera maackii, Amur Honeysuckle

Lonicera sempervirens
Trumpet Honeysuckle

Trumpet Honeysuckle is one of our most common native twining vines. The species is found in shady woods all over its native range. In full sun, it develops into a dense-foliaged vine. The 1- to 3-in.-long, blue-green leaves serve as a great background for the narrow, trumpet-shaped, 1½- to 2-in.-long, orange-red to red flowers, which occur in terminal panicles during May and June and have no fragrance. The ¼-in.-diameter, red berries ripen in September to November. Prefers moist, well-drained, acid to near neutral soils. Leaf drop caused by the *Pseudomonas* bacterium results in a less-than-satisfactory appearance toward the end of summer. The leaves abscise, but this does no permanent damage. Aphids occur on succulent new growth. Utilize on fences, trellises, drain spouts, rock piles, or even as a groundcover. Grows 10 to 20 ft. high. Zones 4 to 9. Connecticut to Florida, west to Nebraska and Texas.

Several other species of climbing European honeysuckles are available. *Lonicera caprifolium*, Italian Honeysuckle, has fragrant, 1¾- to 2-in.-long, yellowish white flowers tinged with purple, and orange-red fruit. It has disklike leaves subtending the flower. Similar to and often confused with *L. caprifolium* is *L. periclymenum*, Woodbine Honeysuckle. Its 1½- to 2-in.-long, fragrant flowers are typically yellowish white with a purple tinge, but it lacks the disklike leaf found on the previous species. It bears red fruit. The most spectacular flowering honeysuckle is *L.* ×*tellmanniana*, Tellmann Honeysuckle. It has almost fluorescent yellow-orange flowers that are blushed with red in the bud stage. Each flower averages 2 in. long and 1 in. across at the mouth of the corolla. All these species can be used in the landscape like *L. sempervirens*, Trumpet Honeysuckle. They are adaptable from Zones 5 to 7(8).

Cultivars and Varieties. 'Sulphurea' is a beautiful yellow-flowered form of *Lonicera sempervirens* that produces a shower of flowers and bright green foliage.

Lonicera sempervirens, Trumpet Honeysuckle

Lonicera sempervirens flowers

Lonicera sempervirens 'Sulphurea' flowers

Lonicera tatarica

Tatarian Honeysuckle

In recent years, the Russian aphid has decimated this species in midwestern gardens, and the aphid is becoming increasingly apparent in eastern landscapes. Aphid infestation causes the growth to become distorted and bunchy with smallish leaves and stems. Several institutions are breeding and selecting for resistance. Typical *Lonicera tatarica* is an upright-oval to rounded, multistemmed shrub. It has 1½- to 2½-in.-long, blue-green leaves and white to pink, ¾- to 1-in.-long flowers in May. Bright red berries ripen from late June to August. Many cultivars offer different flower and fruit colors. This species, like most honeysuckles, leafs out extremely early in spring. Unfortunately, like *L. maackii*, it has become a weed, particularly in the East and Midwest. It was once a common screen and hedge plant in the Midwest and East. Grows 10 to 12 ft. high, 10 ft. wide. Zones 3 to 8. Central Asia to southern Russia.

Lonicera tatarica, Tatarian Honeysuckle, fruit

Lonicera tatarica flowers

Lonicera xylosteum

European Fly Honeysuckle

Arguably, this species and a few selected cultivars may be the most acceptable choices for the conditions of the Midwest and Plains states. *Lonicera xylosteum* is a rounded-mounded shrub with spreading, arching branches. The grayish green, 1- to 2½-in.-long leaves are the most pubescent of the species presented here. The white to yellowish white, ⅝-in.-long flowers produce minimal effect when they bloom in May. The dark red berries offer some color in July and August. A tough, durable honeysuckle for difficult environments. Grows 8 to 10 ft. high, 10 to 12 ft. wide. Zones 4 to 6. Europe to the Altai Mountains of Asia.

Cultivars and Varieties. 'Emerald Mound' ('Nana') is a fine selection, with rich bluish green foliage and a low-growing, mounded habit. Prefers colder climates. Grows 3 to 4 ft. high, 4½ to 6 ft. wide.

'Miniglobe' is more compact and has greater cold hardiness than 'Emerald Mound'. It displays dense, dark green foliage. Grows 3 to 4 ft. high and wide.

Lonicera xylosteum, European Fly Honeysuckle

Lonicera xylosteum fruit

Lonicera xylosteum 'Emerald Mound'

Maackia amurensis
Amur Maackia

Unheralded and unknown except in the gardens of a fortunate few. No singular quality sets this small tree apart, but the sum of its features contributes to a pleasing landscape presence. A dapper, round-headed tree of uniform proportions in youth and at maturity. New foliage is dusted with grayish pubescence that yields to rich green. The leaves are composed of five to seven leaflets, each 1½ to 3½ in. long. Fall color is virtually nonexistent and the leaves die off green. Dull white, pealike flowers appear in 4- to 6-in.-long racemes (sometimes panicles) in June or July. Their fragrance could be likened to that of new-mown alfalfa. The shiny, amber-colored bark peels with age into loose flakes and curls. When backlighted by the setting sun, the bark has the color of a rich brown ale. Performs best in loose, acid or alkaline, well-drained soils. An excellent small tree for streets, planters, lawns, and patios. Grows 20 to 30 ft. high and wide. Zones 4 to 7. Northeastern China.

Maackia amurensis young foliage

Maackia amurensis, Amur Maackia

Maackia amurensis flowers

Maackia amurensis bark

Maclura pomifera

Osage-Orange

Not many gardeners or nursery people become overly excited about this species. For the drier parts of the Midwest, however, it has merit. The species not only withstands but thrives in the harshest conditions. The use of Osage-Orange in the Midwest for hedgerows and fence lines is evident even today. With selection for thornless and fruitless forms, this could become a popular landscape tree. Rounded in youth and old age, with a low trunk. The crown is composed of stiff, spiny, interlacing branches. The glossy, medium to dark green, 2- to 5-in.-long leaves turn a good yellow in fall. Fruit on female trees are green, round, and 4 to 6 in. in diameter. As projectiles they are dangerous, as well as messy. Newton's Law of Gravity had nothing to do with falling apples; falling osage-oranges prompted the theory. The wood is rot resistant and can be used for stepping rounds. Grows 20 to 40 ft. high, similar spread; can grow to 60 ft. high. Zones 4 to 9. Arkansas to Oklahoma and Texas.

Maclura pomifera bark

Maclura pomifera, Osage-Orange

Maclura pomifera fruit

Magnolia acuminata, Cucumbertree Magnolia

Magnolia acuminata

Cucumbertree Magnolia

Seldom seen in North American gardens for want of flashy flowers. It is a large native tree with dark green, 4- to 10-in.-long leaves. Yellow-green flowers appear after the leaves and are followed by small, irregular, cucumber-shaped fruit. Cucumbertree Magnolia will never rival a Saucer Magnolia or Star Magnolia for flower effect, but as a shade tree it deserves consideration. Distinctly pyramidal when young, it becomes round-headed with age, bearing massive, wide-spreading branches. Transplant young specimens into deep, moist, acid or high pH soils. Superb specimens are found in the calcareous soils of the Midwest. This species is only for large properties. Grows 50 to 80 ft. high, similar spread. Zones 4 to 8. New York to Illinois, south to Georgia and Arkansas.

Magnolia acuminata bark and branching pattern

Magnolia acuminata fruit

Magnolia acuminata flower

Magnolia denudata (M. heptapeta)
Yulan Magnolia

More famous as a parent of *Magnolia ×soulangiana*, Saucer Magnolia, than in its own right. The nine-tepaled, 5- to 6-in.-wide, creamy white, fragrant flowers open early and, unfortunately, are often hurt by spring freezes. When undamaged by weather, the floral display is a beautiful sight in March and April. The dark green leaves average 4 to 6 in. long. It is a rounded tree and has smooth gray bark. Excellent specimen magnolia, but often frustrating to grow because of its vulnerability to spring frosts. In hybridization work, it has served as a parent of many fine crosses, including the creamy yellow-flowered 'Elizabeth', which resulted from a cross with *M. acuminata*. Grows 20 to 30 (to 40) ft. high. Zones (4)5 to 8. China.

Magnolia denudata, Yulan Magnolia

Magnolia denudata flower

Magnolia denudata fruit

Magnolia kobus
Kobus Magnolia

Seldom used in contemporary landscapes because of the time it takes for it to flower from seed; some take as long as 30 years to reach full flower. The six- to nine-tepaled, white, slightly fragrant flowers, 3 to 4 in. in diameter, appear before the leaves in March and April. Beautiful when right. In youth the habit is pyramidal; it becomes rounded at maturity. The dark green, 3- to 6-in.-long leaves develop appreciable yellow-brown fall color. The silver-gray bark is a lovely addition to the winter landscape. Very adaptable species. Grows 30 to 40 ft. high. Zones 5 to 7(8). Japan.

Cultivars and Varieties. var. *borealis* is more cold hardy (Zone 4) and more treelike in habit than the species. A plantsman in Maine noted that seedling trees of var. *borealis* did not flower until their 18th year.

Magnolia kobus, Kobus Magnolia

Magnolia ×loebneri
Loebner Magnolia

Magnolia kobus flower

Magnolia ×loebneri 'Ballerina' flower

Magnolia ×loebneri 'Spring Snow' flower

A hybrid between *Magnolia kobus* and *M. stellata*, this small tree embodies the best characteristics of each of its parents. Normally forms a round-headed crown of dense branches. The flowers are typically white, fragrant, and have 12 to 15 tepals, and they open in April, about seven to ten days ahead of those of *M. ×soulangiana*. Leaves are dark green, 3 to 5 in. long, and turn mellow yellow-brown in fall. Grows 20 to 30 ft. high. Zones (4)5 to 8.

Cultivars and Varieties. 'Ballerina' has flowers with 30 tepals, pure white and pinkish in the center. It is pyramidal-oval in habit. Grows to 25 ft. high.

'Leonard Messel' produces 12- to 15-tepaled flowers, flushed purple-pink on the outside. Habit is smaller than that of other cultivars mentioned here. Grows 15 to 20 ft. high.

'Merrill' has 3- to 3½-in.-diameter flowers with 15 tepals, borne profusely on a densely branched plant.

'Spring Snow' has 12-tepaled, creamy white flowers. Grows 25 ft. high and wide.

Magnolia ×loebneri, Loebner Magnolia

Magnolia macrophylla
Bigleaf Magnolia

Although seldom available in commerce other than from specialty nurseries, this large, coarse species makes an interesting novelty specimen for parks, campuses, and large open spaces. At maturity, it is a cumbersome giant, seemingly too tired to lift its leafy arms skyward. And with good reason: its dark green, silver-undersided leaves are 12 to 32 in. long, truly almost too heavy to lift. The leaf litter from this tree, with some leaves facing up and others showing their silver undersides, makes a great autumn sight. No rake is large enough! Six-tepaled, creamy white, fragrant flowers, 8 to 10 (to 14) in. in diameter, open in June at the ends of the branches. The 3-in.-long, roundish, egg-shaped, rose-colored fruit ripen in September. Plant in moist, deep, organic-laden, slightly acid soils for best growth. Will grow in sun or partial shade. Very difficult to use in the average residential landscape; it requires space to flex its muscles. Grows 30 to 40 ft. high and wide. Zones 5 to 8. Ohio to Florida, west to Arkansas and Louisiana.

Several closely related species include *Magnolia ashei*, Ashe Magnolia; *M. fraseri*, Fraser Magnolia; and *M. tripetala*, Umbrellatree Magnolia. These species vary in their mature size, the shape of the leaf base, and the degree of bud pubescence. All have quite large leaves.

Magnolia ×*soulangiana*
Saucer Magnolia

This quintessential hybrid magnolia is as common as fertilizer at every garden center. It is a precocious, large-flowered tree, reliable year in and year out. A specimen in full flower is one of spring's greatest spectacles. The cup-shaped, pinkish purple, nine-tepaled, fragrant flowers, 5 to 10 in. in diameter, open in April on bare stems. Unfortunately, like the flowers of *Magnolia denudata*, they are subject to the vagaries of spring weather. The habit is generally low branched, with upright-arching branches forming a rounded outline. The dark green, 3- to 6-in.-long leaves are handsome into fall, but they seldom produce anything but a muddied yellow fall color. The smooth gray bark is a pleasant addition to the winter landscape. Saucer Magnolia is extremely adaptable to a wide range of soils. An excellent specimen plant. The hybrid was first made in France. Grows 20 to 30 ft. high, variable spread. Zones 5 to 9.

Cultivars and Varieties. 'Alexandrina' produces tepals that are flushed light rose-purple outside, pure white inside. It is one of the larger- and earlier-flowering cultivars. There are at least three clones masquerading as 'Alexandrina' in the nursery trade, one with darker rose-purple flowers.

Magnolia macrophylla, Bigleaf Magnolia

Magnolia macrophylla foliage

Magnolia macrophylla flower

'Brozzonii' offers white tepals tinged pale purplish rose at the base. Each flower is fully 10 in. across when open. This large cultivar is about the last to flower. Grows 25 to 30 ft. high.

'Lennei' bears dark purplish magenta flowers fashioned in an almost goblet shape. Leaves are darker green than those of the species, and the growth habit is that of a stiff, broad shrub.

'Lennei Alba' offers pure white flowers on a framework similar to that of the above.

'Rustica Rubra' ('Rubra') has rose-red, $5\frac{1}{2}$-in.-diameter flowers.

'Verbanica' is a late-flowering cultivar, with rose (wine-red) tepals that grade to white at their tips. It bears abundant buds as a young plant. Habit is large and rounded.

Magnolia ×*soulangiana* 'Alexandrina' flowers

Magnolia ×*soulangiana*, Saucer Magnolia

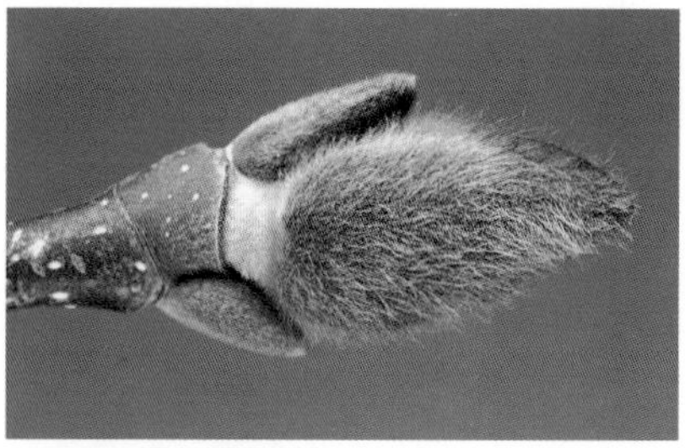

Magnolia ×*soulangiana* flower bud

Magnolia ×*soulangiana* 'Brozzonii' flowers

Magnolia ×*soulangiana* 'Lennei' flower

Magnolia stellata
Star Magnolia

Although more shrublike than treelike, this species can attain a good size. When the basal branches are removed to expose the smooth gray bark, the result is a handsome large shrub or small tree. Typically, Star Magnolia is a dense, oval to rounded, twiggy shrub. The 2- to 4-in.-long, dark green leaves turn handsome yellow to bronze-yellow in autumn. Fragrant, 12- to 18-tepaled, 3- to 4- (to 5-) in.-diameter flowers open in March and April, usually before those of *Magnolia* ×*soulangiana*. Flowering may last for 10 to 20 days, because not all buds open at the same time. The leaves may even reach full size with some flowers still present. This is possibly the most cold- and heat-tolerant species for general ornamental use. Displays excellent adaptability to varied soils, and prospers from Maine to Minnesota to Georgia. Grows 15 to 20 ft. high, 10 to 15 ft. wide. Zones 4 to 8. Japan.

Cultivars and Varieties. Many excellent cultivars are available—I have never observed a bad one.

'Centennial' is an excellent selection that commemorates the 100th anniversary of the Arnold Arboretum. Its flowers have 28 to 32 tepals, with each open flower up to 5½ in. wide. This form has a strong central leader and is the most vigorous of all *Magnolia stellata* types. It is also cold hardy to at least –30°F.

'Rosea' is a true pink-flowered form. Unfortunately, many impostors are sold under this name. Buy in flower, if possible.

'Royal Star' is a dense, oval to rounded, shrubby form. It has 25 to 30 nearly pure white tepals that open to 3- to 4-in.-wide flowers. Reports have indicated hardiness to –35°F. This form is slower growing than 'Centennial'. It is consistently one of the earliest to flower. Matures around 10 to 12 ft. high.

'Waterlily' has rich pink buds that open white with 14 to 24 tepals (on one occasion I counted 33). Flowers are highly fragrant. The habit is upright-bushy. Probably more than one clone in cultivation. Grows 15 ft. high; can grow larger.

Magnolia stellata, Star Magnolia

Magnolia stellata flowers

Magnolia stellata 'Centennial'

Magnolia stellata 'Waterlily'

Magnolia virginiana
Sweetbay Magnolia

Although common in wet areas throughout the Coastal Plain of the southeastern United States, this native species occurs as far north as Massachusetts. Always a favorite of mine, Sweetbay Magnolia is at its best on a June day, when the silvery backed leaves are tousled by the wind and sparkle like diamonds and the lemony sweet fragrance rides on every current of air. The habit varies from a single-stemmed tree to a large, multistemmed, round-headed shrub. The dark green, 3- to 5-in.-long leaves are silvery on their undersides, and the bark is a silvery gray. The leaves are deciduous in northern latitudes, evergreen in the deep South. Creamy white, 2- to 3-in.-diameter, sweetly fragrant flowers, each with 9 to 12 tepals, appear in May and June. Use the species in outdoor living areas by patios, pools, and decks. Grows 10 to 20 ft. high and wide in the North; 60 ft. high in north Florida. Zones 5 to 9. Massachusetts to Florida and Texas.

Magnolia virginiana flower

Magnolia virginiana fruit

Magnolia virginiana, Sweetbay Magnolia

Magnolia Hybrids

Magnolia 'Elizabeth'

Magnolia 'Pristine'

Any treatment of magnolias in this volume will necessarily be somewhat superficial, but it would be difficult to ignore the more recent hybrids that have found a place in mainstream gardening. A few of the most notable ones are presented here.

'Elizabeth', mentioned under the entry for *Magnolia denudata*, is still not the pure yellow that the breeders are seeking. Under cool spring conditions, the emerging buds are indeed yellow, but they open to creamy yellow at best. 'Butterflies' and 'Goldfinch', other hybrids involving *M. denudata* and *M. acuminata*, are two newer cultivars with deeper yellow tepals and are increasingly available in commerce.

'Galaxy' and 'Spectrum' are sister seedlings from crosses between *Magnolia liliiflora* and *M. sprengeri* 'Diva'. They are upright-pyramidal trees in youth, becoming more rounded with age, and have smooth grayish bark. The tepals, backed with rich reddish purple, open in April to expose 6-in.-diameter pinkish centers. Mildew can be a problem in moist, humid climates. 'Galaxy' develops water sprouts, a legacy from its *M. liliiflora* parentage. Both make great specimen plants and are possible street trees in suburban areas. Grows 25 to 30 ft. high, slightly less in spread. Zones 5 to 8(9).

'Pristine' is, unfortunately, unknown to most gardeners, but it is certainly worthy of acquisition. A hybrid between *Magnolia denudata* and *M. stellata*, this cultivar bears ivory-white, lily-shaped, fragrant flowers, each with 15 to 18 tepals, that open in April. The habit is pyramidal and the foliage is a handsome dark green. Grows 15 to 25 ft. high, slightly less in spread. Zones 5 to 9.

Magnolia 'Spectrum'

Mahonia aquifolium
Oregon Grapeholly

One of the more cold-hardy and functional broadleaf evergreens, this species offers pretty golden yellow flowers and blue fruit, as well as excellent shade tolerance. Several growth habits are evident, from a compact-mounded, suckering type to a taller, upright, irregular, and open form. The foliage is certainly spectacular, especially the newly emerging leaves, which range from lustrous, bright apple-green to bronzy orange. The leaves mature to lustrous dark green and assume bronze-purple tints in winter. The fragrant flowers open in March and April in 2- to 3-in.- long and wide terminal inflorescences. The ½-in.-long, grapelike fruit ripen in summer. It prefers moist, acid, well-drained soils and a shady environment, sheltered from winter sun and wind. Plants often appear ragged in exposed locations. Use as a mass, in groupings, or as a specimen. Grows 3 to 6 ft. high and wide. Zones (4)5 to 8. British Columbia to Oregon.

Cultivars and Varieties. Many cultivars have been developed, but only a few are commonly available.

'Compactum' is a beautiful mounded form with extremely glossy dark green leaves and bronze winter color. Grows 2 to 3 ft. high.

'King's Ransom' is upright in habit, with blue-green foliage that turns red-purple in winter. It has become more popular in recent years.

Mahonia aquifolium, Oregon Grapeholly

Mahonia aquifolium new foliage

Mahonia aquifolium flowers

Malus, Flowering Crabapple

Without question, the flowering crabapples are the dominant spring-flowering trees in the northern tier of states, where cherries, dogwoods, and magnolias are often relegated to second-class status. As a small- to medium-sized, cold-hardy tree, Malus *has few competitors. Over 800 cultivars are known, with new selections added yearly. One wholesale producer on the West Coast alone offers 50 cultivars. Many flowering crabapples are susceptible to foliar diseases and fireblight and should be discarded. The newer selections have been chosen for disease resistance, annual flowering, and persistent fruit. Those presented here are selected on the basis of my observations and those of researchers at Ohio State University, the University of Wisconsin, and the Morton Arboretum in Lisle, Illinois. Several older but commercially available cultivars are also discussed. These crabapple species and cultivars represent a range of habits, sizes, and flower and fruit colors. All should be adaptable in Zones 4 to 8.*

Malus, Crabapple, displaying its habit in the winter landscape

Malus floribunda
Japanese Flowering Crabapple

This species is an old favorite. It has carmine buds and 1- to $1\frac{1}{2}$-in.-diameter, white flowers. The $\frac{3}{8}$-in.-diameter fruit are yellow to red. Broad-rounded habit. Good disease resistance. Grows 15 to 25 ft. high.

Malus floribunda, Japanese Flowering Crabapple

Malus floribunda flowers

Malus floribunda fruit

Malus hupehensis
Tea Crabapple

This species has the most elegant vase-shaped growth habit of any crabapple. Unfortunately, it is susceptible to fireblight. Dark pink buds open to 1½-in.-diameter, white flowers. It bears ⅜-in.-diameter, yellow to red fruit. Grows 20 to 25 ft. high and wide.

Malus hupehensis flowers

Malus hupehensis, Tea Crabapple

Malus hupehensis fruit and fall color

Malus sargentii
Sargent Crabapple

A mounded, densely branched, shrubby species. Red buds open to ¾- to 1-in.-diameter, white flowers. It bears ⅜-in.-diameter, bright red fruit. Good disease resistance. Grows 6 to 10 ft. high.

Cultivars and Varieties. 'Tina' is a compact form of the species, with the same desirable features. Grows 5 ft. high.

Malus sargentii, Sargent Crabapple

Malus sieboldii var. *zumi* 'Calocarpa'

This crabapple has deep red buds, 1⅓-in.-diameter white flowers, and ½-in.-diameter bright red fruit. Dense and rounded in habit. Resistant to scab, but susceptible to fireblight. Grows 25 ft. high and wide.

Malus sargentii flowers

Malus sargentii fruit

Malus sieboldii var. *zumi* 'Calocarpa' fruit

Malus sieboldii var. *zumi* 'Calocarpa'

Malus Cultivars

'Adams' offers 1½-in.-diameter, rose-colored flowers and ⅝-in.-diameter, red fruit. The habit is rounded. This cultivar exhibits high resistance to scab. Grows 24 ft. high.

'Amberina' has deep red buds that open to white flowers. Fruit is brilliant orange-red and persistent. Upright, semidwarf habit. High scab resistance. Grows 10 ft. high.

'Centurion' produces red buds that open to rose-red flowers. Glossy cherry-red fruit are ⅝ in. in diameter. Habit is upright in youth, rounded at maturity. Highly resistant to diseases. Grows 25 ft. high, 15 to 20 ft. wide.

'Christmas Holly' has red-budded, 1½-in.-diameter, white flowers and bright red, ½-in.-diameter fruit that persist into December. It has a small, spreading stature. Resistant. Grows 10 to 15 ft. high.

'Donald Wyman' offers rich red buds that unfurl to 1¾-in.-diameter, white flowers. Glossy bright red, ½-in.-diameter fruit persist into winter. Large, rounded habit. Highly resistant. It tends toward alternating cycles of heavy and light flowering. Grows 25 ft. high.

'Harvest Gold' is pink in bud, white in flower. Golden, 3/5-in.-diameter fruit persist in good condition into December or later. Upright-spreading habit. Highly resistant. Grows 25 ft. high and wide.

'Indian Summer' has rose-red flowers and long-persistent, bright red fruit, ⅝ to ¾ in. in diameter. Habit is a broad globe

Malus 'Adams' flowers

Malus 'Centurion' fruit

Malus 'Centurion' flowers

Malus 'Christmas Holly' flowers

Malus 'Donald Wyman'

MORE ➤

Malus 'Donald Wyman' flowers

Malus 'Harvest Gold' fruit

shape. Good resistance. Grows 18 ft. high, 19 ft. wide.

'Jewelberry' is a small but impressive tree with pink buds that open to white flowers. The ½-in.-diameter, glossy red fruit persist into fall. Good resistance. Grows 8 to 12 ft. high.

'Liset' has dark crimson buds that produce 1½-in.-diameter, rose-red to light crimson flowers. The maroon-red fruit average ½ in. in diameter. Rounded and dense in habit. Resistant to scab. Grows 15 to 20 ft. high.

'Mary Potter' is one of my favorites, but this cultivar may suffer from disease problems. Pink-red buds produce prodigious 1-in.-diameter, white flowers. Fruit are bright red and ½ in. in diameter. Broad-mounded habit. Grows 10 to 15 ft. high, 15 to 20 ft. wide.

'Narragansett' is a recent National Arboretum release that prospers in heat. Northern reports indicate good disease resistance. Red buds open to white flowers with pink tinges. Cherry-red fruit are ½ in. in diameter. A broad-crowned

Malus 'Jewelberry'

Malus 'Liset'

Malus 'Mary Potter'

Malus 'Mary Potter' fruit

Malus 'Prairifire' flowers

small tree with wide crotch angles and leathery, dark green leaves. Grows 13 ft. high.

'Prairifire' is red-budded, with dark pinkish red flowers and $\frac{3}{8}$- to $\frac{1}{2}$-in.-diameter, red-purple fruit. Rounded growth habit. Highly resistant. Grows 20 ft. high and wide.

'Profusion' has red buds that open purplish red and fade to purplish pink on 1$\frac{1}{2}$-in.-diameter flowers. The oxblood-red, $\frac{1}{2}$-in.-diameter fruit are persistent. Good resistance. Small tree. Grows 20 ft. high and wide.

'Red Jade' is an older, weeping cultivar with deep pink to red buds and 1$\frac{1}{2}$-in.-diameter flowers. It tends toward alternate-year flowering. It offers glossy red, $\frac{1}{2}$-in.-diameter fruit. Rounded to broad-rounded, graceful, pendulous habit. Moderately susceptible to scab. Grows 15 ft. high.

'Snowdrift' offers pink buds and 1$\frac{1}{4}$-in.-diameter, white flowers. Orange-red fruit are $\frac{3}{8}$ in. in diameter. It is dense and rounded in habit and has lustrous dark green foliage. Slight susceptibility to scab, severe susceptibility to fireblight. Grows 15 to 20 ft. high and wide.

'Sugar Tyme' has pale pink buds that open to sugar-white flowers. The $\frac{1}{2}$-in.-diameter, red fruit are persistent. Oval-rounded in habit. Very resistant. Grows 18 ft. high, 15 ft. wide.

'Weeping Candied Apple' produces red buds and white flowers. The persistent, cherry-red fruit are $\frac{5}{8}$ in. in diameter. It has broad, pendulous branches. Slight to moderate scab susceptibility. Grows 10 to 15 ft. high.

'White Angel' is pink in bud, opening to 1-in.-diameter, pure white flowers. It has glossy red, $\frac{1}{2}$- to $\frac{5}{8}$-in.-diameter fruit and an irregular, rounded habit. Resistant. Grows 20 ft. high.

Malus 'Profusion' flowers

Malus 'Sugar Tyme' flowers

Malus 'Sugar Tyme' fruit

MORE ➤

Malus Cultivars, continued

Malus 'White Angel'

Malus 'White Angel' flowers

Menispermum canadense
Common Moonseed

This twining, large-leaved vine does maintain a permanent woody super-structure above ground. Like *Aristolochia durior*, Dutchman's Pipe, this species makes a reasonable cover or screen if provided support upon which to climb. The dark green leaves are 4 to 10 in. long and 4 to 7 in. wide. Flowers and fruit are inconspicuous. It is adaptable to any well-drained soil, in partial to heavy shade. Grows 10 to 20 ft. high. Zones 4 to 8. Quebec to Manitoba, south to Georgia and Arkansas.

Menispermum canadense, Common Moonseed, foliage

Metasequoia glyptostroboides
Dawn Redwood

Dawn Redwood was resurrected from near-extinction when a Chinese botanist discovered the plant in 1941. The Arnold Arboretum organized an expedition to collect seeds, and gardeners the world over have benefited. In youth and old age, the habit is pyramidal and feathery. The bark is reddish brown in youth, becoming darker and fissured with age and exfoliating in narrow strips. The trunk becomes buttressed with maturity. The ½-in.-long, bright green needles are borne on small branchlets. In fall, the needles turn orangish brown to reddish brown. Once established, the species withstands dry soils, although it will also grow in wet soils. Plant in a sunny location. A single specimen is an imposing sight, but groupings and groves are also effective. Allow ample room for growth. Under ideal cultural conditions, 2 to 3 ft. of vertical growth per year is common. Many trees planted in the late 1940s are now over 100 ft. tall. Grows 70 to 100 ft. high, 25 ft. wide. Zones 5 to 8. China.

Metasequoia glyptostroboides, Dawn Redwood

Metasequoia glyptostroboides in fall

Metasequoia glyptostroboides bark

Metasequoia glyptostroboides fall color

Morus alba
Common or White Mulberry

Mention "mulberry" to a gardener and be prepared to listen to horror stories about the mess created by fruiting specimens. In the early years of my career, a mulberry had as much net worth as my bank account. With the advent of several fruitless (sterile) selections, the tree deserves a second glance. The typical species is a round-headed, twiggy, often unkempt tree. The 2- to 7-in.-long, lustrous dark green leaves may be lobed or undivided. Foliage may turn a pleasing yellow in fall. The April flowers are not showy, but the ½- to 1-in.-long, ellipsoidal, purplish black fruit can be used for pies or to feed the birds. Common Mulberry is adaptable to any soil, in full sun to partial shade. The species grows in dry, high salt, or high pH soils and is frequently seen in the Southwest. Can become a weed tree as fruit are distributed by birds and other wildlife. The cultivars discussed below make effective short-term, urban-tolerant trees or accent plants. Grows 30 to 50 ft. high and wide. Zones 4 to 8(9). China.

Morus alba, Common Mulberry

Cultivars and Varieties. 'Chaparral' and 'Urbana' are fruitless, weeping trees with lustrous dark green foliage. They are often grafted on a standard to produce a fast-growing, small, weeping tree.

'Mapleleaf' and 'Stribling' are fruitless, fast-growing tree types. The first has large, lobed, maplelike leaves; the second has the typical mulberry foliage and excellent yellow fall color. I have observed a plant of 'Stribling' that was 40 ft. high and 30 ft. wide.

var. *tatarica* is considered the most cold hardy of the various *Morus alba* forms. It is available from specialty nurseries.

Morus alba infructescence

Morus australis (M. bombycis) 'Unryu' ('Tortuosa')

This nomenclatural anomaly is gaining popularity in the United States. It is a vigorous large shrub or small tree, with coarse, twisted, contorted branches. The lustrous dark green, 6- to 7-in.-long leaves turn rich bronzy yellow in autumn. A 1-ft.-high plant set in my garden in 1984 is 20 ft. high and wide. Will prove cold hardy to –10°F and below; I recently saw plants in Vassalboro, Maine, where a temperature of –25°F is common. Zones (4)5 to 8. China.

Morus australis 'Unryu'

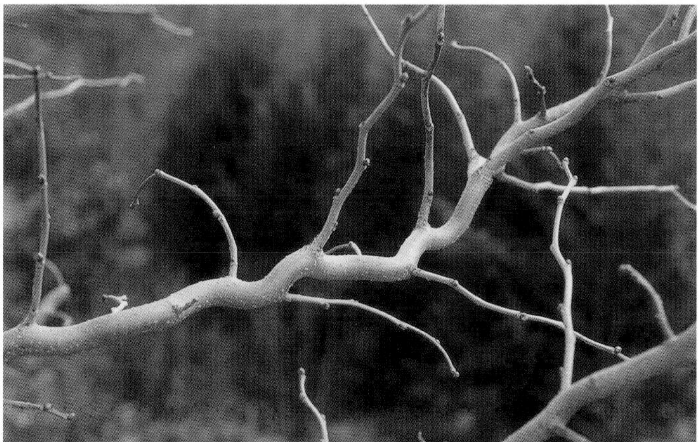

Morus australis 'Unryu' branches

Morus rubra
Red Mulberry

This native tree species is seldom available in commerce but deserves mention because of its wide native range. The habit is upright-spreading. The dark green, 3- to 8-in.-long leaves hang from the branches like large green paper napkins. The edible red fruit turn to dark purple. For best growth, the species requires rich, moist, deep soils. It is often found as an understory or wood's-edge plant in the wild. Grows 40 to 70 ft. high, 40 to 50 ft. wide. Zones 5 to 9. Massachusetts to Michigan, south to Florida and Texas.

Morus rubra, Red Mulberry

Morus rubra fall color

Myrica pensylvanica
Northern Bayberry

A most handsome plant, particularly in its native coastal habitat, where the dark green leaves stand out against the sandy soils. It is amazingly tolerant of salt and infertile soils. Forms great rounded colonies because of its suckering nature. The species is dioecious, bearing minimally showy, yellowish green flowers on male plants and gray, waxy coated, ⅙- to ⅕-in.-diameter drupes on female plants. The fruit ripen in September and may persist until the following April. Transplant from a container into well-drained, preferably acid soils. Withstands clay soils, but will develop chlorosis in high pH soils. Great plant for massing and grouping, in full sun or shade. I have observed it in combination with groundcover junipers, and the textural differences are quite striking. Variable in size. Grows 5 to 12 ft. high, equal or greater in spread. Zones (2)3 to 6. Newfoundland to western New York, south to North Carolina.

Myrica pensylvanica, Northern Bayberry

Myrica pensylvanica flowers

Myrica pensylvanica fruit

Neillia sinensis
Chinese Neillia

In its best form, this species is a refined, delicately branched, rounded shrub that offers rich green foliage and pink flowers, which appear in 1- to 2½-in.-long racemes in May. The leaves are 2 to 4 in. long, with small lobes. Soils should be moist and well drained. Use in the shrub border or in mass plantings, in light shade or full sun. Grows 5 to 6 ft. high and wide. Zones 5 to 7. China.

Neillia sinensis, Chinese Neillia

Neillia sinensis flowers

Neviusia alabamensis
Alabama Snow-Wreath

This shrub is more of a conversation piece than a first-rate, multidimensional landscape plant, although the flower effect can be striking. The quirky, creamy white flowers are apetalous; the stamens are the showy part. Flowers appear in three- to eight-flowered cymes in May and create an effect akin to new-fallen snow covering the branches. The habit is somewhat scraggly with arching branches, developing into a rounded outline. The 1½- to 3½-in.-long leaves are medium green and offer no fall color. In fact, the plant is so nondescript out of flower that few people recognize it. *Neviusia alabamensis* requires moist soils for best growth, but it is an adaptable species and appears to thrive under less-than-ideal conditions. Tolerant of sun or shade. A good choice for the shrub border, or for quizzing your friends to identify. Grows 3 to 6 ft. high and wide. Zones 4 to 8. Alabama.

Neviusia alabamensis flowers

Neviusia alabamensis, Alabama Snow-Wreath

Nyssa sylvatica
Black Tupelo

A true harbinger of autumn. In September, before most trees acknowledge that summer has ended, a smattering of leaves on Black Tupelo trees start to twinkle yellow, orange, and red. It would be among the top five shade trees in the landscape were it not so very difficult to transplant; ideally it should be transplanted as a small tree. The habit is distinctly pyramidal in youth and may maintain that form into old age or become rounded. The dark gray, almost black bark is broken into thick ridges that are divided horizontally, producing a blocky configuration. The 3- to 6-in.-long, lustrous dark green leaves turn fluorescent yellow, orange, scarlet, and maroon in fall. Fall color is often fleeting, for the leaves do not persist like those of maples and oaks. *Nyssa sylvatica* prospers in deep, moist, acid soils, but it is found in dry woods and in swamps throughout its native range. A single specimen is spectacular, but groupings of five to seven trees, each expressing a different fall color, provide pause for reflection. Grows 30 to 50 ft. high, 20 to 30 ft. wide, although size is highly variable. Zones 4 to 9. Maine to Ontario and Michigan, south to Florida and Texas.

Nyssa sylvatica, Black Tupelo

Nyssa sylvatica fall color and fruit

Nyssa sylvatica bark

Nyssa sylvatica in fall

Ostrya virginiana
American Hophornbeam

Although it is a rather handsome small tree, this American native has been relegated to the forest shadows and has never been discovered by the gardening public. It is a graceful, pyramidal tree in youth, becoming more rounded with age. The grayish brown exfoliating bark is attractive in the winter months. The 2- to 5-in.-long, dark green, sharply serrated leaves develop yellow-brown color and drop early in fall. Wormlike, 1½-in.-long, yellow-brown male catkins open in April. American Hophornbeam tolerates dry, acid, and higher pH soils. It prospers in full sun and is also a good understory tree. The species has been used for street and campus plantings. Grows 25 to 40 ft. high, 20 to 40 ft. wide. Zones 4 to 9. Ontario to Minnesota, south to Florida and Texas.

Ostrya virginiana, American Hophornbeam

Ostrya virginiana bark

Ostrya virginiana fruit

Ostrya virginiana male catkins

Oxydendrum arboreum
Sourwood

Northern gardeners would give their best trowel for a specimen Sourwood, a tree that in its native habitat assumes almost blatant commonality. One of our best native trees, and a well-grown specimen rivals even the best dogwoods. The habit is delicately pyramidal with finely textured, drooping branches. Young stems vary from olive-green to rich red, and the brown bark becomes blocky with age. Iridescent green young leaves mature to lustrous dark green, 3 to 8 in. long. The foliage turns yellow, red, and maroon in fall. White, ¼-in.-long, fragrant flowers are borne in 4- to 10-in.- long and wide panicles in June and July. The flowers open over an extended period, perhaps three to four weeks. They are followed by small, ⅓-in.-long, brownish capsules that persist through winter. Sourwood is difficult to produce under typical nursery conditions and is not the easiest plant to move. It is best to work with small, container-grown plants. A great choice for naturalizing in infertile, acid soils, in sun or partial shade. Grows 25 to 30 ft. high, 20 ft. wide; can grow larger. Zones 5 to 9. Southeastern United States.

Oxydendrum arboreum, Sourwood

Oxydendrum arboreum in fall

Oxydendrum arboreum flowers

Oxydendrum arboreum bark

Parrotia persica
Persian Parrotia

I love this tree: the clean summer foliage; the yellows, oranges, and reds of autumn; the cream, green, gray, and brown exfoliating bark; and the small, maroon flowers that glow on a late-winter day. Over the years, my travels have led me to many parrotias, no two alike. A 60-ft.-high specimen in the Jardin des Plantes in Paris and the 100-year-old-plus, 11-trunked national treasure in the Arnold Arboretum are two of the finest specimens I have seen. The developing leaves of *Parrotia persica* are reddish purple to bronze, maturing to lustrous dark green, 2½ to 5 in. long. The foliage is never troubled by insects or diseases. The species prefers moist, well-drained soils. Cooler climates are best, especially those with cooler night temperatures. Utilize as a specimen plant, in the background of borders, or in groupings. Grows 20 to 40 ft. high, 15 to 30 ft. wide; many trees, especially in Europe, are wider than they are tall at maturity. Zones 4 to 8. Iran.

Cultivars and Varieties. 'Pendula' is a confused entity in American horticulture. The true 'Pendula' has a stiff, umbrellalike, weeping habit that results in a dome-shaped configuration. What is commonly offered is a more or less horizontally branched shrub.

Parrotia persica, Persian Parrotia

Parrotia persica fall color

Parrotia persica bark

Parrotia persica flowers

Parrotia persica 'Pendula'

Parthenocissus quinquefolia
Virginia Creeper, Woodbine

No vine is more evident in early fall than Virginia Creeper, when the leaves develop flaming shades of orange and red. This species is a true clinging vine, with five to eight adhesive-tipped tendril branches that cling to any surface, including aluminum siding. The lustrous dark green leaves are composed of usually five serrated leaflets, each 1½ to 4 (to 5) in. long. Yellowish green flowers occur under the leaves, followed by ¼-in.-diameter, blue berries. Adaptable to sandy and heavy clay soils, in full sun or heavy shade. I have observed it growing in pure sand along the Atlantic Ocean. Requires considerable pruning to keep it tidy and in bounds. *Parthenocissus quinquefolia* can function as a groundcover or a high-climbing vine. Used, along with *P. tricuspidata*, to cover campus buildings. Climbs 30 to 50 ft. high. Zones 4 to 9. New England to Illinois, south to Florida and Mexico.

Parthenocissus quinquefolia fall color

Parthenocissus quinquefolia fruit

Parthenocissus quinquefolia, Virginia Creeper

Parthenocissus tricuspidata
Boston Ivy, Japanese Creeper

This species is similar in most respects to *Parthenocissus quinquefolia*, except for the shape of its leaves, which are simple and generally three-lobed and average 4 to 8 in. wide. Zones 4 to 8. Japan, central China.

Cultivars and Varieties. 'Beverly Brooks' has large leaves that turn brilliant shades of red and scarlet in fall.

'Fenway Park', an Arnold Arboretum introduction, has brilliant yellow new growth that mellows to lime-green and turns orange and red in autumn.

Parthenocissus tricuspidata, Boston Ivy

Parthenocissus tricuspidata fall color

Parthenocissus tricuspidata 'Fenway Park' foliage

Paulownia tomentosa flowers

Paulownia tomentosa fruit

Paulownia tomentosa, Royal Paulownia, at Longwood Gardens

Paulownia tomentosa

Royal Paulownia

Royal Paulownia is actually a weed species, much like *Morus alba*, Common Mulberry, and it has escaped from cultivation from New York to Georgia. In the standard frame of reference for shade trees, *Paulownia tomentosa* is a total loser. At Longwood Gardens in Kennett Square, Pennsylvania, however, there is the grandest allée imaginable of 70- to 80-ft. specimens. The habit is rounded with large, stiff, coarse branches. The dark green leaves, which average 5 to 10 in. long, have the endearing characteristic of shedding in summer and fall. A single leaf gives the appearance of a small flying saucer on the lawn. Pale violet (lavender), 2-in.-long, foxglove-shaped flowers occur in 8- to 12-in.-long panicles before the leaves in April and May and give off a vanilla fragrance. The 1- to 2-in.-long, ovoid, pac man–shaped fruit are borne in uncountable quantities, and each fruit houses up to 2000 small, winged seeds. Royal Paulownia is exceedingly adaptable. It has been used to revegetate strip-mined land. For residential landscapes, the species has few redeeming qualities. Grows 30 to 40 ft. high and wide. Zones 5 to 9. China.

Phellodendron amurense
Amur Corktree

Amur Corktree is a boldly branched, broad-spreading tree with a short trunk. Its corky, gray-brown bark accounts for the common name. The dark green leaves are composed of five to eleven leaflets, each 2½ to 4½ in. long. Fall color is often bronzy yellow to rich yellow but is fleeting. The yellowish green flowers are inconspicuous, but the ⅓- to ½-in.-diameter, black fruit are often borne in great profusion on female trees. Plants require moist, acid or near neutral, well-drained soils and full sun. Amur Corktree has received plaudits for its urban tolerance, but my experiences indicate otherwise. I have seen great specimens of this species and its relatives in many arboreta and on campuses, but I do not remember a single quality plant in an urban situation. If the fine trees that I have seen at the Minnesota, Morton, and Arnold Arboreta could be duplicated in the urban landscape, the nursery industry could not produce enough trees to meet the demand. Utilize the species in a broad expanse of lawn where stress is minimal. Grows 30 to 45 ft. high and wide. Zones 4 to 7. Northern and northeastern China, Japan.

Phellodendron lavallei, Lavalle Corktree, and *P. sachalinense*, Sakhalin Corktree, are similar to *P. amurense*, but they grow somewhat larger, as much as 50 to 60 ft. high.

Phellodendron amurense, Amur Corktree

Phellodendron amurense in fall

Phellodendron amurense bark

Phellodendron amurense foliage

Philadelphus, Mockorange

Any treatment of the mockoranges is superficial because of the large number of species (65) and astronomical number of hybrids, but most share the legendary mockorange fragrance. Philadelphus *species thrive with neglect. They withstand heavy clay or lighter soils, acid or high pH. Best in borders.*

Philadelphus coronarius
Sweet Mockorange

This species and its best cultivars offer 1- to 1½-in.-diameter, four-petaled, fragrant, white flowers in May and June. The rest of the garden year, the plant fades into the background. Typical *Philadelphus coronarius* becomes a large, rounded shrub, with stiff, straight, ascending branches that arch with age. Considerable garden space is required. The 1½- to 4-in.-long, dark green leaves are remotely serrated, with three to five main veins. Grows 10 to 12 ft. high and wide. Zones 4 to 8. Southeastern Europe, Asia Minor.

Cultivars and Varieties. 'Aureus' offers yellow foliage and the typical fragrant white flowers. It is used extensively in Europe, where the cooler temperatures keep the foliage more vibrant. More compact than the species. Grows 8 to 10 ft. high.

'Variegatus' has leaves irregularly bordered with creamy white. Somewhat weak growing, but a rather dainty shrub when well grown. Flowers are fragrant.

Philadelphus coronarius flowers

Philadelphus coronarius 'Variegatus'

Philadelphus coronarius, Sweet Mockorange

Philadelphus coronarius 'Aureus'

Philadelphus Hybrids

Philadelphus hybrids offer a great variety of growth habits and floral characteristics. Among the more garden-worthy hybrids are *Philadelphus ×cymosus* (a hybrid of *P. ×lemoinei* and *P. grandiflorus*), *P. ×lemoinei (P. microphyllus × P. coronarius)*, and *P. ×virginalis* (*P. ×lemoinei × P. nivalis* 'Plena'). There is a good selection of flower sizes and colors (many with a purplish blotch in the middle of the corolla), single or double flowers, and tremendous differences in fragrance. When I visited the Edinburgh Botanic Garden in July, many mockoranges were flowering. In a fragrance test, I discovered some had delicious fragrance, others had none. Since fragrance is the main attribute of the plant, I would smell before purchasing.

Several hybrid cultivars with excellent cold hardiness include 'Frosty Morn', 'Minnesota Snowflake', 'Snowdwarf', and 'Snowgoose'. 'Natchez', an 8- to 10-ft.-high shrub, has 1½-in.-diameter, slightly fragrant flowers that completely cover the foliage in May.

Philadelphus 'Natchez'

Philadelphus 'Minnesota Snowflake' flowers

Photinia villosa

Oriental Photinia

Not a well-known shrub, but certainly worthy of consideration, as long as fireblight is not a serious problem. Oriental Photinia offers excellent red fruit and variable yellow, orange, and red fall color. The species is a large, multi-stemmed shrub with an irregular, obovoid crown. It can also be trained as a small tree. The dark green leaves are 1½ to 3½ in. long. White flowers appear in 1- to 2-in.-diameter corymbs in May and June, but they are not particularly effective. The bright red, ⅓-in.-long fruit ripen in October and persist into winter. Provide moist, acid, well-drained soils, in full sun. Best used in the shrub border, although I have seen full-grown specimen plants that were effective. Grows 10 to 15 ft. high, generally less in spread. Zones 4 to 7. Japan, Korea, China.

Photinia villosa, Oriental Photinia

Photinia villosa flowers

Photinia villosa in fall

Physocarpus opulifolius, Common Ninebark

Physocarpus opulifolius
Common Ninebark

Although native to the United States, this species is more common in European gardens, particularly the golden-foliaged forms. Common Ninebark is a tough, durable shrub that becomes dense and rounded with age. The brown bark exfoliates in shaggy sheets and offers winter interest. The medium green, 1- to 3-in.-long leaves, usually with three to five lobes, may develop yellowish to bronze fall color. White to slightly pink-tinged flowers are borne in 1- to 2-in.-diameter corymbs in May and June. The inflated fruit ripen in September and October and vary in color from green to red. The species is adaptable to all conditions, probably even nuclear attacks, and once established, requires a bulldozer for removal. For use as a large foliage mass, screen, or hedge, it has possibilities. Grows 5 to 10 ft. high, 6 to 10 ft. wide. Zones 2 to 7. Quebec to Michigan, south to Virginia and Tennessee.

Cultivars and Varieties. 'Dart's Golden' is more compact than 'Luteus' and has better yellow foliage color. With the heat of summer, however, the color diminishes or is lost completely. Worthwhile for spring and early summer foliage color. Specimens are often cut back to encourage new shoot extensions.

'Luteus', an old standby, has yellowish foliage that gradually changes to yellowish green and finally to almost green. Large shrub. Grows 8 to 10 ft. high and wide.

Physocarpus opulifolius flowers

Physocarpus opulifolius 'Dart's Golden' foliage

Picea abies

Norway Spruce

The most common spruce for general landscape use, *Picea abies* has a pyramidal outline, with a strong central leader, horizontal secondary branches, and pendulous tertiary branches. It is an extremely dominant focal point in the average landscape. Needs ample space to spread its limbs. The lustrous dark green needles average ½ to 1 in. long and maintain their color throughout the winter as well as any evergreen. The 4- to 6-in.-long cones are purple-violet to greenish purple in youth, finally light brown. Transplant balled and burlapped into moderately moist, acid, well-drained soils. This species is tremendously adaptable, except to high heat. Best used in groupings or perhaps as a specimen evergreen. Grows 40 to 60 ft. high, 25 to 30 ft. wide. Zones 2 to 7. Northern and central Europe.

Cultivars and Varieties. Cultivars number in the hundreds, with only a selected few available from the average nursery. (I unearthed one wholesale grower who listed 36 forms.)

'Nidiformis' is appropriately named Bird's Nest Spruce because of the depression in the middle of its tight, compact, mounded habit. Makes a good rock garden or foundation plant. Not exactly dainty. Grows 3 to 6 ft. high and wide.

'Pendula' may be the generic name for a number of weeping types. No two are exactly alike, but all tend to splay their limbs in a wild, often awkward, weeping configuration. Certainly a great novelty plant and a conversation piece at parties.

Picea abies, Norway Spruce

Picea abies cones

Picea abies 'Pendula'

Picea glauca
White Spruce

White Spruce is quite popular in the Midwest, Northeast, and West. Side by side with the more popular Norway and Colorado spruces (*Picea abies* and *P. pungens*, respectively), however, it has no chance with the average consumer. Habit is densely pyramidal, compact, and symmetrical, with ascending branches. The ½- to ¾-in.-long needles are pale green to glaucous green, inspiring little emotion. The cylindrical, pendulous, 1- to 2½-in.-long cones are the smallest of the cones of commonly cultivated spruces. They are green in youth, maturing to pale brown. Culture is essentially like that of *P. abies*, and it withstands wind, heat, cold, drought, and crowding. Useful as a specimen, in a mass planting, or as a hedge or windbreak. Grows 40 to 60 ft. high, 10 to 20 ft. wide. Zones 2 to 5(6). Labrador to Alaska, south to New York, Minnesota, and Montana.

Cultivars and Varieties. 'Conica', often termed Dwarf Alberta Spruce or Dwarf White Spruce, is a broad-conical form, with light green, ¼- to ½-in.-long needles that radiate around the stem like a bottlebrush. It is probably the best-known and most widely sold dwarf conifer in the United States. Grows 10 to 12 ft. high in 25 to 30 years.

Picea glauca, White Spruce

Picea glauca cones

Picea glauca 'Conica'

Picea omorika
Serbian Spruce

Perhaps my favorite spruce, although it is difficult to choose between this and *Picea orientalis*. Mature plants are elegant, and even small plants have character. Serbian Spruce has a remarkably slender trunk and short, ascending or drooping branches on a narrow-pyramidal framework. Considerable variation in habit is evident in any seed-grown population, however. The ½- to 1-in.-long needles are flattish, lustrous dark green, with two silver bands underneath. The 1¼- to 2-in.-long, pendulous cones turn shiny cinnamon-brown at maturity. A formal evergreen best reserved for specimen use, but also quite good in groupings of threes or fives. Quite adaptable and deserving of wider use. Prospers in high pH soils. A good choice for midwestern gardens. Grows 50 to 60 ft. high, 20 to 25 ft. wide. Zones 4 to 7. Southeastern Europe.

Picea omorika needle undersides

Picea orientalis
Oriental Spruce

To see her is to love her. This species matures to a shining, black-green pyramid in an ocean of landscape. It develops a dense, compact, narrow-pyramidal habit, with horizontal or pendulous branches. The lustrous, almost black-green needles are ¼ to ½ in. long, the shortest of the needles of cultivated species. The male flowers are attractive carmine-red, strawberry-shaped cones. Female cones are 2 to 4 in. long and 1 in. wide, reddish purple in youth, maturing to brown. Tolerates infertile, gravelly, or clay soils. Notable specimens occur in the Midwest. Makes a great specimen conifer, but is extremely formal. Grows 50 to 60 ft. high, 10 to 15 ft. wide. Zones 4 to 7. Caucasus, Asia Minor.

Picea orientalis male cones

Picea omorika, Serbian Spruce

Picea orientalis, Oriental Spruce

Picea pungens
Colorado Spruce

A most popular specimen tree, Colorado Spruce is used throughout the northern states. Stiffly conical-pyramidal in habit, with densely set, horizontal whorls of branches that skirt the ground. The plant is so thick and the needles so prickly that it would be impossible to lob a cat through it. The four-sided needles, ¾ to 1¼ in. long, range in color from green to gray-green, blue-green, or silver-blue. The best blue-colored seedlings *(Picea pungens* var. *glauca)* have resulted in the colloquial name "Blue Spruce." Female cones average 2 to 4 in. long, and the tips of the scales are wavy. Withstands virtually any soil, except those that are exceedingly moist. Often used as a specimen plant, although it can detract from the total landscape. Grows 30 to 60 ft. high, 10 to 20 ft. wide. Zones 2 to 7. Western United States.

Cultivars and Varieties. 'Fat Albert' is a cutting-produced clone with a wide, pyramidal habit and excellent, rich blue needle color.

'Hoopsii' is a standard. It has a dense, pyramidal form and extremely glaucous blue needles.

'Moerheimii' is another old cultivar. It, too, has rich blue foliage, but it tends to be more open in habit than some of the others.

'Thompsenii', with its glaucous silver-blue foliage and symmetrical, pyramidal habit, is one of the best.

Picea orientalis young female cones

Picea orientalis mature female cones

Picea pungens var. *glauca* needles

Picea pungens var. *glauca*, Blue Spruce

Picea pungens var. *glauca* 'Thompsenii'

Pieris floribunda
Mountain Pieris

A diminutive species with a broad-mounded outline and dark green leaves. White flowers occur in upright, 2- to 4-in.-long, racemose panicles in April. The floral effect is not as striking as that of *Pieris japonica*, and this species is more difficult to propagate and not as readily available. Once established, Mountain Pieris shows bulldog tenacity. Resistant to lacebug. Useful in shady areas of the garden. Grows 2 to 6 ft. high, equal or greater in spread. Zones 4 to 6. Virginia to Georgia.

Pieris floribunda, Mountain Pieris

Pieris floribunda × *Pieris japonica* Hybrids

The hybrids between *Pieris floribunda* and *P. japonica* share some of the resistance to lacebug that is found in *P. floribunda*. Someone once commented to me that *P. floribunda* would consistently die out in the Atlanta area but the hybrids would persist. Perhaps there is much greater heat tolerance in the hybrids.

Pieris floribunda flowers

Cultivars and Varieties. 'Brouwer's Beauty' offers the best features of both parents. It has yellow-green new foliage that matures to shiny dark green. Deep purplish red buds open to white flowers in horizontal, slightly arched panicles. Grows 6 ft. high and wide.

'Eco-Snowball' and 'Spring Snow' are two other notable hybrids.

Pieris 'Brouwer's Beauty' flowers

Pieris japonica, Japanese Pieris

Pieris japonica

Japanese Pieris

A broadleaf evergreen of the first order that deserves consideration in any garden where shade and moist soil are available. It is one of the best ericaceous plants for the Midwest, particularly in calcareous soils. In its best forms, the habit is dense, almost haystack-shaped, with branches reaching to the ground. The 1½- to 3½-in.-long, lustrous dark green leaves are lovely through the seasons. The new growth displays shades of apple-green, bronze, and rich red, and several cultivars offer excellent red color on new foliage. Urn-shaped, fragrant, white flowers, ¼ to ⅜ in. long, are borne in 3- to 6-in.- long and wide, racemose panicles in March and April, and are effective for two to three weeks. Remove spent flowers. Next year's flower buds are developed by July or August. For maximum performance, provide moist, organic matter–laden soils, in partial shade. Lacebug is a serious pest that sucks the sap from the leaves, often rendering the plant various shades of yellow. Utilize the plant in foundation plantings, borders, groupings, or masses. Grows 8 to 12 ft. high, 6 to 8 ft. wide. Zones 5 to 8. Japan.

Cultivars and Varieties. 'Mountain Fire' offers exceptional fire-red new growth, white flowers, and a compact habit. It is available in commerce.

'Valley Valentine' has rich maroon flower buds that open to deep rose-pink flowers in abundance on a dense, upright plant.

'Variegata' has leaves edged with white. Makes a rather pretty accent in a shady nook of the garden.

Pieris japonica new foliage

Pieris japonica flowers

Pieris japonica 'Mountain Fire' new foliage

Pinus aristata
Bristlecone Pine

A wonderful novelty plant for that special garden niche; however, growth is extremely slow. Generally, this species is dwarf, shrubby, and picturesque in youth, characteristics that make it a first-rate accent plant, and it retains this habit into old age. The 1- to 1¾-in.-long, dark blue-green needles occur in fascicles of five and are covered with resinous exudations. Succeeds in infertile, dry, or rocky soils in a range of pH levels. Best transplanted from a container. One of the oldest trees on earth; specimens range from 4000 to 5000 years old. Expect to pay a tidy sum for a quality plant. Grows 8 to 20 ft. high, variable spread. Zones 4 to 7. Southwestern United States.

Pinus aristata, Bristlecone Pine

Pinus banksiana
Jack Pine

This species has few redeeming features other than its tremendous cold tolerance (to –40°F) and its adaptability to impoverished sandy or clay soils. The habit is pyramidal; open and spreading in youth, often flat-topped at maturity. The ¾- to 2-in.-long, olive-green needles occur in fascicles of two. In winter, needles become a sickly yellow-green. Adaptable for windbreaks, shelterbelts, and mass plantings, particularly in sandy soils. Many better pines are available for normal conditions. Grows 35 to 50 ft. high, spread variable but usually less than the height. Zones 2 to 6. Arctic regions, south to New York and Minnesota.

Pinus banksiana, Jack Pine

Pinus aristata needles

Pinus bungeana
Lacebark Pine

A biological specimen of great beauty. This tree has lustrous, rich green needles and exfoliating, sycamorelike bark. Usually multistemmed, though it may be single-stemmed. The branches reach to the ground; remove lower branches to expose the excellent bark. The bark actually starts to exfoliate on 1- to 2-in.-diameter branches, with color varying from whitish, gray, and green to brownish. The 2- to 4-in.-long, stiff, sharp-pointed needles occur in bundles of three. Growth is quite slow, and consequently, the plant is not abundant in commerce. Transplant balled and burlapped into well-drained soils. Once established, tolerates drought, as well as acid and high pH soils. A fine specimen evergreen or accent plant. Grows 30 to 50 ft. high, 20 to 35 ft. wide. Zones 4 to 8. China.

Pinus cembra
Swiss Stone Pine

I have always considered this to be among the top five pines for landscape use because of its uniform, narrow, densely columnar habit. Mature trees in the wild are looser, more open, and pyramidal. The 2- to 3- (to 5-) in.-long, rich blue-green needles occur in bundles of five. They persist for four to five years, contributing to the overall fullness of the plant. Young stems are covered with a thick, orange-brown pubescence, a characteristic that separates this species from *Pinus flexilis*, *P. peuce*, and *P. strobus*. Provide well-drained, loamy, slightly acid soils, in full sun. Great specimen evergreen; ideal in multiples because of its rigid formality. Unlike a fastigiate *P. strobus*, this species will not outgrow its location. Grows 30 to 40 (to 70) ft. high, 15 to 25 ft. wide. Zones 4 to 7. Mountains of central Europe and southern Asia.

Pinus bungeana, Lacebark Pine

Pinus cembra, Swiss Stone Pine

Pinus bungeana cones

Pinus bungeana bark

Pinus cembra needles

Pinus densiflora
Japanese Red Pine

A mature Japanese Red Pine is indeed majestic, with its wide-spreading, slightly upward-arched branches and plumes of rich green needles. The orange bark develops an exfoliating character. Certainly one of the more picturesque pines. The 3- to 5-in.-long, bright green needles occur in twos. A well-drained soil is necessary, but otherwise the species is quite adaptable. Use as a specimen or in groupings. An open-grown tree qualifies as a botanical sculpture. Every seedling shows character and somewhat irregular growth, and even young plants show no propensity toward the widget mold. Grows 40 to 60 ft. high and wide. Zones (4)5 to 7. Japan, Korea, China.

Cultivars and Varieties. 'Oculus-draconis', commonly known as Dragon's-Eye Pine, has two yellow bands on each needle. When viewed from above, the alternate rings of yellow and green create an "eyeball" effect, hence, the common name. More of a conversation piece or novelty item, but definitely unique.

'Pendula' is a rather effective weeping form that will tend to sprawl and act as a groundcover, unless grafted on a standard or staked to produce a small, weeping tree.

'Umbraculifera' is a beautiful upright, broad-spreading, umbrella-headed form. The branches are upright-spreading, and with time, the habit becomes vase-shaped. The orange bark develops the exfoliating character typical of the species and is superb on old specimens. Amazingly adaptable and heat tolerant. Great accent plant. By no means a small plant. Although listed as a 10-ft. specimen, it can easily reach 20 ft. tall.

Pinus densiflora, Japanese Red Pine

Pinus densiflora 'Oculus-draconis'

Pinus densiflora 'Umbraculifera'

Pinus densiflora 'Umbraculifera' bark

Pinus flexilis
Limber Pine

Limber Pine is often mistaken for *Pinus strobus*, White Pine, but it differs in its needles, which have entire, rather than serrated, margins. In youth it is often a dense pyramid of rich blue-green needles, becoming more open and picturesque with age. The 2½- to 3½-in.-long needles persist for five to six years. Easily transplanted, extremely adaptable, and certainly one of the most beautiful of the five-needled pines. Makes a fine specimen or grouping. Grows 30 to 50 ft. high, 15 to 35 ft. wide. Zones 4 to 7. Western North America.

Cultivars and Varieties. 'Glauca' has a blue-green needle color that is much more intense than that of the species.

'Glauca Pendula' is a wide-spreading, irregular shrub with rich blue-green foliage. Tends to sprawl and scamper rather than truly weep.

Pinus flexilis, Limber Pine

Pinus koraiensis
Korean Pine

Certainly not well known in landscape circles, but one of the most elegant of the five-needled pines. The habit is loosely pyramidal, with branches of densely set needles feathered to the ground. The blue-green (possibly gray-green) needles average 3½ to 4½ in. long and are heavier textured and more coarsely serrated than other five-needled types. Stems are covered with a dense, reddish brown pubescence that becomes dirty brown with age. Quite adaptable, and one of the more cold-hardy pines. Great as a specimen, in groupings, or for screening. Grows 30 to 40 ft. high, 15 to 20 ft. wide. Zones 4 to 7. Korea, Japan.

Pinus koraiensis, Korean Pine

Pinus flexilis 'Glauca' foliage

Pinus mugo

Mugo Pine, Swiss Mountain Pine

Somewhat of an anomaly in American gardening. The dwarf types of this pine are often sold as the typical species, even though the true species can grow to 75 ft. high and the forms in cultivation are generally 10 ft. or less and quite shrubby. In the native populations of the species that I have seen in the Swiss Alps, no two plants were exactly alike. The medium to dark green, 1- to 2- (to 3-) in.-long needles occur in fascicles of two. The species and its cultivars are extremely adaptable and will prosper in Maine, Iowa, or Maryland. Quite adaptable to extremes of soil, pH, and climate. Use for massing and foundation plantings, or in rock gardens, perennial borders, and containers. To maintain a dwarfed condition, prune the new candles (shoots) when the needles are half their mature length. Grows 15 to 20 ft. high and wide; can grow 30 to 80 ft. Zones 2 to 7. Mountains of central and southern Europe.

Cultivars and Varieties. Many cultivars have been named, but they are seldom available in the trade. The variety *mugo* and var. *pumilio* are considered low-growing natural variants. They grow less than 8 ft. high.

Pinus mugo, Mugo Pine

Pinus mugo dwarf form in a Japanese garden

Pinus nigra

Austrian Pine

One of the most popular landscape pines in the Midwest and East because of its densely pyramidal habit, its attractive needles, and its adaptability. In old age the outline is umbelliform, and the bark becomes ridged and furrowed. The flat furrows are scaled in a mosaic of white, gray, and brown. The lustrous dark green, almost black-green needles, 3 to 5 (to 6) in. long, occur in bundles of two and are extremely stiff and sharp pointed. Needles persist for four (occasionally eight) years, giving the branches a full mane of green. *Pinus nigra* is adaptable to high pH, heavy clay soils. It transplants readily and establishes quickly. Used extensively for groupings and screenings. In recent years, this species has been troubled by *Diplodia*, which causes shoot dieback, and the pine nematode. Pine nematode, transmitted by a beetle, plugs the vascular system of the plant and can kill an entire tree, or portions of it, often in a single season. Assess the degree of disease and pine nematode in an area before planting. Grows 50 to 60 ft. high, 20 to 40 ft. wide. Zones 4 to 7. Europe.

Pinus parviflora
Japanese White Pine

A beautifully sculptured tree at maturity, with wide-spreading, artistically arranged branches. In youth it is often reasonably dense with 1- to 2½-in.-long, blue-green needles, which occur in bundles of five. Attractive 1½- to 4-in.-long cones have thick, waxy, greenish scales that mature to brownish red and are borne even on young trees. Japanese White Pine is easily grown and displays reasonable salt tolerance. Perfect tree for restricted spaces. A good accent or specimen conifer. Grows 20 to 50 ft. high, equal or greater in spread. Zones 4 to 7. Japan.

Pinus nigra, Austrian Pine

Pinus parviflora, Japanese White Pine

Pinus nigra bark

Pinus parviflora cones

Pinus peuce
Balkan Pine

A rarity, to be sure, but this five-needled pine makes the true gardener drool. In youth the habit is much like that of *Pinus cembra*, becoming more open with age. A mature specimen at Stourhead in England is easily confused with a giant *P. flexilis* or *P. strobus*. The needles are dark gray-green, 3 to 4 in. long, and have slightly toothed margins. They persist for up to three years. Adaptable to varied soils. Another great specimen or accent plant. Grows 30 to 60 ft. high. Zones 4 to 7. Balkans.

Pinus peuce, Balkan Pine

Pinus pumila
Japanese Stone Pine, Dwarf Siberian Pine

Not very well known except in botanical garden circles, but deserving of consideration in virtually every garden. The plants that I have observed were shrubby, none being taller than 10 ft. The rich bluish green, 1½- to 3- (to 4-) in.-long needles are densely set and occur in fascicles of five. Cones are quite small, averaging 1½ in. long and 1 in. wide. They are purplish when young, turning dull reddish or yellowish brown. Appears to be adaptable and easy to transplant. Great accent plant or as an addition to the shrub or perennial border. Grows 1 to 10 ft. high. Zones 5 to 6. Japan, China, Korea.

Pinus pumila, Japanese Stone Pine

Pinus resinosa
Red Pine

In the past, Red Pine has been utilized throughout the East and Midwest, but this northern United States native is vastly inferior to most other landscape species. Although extolled for the quality of its foliage and growth habit, to find a noble specimen would prove a challenge. The habit is dense in youth and symmetrically oval in old age. The thin, medium green, 5- to 6-in.-long needles, two per fascicle, break or snap when bent. The bark is orange-red and scaly on young trees; on old trunks, it breaks into large, flat, reddish brown, superficially scaly plates. Species is probably best suited to exposed, dry, acid, sandy, or gravelly soils. Use for groves or windbreaks. Grows 50 to 80 ft. high, variable spread. Zones 2 to 5. Newfoundland to Manitoba, south to Michigan and the mountains of Pennsylvania.

Pinus resinosa bark

Pinus resinosa, Red Pine

Pinus strobus
White Pine

If I had to choose one pine for general landscape use, *Pinus strobus* would be it. The soft, plumy texture of the needles, the wide-spreading, horizontally disposed branches, and the hauntingly beautiful asymmetry of ancient trees will make believers out of doubters. Young trees, particularly when pruned, are often full and dense, but they never appear stiff and rigid like Scotch Pine (*P. sylvestris*) or Austrian Pine (*P. nigra*). Needles range in color from light green to medium green to blue-green and average 2 to 4 (to 5) in. in length. The needles, which occur in fascicles of five, persist for a year and a half before abscising in late summer and fall. White Pine is easily transplanted and fast growing. Seems to withstand pruning better than most pines. A great plant as a specimen, in groupings, or for screens and, possibly, hedges. In the Midwest, in high pH soils, iron chlorosis can be a problem. At times, trees die for no explicable reason. In the Northeast, tip moths destroy the terminal shoots, resulting in distorted growth. For the most part, the best species for general use. Grows 50 to 80 ft. high, 20 to 40 ft. wide. Zones 3 to 8. Newfoundland to Manitoba, south to Georgia, Illinois, and Iowa.

Pinus strobus, White Pine

MORE ➤

Cultivars and Varieties. 'Compacta', 'Globosa', 'Nana', and other dwarfish forms are known. All are slower growing than the species and tend toward a rounded or broad-mounded outline. They make choice accent plants.

'Fastigiata' has always been a favorite of mine because of the softly vertical outline that opens somewhat with age. Branches ascend at a 45° angle to the central leader. Specimens over 70 ft. high are known.

'Pendula' is a flailing, arching, pendulous, irregular form that is often staked to provide a semblance of a central leader. Use as an accent plant; one is acceptable, two represent bad taste, and three disgrace.

Pinus strobus cone

Pinus strobus 'Fastigiata'

Pinus strobus 'Pendula'

Pinus sylvestris
Scotch Pine

Common as a Christmas tree in the northern United States. In youth the species forms an irregular pyramid with short, spreading branches, the lower soon dying. At maturity, trees are picturesque, open, wide-spreading, and flat- or round-topped, almost umbrella-shaped. Bark becomes orangish brown and flakes off in small plates and scales. The bluish green, 1- to 3- (to 4-) in.-long needles occur in twos. Each needle is rather flattish, with a slight spiral or twist to its long axis. Many variations of needle size and color according to geographic location. Scotch Pine is easily transplanted and extremely adaptable to varied soils. Often used for screening and massing, particularly in the Midwest. Grows 30 to 60 ft. high, 30 to 40 ft. wide. Zones 2 to 7. Europe, Asia.

Cultivars and Varieties. 'Fastigiata' is frequently listed as the Sentinel Pine because of its pronounced narrow-columnar habit. Subject to snow and ice damage. Grows 25 ft. high or more.

'Watereri' is an old clone, densely pyramidal to flat-topped, with steel-blue needles and handsome orangish brown bark. Slow-growing, it averages about 10 ft. in height, although the original plant is 25 ft. high and wide.

Pinus sylvestris, Scotch Pine

Pinus sylvestris cones

Pinus sylvestris bark

Pinus sylvestris 'Watereri'

Pinus thunbergii
Japanese Black Pine

One of the most salt-tolerant needle evergreens, this species is used from Cape Cod to the Outer Banks of North Carolina. Unfortunately, it is not long lived, and trees over 20 ft. tall are seldom seen. The habit is shrubby, artistic, and picturesque, usually with wide-spreading branches. The stiff, prickle-pointed, lustrous dark green needles occur two to a bundle. A distinguishing characteristic of the species is its elongated, silky white, candlelike buds. Plant in well-drained soils, in full sun. As a young plant, Japanese Black Pine makes for rather pretty groupings. Grows 15 to 25 ft. high, wider at maturity. Zones (5)6 to 8. Japan.

Pinus thunbergii, Japanese Black Pine

Pinus thunbergii needles and bud

Pinus virginiana cone

Pinus virginiana
Virginia or Scrub Pine

Possibly the only redeeming quality of this species is its ability to withstand heat and adverse soil conditions. It will colonize heavy clay soils and is a good cover for such areas. The yellow-green to dark green needles occur in twos and usually turn sickly yellow-green in winter. *Pinus virginiana* develops a broad, open, pyramidal outline, becoming flat-topped with time. Old cones persist, and the tree carries this visual baggage throughout its life. It is a common Christmas tree in the South, but it requires tremendous maintenance—including dyeing the needles—for successful production. A fast-growing tree useful in screens, groupings, or for soil protection, but use with the knowledge that 20 years is probably a long life. Grows 15 to 40 ft. high, 10 to 30 ft. wide. Zones 4 to 8. New York to Alabama.

Pinus virginiana, Virginia Pine

Pinus wallichiana

Himalayan or Bhutan Pine

An elegant pine, considered by some the most beautiful pine species. The habit is broad-pyramidal in youth and old age. The 5- to 8-in.-long, blue-green needles occur in bundles of five and often arch gracefully over their length, providing a fine-textured appearance. Move as a young plant into moist, acid, well-drained soils, and provide shelter from desiccating winds. Only use should be as a specimen. Grows 30 to 50 ft. high, generally equal in spread. Zones 5 to 7. Himalayas.

Cultivars and Varieties. 'Zebrinus' is similar to *Pinus densiflora* 'Oculus-draconis', although the bands on the needles of this Himalayan Pine cultivar tend to be more cream colored.

Pinus wallichiana, Himalayan Pine

Pinus wallichiana needles

Platanus ×acerifolia
London Planetree

London Planetree got its name from extensive use in the city of London, where it is one of the few survivors of the coal-polluted air. No other shade tree has been more widely planted in cities worldwide than *Platanus ×acerifolia* (a hybrid of *P. orientalis* × *P. occidentalis*). It is a massive tree with wide-spreading branches, a fact belied by its tight-pyramidal youthful outline. The cream- to olive-colored bark is one of the winter landscape's bright beacons. The dark green leaves, 6 to 7 in. long and 8 to 10 in. wide, turn yellow-brown in autumn. I have not seen a soil condition that this tree will not tolerate—wet, dry, acid, and alkaline are all acceptable. Anthracnose kills young leaves, especially in moist weather. Stems also die back as a result of anthracnose, resulting in a "brooming" effect. *Platanus ×acerifolia* is certainly more resistant than *P. occidentalis*, however. Use for street plantings, commercial sites, campuses, golf courses, or any large area. In finest form, it is a beautiful and imposing specimen tree. Grows 70 to 100 ft. high, 65 to 80 ft. wide. Zones 4 to 8(9).

Cultivars and Varieties. Several anthracnose-resistant cultivars are available, including 'Bloodgood', which is one of the most common in commerce, 'Columbia', 'Liberty', and 'Yarwood'.

Platanus ×acerifolia, London Planetree

Platanus ×acerifolia bark

Platanus ×acerifolia creating an elegant allée at the Jardin des Plantes, Paris

Platanus occidentalis
American Sycamore

Along with *Liriodendron tulipifera*, Tulip Tree, this species is one of the tallest of the native eastern North American deciduous trees. In southern Ohio, where I grew up, American Sycamore was a common fixture along every stream and river. In most respects, the habit is similar to that of London Planetree, except the bark is more creamy and the 1½-in.-diameter, rounded fruit occur singly (those of *P.* ×*acerifolia* occur in twos). Prefers deep, moist soils and requires abundant space. A great and noble tree. Use for naturalized plantings along streams, in groves, or as a single specimen. Grows 75 to 100 ft. high, similar spread. Zones 4 to 9. Maine to Ontario, south to Florida and Texas.

Platanus occidentalis, American Sycamore

Platanus occidentalis fruit

Platanus occidentalis in winter

Platanus occidentalis bark

Polygonum aubertii
Silver-Vine Fleeceflower

This plant has never ranked in the top 25 vine list, but it keeps surfacing in nursery catalogs as a fast, easy-to-grow cover. It will grow 10 to 15 ft. in a single season. The 1½- to 3½-in.-long, bright green leaves die off green in fall. From July and August into September, fragrant, whitish flowers blanket the foliage in a sea of foam. Will grow in virtually any soil, in sun or shade. Utilize for a quick cover. Flowers when few other plants offer color. Grows 25 to 35 ft. high. Zones 4 to 8. Western China.

Polygonum aubertii, Silver-Vine Fleeceflower

Poncirus trifoliata
Hardy-Orange

I have observed this species used artistically in the Mediterranean garden at Longwood Gardens in Kennett Square, Pennsylvania, and in the collections of the Arnold Arboretum in Boston, Massachusetts. The primary shortcoming of this plant is the 1- to 2-in.-long, stout spines, which are quite sharp, almost lethal. The rich glossy green, trifoliate leaves turn a reasonable yellow in fall. White, five-petaled flowers, 1½ to 2 in. in diameter, appear in April and May and are followed by 1½-in.-diameter, rounded, yellowish fruit that ripen in September and October. The green stems are attractive in the winter months. Extremely adaptable, this species prospers in any well-drained soil. Displays excellent drought tolerance. Could be used to provide an artistic touch to the garden. Take care to plant out of the way of traffic. Grows 8 to 20 ft. high, 5 to 15 ft. wide. Zones 6 to 9. China, Korea.

Polygonum aubertii flowers

Poncirus trifoliata stem and spines

Poncirus trifoliata flower

Poncirus trifoliata, Hardy-Orange

Populus, Poplar

In all my traveling and consulting work, I have never *recommended, at least when conscious, a poplar. The species are susceptible to fungal leaf spots that virtually defoliate trees by late summer. Cankers can also cause injury or death. Poplars are dirty trees, dropping leaves, twigs, and branches with minimal provocation. The genus* Populus *does contain many cold-climate species that harbor an affinity for moisture.*

Populus alba

Silver or White Poplar

Silver Poplar is a wide-spreading tree with an irregular, round-topped crown. The bark is cream-colored. The three- to five-lobed, 2- to 5-in.-long leaves are lustrous dark green above and covered with white, woolly pubescence on the undersides. Although adaptable to dry soils, this species is longer lived in moist situations. For cold climates, it is a possibility, but beware, because diseases can wreak havoc. The species also develops suckers that result in large colonies. Grows 40 to 70 ft. high and wide. Zones 3 to 9. Europe, Asia.

Cultivars and Varieties. 'Pyramidalis', the Bolleana Poplar, is columnar in habit and maintains this trait into old age. Grows 70 ft. high, 12 to 18 ft. wide.

Populus alba 'Pyramidalis', Bolleana Poplar

Populus alba, White Poplar

Populus alba 'Pyramidalis' foliage

Populus alba bark

Populus deltoides
Eastern Cottonwood

As one travels west through Kansas and Nebraska, this species becomes the most common sight along watercourses. It has an upright-spreading, vase-shaped habit and an irregular, ragged branch structure. The ash-gray bark is divided into thick, flattened ridges, separated by deep fissures. The dark green, deltoid leaves, 3 to 5 in. long and wide, may turn a respectable yellow in fall. Where few other trees will grow and for quick cover, Eastern Cottonwood is justified. Several male selections or hybrids (usually with *Populus nigra* as the other parent) are available, and these seedless forms do not produce the cottony froth in spring of the typical species. These forms grow 2 to 4 ft. per year. Grows 75 to 100 ft. high, 50 to 75 ft. wide. Zones 2 to 9. Quebec to North Dakota, south to Florida and Texas.

Cultivars and Varieties. 'Noreaster' and 'Siouxland' are two of the better male cultivars, although the latter tends to shed abundant leaves by late summer in the lower Midwest.

Populus deltoides, Eastern Cottonwood

Populus nigra 'Italica'
Lombardy Poplar

Lombardy Poplar is a common sight throughout the East and Midwest, where it postures like a Titan rocket ready for launching. To most horticulturists, this tree is taboo because of its susceptibility to a devastating canker. Interestingly, in Europe, 80-ft.-tall trees are common in the countryside, suggesting that specimens in Europe may not be as susceptible to the canker. The distinctive columnar, telephone pole–like habit limits contemporary landscape use. The 2- to 4-in.-long, dark green leaves do not color to any degree in fall, although some yellow is possible. Grows 70 to 90 ft. high, 10 to 15 ft. wide in 20 to 30 years. Zones 3 to 9.

Populus nigra 'Italica', Lombardy Poplar

Populus deltoides bark

Populus nigra 'Italica' leaf

Populus tremuloides
Quaking Aspen

Although usually short lived as a cultivated landscape plant, Quaking Aspen has few rivals when it ripens to yellow in the autumn woods of the northern and western states. This species is softly pyramidal in habit, with greenish white to creamy tan bark. The 1½- to 3-in.- long and wide, lustrous dark green leaves have slender, flattened petioles. The slightest breeze induces the "shakes," hence, the name Quaking Aspen. Will grow in a range of soils, from moist, loamy sands to shallow, rocky soils and clay. If native, do not destroy, simply appreciate. Grows 40 to 50 ft. high, 20 to 30 ft. wide. Zones 1 to 6. Labrador to Alaska, south to the mountain regions of Pennsylvania, Missouri, Mexico, and California.

Populus tremuloides showing its yellow autumn color

Populus tremuloides, Quaking Aspen

Populus tremuloides in winter

Potentilla fruticosa

Shrubby Cinquefoil

For northern gardens, the shrubby potentillas can be considered first-class shrubs because of their extended flowering period, from June until frost. Numerous cultivars have been introduced, some of parentage other than *Potentilla fruticosa* but embodying similar landscape attributes. Plants vary in habit from groundcover types to robust shrubs. The leaves are composed of three to seven leaflets and range in color from gray, gray-green, and bright green to dark green. Stems are rich brown and provide winter interest. The number one landscape attribute is the flowers, which are variable in size (usually about 1 in. in diameter) and color, ranging from white to yellow to almost red. Shrubby Cinquefoil is extremely adaptable and withstands any soil condition, except permanently wet. Thrives in dry, calcareous clay soils of the Plains and Midwest states. Requires full sun for maximum flower production, although in some forms, such as 'Red Ace', 'Royal Flush', and 'Tangerine', the flowers bleach in hot sun. Great versatility in the landscape, limited only by the creativity of the gardener. Groundcover types grow 1 to 1½ ft. high; shrub types grow 4 ft. high and wide. Zones 2 to 7. Northern Hemisphere.

Cultivars and Varieties. Cultivars are available in confusing numbers. The following are worth considering, with flower color indicated: 'Abbottswood', white; 'Coronation Triumph', bright yellow; 'Elizabeth', soft yellow; 'Goldfinger', bright yellow; 'Goldstar', deep yellow-gold, flowers up to 2 in. in diameter; 'Jackmanii', bright yellow; 'Katherine Dykes', lemon-yellow; 'Princess', delicate pink; 'Red Ace', red-orange, fades in heat; and 'Tangerine', orange, fades to yellow in heat.

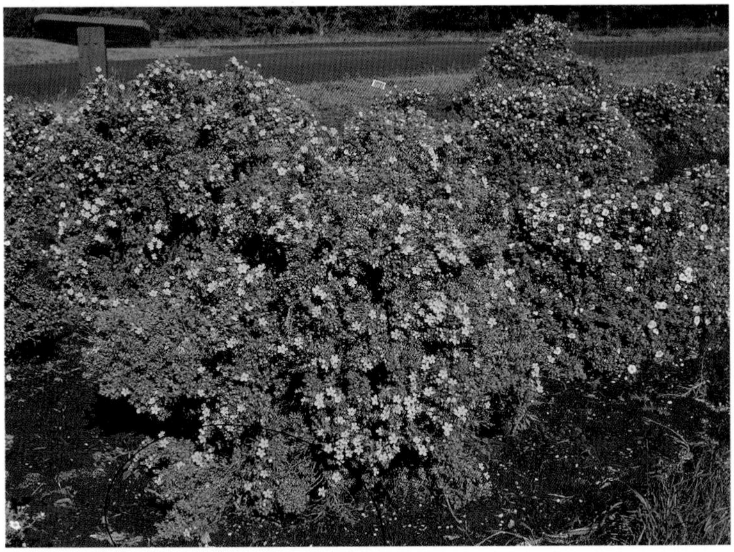

Potentilla fruticosa, Shrubby Cinquefoil

Potentilla fruticosa 'Abbottswood' flowers

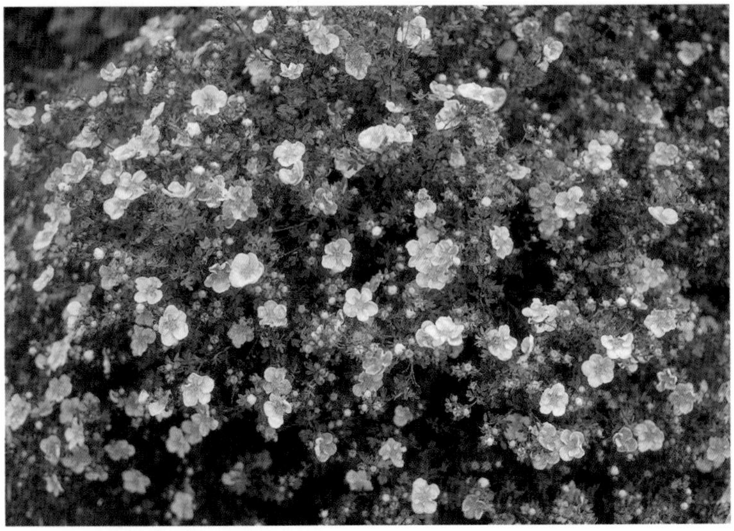

Potentilla fruticosa 'Princess'

Potentilla fruticosa 'Katherine Dykes' flowers

Prinsepia sinensis
Cherry Prinsepia

Virtually unknown in gardens, this is one of the first shrubs to leaf out in spring. It tends to become rather large and unkempt with time, developing a haystack to rounded outline and spiny branches. The bark peels in long, papery strips. The 2- to 3-in.-long, bright green leaves develop minimal yellow fall color. Creamy yellow, ⅗-in.-diameter flowers occur in groups of one to five on previous year's wood in March and April. The ½-in.-long, ovoid, red fruit ripen in July, August, and September. Birds make quick snacks of the fruit. Easily grown. Requires full sun. Perhaps useful as a reminder that hope springs eternal. Grows 6 to 10 ft. high and wide. Zones 3 to 7. Northeastern China.

Potentilla fruticosa 'Red Ace' flower

Potentilla fruticosa 'Tangerine'

Prinsepia sinensis, Cherry Prinsepia

Prinsepia sinensis fruit

Prinsepia sinensis flowers

Prinsepia uniflora
Hedge Prinsepia

This is a much smaller species than the previous one. It has lustrous dark green, 1- to 2-in.-long, distinctly toothed leaves, white flowers, and waxy, dark purplish red, ½-in.-long fruit. The habit is a moderately dense aggregate of light gray, thorny branches and sparse foliage. For the fanatical collector, *Prinsepia uniflora* and *P. sinensis* might have a place. Grows 4 to 5 ft. high and wide. Zones 3 to 5(6). China.

Prinsepia uniflora foliage

Prinsepia uniflora, Hedge Prinsepia

Prinsepia uniflora flowers

Prinsepia uniflora fruit

Prunus, Cherry, Plum

In spring, cherries in white, pink, and rose colors elevate winter souls to the highest level. Unfortunately, countless insects and diseases contribute to the decline of many of these plants. In general, Prunus *species prefer moist, well-drained, acid to near neutral soils. The sweet cherries, such as* Prunus avium *and others, require another clone for cross-pollination and fruit production.*

Prunus avium
Mazzard Cherry

Although used primarily as a rootstock for grafting the more ornamental Oriental cherries, Mazzard Cherry has much to offer in its own right. This large tree is conical to rounded in habit and has reddish brown bark. Leaves emerge bronze, mature to deep green, and turn yellow to bronzy red in fall. The 1- to 1½-in.-diameter, fragrant, white flowers are produced in profusion during April and May. Fruit are reddish black, 1-in.-diameter, rounded, sweetish drupes. Grows 30 to 40 ft. high, similar spread. Zones 3 to 8. Europe, western Asia.

Prunus avium flowers

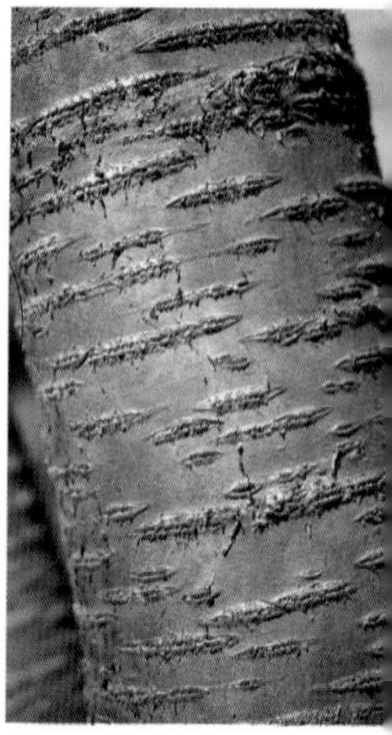
Prunus avium bark

Prunus avium, Mazzard Cherry

Prunus besseyi
Western Sandcherry

A pretty, diminutive shrub with 1- to 2½-in.-long, gray-green leaves and pure white, ½-in.-diameter flowers in April and May. The sweet, purplish black, ¾-in.-long fruit ripen in July and August. Useful in inhospitable hot, dry conditions. Many cultivars have been selected for fruit quality. Grows 4 to 6 ft. high and wide. Zones 3 to 6. Great Plains.

Prunus besseyi, Western Sandcherry

Prunus cerasifera

Myrobalan Plum

This small, white-flowered tree has been used for rootstocks, but the real garden interest lies in the purple-leaf hybrids and cultivars presented below. They usually flower in April, before the leaves emerge. The reddish purple foliage is eye-catching, but use with discretion, for a little travels a long way. Grows 15 to 30 ft. high, 15 to 25 ft. wide. Zones (4)5 to 8. Western Asia, Caucasus.

Prunus ×*blireiana* is a hybrid between *P. cerasifera* 'Atropurpurea' and *P. mume*, Japanese Apricot. It has reddish purple foliage and fragrant, pink flowers. The 10- to 15-petaled, 1¼-in.-diameter flowers open in April, before the leaves. Leaves fade to green with maturity. Grows 20 ft. high and wide. Zones 5 to 8.

Another good purple-leaf hybrid species is *Prunus* ×*cistena*, Purpleleaf Sand Cherry, a cross of *P. cerasifera* 'Atropurpurea' and *P. pumila*. It is a shrub or small tree that displays ruby-purple to reddish purple foliage. Fragrant, pinkish flowers open after the leaves have developed. Grows 10 ft. high, slightly less in spread. Zones 2 to 8.

Cultivars and Varieties. 'Atropurpurea', a cultivar of *Prunus cerasifera*, is the oldest purple-leaf form. Often referred to as the Pissard Plum, it was discovered before 1880 by Mr. Pissard, the gardener to the Shah of Iran. Leaves are reddish purple. Pinkish, ⅓-in.-diameter flowers usually arrive before the leaves. Grows 20 to 25 ft. high.

'Krauter Vesuvius' has dark reddish purple foliage and whitish pink, ½- to ¾-in.-diameter flowers. It is similar to 'Thundercloud', but the flowers arrive earlier and are a lighter pink. Grows 30 ft. high, 20 ft. wide.

'Newport' is a round-headed tree with bronze-purple new growth that matures to dark reddish purple. The pale pink to near white flowers open before the leaves emerge. Grows 15 to 20 ft. high and wide. Zones (4)5 to 8.

'Thundercloud' has single, pink, fragrant flowers that appear before the leaves. It retains its deep purple foliage color throughout the growing season. Easily confused with 'Krauter Vesuvius'. Grows 20 ft. high and wide. Zones 5 to 8.

Prunus cerasifera 'Atropurpurea'

Prunus cerasifera 'Newport'

Prunus cerasifera 'Krauter Vesuvius' foliage

Prunus cerasifera 'Thundercloud' flowers

Prunus glandulosa
Dwarf Flowering Almond

A small, wispy shrub with essentially no redeeming characteristics other than its double, rose-pink flowers that cover the naked branches in April and May. After flowering, the plant is so bland that it practically disappears until the next flowering season. Leaves are bright to medium green. An amazingly durable and adaptable plant. It has somewhat of a suckering tendency and will sneak around the garden and neighborhood, appearing in places it was never planted. Despite all my biases against the plant, I must admit that the floral display is quite pretty. Prune after flowering to rejuvenate the plant. Can be used effectively in a border. Grows 4 to 5 ft. high and wide. Zones 4 to 8. China, Japan.

Prunus glandulosa, Dwarf Flowering Almond

Prunus glandulosa flowers

Prunus 'Hally Jolivette'

Some specimens of this hybrid cultivar form a treelike habit, but most are densely branched shrubs, often wider than they are tall. The small leaves are glossy green and may develop yellow-bronze fall color. The double, 1¼-in.-diameter flowers are pink in bud, opening to pinkish white, and are effective over a 10- to 20-day period in April and May. Fine-textured stems add to the beauty of the plant throughout the seasons. Quite fast growing and adaptable. Grows 15 to 20 ft. high and wide. Zones 5 to 7.

Prunus 'Hally Jolivette'

Prunus 'Hally Jolivette' flowers

Prunus ×*incam* 'Okame'

Okame Cherry

In recent years, this upright-arching flowering cherry has received greater garden press than any other cherry. In youth the outline is distinctly upright and vase-shaped, becoming more rounded with age. The polished, reddish brown bark is covered with horizontal lenticels. Rich pink flowers appear before the leaves in March and April. The 1- to 2½-in.-long, dark green leaves turn bronzy red in autumn. It has demonstrated excellent heat and cold tolerance. In the years ahead, Okame Cherry is likely to become one of the most popular garden cherries. It makes a handsome specimen tree or can be used in groupings of three to five. Hybridized by Collingwood Ingram of England, using *Prunus incisa* and *P. campanulata*. Grows 20 to 30 ft. high. Zones 5 to 8.

Prunus ×*incam* 'Okame', Okame Cherry

Prunus maackii
Amur Chokecherry

Prunus ×incam 'Okame' flowers

On a sunny winter day, Amur Chokecherry is identifiable from a mile away. The glossy, amber to reddish brown to cinnamon-brown bark provides spectacular color in winter. The bark of young trees often exfoliates in shaggy masses, but it loses this quality with age. The habit is distinctly pyramidal in youth, becoming more rounded at maturity. The 2- to 4-in.-long, medium green leaves turn, at best, yellow-green in fall. White flowers are borne in 2- to 3-in. racemes in May and are followed by red fruit that mature to black in August. This species does not tolerate excessive heat and should only be used in colder climates. Grows 35 to 45 ft. high and wide. Zones 2 to 6. China.

Prunus maackii, Amur Chokecherry

Prunus maackii flowers

Prunus maackii bark

Prunus maritima
Beach Plum

Beach Plum is not utilized to any degree in contemporary landscapes, but along the Atlantic Coast this shrub provides a burst of white spring flowers. Edible, ½- to 1-in.-long, yellow-orange fruit ripen to dull purple or crimson in August and are relished for jams and jellies. The 1½- to 3-in.-long, dull dark green leaves may develop slight fall color. Appears to thrive with neglect in sandy, salt-laden environments. Good naturalizing plant. An artistic garden element when the lower branches are removed; I have observed many plants treated this way on Cape Cod, Massachusetts. Can form rather large colonies. Grows 6 ft. high or more. Zones 3 to 6. Maine to Virginia.

Prunus maritima, Beach Plum

Prunus maritima flowers

Prunus padus
European Birdcherry

In early spring, this is one of the first trees to leaf out in the Midwest. The new leaves are combinations of bright and bronzy greens, and they mature to a dull dark green. Autumn foliage color ranges from yellow to bronze. The mature habit is rounded with ascending branches. Fragrant white flowers occur in drooping, loose racemes, 3 to 6 in. long, in April and May. Small, black fruit ripen in July and August. This species is susceptible to black knot disease, which causes grotesque blackish growths on the stems. At its best, European Birdcherry has much to offer the northern landscape. Grows 30 to 40 ft. high and wide. Zones 3 to 6. Europe, northern Asia to Korea and Japan.

Prunus padus, European Birdcherry

Prunus maritima fruit

Prunus persica
Peach

Prunus padus in flower

The number of flowering peach cultivars that have been named over the centuries is astronomical. In flower, they are beautiful, but unfortunately, they are unreliable as garden plants over the long haul. The flowers appear in April before the leaves, and even the worst forms are eye-catching. An entire peach orchard in rich pink spring flower is a spectacular sight. Flower color ranges from white to pink to deep red or multicolored, in singles and doubles. The habit of most trees is rounded. The lustrous dark green, 3- to 6-in.-long leaves die off yellow in fall. For maximum growth and landscape longevity, provide moist, acid, well-drained soils, in full sun. Borers and cankers are troublesome. I cannot remember seeing any truly old trees in landscapes. Use and enjoy with the knowledge that the tree may not be present next year. Grows 15 to 25 ft. high and wide. Zones 5 to 9. China.

Prunus padus flowers

Prunus persica, Peach

Prunus persica flowers

Prunus persica fruit

Prunus sargentii
Sargent Cherry

Many gardeners consider this the crème de la crème of the flowering cherries. The habit is upright-spreading to rounded, with deep reddish brown, polished bark. The 1¼- to 1½-in.-diameter, pink flowers open before the leaves in April and May and are followed by ⅓-in.-long, purple-black fruit in June and July. The reddish tinged new leaves become shiny dark green in summer and bronze-red in autumn. The flowers coincide with daffodils, and Sargent Cherry trees underplanted with bulbs paint a springtime masterpiece. Once established, this species exhibits greater staying power than most *Prunus* species, and old specimens in New England attest to its persistence. Grows 20 to 30 ft. high and wide under landscape conditions. Zones 4 to 7. Japan.

Cultivars and Varieties. 'Accolade' is a rounded, spreading form with 1½-in.-diameter, blush-pink flowers in April. Each flower is composed of 12 to 15 petals. This cultivar is the result of a hybrid between *Prunus sargentii* and *P. subhirtella*. Grows 20 to 25 ft. high.

'Columnaris' is somewhat of a misnomer, for the trees become vase-shaped rather than truly columnar. It possesses the same desirable attributes as *Prunus sargentii*. Grows 25 to 35 ft. high, 10 to 15 ft. wide.

Prunus serotina
Black Cherry

I do not remember ever seeing this native species listed in a nursery catalog, probably because it is almost weedlike over much of the eastern United States. The propensity of Black Cherry to produce thousands of stray seedlings has not endeared it to gardeners. The habit is pyramidal to conical in youth, becoming oval-headed with pendulous branches. New leaves are sparkling bronzy to bright green, turning dark green with maturity and developing reasonable yellow to red fall color. White flowers occur in 4- to 6-in.-long, ¾-in.-diameter racemes in May, followed by prodigious quantities of ⅓-in.-diameter, red to black fruit. Not a good tree for the average garden, but in a native setting it is certainly worth enjoying. Grows 50 to 60 ft. high, 20 to 30 ft. wide. Zones 3 to 9. Ontario to North Dakota, south to Florida and Texas.

Prunus sargentii, Sargent Cherry

Prunus sargentii flowers

Prunus sargentii fruit

Prunus serrulata
Japanese Flowering Cherry, Oriental Cherry

This species, or at least its cultivars, epitomizes to most gardeners all that is sacred about cherries. In its finest forms, the habit is vase-shaped to rounded. Newly emerging leaves vary from fresh spring-green to bronze-green. The lustrous dark green, 2- to 5-in.-long summer leaves turn bronze to subdued red in fall. Fruit are seldom produced. *Prunus serrulata* is used for every imaginable landscape situation, from a single lawn specimen to a street tree to formal allée plantings. Many cultivars are short lived (10 to 15 years); in recent years, 'Kwanzan' has suffered more than most. Viruses lead to gradual decline and, eventually, death. Species grows 50 to 75 ft. high, but the cultivars range from 20 to 35 ft. high. Zones 5 to 8. Japan, Korea, China.

Cultivars and Varieties. 'Amanogawa' develops an upright-columnar habit and produces single to semi-double, pink flowers. Grows 20 ft. high, 4 to 5 ft. wide.

'Kwanzan' ('Sekiyama'), with deep pink, double flowers, is the most common representative of the species.

'Mt. Fuji' ('Shirotae') is rich pink in bud, opening white. New leaves are pale green with a bronze tint. The growth habit is broad-spreading, rather flat-topped. Grows 15 to 20 ft. high and wide.

'Shirofugen' is pink in bud, opening to white, and fading again to pink, with 30 petals per flower. New leaves are deep bronze. A vigorous grower that develops a wide-spreading, flat-topped crown. Grows 25 to 30 ft. high, 20 to 25 ft. wide.

Prunus serotina, Black Cherry

Prunus serotina fruit

Prunus serotina bark

Prunus serrulata, Japanese Flowering Cherry, fall color

MORE ➤

Prunus serrulata continued

Prunus serrulata 'Kwanzan'

Prunus serrulata 'Kwanzan' bark

Prunus serrulata 'Shirofugen' flowers

Prunus serrulata 'Mt. Fuji'

Prunus subhirtella
Higan Cherry

Along with *Prunus sargentii*, this is one of the longest lived flowering cherries. The ½-in.-diameter, white to pinkish flowers arrive before the leaves in April. The habit is typically upright-spreading to rounded. The 1- to 4-in.-long, lustrous green leaves turn yellowish in fall. For the gardener who wants one cherry that will provide many years of enjoyment, this tree and its cultivars are possibly the best choices. Plants, once established, will grow in brick-hard clay. Tolerant of heat, more so than *P. sargentii*. Interestingly, I have observed this species surviving on the campus of the University of Maine at Orono, where most of the desirable flowering cherries are not cold hardy enough. Grows 20 to 40 ft. high, 15 to 30 ft. wide or more. Zones 4 to 8(9). Japan.

Cultivars and Varieties. 'Autumnalis' flowers in fall and spring, producing pinkish white, 10- to 15-petaled flowers, ½ to ¾ in. in diameter. The spring bloom is more potent than the fall bloom.

'Pendula' is greatly variable. It reproduces partially true to type from seed, so many forms are available in commerce. In youth it is a wild and woolly weeping tree, but it calms down with age to produce a rather elegant, dapper, stately character. Flowers may be white but are usually pink. Buy the tree when it is in flower to be sure of flower color. Grows 40 ft. high and wide. There is also a double pink form, 'Pendula Plena Rosea'.

Prunus subhirtella, Higan Cherry

Prunus subhirtella 'Autumnalis'

MORE ➤

Prunus subhirtella continued

Prunus subhirtella 'Autumnalis' flowers

Prunus subhirtella 'Pendula'

Prunus tenella
Dwarf Russian Almond

Certainly not very common in the United States, but the few that I have seen in flower were extremely showy. It is a low, suckering shrub with 1½- to 3½-in.-long, dark green leaves. The rose-red, ½-in.-diameter flowers occur singly or in clusters of two or three from buds of the previous year's growth. Minimal information is available on culture, but well-drained soils and full sun are imperative. Use in the border. Grows 2 to 5 ft. high and wide. Zones 2 to 6. Europe, Asia.

Prunus tenella, Dwarf Russian Almond, in fall

Prunus tomentosa
Manchu or Nanking Cherry

Manchu Cherry is sold for its edible scarlet fruit, but in the northern states it is one of the first shrubs to flower and is worth using for that reason alone. By no means a small shrub, *Prunus tomentosa* is broad-spreading and densely twiggy, becoming more open and picturesque with age. It is not a bad idea to prune the lower limbs to expose the exfoliating reddish brown bark. Fragrant white flowers, ¾ in. in diameter, appear on leafless branches in early to mid-April. The fruit ripen in June and July. The 2- to 3-in.-long, dark green leaves are extremely hairy on their undersides. Very adaptable to soils. Provide full sun. Useful in mass plantings or in the shrub border. Grows 6 to 10 ft. high, may spread to 15 ft. Zones 2 to 6(7). China, Japan.

Prunus tomentosa, Manchu Cherry

Prunus tomentosa flowers

Prunus tomentosa foliage

Prunus triloba var. *multiplex*

Flowering Almond, Double Flowering Plum

For rich pink flower effect in April, this is a most magnificent choice. The 1- to 1½-in.-diameter, double flowers clothe the naked branches in rich rose-pink. The 1- to 2½-in.-long, medium green leaves turn yellow to bronze in fall. An adaptable shrub, but it requires full sun for best flowering. Looks a bit bedraggled in the winter months. Use in a border or mass. Grows 12 to 15 ft. high and wide. Zones 3 to 6.

Prunus triloba var. *multiplex*, Flowering Almond

Prunus triloba var. *multiplex* flowers

Prunus virginiana

Common Chokecherry

This suckering small tree or large shrub is similar to *Prunus padus* in most respects, and the two species are quite difficult to accurately separate. The fruit of Common Chokecherry is used for making jams, jellies, pies, sauces, and wines. Suited only to the colder areas of North America. Tolerates high pH and clay soils. Grows 20 to 35 ft. high, 18 to 25 ft. wide. Zones 2 to 5. Canada, northern United States.

Cultivars and Varieties. 'Schubert' ('Canada Red') is a selection with reddish purple foliage. New growth emerges green. It reproduces true to type from seed. Suitable only for northern climates.

Prunus virginiana, Common Chokecherry

Prunus triloba var. *multiplex* fall color

Prunus virginiana fruit

Prunus virginiana 'Schubert' foliage

Prunus ×yedoensis
Yoshino Cherry

This is the species that dominates the Tidal Basin in Washington, DC. Several years past, I witnessed this rim of billowy white that surrounds the water—never have I seen more cameras aimed at the same subject. It's a shame that the allure and power of a cherry in flower cannot be transferred to the politicians. The habit of Yoshino Cherry is rounded to broad-rounded. The $2\frac{1}{2}$- to $4\frac{1}{2}$-in.-long, dark green leaves develop a semblance of yellow fall color. The $\frac{1}{2}$- to $\frac{5}{8}$-in.-diameter flowers are light pink in bud, opening to clouds of white. Although fleeting, the effect is spectacular. The falling petals are reminiscent of giant snowflakes. Blackish, $\frac{1}{3}$- to $\frac{1}{2}$-in.-diameter fruit ripen in June and July. The species is used extensively for street plantings; in some cities, such as Macon, Georgia, it has become a monoculture, and festivals celebrate the tree's mystique. As a single specimen, Yoshino Cherry provides great beauty in the early spring garden. It flowers reasonably well when used as an understory tree with pines overhead. Grows 40 to 50 ft. high and wide; usually smaller under cultivation. Zones 5 to 8. Japan.

Cultivars and Varieties. 'Akebono' has soft pink flowers and a rounded, spreading growth habit. In youth it is extremely vigorous.

'Shidare Yoshino' is a weeping, white-flowered selection. A 10-year-old plant reaches 15 ft. high and 20 to 25 ft. wide. Often treated as synonymous with f. *perpendens*, but there is no guarantee that plants labeled f. *perpendens* will grow like 'Shidare Yoshino'.

'Snow Fountains' ('White Fountain' by Wayside) is a semi-weeping form with white flowers. Foliage is dark green and turns gold and orange shades in fall. This form has been widely promoted, but it lacks grace. Grows 6 to 12 ft. high and wide.

Prunus ×yedoensis 'Shidare Yoshino'

Prunus ×yedoensis, Yoshino Cherry

Pseudocydonia sinensis (Cydonia sinensis)
Chinese Quince

Perhaps the best feature of this large shrub or small tree is its exfoliating bark in colors of gray, green, orange, and brown. The trunks become fluted or corrugated with age. The leathery, lustrous dark green foliage is also handsome. Soft pink flowers, 1 to 1½ in. across, appear in April and May. The 5- to 7-in.-long, egg-shaped fruit are citron-yellow. Provide well-drained soils, in full sun to partial shade. Fireblight is a significant problem and may limit successful culture. Use as a specimen. Grows 10 to 20 ft. high, 5 to 15 ft. wide. Zones (5)6 to 7. China.

Pseudocydonia sinensis, Chinese Quince, in fall

Pseudocydonia sinensis flower

Pseudocydonia sinensis fall color

Pseudocydonia sinensis bark

Pseudotsuga menziesii
Douglas Fir

I had never seen this magnificent needle evergreen in the wild until I was able to experience it first-hand during a trip along the West Coast. Douglas Fir is a great tree for the northern states and should be used more often. It is a tall, airy, spirelike, soft-textured tree. In youth the habit is uniformly pyramidal with drooping lower branches and ascending upper branches; in old age the top remains irregularly conical and the long, slender bole is branchless. The 1- to 1½-in.-long, flattish, blue-green needles are arranged in a spiral around the stem, so that a small V-shaped groove is evident on the upper side of the branches. The 3- to 4-in.-long cones have extended bracts reminiscent of a horseshoe crab's tail. The species prefers moisture-retentive soils but is quite adaptable. Ideal as a specimen, in groupings, or as a screen. Also makes a fine Christmas tree, because the needles are retained better than those of spruce or fir under hot, dry conditions. Great variation in needle color. Opt for the best bluish green forms, which are considered more cold hardy. Grows 40 to 80 ft. high, 12 to 20 ft. wide. Zones 4 to 6. Western United States.

Pseudotsuga menziesii bark

Pseudotsuga menziesii, Douglas Fir

Young specimen of *Pseudotsuga menziesii*

Pyracantha coccinea
Firethorn

For fruit display in the winter garden, few plants rival pyracanthas. Framed by the dark leaves, or nestled among them, the bright orange-red fruit provide spectacular fall and winter color. Typically, Firethorn is a large, unkempt and splaying evergreen shrub with stiff, thorny branches. The 1- to 2½-in.-long, lustrous dark green leaves may develop bronzy off-green colors in extremely cold weather. Slightly malodorous white flowers smother the plant in May and June. The fruit ripen in September and October and persist into winter. Transplant from a container into any well-drained soil. Pyracanthas are amazingly adaptable and make good choices for dry soils. They require full sun for best fruiting but will do well in partial shade. Many uses, including barrier, mass, hedge, and espalier. Select cold-hardy cultivars. Grows 6 to 18 ft. high and wide. Zones (5)6 to 8. Italy to Caucasus.

Cultivars and Varieties. 'Chadwickii' develops a more compact, spreading habit and orange-red fruit. Shows good hardiness. Grows 6 ft. high.

'Fiery Cascade', an 8-ft.-high and 9-ft.-wide cultivar with small red fruit, 'Gnome', a compact (6 ft. by 8 ft.) shrub with orange fruit, and 'Rutgers', a selection that grows 3 ft. by 9 ft. and bears orange-red fruit, are cold hardy to about 0°F.

'Lalandei' is a large, shrubby form. It offers orange-red fruit and good cold hardiness. Grows 10 to 15 ft. high.

'Wyattii' is another vigorous form with orange-red fruit and good cold tolerance. Grows 9 to 12 ft. high and wide.

Pyracantha coccinea, Firethorn

Pyracantha coccinea fruiting

Pyrus calleryana

Callery Pear

True *Pyrus calleryana* is a thorny, coarse, irregular tree of which the only redeeming characteristic is the early spring white flowers, but even they are mildly disagreeable in their odor. The true species is generally used as an understock for budding the more desirable cultivars, the tree's main representatives in the landscape. The species was used as breeding stock in an attempt to incorporate fireblight resistance into *P. communis*, Common Pear; this experiment did not work, but gardeners have benefited from the ornamental attributes of the resulting cultivars. The most notable cultural aspect of *P. calleryana* is its tremendous tolerance of heat, drought, and compacted soils. Zones 5 to 8(9). Korea, China.

Cultivars and Varieties. 'Aristocrat' is a pyramidal to broad-pyramidal form, with coarse, horizontal branches. The lustrous dark green, wavy margined leaves turn persimmon-orange in fall. The white flowers are not as profuse as those of 'Bradford', but this cultivar is more structurally sound. Better suited to the North; fireblight has been problematic in the South. Grows 40 ft. high, 20 to 25 ft. wide.

'Bradford', introduced in the early 1960s, is as common as mud in landscapes across the United States. It is densely branched and foliaged, broad-conical in habit in youth and maturity. A profusion of white flowers appear in April, and the leathery, 1½- to 3-in.-long and wide, dark green leaves turn fluorescent orange and red in fall. Despite all its desirable attributes, however, 'Bradford' suffers from a fatal genetic flaw that causes it to self-destruct, literally falling apart with time—the many branches will cause the tree to split in half after 10 to 15 years. For short-term use, it is acceptable, but to plant entire streets with this cultivar is playing biological Russian roulette. Trees that survived 20 years were 50 ft. high and 40 ft. wide. 'Bradford' is highly resistant to fireblight.

'Capital' has an upright-columnar habit like that of *Populus nigra* 'Italica', Lombardy Poplar. It bears lustrous dark green leaves. Probably suitable only for northern states; fireblight has been a tremendous problem in the South. Grows 32 ft. high and 8 ft. wide in 15 years.

'Chanticleer' (also 'Select', 'Cleveland Select', or 'Stone Hill') is an upright-pyramidal form that, unlike some of the other cultivars, has not shown the propensity to break apart with age. It flowers heavily, but its reddish purple fall color does not measure up to that of 'Bradford'. Displays good fireblight resistance. Grows 35 ft. high and 16 ft. wide in 15 years.

Pyrus calleryana, Callery Pear

Pyrus calleryana 'Aristocrat' fall color

MORE ➤

Pyrus calleryana **continued**

'Redspire' originated as a seedling of 'Bradford', but its pyramidal outline lacks the inherent stiffness of that of its parent. Flowers are less profuse, and fall color is yellow-orange to red. Fireblight has been devastating in the South, but I have not noticed the problem in the North.

'Whitehouse', intermediate between 'Capital' and 'Bradford' in growth habit, has never proven popular because of its susceptibility to leaf spot. It is tightly pyramidal. Not as heavy flowering as 'Bradford'. Grows 35 ft. high and 14 ft. wide after 14 years.

Pyrus calleryana 'Bradford' fall color

Pyrus calleryana 'Bradford' flowers

Pyrus calleryana 'Bradford' fruit

Pyrus calleryana 'Chanticleer'

Pyrus communis
Common Pear

Gardeners rarely utilize the fruiting pear for ornamental purposes, but many older residences and farmsteads have a tree or two. The 1- to 1½-in.-diameter, white flowers open in April and are quite disagreeable to the olfactory sense. Habit is irregularly pyramidal, and the lustrous dark green leaves often turn rich red in fall. Fruit are 3- to 4-in.-long pomes. Grows 20 to 30 ft. high, generally less in spread. Zones 4 to 8(9). Europe, western Asia.

Pyrus communis fall color

Pyrus communis flowers

Pyrus communis, Common Pear

Pyrus pyrifolia
Chinese Sand Pear

Like *Pyrus ussuriensis*, this attractive species plays second (or, perhaps, third) fiddle to the *P. calleryana* selections. It develops into a dense, broad-pyramidal to rounded tree. The foliage is lustrous dark green in summer and yellow, orange, and red in fall. White flowers blanket the tree in April, and they are followed by hard, 1½-in.-diameter, rounded fruit, which are quite messy. Because of the large fruit, it is doubtful that this species or *P. ussuriensis* will ever become popular in gardening circles. Grows 30 to 40 ft. high and wide. Zones 5 to 8. Central and western China.

Pyrus pyrifolia, Chinese Sand Pear

Pyrus pyrifolia flowers

Pyrus pyrifolia fruit

Pyrus salicifolia
Willowleaf Pear

If fireblight were not so problematic, this gray-leaved species would be as common as *Pyrus calleryana* 'Bradford'. The graceful, fine-textured branches are clothed with 1½- to 3½-in.-long, woolly, gray-green willowlike leaves. Flowers and fruit are not spectacular. Grows 15 to 25 ft. high. Zones 4 to 7. Southeastern Europe, western Asia.

Cultivars and Varieties. 'Pendula' is the most common form of Willowleaf Pear in cultivation. It boasts elegant drooping branches and silvery gray foliage. Grows 15 ft. high.

Pyrus salicifolia, Willowleaf Pear, foliage

Pyrus ussuriensis
Ussurian Pear

Pyrus salicifolia 'Pendula'

Although seldom seen outside of arboreta, this round-headed, white-flowered species has merit, especially in northern gardens (Zones 3 to 4) where the *Pyrus calleryana* types are not cold hardy. The 1⅓-in.-diameter flowers open in April and May and are followed by 1- to 1½-in.-diameter, greenish yellow fruit. The lustrous dark green leaves may turn respectable red to reddish purple in fall. Grows 40 to 50 ft. high. Zones 3 to 6. Northeastern Asia.

Cultivars and Varieties. Prairie Gem™ ('Mordak') is a new selection released by North Dakota State University. It has an oval to rounded habit and thick, glossy dark green leaves.

Pyrus ussuriensis foliage

Pyrus ussuriensis, Ussurian Pear

Quercus acutissima
Sawtooth Oak

This unsung species of the oak world offers great aesthetic benefits for garden and large-area use. The habit is distinctly pyramidal in youth, becoming rounded to broad-rounded with age. The lustrous dark green, prominently serrated leaves turn yellow to golden brown in autumn. They emerge early in spring, color late in fall, and may persist into winter. The bark becomes deeply ridged and furrowed with age, appearing almost corky. The rich brown nuts are enclosed in a scaly cap to about ⅔ of their length. Sawtooth Oak tolerates dry soils but prospers in moist, well-drained, acid soils. Transplants more readily than most oaks. A great choice for campuses, parks, or golf courses. Useful along streets or in medians, but can be a nuisance in autumn when the nuts roll about like marbles. Grows 35 to 45(60) ft. high and wide. Zones 5 to 8. Asia.

Quercus acutissima foliage

Quercus acutissima, Sawtooth Oak, in fall

Quercus acutissima bark

Quercus acutissima acorn

Quercus alba
White Oak

White Oak is the standard by which all other oaks are measured. The majesty of a mature tree warrants pause for reflection. Distinctly pyramidal in youth, the outline becomes oval-rounded to rounded with age. The dark green, almost blue-green leaves often turn a good russet-red to red in fall. Bark is light ash-brown and often breaks into small, vertically arranged, scaly plates. The rich brown, 1-in.-long acorn is ¼ covered by the bumpy scaled cap. Grows best in deep, moist, acid, well-drained soils, but it is adaptable. Unfortunately, it is quite difficult to transplant and must be moved as a small tree, ideally of less than 2½ in. caliper, for best success. White Oak is excellent as a specimen tree and also in groves. Possibly one of America's most handsome native species. Grows 50 to 80 ft. high and wide. Zones 3 to 8. Maine to Minnesota, south to Florida and Texas.

Quercus alba, White Oak

Quercus alba in winter

Quercus alba acorn

Quercus alba fall color

Quercus bicolor
Swamp White Oak

A virtually unknown landscape species that should be utilized more frequently, particularly in areas with moist soils. In a sense, it plays second fiddle to White Oak, but it is easier to transplant. The habit is stiffly pyramidal in youth, becoming rounded at maturity. The secondary branches develop small spur shoots that give the tree a coarse, less-than-pristine appearance. The lustrous dark green leaves are often covered with a white pubescence beneath. Fall color is usually yellowish brown but occasionally russet-red. The brownish black bark is rough and scaly even on young trees, becoming deeply ridged and furrowed with age. Plant in moist, acid soils. Chlorosis will develop in high pH soils. A worthwhile plant for wet areas. Good for naturalizing or for use in parks, golf courses, and large areas. Grows 50 to 60 ft. high and wide. Zones 3 to 8. Quebec to Michigan, south to Georgia and Arkansas.

Quercus bicolor, Swamp White Oak

Quercus bicolor foliage

Quercus bicolor bark

Quercus coccinea
Scarlet Oak

If but one oak could grace my garden, this would be the choice. Unfortunately, the species is seldom available in commerce because of its transplanting difficulty. Also, what is often sold as Scarlet Oak is actually *Quercus palustris*, Pin Oak, or *Q. rubra*, Red Oak. The lustrous, almost reflective, dark green summer leaves yield to brilliant reds and scarlets in the fall. Fall coloration may last three to four weeks. The habit is softly pyramidal in youth, becoming upright-spreading and open with age. The ½- to 1-in.-long acorns are covered to about ½ their length in a bowl-like cap. Scarlet Oak is adaptable, but it prospers in moist, well-drained, acid soils. In the wild, it is often found on dry, sandy soils. Ideally, move as a small, 6- to 10-ft.-high container plant or balled and burlapped specimen. Grows 70 to 75 ft. high, 40 to 50 ft. wide. Zones 4 to 8(9). Maine to Minnesota, south to Florida and Missouri.

Quercus coccinea fall color

Quercus coccinea acorns

Quercus coccinea, Scarlet Oak, in fall

Quercus imbricaria
Shingle Oak

Shingle Oak develops a pyramidal outline in youth, eventually becoming rounded to broad-rounded. The lustrous dark green, 2½- to 6-in.-long leaves are unlobed and, to the casual observer, represent anything but an oak. Leaves turn, at best, yellow-brown to russet-red in fall and often persist into winter. Many gardeners find the persistent leaves objectionable, but others appreciate the rustling sound of the dried leaves. Shingle Oak is relatively easy to transplant and is adaptable to a wide range of soil conditions, from acid to higher pH and moist to dry. Old trees are quite imposing because of the mammoth, spreading branches. Grows 50 to 60 ft. high and wide. Zones 4 to 7. Pennsylvania to Nebraska, south to Georgia and Arkansas.

Quercus imbricaria foliage

Quercus imbricaria, Shingle Oak

Quercus macrocarpa
Bur or Mossycup Oak

Certainly a most impressive species when viewed as an open-grown specimen in a grassy field in the Midwest, but it is perhaps too big, too messy, and too lacking in ornamental characteristics for the average landscape. In its finest form, *Quercus macrocarpa* is a behemoth, with a massive trunk and a broad crown of stout branches. The large (up to 10 to 12 in. long), dark green leaves turn yellow-brown in fall. The gray-brown bark becomes deeply ridged and furrowed with age. Bur Oak is difficult to transplant and, for that reason, is seldom available in commerce. Northern nurseries have recently reported successful transplanting and increased sales. Ideally, transplant young balled and burlapped or container-grown plants to a permanent location. Adaptable to many soils. In nature, the tree is found on sandy plains and moist, alluvial bottoms, in limestone and dry clay soils. Grows 70 to 80 ft. high and wide. Zones 2 to 8. Nova Scotia to Manitoba, south to Texas.

Quercus macrocarpa, Bur Oak, in fall

Quercus muehlenbergii
Chinkapin Oak

Another oak that is seldom offered in commerce because of transplanting difficulties. The habit is weakly rounded in youth, becoming open and rounded with maturity. The lustrous dark green leaves turn yellow to orangish yellow in fall. Massive trees occur in dry, limestone-based soils as well as in rich bottomlands. If native in the area, trees should be protected and enjoyed. As with many of the difficult-to-transplant species, small seedlings can be successfully established. Chinkapin Oak is a fine park or large-area tree. Grows 40 to 50 ft. high and wide under landscape conditions; will reach 70 to 80 ft. high in the wild. Zones 4 to 7. Vermont to Nebraska, south to Virginia, Texas, and Mexico.

Quercus muehlenbergii foliage and acorns

Quercus macrocarpa foliage

Quercus palustris
Pin Oak

Quercus muehlenbergii, Chinkapin Oak

In a popularity poll by *American Nurseryman* magazine, this species was the most commonly planted shade and street tree. Pin Oak has consumer recognition, and it is also one of the easiest oaks to grow and transplant, which contributes to its popularity. The habit is strongly pyramidal, usually with a central leader. The lower branches are pendulous; the middle are horizontal; and the upper branches are upright. The lustrous dark green leaves turn russet-red to red in fall. Pin Oak requires acid soils for best performance. Chlorosis is common throughout the Midwest on plants in calcareous soils. One major maintenance problem is that the lower branches hang down and must be removed to facilitate vehicular and pedestrian traffic. Use for street and lawn plantings. Grows 60 to 70 ft. high, 25 to 40 ft. wide. Zones 4 to 7. Massachusetts to Wisconsin, south to Delaware and Arkansas.

Cultivars and Varieties. 'Crownright' and 'Sovereign' do not develop the weeping lower branches of the species.

Quercus palustris, Pin Oak

Quercus palustris fall color

Quercus palustris acorns

Quercus phellos, Willow Oak

Quercus phellos fall color

Quercus phellos
Willow Oak

The most popular tree in the Southeast for streets, parks, estates, and residential properties, Willow Oak is also grown as far north as Cape Cod with reasonable success. The fine-textured, oval to rounded habit makes this species one of the most desirable oaks for general use. The 2- to 5½-in.-long, narrow, willowlike leaves are lustrous dark green in summer, changing to brownish yellow and occasionally orangish yellow in fall. Acorns are ½ in. long or less, and not as messy as those of *Quercus alba*, *Q. macrocarpa*, and *Q. rubra*. Transplant in late winter, when dormant, into moist, well-drained soils. Once established, *Q. phellos* is extremely tolerant of heat, drought, and stress. Beautiful specimen oak and an excellent street tree. Grows 40 to 60 ft. high, 30 to 40 ft. wide or equal in spread. Zones 6 to 9. New York to Florida, west to Missouri and Texas.

Quercus phellos acorns

Quercus robur
English Oak

A trip through the English countryside will provide sufficient reason for bringing an English Oak into the garden. The broad-rounded habit, the wide-spreading, ridged and furrowed branches, and the sturdy, imposing trunk provide architectural elegance. The three- to seven-lobed, 2- to 5-in.-long, rich blue-green leaves hold late in fall but seldom develop good color. English Oak is easier to transplant than White Oak or Bur Oak. Tolerates dry, high pH soils. It is quite adaptable and has been successful from North Dakota to Utah to Georgia. Mildew is often a problem but can be controlled by an appropriate fungicide. The species is great for large areas; the fastigiate cultivars can be used in more restricted planting spaces. Grows 40 to 60 ft. high and wide. Zones 3 to 7. Europe, northern Africa, western Asia.

Cultivars and Varieties. 'Fastigiata' is perhaps the finest form. It is upright-columnar in habit with dense branches. Grows 60 ft. high, but only 10 to 15 ft. wide.

Several forms with colored foliage are available, including 'Atropurpurea' (purple leaves), 'Concordia' (yellow), and 'Variegata' (white-margined).

Upright selections include 'Attention', 'Rose Hill', and 'Skyrocket'; the latter two have mildew-resistant and more handsome foliage. More uniform in habit than 'Fastigiata', which is often grown from seed.

Quercus robur acorn and foliage

Quercus robur, English Oak

Quercus robur 'Fastigiata'

Quercus robur bark

Quercus rubra
Red Oak

Unique among the landscape oaks because of its rounded growth habit in youth and maturity. Red Oak is a superb tree that rivals Pin Oak for ease of transplanting. The seven- to eleven-lobed, lustrous dark green leaves change to russet-red and red in fall. New spring growth is a dusty bronze-red color, and the effect can be as handsome as the spring-flowering trees. Its ¾- to 1-in.-long, medium brown acorns are among the first of the landscape oaks to ripen, providing an early harvest for animals. Red Oak is adaptable to extremes of soil, but it prefers acid, well-drained sites. The root system is shallow compared to that of most oaks, and in extreme drought, trees may suffer. A superb large-area tree, it has also been used effectively as a street tree, particularly along the VFW Parkway and the Arborway in Boston, Massachusetts. Grows 60 to 75 ft. high and wide. Zones 4 to 7. Nova Scotia to Pennsylvania, west to Minnesota and Iowa.

Quercus rubra bark

Quercus rubra, Red Oak

Quercus rubra acorn

Quercus rubra fall color

Rhamnus frangula
Glossy Buckthorn

In the Midwest, the Glossy Buckthorn 'Columnaris' was becoming the most popular hedging and screening plant, but canker and other stress-related maladies slowed its advance. The species has minimal use in contemporary landscapes. The habit is upright-spreading with long, arching branches, which results in a gangly, open appearance. The 1- to 3-in.-long, glossy dark green leaves develop, at best, greenish yellow fall color. The creamy green flowers are not showy. The ¼-in.-diameter fruit pass from red to purple-black as they mature. Birds devour the fruit, and stray seedlings are common. Glossy Buckthorn is easy to transplant and grow, but compacted soils and other high-stress situations should be avoided. Although the species has minimal appeal, the cultivars are worth considering. Grows 10 to 12 (to 18) ft. high and wide. Zones 2 to 7. Europe, eastern Asia, North Africa.

Cultivars and Varieties. 'Asplenifolia' offers a fine-textured, almost fernlike appearance. The leaves are reduced to elongated ribbons with an irregular margin. Grows 10 to 12 ft. high, 6 to 10 ft. wide.

'Columnaris' is a narrow, columnar shrub that has been overused for hedges and screens. Grows 10 to 15 ft. high, 5 ft. wide.

Rhamnus frangula, Glossy Buckthorn

Rhamnus frangula fruit

Rhamnus frangula 'Asplenifolia' foliage

Rhododendron, Rhododendron, Azalea

For many gardeners, this genus epitomizes all that is great about gardening. The colorful flowers are often spectacular. Plants range from small, groundcover-type shrubs to 60-ft.-tall trees. Rhododendron *species thrive in well-drained, organic-laden, acid, moist soils. Provide as much light as possible to foster maximum growth and flower bud set. Many insects and diseases, particularly root rot or wilt-type diseases, wreak havoc on rhododendrons and azaleas. One of the keys to successful culture is excellent drainage. I know gardeners who break up the ground, set the plant on top, and cover its roots with an organic substrate, like pine bark.*

Rhododendron atlanticum

Coast Azalea

A delightful small, suckering shrub with glaucous, blue-green leaves and fragrant, white to light pink flowers. Flowers occur with or slightly before the leaves in May. Makes a lovely addition to the shrub border. Grows 6 to 8 ft. high and wide. Zones 5 to 8. Delaware to South Carolina.

Rhododendron atlanticum, Coast Azalea

Rhododendron atlanticum flowers

Rhododendron atlanticum foliage

Rhododendron calendulaceum
Flame Azalea

One of the finest deciduous native azaleas, this species bears yellow to orange to red, nonfragrant flowers in May and June. Medium green summer foliage develops yellow to bronze to reddish fall color. Grows 4 to 8 ft. high and wide; can grow 12 to 15 ft. Zones 5 to 7. Mountains of Pennsylvania, south to Georgia.

Rhododendron carolinianum
Carolina Rhododendron

A rounded evergreen shrub of gentle proportions. The 3-in.-diameter inflorescences vary in color from pale rose to rose and lilac-rose. Not used a great deal in modern landscapes, but beautiful in a woodland setting. One of the parents of *Rhododendron* 'PJM'. Grows 3 to 6 ft. high and wide. Zones (4)5 to 8. North and South Carolina, Tennessee.

Rhododendron calendulaceum, Flame Azalea

Rhododendron carolinianum, Carolina Rhododendron

Rhododendron calendulaceum fall color

Rhododendron calendulaceum flowers

Rhododendron carolinianum flowers

Rhododendron catawbiense
Catawba Rhododendron

A large, bold, broadleaf evergreen with a dense, oval-rounded to rounded outline. Considered the most durable and easy-to-grow rhododendron for everyday gardening purposes. The typical species flower is lilac-purple and occurs in 5- to 6-in.-diameter inflorescences in May and June. At the edges of woodlands, in naturalized situations, or in the shrub border, this species makes a stunning show. Numerous cultivars in a variety of flower colors are available; check with the local nursery for those best adapted to the area. Grows 6 to 10 ft. high and wide. Zones 4 to 8. Southern Appalachians.

Rhododendron catawbiense, Catawba Rhododendron

Rhododendron catawbiense foliage

Rhododendron maximum
Rosebay Rhododendron

Although seldom available in commerce, this large-leaved (4 to 8 in. long) evergreen rhododendron offers possibly the greatest cold hardiness of any native species. It develops into a massive, rounded shrub. The pink-budded flowers open white, with an olive-green spot in the center. Flowers occur in 4- to 6-in.-wide inflorescences in June and July. Use only for naturalizing purposes. Grows 15 to 20 ft. high and wide in the wild. Zones 3 to 7. Nova Scotia to Ontario, south to Georgia and Alabama.

Rhododendron maximum foliage

Rhododendron maximum flowers

Rhododendron mucronulatum
Korean Rhododendron

Korean Rhododendron is a deciduous shrub that offers bright rose-purple, 1½-in.-long and wide flowers on naked stems from March to early April. It was a welcome sight in my Illinois garden after the hostilities of the midwestern winter. Use in a shrub border or grouping framed by an evergreen background. Grows 4 to 8 ft. high and wide. Zones 4 to 7. Northern and northeastern China, Korea, northern Japan.

Cultivars and Varieties. 'Cornell Pink' has phlox-pink flowers.

Rhododendron maximum, Rosebay Rhododendron

Rhododendron mucronulatum, Korean Rhododendron

Rhododendron mucronulatum flowers

Rhododendron periclymenoides (R. nudiflorum)
Pinxterbloom Azalea

A deciduous, fragrant-flowered species that forms a many-branched, rounded to spreading shrub. The 1½-in.-diameter flowers occur in May in clusters of 6 to 12, before the leaves. Colors range from near white to pale pink to violet. Grows 4 to 6 (to 10) ft. high. Zones 4 to 8. Massachusetts to North Carolina and Ohio.

Rhododendron periclymenoides, Pinxterbloom Azalea

Rhododendron periclymenoides flowers

Rhododendron prinophyllum (R. roseum)
Roseshell Azalea

A wonderfully fragrant, pink-flowered, deciduous shrub. Five to nine flowers are borne on each inflorescence in May. Summer foliage is bright green; fall foliage is bronze. The habit is tremendously variable, but plants in full sun are dense and rounded. Grows 2 to 8 (to 15) ft. high and wide. Zones 4 to 8. Southern Quebec to Virginia, west to Missouri.

Rhododendron prinophyllum, Roseshell Azalea

Rhododendron prinophyllum flowers

Rhododendron schlippenbachii
Royal Azalea

Possibly the most handsome of all azaleas when the soft pink, fragrant flowers cover the shrub in May. Three to six flowers are present in each 2½- to 3-in.-diameter inflorescence. Foliage is dark green in summer, developing subdued yellow, orange, and red tints in autumn. Grows 6 to 8 ft. high and wide. Zones 4 to 7. Korea, northeastern China.

Rhododendron schlippenbachii flowers

Rhododendron schlippenbachii, Royal Azalea

Rhododendron schlippenbachii foliage

Rhododendron schlippenbachii fall color

Rhododendron vaseyi

Pinkshell Azalea

This species offers abundant $1\frac{1}{2}$-in.-diameter, pink flowers before the leaves in May. The medium to dark green leaves develop excellent reddish fall color. Several white-flowered selections are available, including 'Alba'. Grows 5 to 10 ft. high. Zones 4 to 8. North Carolina.

Rhododendron vaseyi flowers

Rhododendron vaseyi, Pinkshell Azalea

Rhododendron viscosum

Swamp Azalea

This is a wonderful native species that has been used by hybridizers to produce summer-blooming azaleas. The white, rarely pink, flowers have a clovelike fragrance. They occur in four- to nine-flowered inflorescences after the leaves have fully matured. The flowers are not particularly striking, but the fragrance more than compensates for the lack of show. The lustrous dark green leaves have a glaucous cast on their undersides. A rather open shrub. Grows 5 to 8 ft. high, wider at maturity. Zones 3 to 9. Maine to South Carolina, Georgia, and Alabama, in swamps.

Rhododendron viscosum, Swamp Azalea

Rhododendron viscosum flowers

Rhododendron yakushimanum
Yakushima Rhododendron

A slow-growing, dense, mounded evergreen shrub. The dark green leaves are covered with a light gray-brown, woolly pubescence on their undersides. Flowers are spectacular, varying from bright rose to red in bud and opening to white in full flower. Inflorescences average 3 to 6 in. in diameter. Used extensively in breeding; many cultivars are available. Hardy to –5 to –15°F. A compact shrub. Grows 3 ft. high and wide after 20 years. Zones 5 to 6(7). Yakushima Island, Japan.

Rhododendron yakushimanum, Yakushima Rhododendron

Rhododendron yakushimanum flowers

Rhododendron yedoense var. *poukhanense*
Korean Azalea

Korean Azalea displays excellent flower bud hardiness (–20 to –25°F). It is a compact shrub with a mounded-rounded outline. The 2-in.-diameter, rose to lilac-purple, slightly fragrant flowers appear in May. The dark green foliage often develops orange to red-purple fall color. Grows 3 to 6 ft. high and wide. Zones 4 to 8. Korea.

Rhododendron yedoense, Yodogawa Azalea, has double flowers of a similar color.

Rhododendron yedoense var. *poukhanense*, Korean Azalea

Rhododendron yedoense var. *poukhanense* flowers

Rhododendron yedoense, Yodogawa Azalea, flowers

Rhododendron Hybrid Groups

Exbury, Ghent, Knap Hill, Ilam, Mollis, Northern Lights, Windsor

These hybrids are spectacular deciduous shrubs that are covered with flowers in white, yellow, orange, red, and all shades in between during May and June. Flowers generally occur before the leaves emerge, although this is variable. Habit is shrubby. The medium green leaves may develop yellow, orange, and red fall color. Numerous selections are available with flower bud hardiness to about –15 to –20°F. Grows 8 to 12 ft. high and wide. Zones 4 to 8.

Rhododendron Exbury Hybrids

Rhododendron Exbury Hybrid flowers

Rhododendron 'PJM'

Since its origination in about 1943, 'PJM' has become the standard by which all small, broadleaved, cold-hardy rhododendrons are judged. I am told it is the only broadleaf evergreen rhododendron that flowers in the Minnesota Landscape Arboretum. The habit is dense and rounded. Vivid lavender-pink flowers occur in mid- to late April. The dark green leaves turn reddish purple in winter. This hybrid, a result of crosses involving *Rhododendron carolinianum* and *R. dauricum* var. *sempervirens*, was introduced by Weston Nurseries, Hopkinton, Massachusetts. Grows 3 to 6 ft. high and wide. Zones 4 to 7.

Cultivars and Varieties. Weston Nurseries has introduced other hybrids with excellent cold hardiness and varying foliage and flower colors. Consult my *Manual of Woody Landscape Plants* (Champaign, IL: Stipes, 1990) or Homer Salley and Harold Greer's *Rhododendron Hybrids*, second edition (Portland, OR: Timber Press, 1992) for specifics.

Rhododendron 'PJM' flowers

Rhododendron Knap Hill Hybrid flowers

Rhododendron 'PJM'

Rhodotypos scandens
Black Jetbead

An old-fashioned shrub, Black Jetbead is seldom available in commerce, but it is receiving increasing attention because of its tremendous urban tolerance and its adaptability to shady habitats. In the best form, it develops into a mounded, loosely branched shrub with ascending and arching branches. The bright green, 2¼- to 4-in.-long leaves look like raspberry foliage. The leaves are among the first to emerge in spring, and they hold late into fall. Four-petaled, white, 1- to 2-in.-diameter flowers open in May and June, with scattered flowers often into the summer. The ⅓-in.-long, ovoid fruit are shining black, hard as a rock, and persistent through winter. Extremely adaptable; in fact, it is almost impossible to kill once established. Use as a foliage filler in shady borders, on banks, or in hostile soil areas. Never sensational, but certainly functional. Grows 3 to 6 ft. high, 4 to 9 ft. wide. Zones 4 to 8. Japan, central China.

Rhodotypos scandens, Black Jetbead

Rhodotypos scandens flower

Rhodotypos scandens foliage

Rhus aromatica
Fragrant Sumac

Fragrant Sumac is a useful shrub for groundcover and massing situations. It is adapted to the hottest, driest conditions and has proven a great plant for midwestern landscapes. Habit varies from a low groundcover to an irregular, spreading shrub with lower branches that turn up at the tips. Produces suckers and will create an almost impenetrable tangled mass of stems and leaves. The trifoliate, near blue-green leaves are often glossy on the upper surface. They develop orange to red to reddish purple fall color. Yellowish catkins open on naked stems of male plants in late March and April. Red, hairy, ¼-in.-diameter fruit ripen on female plants in August and September. Extremely adaptable to varied soils. Withstands sun or shade. Nice shrub for naturalizing, groundcover, or border use. Grows 2 to 6 ft. high, 6 to 10 ft. wide. Zones 3 to 9. Vermont to Ontario and Minnesota, south to Florida and Louisiana.

Cultivars and Varieties. 'Gro-Low' is a wide-spreading form with excellent glossy green foliage and orange-red fall color. It is a female and bears yellow flowers and hairy red fruit. Grows 2 ft. high, 6 to 8 ft. wide.

Rhus aromatica, Fragrant Sumac

Rhus aromatica fruit

Rhus chinensis
Chinese Sumac

This species ranges from a large, multistemmed shrub to a small tree. In northern latitudes, it is often shrubby. The bright green leaves are composed of 7 to 13 leaflets, each 2 to 5 in. long, and develop respectable yellow, orange, and red fall color. The real show occurs in August and September when 8- to 16-in.-long and wide, fleecy, white panicles smother the foliage. Flowers last for two to three weeks or longer. Chinese Sumac is ideal for dry, infertile soils. Requires full sun for maximum flowering. Suckers do develop; to keep the plant in bounds, simply mow them off. A good choice for use where walls, walks, and roads will limit its spread. Grows 20 to 25 ft. high, spreads indefinitely. Zones 5 to 7(8). China, Japan.

Cultivars and Varieties. 'September Beauty' was selected by Elwin Orton of Rutgers University for its larger flowers and tree-type habit. It is stunning in flower.

Rhus chinensis flowers

Rhus aromatica fall color

Rhus copallina

Flameleaf or Shining Sumac

Rhus chinensis, Chinese Sumac

At one time, I considered this species the best of the large-growing, suckering native sumacs, but now I defer to *Rhus typhina* 'Laciniata', primarily because of availability. The Flameleaf Sumac is a large, suckering, colonizing shrub with invasive qualities similar to that of the other sumacs. The leaves are composed of 9 to 21 lustrous dark green leaflets, each 1¾ to 4 in. long. Foliage changes to rich red, crimson, scarlet, and maroon in autumn. Greenish yellow flowers are borne in 4- to 8-in.-long, 3- to 4-in.-wide, feathery panicles in July and August. The crimson fruit ripen in September and October, but they are not as showy as those of *R. glabra* or *R. typhina*. As with the other species, Flameleaf Sumac will grow in any soil except one that is permanently moist. Grows 20 to 30 ft. high and wide. Zones 4 to 9. Maine to Ontario and Minnesota, south to Florida and Texas.

Cultivars and Varieties. 'Creel's Quintet' is a compact form. Its lustrous dark green leaves, composed of 5 leathery leaflets, are closely spaced along the stems and produce red-purple fall color. Grows 5 to 8 ft. high.

Rhus chinensis fall color

Rhus copallina fall color

Rhus copallina, Flameleaf Sumac

Rhus glabra
Smooth Sumac

Perhaps no native plant is as flamboyant as Smooth Sumac in autumn, when large colonies create blankets of fluorescent yellows and reds along the highways and byways of America. Most gardeners consider this species a pernicious weed, however, and would not give it a second thought for general landscape use. The habit is colonizing, suckering, rampant, spreading. The deep green leaves consist of 11 to 31 leaflets, each 2 to 5 in. long, with evenly serrated margins. Flowers are yellowish green and appear in June and July. The fruit, which occur on female plants, are small, hairy, red drupes arranged in a conical, 6- to 10-in.-long panicle. Culture is abysmally easy. Once the plant is invited to the garden, it is like an unwanted guest—difficult to get rid of. Even root pieces will regenerate quickly. Use for naturalizing, on difficult slopes and banks, or in large areas. Seems to outcompete other woody vegetation. Grows 10 to 15 ft. high, considerably greater in spread; I have observed 20-ft.-tall tree forms that were quite attractive. Zones 2 to 9. Most of the United States, parts of Canada.

Cultivars and Varieties. 'Laciniata' is a pretty form, with deeply cut leaflets reminiscent of a fern frond. It is a female and carries the same handsome fruit as the species.

Rhus glabra, Smooth Sumac

Rhus glabra in fall

Rhus typhina
Staghorn Sumac

Rhus glabra fruit

Staghorn Sumac is very similar to the previous species in both appearance and habit. The principal difference is the hairy stems of *Rhus typhina*, as opposed to the non-hairy (glabrous) stems of *R. glabra*. Not as widespread in nature, but this species appears as adaptable as Smooth Sumac under cultivation. Mature size is larger, generally 15 to 25 ft. high, although it can grow 30 to 40 ft. Zones 3 to 8. Quebec to Ontario, south to Georgia and Iowa.

Cultivars and Varieties. 'Laciniata' offers divided leaflets that create a fine-textured, ferny appearance. It is a female.

Rhus glabra 'Laciniata' foliage

Rhus typhina, Staghorn Sumac

Rhus typhina fall color

Rhus typhina 'Laciniata' in fall

Rhus typhina fruit

Ribes alpinum
Alpine Currant

Alpine Currant is a choice shrub for colder climates, where it is often used for masses, hedges, and groupings. The habit is densely twiggy and rounded with stiffly upright stems and spreading branches. The three- to (rarely) five-lobed, bright green leaves, 1 to 2 in. long and wide, develop minimal yellow fall color. The leaves emerge early in spring. Flowers are rather inconspicuous greenish yellow catkins. Fruit are $\frac{1}{4}$- to $\frac{1}{3}$-in.-diameter, scarlet berries that ripen in June and July; they occur on female plants only. Their effect is masked by the foliage, and the fruit are eaten by birds. *Ribes alpinum* is readily transplanted. It is adaptable to virtually any well-drained soil and withstands sun or shade. Does not perform well in high heat. Great plant for northern landscapes. Grows 3 to 6 (to 10) ft. high and wide. Zones 2 to 7. Europe.

Cultivars and Varieties. 'Green Mound' is a dense, dwarf form that is used frequently in the upper Midwest. Grows 2 to 3 ft. high and wide. I have also seen 'Nana', 'Pumila', and 'Compacta' listed.

Ribes alpinum, Alpine Currant

Ribes odoratum
Clove Currant

A rare gem in the shrub world, this species offers wonderfully fragrant, golden yellow flowers in early to mid-April. The habit is upright-arching, usually prolifically suckering. The 1- to 3-in.-wide, three- to five-lobed, rich blue-green leaves turn yellowish to reddish in fall. The flowers have the fragrance of cloves. Quite adaptable to varied soils, in full sun or partial shade. Use in a shrub border or combine with bulbs and wildflowers. Grows 6 to 8 ft. high, greater in spread. Zones 4 to 6(7). Minnesota and South Dakota, south to Arkansas and Texas.

Ribes odoratum, Clove Currant

Ribes odoratum fall color

Ribes odoratum flowers

Ribes alpinum fruit

Robinia hispida

Bristly or Roseacacia Locust

For landscape purposes, the effect of this suckering shrub and that of *Robinia fertilis* are very similar, and their characteristics are almost identical. The one major difference is that *R. hispida* does not set fruit. For both, the branches, petioles, and floral stalks are covered with brown, bristly pubescence. The dark blue-green leaves are composed of 9 to 15 leaflets, each 1 to 2 in. long. Rose to rose-lavender, nonfragrant flowers occur in 2- to 4-in.-long racemes in May and June. Fruit of *R. fertilis* are 2- to 4-in.-long, bristly pods; *R. hispida* lacks fruit. Extremely adaptable, even in infertile, dry soils. Fixes atmospheric nitrogen. A good plant to reclaim waste soil areas. Grows 6 to 10 ft. high, spreads indefinitely. Zones 5 to 8. Southeastern United States.

Robinia hispida, Bristly Locust

Robinia hispida flowers

Robinia pseudoacacia
Black Locust

Black Locust qualifies as a weed tree in many sections of the United States because of its ability to seed and establish quickly on infertile soils. Growth habit varies from a suckering shrub to an upright tree with a narrow, oblong crown. The bluish green leaves seldom change color in fall and die off yellowish brown, at best. The grayish to brownish black bark becomes deeply ridged and furrowed with age. Creamy white, fragrant flowers occur in 4- to 8-in.-long racemes in May and June. Virtually any soil is suitable, but the plant requires full sun for best growth. Black Locust is a great choice for sandy, infertile soils, and it shows respectable salt tolerance. Grows 30 to 50 ft. high. Zones 3 to 8. Pennsylvania to Iowa, south to Georgia and Oklahoma.

Cultivars and Varieties. 'Frisia' offers golden yellow leaves that become green with the heat of summer.

'Umbraculifera' forms a dense, globe-headed outline. Grows 20 ft. high and wide.

Robinia pseudoacacia, Black Locust

Robinia pseudoacacia 'Frisia'

Robinia pseudoacacia foliage

Robinia pseudoacacia bark

Rosa, Rose

With hundreds of species and thousands of cultivars of roses in the world, providing literary and photographic justice to the genus Rosa *is nearly impossible. For the purposes of this book, I will focus on several adaptable shrub species that make excellent additions to borders and are effective in masses or groupings. Some shrub roses are useful as soil-stabilizing agents. Many species-type roses are more resistant to the problems that typically beset the hybrids, but even these shrub species are not without their problems—diseases and pests can take their toll. I remember vividly the excitement of planting* Rosa chinensis *'Mutabilis',* R. roxburghii, R. rubrifolia, *and* R. rugosa *in my Georgia garden. Unfortunately, today only 'Mutabilis' remains, and it is defoliated by black spot in the warm, humid summers. A new wave of "carefree" roses has been introduced that offer greater disease resistance, but these lower maintenance roses are still far from perfect. The Meidiland series has received the most press and indeed are worthy garden subjects. Do not be misled, however, for some disease will develop if climatic conditions are optimal. Use roses with the knowledge that at certain times of the gardening cycle they appear less than pristine.*

Rosa carolina, Carolina Rose

Rosa carolina

Carolina or Pasture Rose

This rather lax, erect-arching species offers lustrous, rich green summer foliage that turns dull red in fall. The 2- to 2½-in.-diameter, single, pink flowers appear in June and July. Red, pear-shaped fruit, ⅓ in. in diameter, ripen in fall and may persist into winter. Grows 6 to 7 ft. high. Zones 4 to 9. Maine to Wisconsin, south to Florida and Texas.

Rosa moyesii, Moyes Rose

Rosa moyesii

Moyes Rose

A beautiful large, rounded shrub with lustrous dark green leaves and 2- to 2½-in.-diameter, blood-red flowers in June and July. Common in European gardens, this is one of the most beautiful of all shrub species in flower. The bright red fruit are 1½ in. long. Grows 6 to 10 ft. high. Zones 5 to 7. Western China.

Cultivars and Varieties. 'Geranium' produces geranium-red flowers and is showier than the typical species.

Rosa moyesii fruit

Rosa moyesii 'Geranium' flower

Rosa rubrifolia (R. glauca)

Redleaf Rose

One of my favorites because of its leaves: glaucous bluish green overcast with reddish purple. New leaves are reddish purple upon emergence. Pink, 1½-in.-diameter flowers bloom in June and are not particularly potent. Flowers on seed-grown plants vary from light to deep pink. The ½-in.-long fruit mature to dark red. Habit is upright-spreading, eventually rounded. Great choice for a colorful addition to a shrub or perennial border. Grows 5 to 7 ft. high. Zones 2 to 8. Mountains of central and southern Europe.

Rosa rubrifolia foliage and flower

Rosa rubrifolia, Redleaf Rose

Rosa rugosa

Rugosa or Saltspray Rose

Perhaps the best known and loved of all shrub roses because of its tenacious constitution, deliciously fragrant flowers, and large, orange-red fruit. Develops into a rounded, suckering shrub that colonizes large areas if not restrained. The leathery, lustrous dark green leaves turn yellow to bronze to orange and red in autumn. White to rose-purple flowers, 2½ to 3½ in. in diameter, open from June through August, and sporadically into September and October. The 1-in.-diameter, tomatolike fruit ripen from August through fall. The species has been utilized in breeding because of its disease resistance. Many single- and double-flowered forms are known. Grows 4 to 6 ft. high. Zones 2 to 7. Northern China, Korea, Japan.

Cultivars and Varieties. Some of the better cultivars include: 'Albo-plena' (double, fragrant, pure white), 'Belle Poitevine' (semidouble, slightly fragrant, light mauve-pink with showy yellow stamens), 'Blanc Double de Coubert' (double, fragrant, pure white), and 'Frau Dagmar Hastrup' (prolific bloomer, fragrant, light pink flowers, large red fruit).

Rosa rubrifolia fruit

Rosa rugosa flower

Rosa rugosa fruit

Rosa spinosissima
Scotch Rose

The overwhelming variation in this species contributes to taxonomic nightmares but also serves as a gardener's delight. The only common feature I can find is the bright green leaves that are composed of five to eleven rounded, delicate leaflets, each ½ to 1 in. long. The plant varies in habit from groundcoverlike to 3- to 4-ft.-high, mounded shrubs. White, yellow, or pink, 1- to 2-in.-diameter, single flowers are borne in profusion on short branches along the stems in May and June. Blackish to dark brown fruit range from ½ to ¾ in. in diameter. One of the most widely distributed rose species in its native range. Zones 4 to 8. Europe, western Asia.

Rosa rugosa, Rugosa Rose

Rosa rugosa 'Frau Dagmar Hastrup' flower

Rosa rugosa 'Frau Dagmar Hastrup' fruit

Rosa spinosissima, Scotch Rose

Rosa spinosissima flowers

Rosa virginiana
Virginia Rose

A lovely native species, Virginia Rose bears 2- to 2½-in.-diameter, pink flowers. The glossy dark green foliage develops excellent yellow to red fall color. Bright red, ½-in.-diameter fruit persist into winter, and the reddish canes also provide winter interest. Very adaptable and at home by the sea or inland. I have never observed black spot on this species. Grows 4 to 6 ft. high. Zones 3 to 7(8). Newfoundland to Virginia, Alabama, and Missouri.

Rosa virginiana, Virginia Rose

Rosa virginiana flower

Rosa virginiana fruit

Rosa Hybrids
Lower Maintenance Roses

As mentioned earlier, breeders and nursery people are working to develop low-maintenance roses that require little or no care. Gardeners should be alert for new introductions in their particular region of the United States.

Cultivars and Varieties. The Meidiland series offers colors of white, pink, and red, in single and double forms. The old standards 'The Fairy' (pink) and 'Seafoam' (white), seen throughout New England, are excellent plants for low masses or groundcover and provide good color in June and July.

'Carefree Beauty' and 'Carefree Wonder' are impressive forms with fragrant, pink, semidouble flowers from June until frost. In tests conducted in Wisconsin and in Massachusetts, plants were completely free of mildew and black spot; black spot is problematic in Zones 7 and 8.

'Nearly Wild' has single, pink, dogwood-like flowers all season long. It is disease resistant.

Agricultural Canada has introduced a whole range of disease-resistant, cold-hardy cultivars, including 'Champlain' (dark red flowers), 'Charles Albanel' (medium red), 'J. P. Connell' (yellow), 'John Davis' (medium pink), 'Rugosa Ottawa' (purple, excellent disease resistance), 'William Baffin' (deep pink, climber), and others.

Rosa 'Carefree Beauty' flowers

Rosa 'Carefree Beauty'

Rosa 'The Fairy'

Rosa 'Nearly Wild' flowers

Salix alba 'Tristis'

Weeping-Gold White Willow

This is one of the best loved and most hated trees in landscape history. The graceful weeping habit and the long, trailing, supple stems, golden in the winter sun, have inspired poets and artists along with gardeners. This cultivar develops a rounded outline with age, and it can overtake portions of real estate thought to be uninhabitable. The lustrous rich green, 1½- to 4-in.-long summer leaves may turn shimmering yellow in fall. Interestingly, it is one of the first trees to leaf out and one of the last to shed its leaves. Bark on mature trunks is yellowish brown to brown in color and corky in texture. Plant in moist soils alongside a stream or lake where the long branches can brush the surface of the water. Susceptible to canker. Can be a messy tree, as the small branches and twigs constantly litter the ground. Grows 50 to 70 ft. high and wide. Zones 4 to 9. Southern Europe to western Siberia, central Asia, China.

Salix alba 'Tristis' catkins

Salix alba 'Tristis', Weeping-Gold White Willow, in fall

Salix babylonica

Babylon Weeping Willow

Although many weeping willows are sold under this name, very few, if any, are the real thing. The true form is a graceful, refined tree with a short, stout trunk and a broad-rounded crown of weeping branches that sweep the ground. The supple stems are reddish brown in winter, never yellow like those of *Salix alba* 'Tristis'. Grows 30 to 40 ft. high and wide. Zones 6 to 8. China.

Cultivars and Varieties. 'Crispa' ('Annularis') is an unusual form, with spirally curled leaves.

Salix babylonica 'Crispa' leaves

Salix caprea
Pussy or Goat Willow

Salix babylonica, Babylon Weeping Willow

When winter has lulled many people into a blue-gray funk, this species offers hope that, yes, spring is just around the corner. In Washington, DC, I have seen Pussy Willow in flower as early as late February. The habit is distinctly upright, almost oval in outline. Although considered a shrub, more often the species has the habit of a small tree. The 2- to 4-in.-long, dark green leaves have slightly crisped and crimped margins. Yellowish brown to dark brown stems are studded with ¼- to ⅓-in.-long, purple-brown buds that open to expose soft, furry, 1- to 2-in.-long, grayish male catkins in March and April. The branches can be cut and forced earlier for use in arrangements. The species grows in virtually any soil, particularly those that are moist, and prefers full sun. In most cases, it is short lived because of insect and disease problems. Use in moist or wet areas of the landscape. Could be used in a shrub border. Grows 15 to 25 ft. high, 12 to 15 ft. wide. Zones 4 to 8. Europe.

Salix chaenomeloides, Japanese Pussy Willow, is similar in most respects to *S. caprea*. It is a large shrub with stout, reddish purple stems and fat, ½-in.-long, red buds that open to silver-gray catkins.

Cultivars and Varieties. 'Pendula' is a weeping form of *Salix caprea* that is often grafted on a standard. Makes a handsome accent for the small garden.

Salix caprea, Pussy Willow

Salix caprea leaf

Salix caprea male catkins

Salix elaeagnos *(S. rosmarinifolia)*
Rosemary Willow

A virtual unknown among shrubby willows, but an ideal plant for foliage effect in the border or along streams and other moist areas. Rosemary Willow develops a strongly multistemmed, oval-rounded habit. The 3- to 4-in.-long leaves are only ⅛ to ⅞ in. wide. They are dark green above and covered with white, woolly pubescence below. From a distance, the effect is a pleasing gray-green color. Like all willows, *Salix elaeagnos* is easy to grow and thrives in moist areas. Longwood Gardens prunes the plant to within 6 to 12 in. of the ground each spring to force long shoots during the growing season. Grows 6 to 10 ft. high and wide. Zones 4 to 7. Mountains of central and southern Europe, Asia Minor.

Salix elaeagnos, Rosemary Willow

Salix elaeagnos leaves

Salix gracilistyla
Rosegold Pussy Willow

Another pussy willow type, this species offers 1¼-in.-long, grayish catkins tinged with pink that open in March and April. The pinkish character seems to be variable from plant to plant. The 2- to 4-in.-long, grayish green leaves provide a diversion from the typical green. A mounded, wide-spreading shrub. Grows 6 to 10 ft. high. Zones 5 to 7. Japan, Korea.

Cultivars and Varieties. 'Melanostachys' is often referred to as Black Pussy Willow because of its deep purple-black male catkins. The stems also assume a rich purple-black color in winter. The catkins are smaller than those of typical *Salix gracilistyla*. Sometimes listed as *Salix* 'Melanostachys' or *S. melanostachys*, it is most likely a hybrid or cultivar of *S. gracilistyla*.

Salix gracilistyla, Roseglow Pussy Willow

Salix gracilistyla catkins

Salix matsudana
Hankow Willow

The species is seldom seen in cultivation, but it is represented by several cultivars, of which 'Tortuosa' is the most common. Grows 40 to 50 ft. high. Zones 5 to 8. China.

Cultivars and Varieties. 'Golden Curls' is a hybrid between *Salix alba* 'Tristis' and *S. matsudana* 'Tortuosa'. It has slightly contorted, golden stems and somewhat curled leaves. Growth habit is semipendulous.

'Scarlet Curls' has contorted stems that are reddish in winter and curled leaves.

'Tortuosa', Contorted Hankow Willow, is the most commonly encountered Hankow Willow in the United States. Habit is upright-oval to rounded, with slender, yellow-brown, gnarled and contorted branches. The more vigorous the growth, the more contorted the stems. Leaves are similar to those of *Salix alba*. In many parts of the United States, this is a short-lived tree. Use as a short-time investment or cut back heavily (pollard) to encourage vigorous shoots. Provide moist soil. Grows 30 to 40 ft. high.

Salix matsudana 'Tortuosa', Contorted Hankow Willow

Salix purpurea
Purpleosier Willow

This is a good choice for stabilizing stream banks and covering large, moist areas. *Salix purpurea* is a rounded, dense, finely branched shrub that becomes unsightly if not occasionally pruned back to the ground. The dark blue-green leaves are 2 to 4 in. long and ⅛ to ⅓ in. wide and hold late in fall. Grows 8 to 10 (to 18) ft. high and wide. Zones 3 to 6(7). Europe, northern Africa, Asia.

Cultivars and Varieties. 'Nana' is a compact form with dark blue-green leaves. Grows 5 ft. high and wide.

'Pendula' is a more or less wide-spreading, weeping form that is often grafted on a standard.

Salix purpurea, Purpleosier Willow

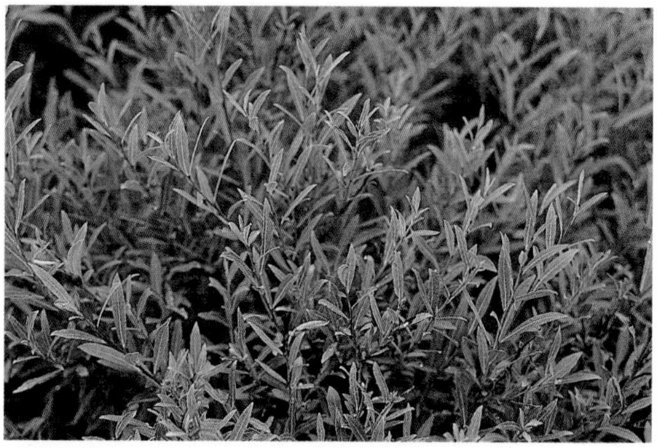

Salix purpurea foliage

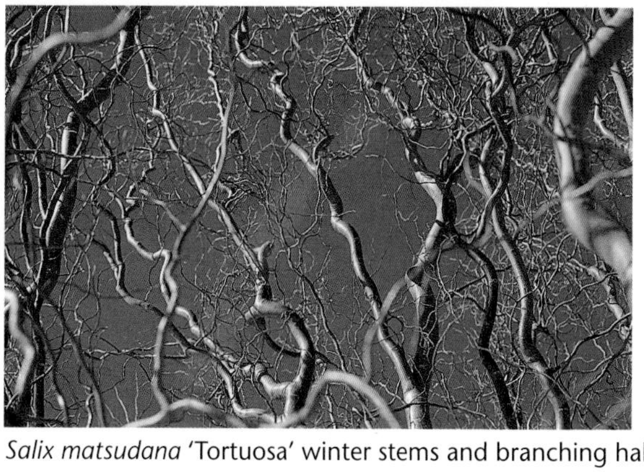

Salix matsudana 'Tortuosa' winter stems and branching habit

Salix sachalinensis 'Sekka'

Japanese Fantail Willow

This interesting cultivar has fasciated, flat, and twisted branches that can be utilized in floral arrangements. To maximize this condition, prune severely in late winter. The lustrous dark green leaves are 4 to 6 in. long and 3/4 in. wide. 'Sekka' is a male clone with pretty, 1/2- to 3/4-in.-long, grayish catkins in March. It develops into a broad-rounded shrub. Definitely not a choice for the small property. Grows 10 to 15 ft. high and wide. Zones 4 to 7. Japan.

Salix sachalinensis 'Sekka', Japanese Fantail Willow

Salix sachalinensis 'Sekka' branch and buds

Salix sachalinensis 'Sekka' catkins

Sambucus canadensis

American Elder, Elderberry

Perhaps no shrub is more common than *Sambucus canadensis* along roadways, where it often inhabits moist ditches. Large and scruffy, usually broad-rounded in outline, American Elder is only suitable for rough areas of the garden. The bright green leaves are composed of seven 2- to 6-in.-long leaflets. The chief merits are the 6- to 10-in.-diameter, creamy cymes of flowers in June and July and the 1/4-in.-diameter, purple-black fruit in August and September, which can be used for jellies and wine. Prefers moist soils and full sun. Grows 5 to 12 ft. high and wide. Zones 3 to 9. Nova Scotia and Manitoba, south to Florida and Texas.

Sambucus canadensis, American Elder

Sambucus nigra

Common or European Elder

This species does not appear to be as well adapted to the heat of North America as *Sambucus canadensis*. The general characteristics of the two shrubs are similar, except the inflorescences of European Elder are smaller, about 5 to 8 in. in diameter, and the leaves are composed of three to seven (usually five) leaflets. Like *S. canadensis* in America, *S. nigra* is a weed species in Europe, inhabiting moist or wet areas and flowering in June and July. Grows 10 to 20 ft. high; may develop into a small tree, and 30-ft.-tall plants are known. Zones 5 to 6(7). Europe, northern Africa, western Asia.

Cultivars and Varieties. Several cultivars with variegated foliage are available. The most interesting is 'Laciniata', which has finely dissected leaflets.

Sambucus canadensis foliage

Sambucus canadensis fruit

Sambucus nigra flowers

Sambucus nigra 'Laciniata' foliage

Sambucus nigra, European Elder

Sambucus racemosa
European Red Elder

Another dubious species for culture in the heat of North America; best where summers are cool. White flowers occur in pyramidal panicles and are followed by red fruit. Grows 8 to 12 ft. high and wide. Zones 3 to 6(7). Europe, western Asia.

Cultivars and Varieties. 'Plumosa Aurea' is a handsome form with finely cut leaflets and bright yellow new leaves that mature to green.

'Sutherland Golden' is similar to the previous cultivar, but it is probably more cold hardy.

Sambucus racemosa, European Red Elder

Sambucus racemosa flowers

Sambucus racemosa fruit

Sambucus racemosa 'Plumosa Aurea'

Sarcococca hookerana

Himalayan Sarcococca, Sweetbox

A wonderful plant for a shady environment, this shrub offers lustrous dark green evergreen foliage and small, cream-colored, sweetly fragrant flowers in March and April. The habit is variable; generally a multistemmed, suckering shrub. Fruit are $\frac{1}{3}$-in.-diameter, shiny black drupes, normally not produced in great quantities. Prefers organic, moist, well-drained soils, but I have observed it looking rather prosperous under severe water stress. Possibly more stress tolerant than it is generally given credit for. Use in combination with ericaceous and other shade-loving plants. Grows 4 to 6 ft. high, greater in spread. Zones (5)6 to 8. Western Himalayas, Afghanistan.

Cultivars and Varieties. var. *humilis* is the most common form of Himalayan Sarcococca in the commercial sector. The habit is more uniform than that of the species. For groundcover use in shade, it is a first-rate plant. Grows $1\frac{1}{2}$ to 2 ft. high. Zones 5 to 8.

Sarcococca hookerana, Sweetbox

Sarcococca hookerana foliage

Sarcococca hookerana flowers

Sarcococca hookerana var. *humilis*

Sassafras albidum
Common Sassafras

If a third grader had to pick but one tree to include in his or her leaf collection, this would be it. The leaves are entire, three-lobed, or mitten-shaped. The "mittens" come in left- and right-hand versions. The bright green foliage turns brilliant shades of yellow, orange, and red in autumn. Next to *Nyssa sylvatica*, Black Tupelo, this may be the best native tree for fall color. The growth habit varies from pyramidal to highly irregular. Many short, stout, contorted branches spread to form a flat-topped, irregular, round-oblong head at maturity. The dark cinnamon to reddish brown bark is deeply ridged and furrowed. Yellow flowers appear in April before the leaves. Female plants produce ½-in.-long, oblong, dark blue fruit. Unfortunately, Common Sassafras is almost impossible to transplant and must be moved as a small container-grown plant. Adaptable to varied soils with low pH. Great tree for naturalistic plantings. Grows 30 to 60 ft. high, 25 to 40 ft. wide. Zones 4 to 8. Maine to Ontario and Michigan, south to Florida and Texas.

Sassafras albidum, Common Sassafras, in fall

Sassafras albidum foliage

Sassafras albidum fall color

Schizophragma hydrangeoides
Japanese Hydrangea-Vine

Sassafras albidum flowers

Sassafras albidum fruit

Schizophragma hydrangeoides foliage

Schizophragma hydrangeoides 'Roseum' flowers

In recent years, this species has achieved cult status, particularly the silvery leaved cultivar 'Moonlight'. A true clinging vine, this species is similar to *Hydrangea anomala* subsp. *petiolaris*, Climbing Hydrangea. Japanese Hydrangea-Vine offers lovely lustrous dark green, 2- to 4-in.-long, coarsely serrated leaves and 8- to 10-in.-wide, flattish inflorescences in June and July. One major difference between Japanese Hydrangea-Vine and Climbing Hydrangea is the shape of the sepals: the sepals of the former are single and ovate; those of the latter are three to five parted. Uses and culture are similar to that of *H. anomala* subsp. *petiolaris*. Grows to 30 ft. Zones 5 to 7(8). Japan.

Cultivars and Varieties. 'Roseum' has rich pink to rose-colored, showy sepals. When the color is fully developed, the effect is striking.

Schizophragma hydrangeoides, Japanese Hydrangea-Vine

Sciadopitys verticillata
Japanese Umbrellapine

An oddly textured needle evergreen, like a relic from the past. Certainly a unique and artistic specimen plant where it can be grown. Habit is variable, from spirelike to broadly pyramidal. The 2- to 5-in.-long, dark green needles spread in whorls from the ends of the branches. The bark on old specimens is orangish to reddish brown and exfoliates in plates and strips. Not a fast-growing evergreen; expect about 6 in. per year. Plant in moist, well-drained soils, in full sun to partial shade. Magnificent specimens are found in the New England states. Great for specimen use or perhaps in a border. Patience is the key. Grows 20 to 30 ft. high, 15 to 20 ft. wide. Zones 4 to 8. Japan.

Sciadopitys verticillata, Japanese Umbrellapine

Sciadopitys verticillata needles

Sciadopitys verticillata bark

Shepherdia argentea
Silver Buffaloberry

Many people express excitement about this species, but I have yet to see one that stimulates my gardening juices. The plant is typically an open shrub, with leafy branches terminating in 1- to 2-in.-long spines. The slender, 1- to 2-in.-long leaves are covered with silvery scales on both surfaces. Small, yellowish flowers are followed by orange to red fruit. Utilize in infertile, dry, alkaline soils. Prefers sunny, open areas. Most plants growing on the East Coast are smaller than the typical Midwest version. Grows 6 to 10 (to 18) ft. high. Zones 2 to 6. Plains States.

Shepherdia argentea, Silver Buffaloberry

Shepherdia canadensis, Russet Buffaloberry

Shepherdia canadensis foliage

Shepherdia argentea branch and foliage

Shepherdia canadensis
Russet Buffaloberry

This is a variable species, generally loosely branched and rounded in outline, with ½- to 2-in.-long leaves that are dark green above and silver below. Essentially like *Shepherdia argentea* in flower and fruit. No great redeeming characteristics, however. Grows 6 to 8 ft. high, 3 to 9 ft. wide. Zones 2 to 6. Newfoundland to Alaska, south to Maine, Ohio, and northern Mexico.

Skimmia japonica
Japanese Skimmia

An absolutely magnificent plant in its finest forms. Unfortunately, this shrub is better adapted to the cool, moist climate of Europe than to the vagaries of midwestern and eastern North America. Habit is rounded to haystack-shaped, and it is clothed by dark green, 2½- to 5-in.-long evergreen leaves. Creamy white flowers occur in 2- to 3-in.-long, 1- to 2-in.-wide, upright terminal panicles in April. Globose, ⅓-in.-diameter, bright red fruit occur only on female plants. If the plant is under drought stress, mite infestations are problematic. Transplant from a container into organic-laden, moist, well-drained soils, in shady environments. A great plant for shady nooks of the garden. Use in combination with rhododendrons and azaleas. Grows 3 to 4 ft. high and wide. Zones 6 to 8. Japan.

Cultivars and Varieties. 'Rubella' and several other cultivars have deep maroon-red flower buds that are actually more attractive than the open white flowers.

Skimmia japonica, Japanese Skimmia

Skimmia japonica fruit

Skimmia japonica flowers

Skimmia japonica 'Rubella' flower buds

Skimmia reevesiana
Reeves Skimmia

This shrub is lower growing, more loose and open, and less attractive than the previous species, but it does have the advantage of being perfect-flowered. The 1- to 4-in.-long, dark green evergreen leaves are narrower than those of *Skimmia japonica*. The white, fragrant flowers are followed by oval to pear-shaped, ⅓-in.-long, crimson fruit that persist into winter. Culture is similar to that of the previous species. Considered more cold hardy than *S. japonica*, but there is no hard evidence to support this. Grows 1½ to 3 ft. high, 2 to 3 ft. wide. Zones 6 to 7. China.

Skimmia reevesiana, Reeves Skimmia, foliage, fruit, and flower buds

Sophora japonica
Japanese Pagodatree, Scholar-Tree

In the scheme of great trees, the Japanese Pagodatree ranks in the first order. A full-grown tree is an impressive sight, with branches that seem to stretch to infinity, rich green leaves without a care in the world, and fragrant, cream-colored flowers that create a frothy mass over the canopy. Even young trees, particularly the better cultivars, display a dense, rounded, full crown and make their presence known. With age the tree assumes an upright-spreading to broadly rounded crown. The lustrous green leaves do not develop significant fall color. In July and August, the creamy panicles, 6 to 12 in. high and wide, cover the foliage in a lacy veil. The fruit are 3- to 8-in.-long pods that change from pea-green to yellow and brown. They can be somewhat messy when they abscise. Soils should be well drained; otherwise, the species is quite adaptable. Japanese Pagodatree requires tremendous space and is best reserved for large-area use. Grows 50 to 70 ft. high and wide. Zones 4 to 7. China, Korea.

Cultivars and Varieties. 'Pendula' is a weeping type that should not be used by the faint of heart—the branches are rather frightening, particularly in the winter landscape.

'Regent' has excellent vigor and a handsome oval-rounded form. It flowers at an early age.

Sophora japonica, Japanese Pagodatree

Sophora japonica flowers

Sophora japonica fruit

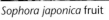

MORE ➤

Sophora japonica continued

Sophora japonica 'Pendula'

Sorbaria aitchisonii
Kashmir Falsespirea

Sorbaria arborea
Tree Falsespirea

I have great difficulty distinguishing between these two species. Both shrubs bear immense (12 to 15 (to 18) in. long and 8 to 14 in. wide), fleecy panicles of creamy white flowers in July and August. The flowers are spectacular, but they mature to a rather dirty brown and should be removed. The leaves of *Sorbaria aitchisonii* are composed of 11 to 23 leaflets, each 2 to 4 in. long and ¼ to ⅝ in. wide; those of *S. arborea* are composed of 13 to 17 leaflets, generally wider than those of the former. Both require well-drained soils, full sun, and plenty of real estate. The best specimens I have observed were on Cape Cod, growing in essentially pure sand. Like *S. sorbifolia*, they appear to be quite heat and drought tolerant. Both grow 10 to 15 ft. high and wide. Zones 5 to 7. Asia.

Sorbaria aitchisonii, Kashmir Falsespirea

Sorbaria aitchisonii flowers

Sorbaria arborea flowers

Sorbaria sorbifolia
Ural Falsespirea

Sorbaria arborea, Tree Falsespirea

This rather obscure plant offers a gorgeous display of creamy white flowers on a suckering, multistemmed shrub. The 8- to 12-in.-long leaves are composed of 13 to 25 deep green leaflets, each 2 to 4 in. long. New growth has a reddish tinge before maturing. Flowers occur in 4- to 10-in.-long, fleecy terminal panicles in June and July. Plant in well-drained soils, in full sun. Appears to be a good choice for dry soils, especially where mass-type cover is required. One of the first shrubs to leaf out in spring. Can become somewhat invasive because of its spreading, suckering nature. Grows 5 to 10 ft. high, wider at maturity. Zones 2 to 7. Northern Asia to Japan.

Sorbaria sorbifolia new foliage

Sorbaria sorbifolia flowers

Sorbaria sorbifolia, Ural Falsespirea

Sorbus, Mountainash

In general, mountainashes are among the most beautiful trees for fruit effect, but they are beset with borer and canker problems, which limits their use in hostile environments. All species discussed here prefer cool climates for best growth.

Sorbus alnifolia
Korean Mountainash

Korean Mountainash is generally more adaptable than the other mountainashes. The habit is softly pyramidal in youth, becoming pyramidal-oval to rounded with age. The simple, beechlike foliage is atypical for a mountainash. Leaves emerge a bright, fresh spring green, turn lustrous dark green, and then mellow to yellow, golden brown, and orange in fall—truly inspirational! Young stems develop diamond-shaped lenticels; older branches become smooth and gray, resembling beech bark. White flowers occur in 2- to 3-in.-diameter corymbs in May, somewhat alternate in abundance from year to year. Fruit can be spectacular, ripening with the fall foliage in September and October, in colors ranging from pinkish red to orangish red and scarlet. At its best, this species has perhaps the most magnificent fruit display of all the *Sorbus* species. Easily grown in well-drained soils and full sun. The species is not borer resistant, and excessive stress, such as urban settings, will induce problems. Use against an evergreen background to maximize ornamental effects. Grows 40 to 50 ft. high, 20 to 30 (to 50) ft. wide. Zones 3 to 6(7). Central China, Korea, Japan.

Sorbus alnifolia, Korean Mountainash

Sorbus americana
American Mountainash

This species is native to eastern North America, but it is seldom available in commerce. Variable in habit, American Mountainash can grow as a shrub or as a small tree with a short trunk and spreading, slender branches that form a rounded crown. Foliage, flowers, and fruit are similar to those of *Sorbus aucuparia* (although the fruit may be redder). Grows along the borders of cold swamps and bogs, as well as on the sides of mountaintops in relatively dry soils. If native, this species is worth preserving. It is certainly handsome in fruit. Grows 10 to 30 ft. high and wide. Zones 2 to 5. Newfoundland to Manitoba, south to Michigan and in the southern Appalachians to Georgia.

Sorbus alnifolia flowers

Sorbus alnifolia fruit

Sorbus alnifolia fall color

Sorbus americana foliage and flowers

Sorbus americana, American Mountainash

Sorbus americana fruit

Sorbus aria
Whitebeam Mountainash

Although rarely utilized in the United States, this species enjoys popularity in European gardens. It has many of the same requirements and difficulties as *Sorbus aucuparia*, European Mountainash, and using Whitebeam Mountainash in the average landscape is like a roll of the dice. However, the silvery backed, simple leaves and the large, orange-red to scarlet fruit have tempted more than one gardener to take that chance. The habit is oval to broad-pyramidal. The foliage effect is beautiful, especially on windy days when the leaves are buffeted about. A worthwhile tree in the Pacific Northwest, perhaps in the Northeast and Canada as well. Grows 35 to 45 ft. high. Zones 4 to 5. Europe.

Sorbus aria, Whitebeam Mountainash

Sorbus aria leaf

Sorbus aucuparia
European Mountainash

This is the most widely available mountainash species in the United States, and the brilliant display of orange-red fruit justifies any attempt to grow it. The habit is erect and oval in youth, becoming ovate or spherical with age. The leaves are composed of 9 to 15 dark green leaflets, each ¾ to 2½ in. long. Foliage changes to yellow, red, and reddish purple in fall. Bark is shiny gray-brown and smooth, becoming slightly roughened on old trunks. White, rather malodorous flowers occur in 3- to 5-in.-diameter corymbs in May. The fruit ripen in late August and September, but they make palatable bird food and seldom last very long. Provide acid or high pH, moist, well-drained soils; keep stress to a minimum. When right, it makes a very pretty fruiting tree. Grows 20 to 40 (to 60) ft. high, 15 to 25 (to 40) ft. wide. Zones 3 to 6(7). Europe, western Asia, Siberia.

Cultivars and Varieties. 'Beissneri' displays rich copper-brown bark.

'Pendula', a weeping form, bears orange fruit.

Sorbus aucuparia flowers

Sorbus aucuparia fruit

Sorbus aucuparia, European Mountainash

Spiraea albiflora, Japanese White Spirea

Spiraea, Spirea

Spireas grow best in well-drained, preferably acid soils, in full sun. These plants are not seriously troubled by insects or diseases, although aphids are an occasional problem. If pruning is necessary, Spiraea albiflora, S. ×bumalda, *and* S. japonica *should be pruned in late winter, since these species flower on new growth of the season; all other* Spiraea *species discussed here should be pruned after flowering, since flowers are formed on the previous year's growth.*

Spiraea albiflora

Japanese White Spirea

This species is often listed as 'Albiflora', a selection of *Spiraea japonica*, but it is treated separately here for emphasis. It is a low, mounded, densely branched shrub with 2½-in.-long, almost blue-green leaves. The foliage is topped with 2- to 3-in.-diameter, white, flattish inflorescences in June. *Spiraea albiflora* is a great filler in a perennial or shrub border and is wonderful in groupings or masses. This and many of the other compact spireas make excellent large groundcover masses, particularly because of their late spring to summer flowering. Grows 2 to 3 ft. high and wide. Zones (4)5 to 8. Japan.

Spiraea ×bumalda
Bumald Spirea

This category includes the hybrids of *Spiraea albiflora* and *S. japonica*. Since *S. ×bumalda* does not occur in cultivation, only the cultivars are discussed. Zones 4 to 8.

Cultivars and Varieties. 'Anthony Waterer' is the old standard. It has 4- to 6-in.-wide, carmine-pink inflorescences. Often produces yellow to cream branch reversions. Be careful when buying this cultivar; several forms are sold under this name. Grows 3 to 4 ft. high, 5 to 6 ft. wide.

'Crispa' is a cutleaf form, but in most other respects it is similar to 'Anthony Waterer'. It develops branch reversions of cream to yellow. Subject to aphids and chlorosis. 'Dolchica' is similar.

'Froebelii' is supposedly smaller than 'Anthony Waterer' and has deeper carmine-pink flowers. Most 'Froebelii' I have seen in cultivation, however, have lighter pink flowers. I have not observed branch reversions.

'Goldflame' is an old reliable cultivar with russet-orange to bronze-red new growth that changes to soft yellow, yellow-green, and finally green. The cooler the temperatures, the more intense the yellow coloration. The pink flowers are a little difficult to digest next to the yellow foliage. Produces green and gold shoots. May produce excellent bronze-red to red fall color.

Spiraea ×bumalda 'Anthony Waterer'

Spiraea ×bumalda 'Anthony Waterer' flowers

Spiraea ×bumalda 'Crispa' foliage

Spiraea ×bumalda 'Goldflame'

Spiraea ×bumalda 'Goldflame' fall color

Spiraea cantoniensis 'Lanceata'

Double Reeves Spirea

At its best, this plant provides excellent early spring foliage and a profusion of white, buttonlike, double flowers. Unfortunately, the leaves and flower buds, which open in March and April, are often severely hurt by low temperatures. The habit is gracefully arching, forming a mounded outline. The 1- to 2½-in.-long, bluish green leaves are handsome throughout the seasons and hold into late fall. The ½-in.-wide flowers appear in terminal corymbs in April and are effective for two to three weeks. Utilize in a border or in groupings. Grows 4 to 6 ft. high and wide. Zones 6 to 9. China, Japan.

Spiraea cantoniensis 'Lanceata', Double Reeves Spirea

Spiraea japonica

Japanese Spirea

This species is very similar to *Spiraea* ×*bumalda*, and the two are often confused for one another. Japanese Spirea tends to be more upright in habit. The leaves range from 1 to 3 in. long and have distinct sharp serrations. Flowers range from white to pink (occasionally red) and are borne in flat-topped corymbs in June. Grows 4 to 5 ft. high. Zones 4 to 8. Japan, China, Korea.

Spiraea cantoniensis 'Lanceata' flowers

Cultivars and Varieties. var. *alpina* is a dainty, fine-textured, low-growing, wide-spreading form with pink flowers and blue-green foliage. Grows 1 to 2½ ft. high.

'Goldmound' has rich golden yellow leaves, and the foliage color holds much better than that of *Spiraea* ×*bumalda* 'Goldflame' in the heat. Flowers are pink. Grows 2½ to 3½ ft. high. 'Golden Princess' and 'Limemound' are similar golden-foliaged cultivars.

'Little Princess' is a large version of var. *alpina*, with pink flowers and a more rounded habit. Grows 2½ ft. high or more.

'Shibori' ('Shirobana') may be the best of the *Spiraea japonica* types. It offers deep rose, pink, and white flowers on the same plant. After a time, the pink flowers seem to dominate. A vigorous, rounded cultivar with lustrous dark green leaves and a recurrent flowering habit. Leafs out earlier than other cultivars. Grows 3½ to 4 ft. high and wide.

Spiraea japonica, Japanese Spirea

MORE ➤

Spiraea japonica continued

Spiraea japonica 'Goldmound'

Spiraea japonica 'Little Princess'

Spiraea japonica 'Shibori' flowers

Spiraea nipponica 'Snowmound'

Snowmound Nippon Spirea

For some strange reason, this selection is commonly used in the Midwest but seldom in great quantities anywhere else. The tight-knit branches are covered with 1- to 1½-in.-long, dark blue-green leaves. White flowers cover the branches in May and June. It is a superb plant for use on banks, in masses, or in groupings. With time, it develops into a shapely, rounded shrub. Grows 3 to 5 ft. high and wide. Zones 4 to 8. Japan.

Spiraea prunifolia

Bridalwreath Spirea

Along with *Spiraea* ×*vanhouttei*, this is the spirea species with which the general gardening public is most familiar. To my mind, it does not measure up to the newer, more compact spireas (such as the *S.* ×*bumalda* and *S. japonica* types), but it has withstood the test of time around farmsteads and residences for over 100 years. The habit is open, straggly, and leggy, with the bulk of the foliage on the upper half of the plant. The 1- to 2-in.-long, lustrous dark green leaves turn yellow-orange to purplish brown in fall. Double, white, ⅓-in.-diameter flowers occur three to six together along the naked stems in April. Probably of little value in modern gardens compared to some of the other spireas. Grows 4 to 9 ft. high, 6 to 8 ft. wide. Zones 4 to 8. Korea, China, Taiwan.

Spiraea prunifolia flowers

Spiraea nipponica 'Snowmound', Snowmound Nippon Spirea

Spiraea prunifolia, Bridalwreath Spirea

Spiraea prunifolia foliage

Spiraea thunbergii
Thunberg Spirea

I take great delight in this wispy, fine-textured shrub. It offers light green, willow-like leaves, five-petaled, single, white flowers, and a bulldog's tenacity that allows it to prosper in virtually any environment. The ultimate form is gracefully arching with a rounded-mounded outline. The yellowish green leaves are 1 to 1½ in. long and ⅛ to ¼ in. wide and turn orange and bronze in autumn. The ⅓- to ½-in.-diameter flowers appear on naked branches in March and April, well ahead of the majority of flowering shrubs. Makes a great mass effect, or it can be used for color and textural purposes in the shrub border. Grows 3 to 5 ft. high and wide. Zones 4 to 8. Japan, China.

Spiraea ×*arguta*, Garland Spirea, is closely related, but it flowers later and grows slightly larger. The leaves are entire at the base, while those of *S. thunbergii* are serrated to the base.

Spiraea thunbergii, Thunberg Spirea

Spiraea thunbergii flowers

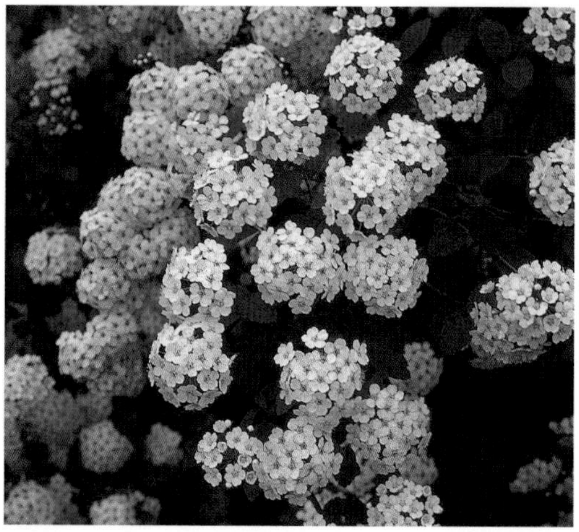

Spiraea ×*vanhouttei* flowers

Spiraea thunbergii foliage

Spiraea ×*vanhouttei*
Vanhoutte Spirea

The granddaddy of all spireas, Vanhoutte Spirea has greater representation in the gardens of America than any other *Spiraea* species or cultivar. The habit is distinctly arching and fountainlike. The ¾- to 1¾-in.-long leaves are often three lobed and have a distinct blue-green color. White flowers, which appear in May after the leaves, are raised above the foliage in 1- to 2-in.-diameter inflorescences. In flower, the shrub is extremely showy, one of the main reasons for its great popularity. Extremely durable, and in some respects it can be like an uninvited guest—unwanted after a period of time. Grows 6 to 8 (to 10) ft. high, 10 to 12 ft. wide. Zones 3 to 8(9).

Spiraea ×*vanhouttei*, Vanhoutte Spirea

Stachyurus praecox

I have always waffled about the merits of this coarse, almost cumbersome shrub, but after observing a number of specimens in respectable flower, I believe it merits consideration. It forms a broad-mounded outline and bears 3- to 7-in.-long, lustrous dark green leaves. No appreciable fall color develops. Small, pale yellow (yellow-brown) flowers appear in 2- to 3-in.-long, pendulous racemes from each axil in April. The flowers occur on naked stems and resemble long beaded chains. The U.S. National Arboretum has a particularly long-flowered form (6-in. racemes) that is definitely superior to the typical species. Site in moist, acid, organic, well-drained soils, in partial shade; plants in hot, dry sites and full sun will never prosper. This is not a shrub for every garden, but in a woodland or naturalized setting, it might prove a good fit. Grows 4 to 6 (to 8) ft. high, possibly wider at maturity. Zones 6 to 8. Japan.

Stachyurus praecox

Stachyurus praecox flowers

Stephanandra incisa

Cutleaf Stephanandra

This shrub forms a graceful mass of spreading, arching branches, and it suckers freely from the base. Yellowish white flowers appear in May and June and are not showy. Prefers acid, well-drained soils, in full sun or partial shade. The species is seldom used in contemporary landscaping, having been replaced by the cultivar 'Crispa'. Grows 4 to 7 ft. high, equal or greater in spread. Zones 3 to 7. Japan, Korea.

Cultivars and Varieties. 'Crispa' has 1- to 2-in.-long, bright green, deeply cut leaves that produce a fine texture. It forms a thick tangle of branches that root along their length, resulting in a wide-spreading groundcover. Grows 1½ to 3 ft. high.

Stephanandra incisa, Cutleaf Stephanandra

Stephanandra incisa 'Crispa'

Stewartia koreana
Korean Stewartia

Many people insist that Korean Stewartia is distinctly different from *Stewartia pseudocamellia*, Japanese Stewartia, but from all landscape standpoints, they are similar. I have looked at enough plants of each species and I simply cannot reliably distinguish them. On selected specimens of this species, more vivid red fall color and perhaps greater exfoliation of the bark are evident. Forms a pyramidal outline. Several nursery professionals have advised me that this species is considerably more heat tolerant than *S. pseudocamellia*. E. H. Wilson introduced the species from Korea in 1917. Grows 20 to 30 ft. high. Zones 5 to 7. Korea.

Stewartia koreana, Korean Stewartia, in fall

Stewartia koreana fall color

Stewartia monadelpha
Tall Stewartia

In terms of culture, Tall Stewartia is the easiest of the genus. It is also one of the most heat-tolerant species, and it withstands dry soils better than *Stewartia koreana* or *S. pseudocamellia*. The habit is shrubby and multistemmed, although some specimens may develop a single trunk and oval-rounded outline. In shade, the habit is open with wide-spreading branches. The 1½- to 3-in.-long, dark green leaves develop excellent deep reddish fall color. Leaves hold late, and severe cold may reduce or eliminate fall color expression. White, 1- to 1½-in.-diameter flowers open from late June into July and are almost lost among the leaves. The bark is a rich mosaic of gray, brown, and cinnamon flakes that expose a rich brown underbark. Although not as spectacular as the best forms of Japanese Stewartia or Korean Stewartia, it is still a choice ornamental for the discriminating gardener. Grows 20 to 30 ft. high and wide after 30 years. Zones 5 to 8. Japan.

Stewartia monadelpha flower

Stewartia monadelpha fall color

Stewartia koreana bark

Stewartia monadelpha bark

Stewartia pseudocamellia
Japanese Stewartia

Stewartia monadelpha, Tall Stewartia

I suspect that there is not a gardener who, upon seeing this species, would not opt for one in the garden. Flowers and fall foliage can be memorable, but the exquisite lightning-bolt pattern of the exfoliating bark is the real show, bringing pizazz to the winter garden. Generally pyramidal-oval in youth, the habit becomes more open and rounded with maturity. The character of the bark is not particularly dazzling until the branches reach 2 to 3 in. in diameter, at which time the bark exfoliates in striking patterns of gray, orange, and red-brown. The 2- to 3½-in.-long, medium to dark green leaves have serrated margins. Leaves emerge bronzy purple and, in fall, may develop excellent orange to red to bronze-red color. The five-petaled, white flowers, 2 to 2½ (to 3) in. in diameter, have a central golden orange mass of anthers. Flowers open in July. The fruit is a five-valved, brownish capsule that splits at maturity to expose the brown seeds. Ideally soils should be moist, well drained, and on the acid side. Plants prefer full sun but also perform well in partial shade. High summer heat and dry soil conditions limit the growth of the species. Japanese Stewartia is ideal as an accent or focal point. Several trees in a grovelike setting are terrific. Expect, at best, 6 to 12 in. of growth per year until well established. Grows 20 to 40 ft. high and wide at mature landscape size. Zones (4)5 to 7. Japan.

Stewartia pseudocamellia, Japanese Stewartia

Stewartia pseudocamellia flower

Stewartia pseudocamellia bark

MORE ➤

Stewartia pseudocamellia continued

Stewartia pseudocamellia in fall

Stewartia sinensis

Chinese Stewartia

A truly magnificent species. Chinese Stewartia has been described by W. J. Bean as having bark "as smooth as polished alabaster and the color of weathered sandstone." In my travels, I have come across many specimens that give little credence to this description; however, 25- to 30-ft.-high specimens at Wakehurst Place, England, and Rowallane, Northern Ireland, made a believer out of me. The medium green leaves average 1½ to 4 in. long and seldom develop appreciable fall color. The white, fragrant flowers average 1½ to 2 in. across, but they are not overwhelming since they open over a long period. Culture is similar to that of *Stewartia pseudocamellia*; in more northerly locations, plants should be protected from harsh weather. Grows 15 to 25 ft. high. Zones 5 to 7. China.

Stewartia sinensis trunk at Wakehurst Place, England

Stewartia sinensis bark

Stewartia sinensis flower

Stewartia sinensis, Chinese Stewartia

Styrax americanus
American Snowbell

An underappreciated, underutilized native shrub with delicate leaves and white, bell-shaped flowers with highly reflexed petals. The habit is oval-rounded to rounded. The bright green, 1½- to 3½-in.-long leaves do not develop appreciable fall color. Flowers occur in great abundance from the leaf axils in June and July. Prefers moist soils and partial shade. A good shrub for naturalizing; in the wild, it occurs in lowlands bordering streams. Grows 6 to 8 (to 10) ft. high; a specimen in the Arnold Arboretum is 15 ft. high. Zones (5)6 to 9. Virginia to Florida, west to Missouri and Louisiana.

Styrax americanus, American Snowbell

Styrax japonicus
Japanese Snowbell

For years I chased this plant, until I was finally able to secure one for my Illinois garden. A 25-ft.-high tree sited next to a wall at Longwood Gardens, Pennsylvania, provided my first introduction to the consistently superb flower display. A delicate beauty, Japanese Snowbell is best viewed from below so that one can most appreciate the medium to dark green leaves perched like butterflies above the white, bell-shaped flowers. The five-lobed, slightly fragrant flowers occur three to six together on short lateral shoots and appear in May and June. Leaves are 1 to 3½ in. long. The smooth gray bark is quite pleasing when framed by evergreens or another dark background. *Styrax japonicus* prefers moist, acid, well-drained soils abundantly supplied with organic matter. Full sun to partial shade is suitable. It does not tolerate high heat or extremely dry conditions. At –20°F, young trees die back to the snowline, while on older plants the stems die back and the flower buds will perish. Great in the shrub border or as an understory or hillside plant, where flowers can be viewed by passersby. Grows 20 to 30 ft. high and wide. Zones 5 to 8. China, Japan.

Cultivars and Varieties. 'Emerald Pagoda' ('Sohuksan') was introduced from Korea in 1985 by J. C. Raulston and the U.S. National Arboretum. I am fantastically impressed by this treasure. It has larger, more leathery, lustrous dark green leaves and heavy textured, waxy, 1-in.-wide flowers.

'Pendula' ('Carilon') has a weeping habit. Leaves and flowers are similar to those of the species.

'Pink Chimes' offers pink flowers on a small, graceful tree. High heat reduces the intensity of the pink coloration.

MORE ➤

Styrax americanus flowers

Styrax japonicus, Japanese Snowbell

Styrax japonicus **continued**

Styrax japonicus flowers

Styrax japonicus 'Emerald Pagoda'

Styrax japonicus in winter

Styrax obassia

Fragrant Snowbell

My wife Bonnie and I have always admired this large-leaved, white-flowered tree, and it occupies a place of prominence in our garden. In winter, Fragrant Snowbell has a certain sculptural quality because of its architecturally elegant smooth gray branches. The dark green leaves, to 8 in. long, provide a bold textural effect. The fragrant, 4- to 8- (to 10-) in.-long flowers open as the leaves mature, generally in May and June. Moist, well-drained, acid soils are best, in full sun to partial shade. Use for specimen effect only; an isolated plant makes a striking landscape element. It is hardier than *Styrax japonicus*, with an estimated cold hardiness of –25°F. Appears slightly more heat tolerant as well. Grows 20 to 30 ft. high, slightly less in spread. Zones (4)5 to 8. Japan, Korea, northeastern China.

Styrax obassia flowers

Symphoricarpos albus
Common Snowberry

A native species with attractive white fruit in autumn and excellent shade tolerance. Common Snowberry is a rounded to broad-rounded shrub, with numerous ascending, fine, twiggy shoots. It suckers profusely and can develop large colonies. The ¾- to 2-in.-long, dark, almost blue-green leaves remain into fall. Flowers are pinkish and not showy. The white, ½-in.-diameter, popcornlike fruit ripen in September and persist into November. Very adaptable plant that prospers in limestone, clay soils. Provide a shady environment. Good as a filler or in mass plantings. *Symphoricarpos albus* can become rather unkempt and should be pruned in late winter to bring it back to summer respectability. Grows 3 to 6 ft. high and wide. Zones 3 to 7. Nova Scotia to Alberta, south to Virginia and Minnesota.

Styrax obassia, Fragrant Snowbell

Symphoricarpos albus, Common Snowberry

Styrax obassia leaf

Styrax obassia fruit

Symphoricarpos albus foliage

Symphoricarpos albus fruit

Symphoricarpos ×chenaultii
Chenault Coralberry

This hybrid develops a low, spreading, arching habit. Flowers and fruit are not significant. Grows 3 to 6 ft. high and wide. Zones 4 to 7.

Cultivars and Varieties. 'Hancock' is a beautiful low-growing type with small, blue-green leaves. A 12-year-old plant may be 2 ft. high and 12 ft. wide.

Symphoricarpos ×chenaultii, Chenault Coralberry

Symphoricarpos ×chenaultii fruit

Symphoricarpos orbiculatus fruit

Symphoricarpos ×chenaultii 'Hancock'

Symphoricarpos orbiculatus
Indiancurrant Coralberry, Buckbrush

I have seen fields of this plant in Virginia, where it qualifies for weed status. Attractive purplish red, ⅙- to ¼-in.-diameter fruit mature in October and persist into winter. The yellowish white flowers are flushed with pink and are borne in short axillary clusters on terminal spikes. Unfortunately, the species is quite susceptible to mildew. Similar to *Symphoricarpos albus* in growth habit. It is an inherently durable shrub for difficult areas of the garden. Grows 2 to 5 ft. high, 4 to 8 ft. wide. Zones 2 to 7. New Jersey to South Dakota, south to Georgia and Texas.

Symphoricarpos orbiculatus, Indiancurrant Coralberry

Symplocos paniculata
Sapphireberry

In September, when the sapphire-blue fruit ripen, one questions why this shrub is not more abundant in commerce. Sapphireberry is a large, rounded to broad-rounded shrub that could easily be grown as a small tree. The 1½- to 3½-in.-long, dark green leaves offer no appreciable fall color. White, ½-in.-diameter flowers are borne in 2- to 3-in.-long panicles in May and June. They are slightly fragrant and occur in great profusion. The real treasure is the ⅓-in.-long, ellipsoidal, turquoise-blue fruit. They generally ripen in September and persist into October, if the birds do not eat them earlier. The gray bark is quite appealing, having a ridged and furrowed character. Provide well-drained soils and full sun for best growth; will tolerate light shade. An excellent plant for attracting birds. Use as a single specimen, in the shrub border, or in groupings. Grows 10 to 20 ft. high, similar spread. Zones 4 to 8. Himalayas, China, Japan.

Symplocos paniculata, Sapphireberry

Symplocos paniculata flowers

Symplocos paniculata fruit

Syringa, Lilac

Lilacs can be magnificent flowering shrubs or trees, but they are not without their shortcomings. The fragrant flowers are certainly delightful additions to any garden; after flowering, however, most lilacs offer limited interest. Transplant Syringa *from a container or as a balled and burlapped specimen in late winter or early spring. Provide well-drained, near neutral soils, although plants perform well in acid soils. The oldest branches should be pruned out on a regular basis to ensure vigorous, flower-producing shoots. Remove spent flowers to prevent seed set. Lilacs make great border shrubs and should not be isolated in an expanse of lawn. Mildew, scale, borers, leaf roll necrosis, and other maladies affect the plants. Countless hybrids are known.*

Syringa ×chinensis 'Saugeana' flowers

Syringa ×chinensis, Chinese Lilac

Syringa ×chinensis
Chinese Lilac

A large, broad-spreading, relatively fine-textured shrub, *Syringa ×chinensis* is a common inhabitant of Midwest landscapes. Its 1½- to 3-in.-long, dark green leaves are less susceptible to mildew than those of *S. vulgaris*, Common Lilac. Fragrant, purple-lilac flowers are borne in 4- to 6-in.-long panicles in May. Grows 8 to 15 ft. high and wide. Zones 3 to 7.

Cultivars and Varieties. 'Saugeana', with lilac-red flowers, is more colorful than the species.

Syringa laciniata, Cutleaf Lilac

Syringa laciniata
Cutleaf Lilac

Comparable to *Syringa ×persica*, Persian Lilac, in most characteristics, except for the leaves, which are generally three- to nine-lobed and not susceptible to mildew. Fragrant, pale lilac flowers are borne in 3-in.-long, loose panicles all along the stems in May. Bears reasonable flowers in partial shade. Forms a graceful, rounded-mounded outline. *Syringa laciniata* is one of the most heat-tolerant lilacs. Grows 6 to 8 ft. high and wide. Zones 4 to 8. Turkmenistan, China.

Syringa meyeri
Meyer Lilac

Syringa laciniata foliage

Another midwestern favorite. Although many dismiss this species as inferior to *Syringa vulgaris*, I consider it a superior choice because of its reliably heavy bloom, clean foliage, and compact habit. The plant is not small, and it develops a broad-rounded outline and excellent branch structure. The ¾- to 1¾-in.-long, dark green leaves are almost rounded in outline. Meyer Lilac generally flowers before the leaves are fully developed. The purplish pink, fragrant flowers occur in 4-in.-long and 2½-in.-wide panicles in May. They literally cover the entire shrub from top to bottom and remain effective for 10 to 14 days. A great choice for the border, especially if backed by evergreens. Grows 4 to 8 ft. high, 6 to 12 ft. wide. Zones 3 to 7. Northern China.

Cultivars and Varieties. 'Palibin' is a compact form with reddish purple buds that open to icy pink flowers. Grows 4 to 5 ft. high, 5 to 7 ft. wide.

Syringa laciniata flowers

Syringa meyeri flowers

Syringa meyeri foliage

Syringa meyeri, Meyer Lilac

Syringa microphylla

Littleleaf Lilac

Littleleaf Lilac is a handsome broad-spreading shrub. It has grayish green, ½- to 2-in.-long leaves and fragrant, rosy lilac flowers. The flowers are borne in 2- to 4-in.-long, 1½- to 2-in.-wide panicles in May and June. Often flowers sporadically in late summer and early fall. Grows 6 ft. high, 9 to 12 ft. wide. Zones 4 to 7(8). Northern and western China.

Cultivars and Varieties. 'Superba' has single, deep pink flowers and is more colorful than the species.

Syringa microphylla, Littleleaf Lilac

Syringa microphylla foliage

Syringa microphylla flowers

Syringa oblata var. *dilatata*

Early Lilac

The common name for *Syringa oblata* is appropriate, for this is the first species to flower in the Arnold Arboretum's extensive collection.The variety *dilatata* is shrubbier than the species form and has longer leaves and a longer, more slender corolla tube. Plants in cultivation appear to be this variety rather than the species. The fragrant, pale lilac to purple-lilac flowers occur in broad, 2- to 5-in.-long panicles from the uppermost nodes of the previous year's wood. The dark blue-green leaves, 2 to 4 in. long and wide, are free from mildew. Foliage turns muted reddish to reddish purple in fall. Forms an oval-rounded shrub or small tree. Like all lilacs, Early Lilac requires well-drained soils and full sun. Displays more heat tolerance than *Syringa vulgaris*, Common Lilac, and is probably a better choice where heat stress is prevalent. The floral fragrance is not as sweet as that of *S. vulgaris*. Grows 10 to 12 ft. high. Zones 3 to 6(7). Korea.

Syringa oblata var. *dilatata* flowers

Syringa patula
Manchurian Lilac

This species is frequently confused with *Syringa meyeri* and *S. microphylla*, but it has larger (2 to 5 in. long), leathery, dull dark green leaves. The habit is oval-rounded. Lilac-purple, fragrant flowers open in May and June. Grows 8 to 10 ft. high. Zones 3 to 8. Northern China, Korea.

Cultivars and Varieties. 'Miss Kim' is a lovely oval-rounded selection with purple flower buds and icy pink flowers. It is extremely dense in habit. The leaves often turn a respectable reddish purple fall color. Grows 10 ft. high.

Syringa oblata var. *dilatata*, Early Lilac, in fall

Syringa patula, Manchurian Lilac, flowers

Syringa patula foliage

Syringa patula 'Miss Kim'

Syringa ×persica
Persian Lilac

Another shrub that was planted extensively in older gardens of the East and Midwest. Persian Lilac develops into a graceful, rounded shrub. It has 1- to 2½-in.-long, dark blue-green leaves and fragrant, pale lilac flowers. The flowers occur in May in 2- to 3-in.- long and wide panicles from the upper nodes of the previous season's growth. The leaves are often infected by mildew. Grows 4 to 8 ft. high, 5 to 10 ft. wide. Zones 3 to 7.

Syringa ×persica, Persian Lilac

Syringa ×persica flowers

Syringa reticulata
Japanese Tree Lilac

Japanese Tree Lilac is possibly the most adaptable lilac for difficult sites. It develops into a large shrub or small tree with an oval to rounded crown. The bark is lustrous brown, with horizontal lenticels reminiscent of cherry bark. The dark green, 2- to 5½-in.-long leaves develop no appreciable fall color. White flowers are borne in May and June in panicles 6 to 12 in. long and 6 to 10 in. wide; the fragrance is almost privet-like. This species is highly resistant to mildew, scale, and borers. Attractive as a small landscape tree or large shrub. Use as a specimen. Grows 20 to 30 ft. high, 15 to 25 ft. wide. Zones 3 to 7. Japan.

Cultivars and Varieties. 'Ivory Silk', 'Regent', and 'Summer Snow' should be used, if available, instead of the species because of superior flower production, more uniform habit, and superior foliage.

Syringa reticulata, Japanese Tree Lilac

Syringa reticulata flowers

Syringa reticulata bark

Syringa villosa
Late Lilac

Certainly not a force in the world of landscape lilacs, but it has been utilized in breeding because of its late flowering time. Typically, Late Lilac is a large, bushy shrub with erect or ascending, stout, stiff branches. Most older specimens become leggy and open at the base. The medium green leaves range from 2 to 7 in. long and have deeply impressed veins, resulting in a pleated appearance. The rosy lilac to white flowers occur in 3- to 7-in.-long panicles at the end of the shoots of new growth of the season in May and June. The fragrance is somewhat similar to that of the privet and definitely not the sweet perfume associated with *Syringa vulgaris*. Grows 6 to 10 ft. high, 4 to 10 ft. wide. Zones 2 to 7. China.

Syringa villosa, Late Lilac

Syringa villosa foliage

Syringa vulgaris
Common Lilac

It is unfortunate that such a treasured shrub with such wonderfully fragrant flowers should have so many flaws. Common Lilac is a large, cumbersome shrub of irregular outline, often becoming leggy at the base. The 2- to 5-in.-long, dark green to blue-green leaves may contract significant mildew by summer. Undeniably, the deliciously fragrant lilac flowers make all the other liabilities seem tolerable. Flowers occur at the ends of the shoots in 4- to 8-in.-long panicles in May, before or as the leaves mature. They make wonderful cut flowers for the home. Plant in the border or even in the vegetable garden, wherever the fragrance can be enjoyed. It's anybody's guess as to the number of cultivars, but 2000 is a current estimate. Grows 8 to 15 (to 20) ft. high, 6 to 12 (to 15) ft. wide. Zones 3 to 7. Southern Europe.

Cultivars and Varieties. var. *alba* ('Alba'), with white flowers, is common throughout the northern states.

Syringa vulgaris, Common Lilac

Syringa vulgaris flowers

MORE ➤

Syringa vulgaris continued

Syringa vulgaris var. *alba*

Syringa vulgaris 'Charles Joly' flowers

Syringa vulgaris 'Sensation' flowers

Tamarix ramosissima

Five-Stamen Tamarix

This species is often used in coastal landscapes or alkali soil areas because of its excellent salt tolerance. I have encountered plants growing on the beaches of Georgia and the Carolinas, in the heavy clays of Michigan, and in the deserts of Arizona. Amazingly, all were prospering. It is a large, irregular shrub or small tree. The foliage is scalelike, almost like that of junipers, and usually light green to gray-green in color. Rose-pink flowers occur in large panicles in June and July on new growth of the season. The flowers persist for four to six weeks, but they show their age toward the end of the cycle. It is probably best to prune the plant back in late winter to induce long, feathery growth and summer flowers. Transplant from a container; the root system is sparse. Provide full sun for best flower. Grows 10 to 15 ft. high; I have observed 20- to 25-ft.-high forms. Zones 2 to 8. Southeastern Europe to central Asia.

Tamarix ramosissima, Five-Stamen Tamarix

Tamarix ramosissima flowers

Taxodium ascendens (T. distichum var. *nutans)*
Pond Cypress

Taxonomically, this species has been juggled over the years; *Hortus Third* (New York: Macmillan, 1976) places it as a variety of *Taxodium distichum*. From a landscape standpoint, it is more columnar than *T. distichum*. Secondary branches originate at right angles to the central leader, and the soft, appressed, rich green needles produce a foliage effect similar to that of *Cryptomeria* or juniper. Uses are similar to that of *T. distichum*. Grows 70 to 80 ft. high, 15 to 20 ft. wide. Zones (5)6 to 9. Virginia to Florida and Alabama.

Tamarix ramosissima fall color

Taxodium ascendens fall color

Taxodium ascendens, Pond Cypress

Taxodium distichum
Common Baldcypress

Europeans consider the Common Baldcypress one of the finest North American trees, and its use in Europe, particularly in German gardens, borders on the fantastic. This deciduous conifer is a tall, airy spire, columnar to softly pyramidal in habit; the western populations are more open and treelike. The rich green foliage appears on featherlike branches and turns rusty orange to brown in autumn. The fibrous, reddish brown to gray-brown bark sparks winter interest. Transplants with some difficulty because of its large taproot; use container-grown plants or small balled and burlapped plants. Found in swamps and moist areas throughout its native range, this species performs admirably in drier soils and is adaptable to a variety of soil conditions, except high pH, which causes chlorosis of foliage. Knees generally develop around trees that grow in or near water. Ideal for use near water or in moist areas where few other trees will prosper. Makes its greatest statement in groupings or groves. Also good as a street tree. Grows 50 to 70 ft. high, 20 to 30 ft. wide; can grow to 100 ft. or more. Zones 4 to 9. Delaware to Illinois, south to Florida and Texas.

Cultivars and Varieties. 'Shawnee Brave' is a narrow-pyramidal form with blue-green foliage. It is resistant to gall mite. Original parent tree was 75 ft. high and 18 ft. wide when the selection was made.

Taxodium distichum, Common Baldcypress

Taxodium distichum in fall

Taxodium distichum knees growing out of the water

Taxodium distichum cones

Taxus, Yew

Too often mutilated by the pruning shears, yews may assume a disgusting regularity. Left to their own genetic devices, however, Taxus *species make splendid, artistic trees and shrubs. Not so much in this country, but in England, where the large native trees have not been pruned, the stately, dark green, somber yew trees with a broad pyramidal habit grow 40 to 60 ft. high. Yews are fantastically adaptable. They thrive in sun or shade, in moist or dry soils. Good drainage is essential for successful culture. Transplant balled and burlapped. For function and aesthetics, yews rank in the first order of needle evergreens. The abundant uses for these trees include foundation plantings, screens, hedges, masses, and accents. Yews are generally free of significant insects and diseases.*

Taxus baccata

English Yew

Typical English Yew is an immense plant, but the cultivars are more in scale with contemporary landscapes. The height of all forms is easily controlled by pruning. The ½- to 1¼-in.-long, dark green needles maintain their color through the seasons, although some discoloration is common in cold, windy climates. The reddish brown, furrowed, scaly, flaky bark is beautiful, particularly on mature trees. The ¼- to ⅜-in.-long, football-shaped seeds have a fleshy red covering called an aril. Seeds occur on female plants. Grows 30 to 60 ft. high, 15 to 25 ft. wide. Zones (5)6 to 7. Europe, northern Africa, western Asia.

Taxus baccata seeds

Taxus baccata bark

MORE ➤

Taxus baccata continued

Cultivars and Varieties. 'Adpressa' has short, 1/4- to 1/2-in.-long, dark green needles densely set along the stems. Makes a large shrub or small tree. Plants as large as 30 ft. tall are known.

'Adpressa Fowle' is more compact than 'Adpressa' and smaller in stature.

'Aurea' ('Aurescens') is a golden-needled form. Similar types exist under this name. The ones I have observed display rich golden yellow new growth that gradually fades to green.

'Fastigiata' is commonly known as the Irish Yew, although other upright forms masquerade with this title. Decidedly columnar in habit with strongly vertical branches. Grows 15 to 30 ft. high, 4 to 8 ft. wide.

'Repandens' is frequently used in North American gardens because of its greater cold hardiness. A superb wide-spreading form. The tips of the branches are slightly pendulous. Grows 2 to 4 (to 6) ft. high, 12 to 15 ft. wide.

Taxus baccata, English Yew

Taxus baccata grown as a hedge

Taxus baccata 'Repandens'

Taxus canadensis
Canadian Yew

Similar to *Taxus baccata* except for its size and winter color. This species is not used to any degree because its needles turn an inferior reddish brown in winter. Plants in the wild are often prostrate, loose, and straggling. For heavy shade situations in a naturalistic garden, it is worthy of consideration. Grows 3 to 6 ft. high, 6 to 8 ft. wide. Zones 2 to 6. Newfoundland to Manitoba, south to Virginia and Iowa.

Taxus canadensis, Canadian Yew

Taxus cuspidata
Japanese Yew

In most respects, this species could be considered the Japanese equivalent of English Yew. The numerous cultivars are better choices for colder climates. Size is variable, depending on the cultivar. Zones 4 to 7. Japan, northeastern China.

Cultivars and Varieties. 'Capitata' is a tree form often used for screening and hedging in the East and Midwest. The habit is pleasingly pyramidal. Unless pruned, it grows 40 to 50 ft. high.

'Densa' makes a broad mound, almost twice as wide as it is high, and is clothed with extremely dark green needles. Grows 4 ft. high, 8 ft. wide.

'Nana' is another compact form with dark green needles. Grows 3 ft. high, 6 ft. wide.

Taxus cuspidata seeds

MORE ➤

Taxus cuspidata continued

Taxus cuspidata, Japanese Yew

Taxus ×media

English-Japanese Yew

Plants included in this grex are hybrids between the English and Japanese species. Many selections have been made, and these cultivars represent the better choices for modern landscapes. Most are shrubby, but there are several distinctly upright types. In Midwest and Northeast landscapes, *Taxus ×media* selections predominate. Zones (4)5 to 7.

Cultivars and Varieties. 'Brownii' is an old clone with a dense, rounded outline and dark green needles. Grows 9 ft. high, 12 ft. wide in 15 to 20 years.

'Densiformis' is one of the more popular forms. Grows twice as wide as tall.

'Hatfieldii' is a male form with dark green needles. Dense and broadly pyramidal-columnar in

Taxus ×media, English-Japanese Yew

habit. A 20-year-old plant may be 12 ft. high and 10 ft. wide.

'Hicksii' might be considered a replacement for *Taxus baccata* 'Fastigiata', Irish Yew, in colder climates. Makes a good hedge or screening plant. Grows 15 to 20 ft. high, 5 to 8 ft. wide.

'Wardii' is a wide-spreading, flat-topped, densely branched cultivar with dark green needles. Usually grows about two to three times wide as it is tall. A 20-year-old plant was 6 ft. high by 19 ft. wide.

Taxus ×*media* 'Brownii'

Thuja occidentalis
American Arborvitae

In northern landscapes, this species and its cultivars are as common as grass. Plants are used around foundations, in groupings, as screens or hedges, and occasionally as free-standing specimens. The rather stiff, narrow- to broad-pyramidal habit makes the plant useful for hedging. The foliage is rich green in summer, often yellowish green to brownish green in winter, especially on plants exposed to winter sun and wind. Amazingly durable and can be grown in virtually any soil. In the wild, it is found in rocky and marshy soils. Takes pruning with grace and dignity, and makes, as hedges go, a fine green wall. Grows 40 to 60 ft. high, 10 to 15 ft. wide. Zones 2 to 7. Eastern North America.

Taxus ×*media* 'Hatfieldii' pruned as a hedge

Cultivars and Varieties. Numerous cultivars confound and confuse, but several are good for general landscape use.

'Emerald' ('Smaragd') is a compact pyramid of lustrous emerald-green foliage. Does not discolor in winter. Displays excellent heat tolerance and is described as

Thuja occidentalis pruned as a hedge

MORE ➤

Thuja occidentalis continued

hardy to –40°F. Slower growing than the species. Grows 10 to 15 ft. high, 3 to 5 ft. wide.

'Nigra' has good dark green foliage throughout the seasons. Grows 20 to 30 ft. high.

'Techny' ('Mission') is a broad-based pyramidal form with excellent dark green foliage throughout the seasons. Grows slowly, to 15 ft. or more.

'Woodwardii' is a common sight in midwestern landscapes. It has a broad-rounded habit. The dark green summer foliage may turn ugly brown in winter. Grows 8 to 10 ft. high, 16 to 20 ft. wide.

Thuja occidentalis, American Arborvitae

Thuja occidentalis cones

Thuja orientalis (Platycladus orientalis)
Oriental Arborvitae

An amazing plant with a modicum of cold tolerance and even greater heat tolerance (to Key West, Florida, in Zone 11). The habit is densely pyramidal with a rotund base and vertically arranged sprays of foliage. The rich grass-green leaves will discolor in cold weather. Like the previous species, it is ideal for miserable soils and can be utilized for a wide range of landscape needs. Grows 18 to 25 ft. high, 10 to 15 ft. wide. Zones (5)6 to 10(11). Korea, northern and northeastern China.

Cultivars and Varieties. 'Aurea Nana', Berckman's Golden Arborvitae, represents the most common form in cultivation. It is dense, compact, and ovoid-pyramidal in habit. The rich golden yellow new foliage fades to a lighter yellow-green. Although considered smallish, it grows 10 ft. high and more. Easily kept under control with pruning.

'Baker', 'Blue Cone', and 'Fruitlandii' are quality green-foliaged forms that are preferable to the typical species.

Thuja orientalis, Oriental Arborvitae

Thuja plicata

Western or Giant Arborvitae

Over the years, I pushed and promoted the better forms of *Thuja occidentalis*, American Arborvitae, and missed the truly noble member of the genus. Typically, the habit of *T. plicata* is narrow- to broad-pyramidal. The lustrous, rich dark green foliage is the most beautiful of all the arborvitaes, elegantly postured, like a lady's hand outstretched for a kiss. The foliage does not discolor in winter to the degree of that of *T. occidentalis* or *T. orientalis*. Moist, acid, well-drained soils are preferred, but plants prosper in heavy clays in the Midwest as well. Although native to the Pacific Northwest, where it grows 180 to 200 ft. high, Western Arborvitae prospers from Boston to Cincinnati to Raleigh. On the Isle of Mainau in Germany and at Stourhead, England, reside the most magnificent 80-ft.-high specimens, with layered lower branches that provide a density belied by the aging specimens. Grows 50 to 75 ft. high, 15 to 25 ft. wide. Zones 5 to 7. Alaska to California.

Cultivars and Varieties. 'Atrovirens' is possibly the best of the large pyramidal forms. Superb, shining dark green foliage.

'Fastigiata' ('Hogan') is a good columnar-pyramidal form with a straight, slender trunk and dense, dark green foliage. It has grown remarkably well under high summer heat and drought.

'Zebrina' seldom appears in garden centers, but its yellowish striped foliage sprays (flattened fronds) provide a less-than-offensive golden hue. Broad-pyramidal habit. Grows 30 ft. high.

Thuja orientalis 'Aurea Nana', Berckman's Golden Arborvitae

Thuja plicata, Western Arborvitae

Thuja plicata foliage

Thuja plicata trunks, on the Isle of Mainau in Germany

Thujopsis dolobrata
Hiba Arborvitae

Hiba Arborvitae is truly a great conversation piece in the garden, since few people have any idea of its identity. The broad-pyramidal habit is reminiscent of that of typical *Thuja*, but the individual segments of the foliage are wider and darker green above, with distinct silvery white markings below. The species makes a good garden plant. Quite adaptable, requiring only well-drained soils. Withstands full sun and partial shade. Generally does not discolor in winter. Cuttings root readily, and I see no reason for its paucity in commerce. Use as a specimen evergreen, for it is too beautiful to mutilate with pruning shears. Grows 30 to 50 ft. high, 10 to 20 ft. wide. Zones 5 to 7. Japan.

Cultivars and Varieties. 'Nana' is a great evergreen plant for the rock garden, the shrub border, or as an accent. It has a rounded-mounded outline. Grows 3 ft. high and wide.

'Variegata' has sprays marked with creamy white.

Tilia americana
American Linden, Basswood

Not used to any great degree in American landscapes, but found in the wild over much of eastern and midwestern North America. The habit is sturdy and imposing—pyramidal in youth, oval-rounded with arched and spreading branches at maturity. The gray to brown bark is smooth and shiny on young trees, developing flat, scaly ridges with age. The 4- to 8-in.-long, lustrous dark green leaves turn, at best, yellow-green in fall. Cream-yellow, fragrant flowers appear in June and are followed by rather inconspicuous hard-shelled nutlets. Provide moist, deep, well-drained soils, in full sun. If native in an area, make every effort to keep the plant. The smaller-leaved lindens that follow are more suited to traditional landscapes. Grows 60 to 80 ft. high, 20 to 40 ft. wide. Zones 2 to 8(9). Maine to Florida.

Thujopsis dolobrata, Hiba Arborvitae

Thujopsis dolobrata 'Nana'

Thujopsis dolobrata foliage

Tilia heterophylla, *T. michauxii*, and *T. neglecta* have many of the same traits as *T. americana*, and the labeling of these species can be confused.

Cultivars and Varieties. 'Redmond', often described as a hybrid between *Tilia americana* and *T. ×euchlora*, resembles the former in most respects. It has a distinctly pyramidal outline and is more densely branched than *T. americana*. Common in commerce, especially in the Midwest.

Tilia americana, American Linden

Tilia americana leaf

Tilia cordata

Littleleaf Linden

Truly a cool-climate shade and street tree; plants in the Southeast simply languish. Popular and fashionable because of the numerous reliable selections that have been made, Littleleaf Linden is a staple from New Hampshire to the Midwest and south to just below the Mason-Dixon line. Distinctly pyramidal in youth, becoming pyramidal-rounded with age. Densely branched and foliaged, it makes an ideal landscape tree. The 1½- to 3-in.-long, dark green leaves may turn a reasonable yellow in fall. Yellowish, fragrant flowers occur in June. Relatively easy to transplant. Its tolerance of harsh soil conditions is legendary. The species thrives in heavy clays and acid to higher pH soils; tolerates drier soils better than many trees. Japanese beetles (which plague all lindens), aphids, and sooty mold (a fungus that feeds on aphid excrement) are serious problems. Nevertheless, it is without question a first-rate lawn, street, or shade tree. The numerous selections are superior to the species. Site with care, because the abundant flowers often attract bees. Grows 60 to 70 ft. high, 30 to 45 ft. wide. Zones 3 to 7. Europe.

Cultivars and Varieties. 'Chancellor', 'Corinthian', 'Glenleven', 'Greenspire', and 'June Bride' are good selections. 'Greenspire' is the most popular because of its central leader and uniform branching habit.

Tilia cordata, Littleleaf Linden

MORE ➤

Tilia cordata continued

Tilia cordata in fall

Tilia cordata foliage

Tilia ×euchlora foliage

Tilia ×euchlora
Crimean Linden

Little used in commercial landscaping because of competition from *Tilia cordata* (one of its parents), but this hybrid is still a handsome tree. Habit is softly pyramidal, with branches that skirt the ground. The 2- to 4-in.-long leaves are lustrous, polished dark green. The leaf margins have elongated, mucronate serrations, almost like bristles, a trait that separates this species from Littleleaf Linden. Tends to sucker from the base, producing unwanted shoots that need to be removed. Supposedly more resistant to aphids than *T. cordata*. A fine tree for parks, campuses, and large areas. Do not limb up the lower branches, since they add much to the character of a mature tree. Crimean Linden is a hybrid between *T. cordata* and *T. dasystyla* that originated about 1860. Grows 40 to 60 ft. high, 20 to 30 ft. wide. Zones 3 to 7.

Tilia ×euchlora, Crimean Linden

Tilia petiolaris (*Tilia* 'Petiolaris')
Pendent Silver Linden

A noble tree of weeping habit, with all the fine attributes of *Tilia tomentosa*, Silver Linden. In my opinion, this pyramidal-oval to oval-rounded, weeping form is probably nothing more than a selection of *T. tomentosa*. The fall color is often striking yellow. Great specimen tree, deserving of space in every park, campus, or golf course. Grows 60 to 80 ft. high, 30 to 40 ft. wide. Zones 5 to 7.

Tilia petiolaris flowers and foliage

Tilia petiolaris, Pendent Silver Linden

Tilia petiolaris fall color

Tilia platyphyllos
Bigleaf Linden

The common name does not really reflect the actual leaf size of this species. Averaging 2 to 5 in. in length, the leaves of Bigleaf Linden are not a great deal larger than those of Littleleaf Linden. This species is occasionally grown in the United States, most often in the Midwest and Northeast, but in Europe, it appears everywhere, particularly in formal allées and along streets. The stems are covered with long pubescence, a characteristic that separates the species from the others presented here. The habit is densely broad-pyramidal. With its dark green leaves and yellowish white flowers, this makes a tree of great beauty. Grows 60 to 80 ft. high, 20 to 40 ft. wide. Zones 2 to 6. Europe.

Tilia platyphyllos, Bigleaf Linden

Tilia platyphyllos leaf

Tilia tomentosa
Silver Linden

In the world of lindens, this species deserves the beauty-queen title. Stunning, lustrous dark green, 2- to 5-in.-long, silver-backed leaves reflect like silver dollars in the summer sun. This has always been one of my favorite lindens, but unfortunately, it is not widely available in commerce. The habit is distinctly pyramidal in youth, tightly broad-pyramidal with a uniform branching structure in old age. The smooth, light gray bark borders on silver-gray, carrying the plant's common name into the winter months. Silver Linden is generally the last of the cultivated lindens to bloom. Yellowish white flowers open in late June and early July. Requires ample moisture in the early years of establishment. Use as a lawn, street, or specimen tree. Grows 50 to 70 ft. high, 25 to 45 ft. wide. Zones 4 to 7. Southeastern Europe, western Asia.

Cultivars and Varieties. 'Sterling Silver' is an impressive new selection. It has a sculptured, broad pyramidal crown, with the fine foliage and bark features found in the species. The parent tree was 45 ft. high and 24 ft. wide after 30 years.

Tilia tomentosa, Silver Linden

Tilia tomentosa foliage

Tilia tomentosa branches in winter

Tsuga canadensis, Eastern Hemlock

Tsuga canadensis
Canadian or Eastern Hemlock

What a grand needle evergreen—softly pyramidal in outline, deep green needles, good tolerance of shade or sun, and many landscape uses. I have never met a specimen I did not appreciate. Unfortunately, on the East Coast *Tsuga canadensis* has suffered from attacks of the woolly adelgid. The ½- to ¾-in.-long needles have two silver bands on their undersides. The ½- to ¾-in.-long, ovoid, brown cones look like dangling ornaments. The rich brown bark is ridged and deeply furrowed on old trees. Transplant balled and burlapped or from a container into cool, moist, acid, well-drained soils. Protect from desiccating winter winds. Does not display great tolerance to heat or urban stress. Use as a specimen or in screens, groupings, or hedges. This species produces a magnificent hedge. Grows 40 to 70 ft. high, 25 to 35 ft. wide. Zones 3 to 7. Nova Scotia to Minnesota, south in the mountains to Alabama and Georgia.

Cultivars and Varieties. The number of cultivars is astronomical, and only specialized treatises can do justice to the broad range. One of the most notable is mentioned here.

'Sargentii' (var. *sargentii*) is one of the best weeping evergreens for general use. It is commercially common and reasonably priced. As a free-standing specimen in a lawn, by the edge of a stream, or cascading over rocks, or as a container plant, it has great worth. The broadly weeping habit can be controlled with judicious pruning. Grows 10 to 15 ft. high, 20 to 30 ft. wide; an old specimen at the Biltmore estate in Asheville, North Carolina, is 25 to 30 ft. high.

Tsuga canadensis 'Sargentii'

Tsuga canadensis needle undersides

Tsuga canadensis cones

Tsuga caroliniana
Carolina Hemlock

Many gardeners rave about this species, but to my mind, it is inferior when compared to *Tsuga canadensis*. I have observed several young and mature specimens, and my heart never missed a beat. The habit is supposedly more compact and more narrowly pyramidal than that of *T. canadensis*, but trees I have observed are more open foliaged. The ¼- to ¾-in.-long, dark green needles have two white bands on their undersides, and they are entire along the margin, a detail that separates this species from the previous. Also, the 1- to 1½-in.-long, 1-in.-wide cones have scales that radiate out from the central axis, as opposed to overlapping like those of *T. canadensis*. Supposedly more tolerant of urban conditions, but I know of no quantitative data that authenticates this. Makes a respectable specimen plant. Not common in commerce. Grows 45 to 60 ft. high, 20 to 25 ft. wide. Zones 4 to 7. Southeastern United States.

Tsuga caroliniana, Carolina Hemlock

Tsuga caroliniana foliage and young cones

Tsuga caroliniana cone

Ulmus americana
American Elm

A fantastic, majestic, almost-perfect native tree that once permeated the consciousness of every American. Unfortunately, Dutch elm disease stripped our cities, towns, and gardens of this green beauty. Considerable effort has been made to breed clones that are resistant to Dutch elm disease, and the U.S. National Arboretum in Washington, DC, has released 'Valley Forge' and 'New Harmony'. Majestic in habit, American Elm has an upright-spreading outline and semipendent outer branches. Trees planted along boulevards meet to form cathedral ceiling–like archways. The 3- to 6-in.-long, leathery, dark green leaves turn butter-yellow to rich yellow in autumn. This elm species and those that follow are very easy to transplant and withstand extremes of soil conditions and pH. From a pragmatic viewpoint, it is difficult to recommend this species because of the disease problem. If the newer, resistant selections prove successful, then I would consider planting, but still in a cautious vein. Grows 60 to 80 ft. high, 30 to 50 ft. wide. Zones 2 to 9. Newfoundland to Florida, west to the Rockies.

Ulmus americana, American Elm

Ulmus americana fruit

Ulmus americana in fall

Ulmus carpinifolia
Smoothleaf Elm

Probably, if one took the time and searched every nursery catalog in the United States, this elm or one of its cultivars might be offered in one or two. At one time, Smoothleaf Elm was widely planted, particularly in the Midwest and Northeast, where it is found on campuses. This species is susceptible to Dutch elm disease, but not to the degree of *Ulmus americana*. The habit is weakly pyramidal-oval, with a straight trunk and slender, ascending branches. The 1½- to 4-in.-long, lustrous dark green leaves develop limited yellow fall color. Damage from the elm leaf beetle (browning of leaves) is also often evident. Grows 70 to 90 ft. high. Zones 5 to 7. Europe.

Ulmus carpinifolia, Smoothleaf Elm

Ulmus glabra
Scotch Elm

Because of Dutch elm disease, elm leaf beetle, and general scruffiness, this species does not deserve planting, at least not in the United States. Several cultivars, however, although not without their foibles, deserve mention. Both cultivars mentioned below are susceptible to Dutch elm disease and elm leaf beetle but, based on the number of extant specimens, are more resistant than the species. Zones 4 to 6(7). Northern and central Europe, western Asia.

Cultivars and Varieties. 'Camperdownii' is a strong weeping form. The dark green, sandpapery leaves seem to hover in the summer landscape. The leaves abscise to expose a handsome silhouette of weeping branches that sweep the ground. It bears few or no fruit. Effective as a character or accent plant. Usually grafted 6 to 7 ft. high on a standard, it grows 20 to 25 ft. high.

'Horizontalis' is often sold as 'Camperdownii', and in many arboreta is labeled as such, but it has smoother leaves, abundant fruit, and branches that are semipendent, never really touching the ground. Grows 15 ft. high, 33 ft. wide.

Ulmus glabra, Scotch Elm

Ulmus glabra 'Camperdownii'

Ulmus glabra 'Camperdownii' in winter

Ulmus glabra 'Horizontalis'

Ulmus parvifolia

Chinese or Lacebark Elm

Without question, this species should become the dominant shade and street tree of the 21st century. Many superior new selections have been introduced and are being produced in commerce. In the past, this tree suffered in popularity because it was often confused with the woeful *Ulmus pumila*, Siberian Elm, and because of the fact that it is an elm, which to many people connotes susceptibility to disease. *Ulmus parvifolia* has proven highly resistant to Dutch elm disease and the elm leaf beetle, facts that have been borne out by scientific research. Unfortunately, seedlings of *U. parvifolia* are so variable that the gardener may end up with a bonsai specimen or a 70-ft. tree. The habit is generally rounded with a finely textured, uniform branching structure. The ¾- to 2½-in.-long, leathery, dark green leaves may turn yellow to burgundy hues in fall. The most endearing ornamental characteristic of this species is the splendid exfoliating bark, which shows colors of gray, green, brown, and orange. The bark is a welcome colorful addition to the winter landscape, and the tree is worth incorporating into the garden for that reason alone. Unbelievably adaptable to extremes of soil and climate, it thrives from Iowa to Florida and from the Atlantic Coast to the Pacific. A great lawn, street, park, or grove tree. Its greatest days lie ahead. Grows 40 to 50 ft. high and wide; the variation in size, however, is phenomenal. Zones 5 to 9. China, Korea, Japan.

Cultivars and Varieties. The cultivars that follow offer great hope for the 21st-century landscape.

Allee® ('Emer II') is perhaps the finest of the recent introductions because of its resemblance to American Elm. It has an upright-spreading outline, dark green leaves, and astounding gray to orange-brown exfoliating bark. The 3-ft.-diameter trunk is fluted (corrugated) and the bark's brilliant mosaic extends from the 2-in.-diameter branches to the exposed surface roots. The parent tree was 70 ft. high and 60 ft. wide in 1992.

Athena® ('Emer I') is a broad-spreading tree with fine-textured branches. The leathery, extremely lustrous dark green leaves abscise early in autumn with a hint of yellow-bronze coloration. The bark develops the typical puzzlelike pattern of gray, gray-green, and orangish brown. The parent tree was 30 to 35 ft. high and 55 ft. wide.

'Dynasty', introduced by the U.S. National Arboretum, has leathery, dark green leaves. The bark, unfortunately, is not particularly outstanding. Grows 30 ft. high and wide after 16 years.

'King's Choice' is a rapid-growing selection with leathery, dark green leaves. The original selection grew 22 ft. high and 16 ft. wide in seven years.

'Milliken' is an oval-rounded form with rich green foliage and prominent exfoliating bark. Parent tree was 50 ft. high, 40 ft. wide in 1992.

Ulmus parvifolia, Lacebark Elm

Ulmus parvifolia Allee® in winter

Ulmus parvifolia fall color

Ulmus parvifolia Athena®

Ulmus parvifolia bark

Ulmus parvifolia 'Milliken'

Ulmus pumila
Siberian Elm

What a disastrous tree—unfortunately, it is still sold and planted. Many arborists made their fortunes from the limb breakage and general decline of this species. Usually I can find a bright light in every tree's closet—not so here. Although highly resistant to Dutch elm disease, the leaves of Siberian Elm are unbelievably susceptible to elm leaf beetle. In fact, the tree often looks like a brown bag in summer because of the incessant beetle feeding. The dark green leaves range from ¾ to 3 in. long and have no appreciable fall color. Admittedly, the species will tolerate miserable climates and soils, and it has been used for hybridizing purposes to impart resistance to Dutch elm disease to other species. With the resistance, however, came the susceptibility to the elm leaf beetle, and the new introductions, such as 'Urban', 'Homestead', and 'Pioneer', are less than satisfactory. Grows 50 to 70 ft. high, 40 to 50 ft. wide. Zones 4 to 9. Eastern Siberia, northern and northeastern China, Korea.

Ulmus pumila, Siberian Elm

Ulmus Hybrids
Elm Hybrids

A select few hybrids, often of complex parentage, were selected for their resistance to Dutch elm disease, but they do not always embody other quality elm traits. 'Cathedral', 'Frontier', 'Jacan', 'New Horizon', 'Prospector', 'Regal', and 'Sapporo Autumn Gold' represent a few of the new selections that gardeners and horticulturists might consider.

Vaccinium angustifolium
Lowbush Blueberry

Lowbush Blueberry is the most economically productive fruit crop in the state of Maine, and native stands of the plant are simply managed to prevent excessive weed growth. The species is rarely planted in cultivation, but the delicate pink flowers and sweet, bluish black berries are justification for use. It is a spreading, stoloniferous shrub, with lustrous dark green to blue-green foliage that turns brilliant scarlet and crimson in fall. Requires nothing but acid, low-fertility soils, in full sun or partial shade. Makes a fine groundcover mass and needs minimal maintenance. Grows ½ to 2 ft. high. Zones 2 to 5. Newfoundland to Saskatchewan, south to the mountains of New Hampshire and New York.

Vaccinium angustifolium, Lowbush Blueberry

Vaccinium angustifolium flowers

Vaccinium angustifolium fruit

Vaccinium angustifolium in fall

Vaccinium angustifolium fall color

Vaccinium corymbosum
Highbush Blueberry

For years, I have touted this most handsome shrub as a fine ornamental that also produces sufficient blueberries for cereal, jams, and pies. It is an excellent choice for incorporating in the border or the back of the vegetable garden. A strong, multistemmed shrub, its spreading branches form a rounded, dense, compact outline, especially when grown in full sun. The winter stems vary from yellow-green to deep red. The 1- to 3½-in.-long, dark green to blue-green leaves may turn yellow, bronze, orange, or red in fall. White or pink-tinged, ⅓-in.-long, urn-shaped flowers are borne in axillary racemes in May. The blue-black, waxy coated, ¼- to ½-in.-diameter fruit ripen in July and August. Fruit are not as sweet as those of *Vaccinium angustifolium*. Provide acid soils. Most blueberry plants are container grown and present no transplanting problem. Grows 6 to 12 ft. high, 8 to 12 ft. wide. Zones 3 to 7. Maine to Minnesota, south to Florida and Louisiana.

Vaccinium corymbosum, Highbush Blueberry

Vaccinium corymbosum in fall

Vaccinium corymbosum flowers

Vaccinium corymbosum fruit

Vaccinium vitis-idaea
Cowberry

Cowberry is an evergreen groundcover that seldom reaches more than 10 in. in height. The lustrous dark green leaves develop metallic mahogany winter color. White or pinkish flowers bloom in May and June and are followed by 3/8-in.-diameter, dark red fruit that ripen in August. Provide moist, peaty, acid soils, in full sun or partial shade. Makes a handsome rock garden plant. Zones 4 to 5. Northern United States, Canada.

Vaccinium vitis-idaea, Cowberry

Vaccinium vitis-idaea fruit

Viburnum acerifolium
Mapleleaf Viburnum

This suckering, colonizing denizen of the woods may be the most obscure of all the viburnums, but it offers tremendous shade tolerance and exquisite fall color. The dark green, three-lobed, 2- to 5-in.- long and wide leaves resemble Red Maple leaves, hence, the common name. The foliage turns fluorescent rose to grape-juice purple in fall. The 1- to 3-in.-diameter, white flower clusters open in June and are followed by 1/3-in.-long, shiny black fruit that ripen in September and persist into winter. Adaptable to difficult dry and shady conditions. Use as a mass or filler. Grows 4 to 6 ft. high, wider at maturity. Zones 3 to 8. New Brunswick to Minnesota, south to Georgia.

Viburnum acerifolium, Mapleleaf Viburnum

Viburnum acerifolium fall color

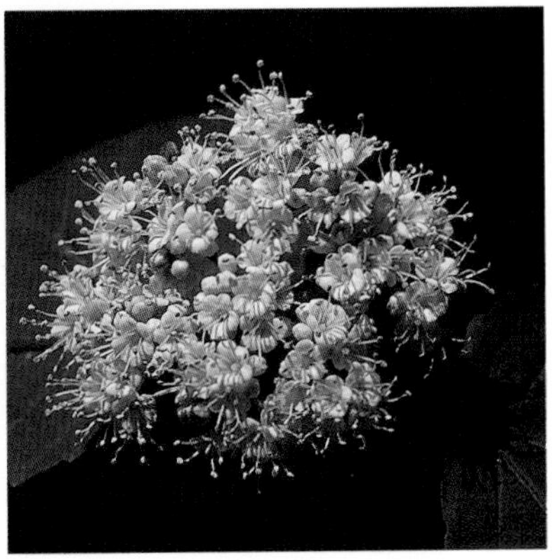

Viburnum acerifolium flowers

Viburnum ×burkwoodii, Burkwood Viburnum

Viburnum ×burkwoodii
Burkwood Viburnum

Viburnum popularity may ebb and flow like the tide, but this hybrid species never goes out of fashion, principally because of its climatic and cultural adaptability. Burkwood Viburnum develops into an oval-rounded shrub with a mass of rather fine stems. The 1½- to 4-in.-long, lustrous dark green leaves persist late in fall and may develop a burgundy color. In April, flower buds emerge pink, opening to 2- to 3-in.-wide, hemispherical, white flowers with the fragrance of Winter Daphne *(Daphne odora)*. Flowers are effective for only seven to ten days. Fruit are red, changing to black, and sparsely produced. Plant in moist, acid to neutral, well-drained soils, in full sun to partial shade. Maximum flowering occurs in full sun. A great plant for the shrub border. Grows 8 to 10 ft. high, slightly less in spread. Zones 4 to 8.

Viburnum ×burkwoodii flowers

Viburnum ×burkwoodii fruit

Viburnum ×burkwoodii fall color

Viburnum ×burkwoodii 'Chesapeake' foliage

Viburnum ×*carlcephalum*
Fragrant Viburnum

This loose, often open shrub offers deliciously fragrant flowers in late April and May. The flowers are pink in bud, finally white, in 5-in.-diameter clusters of half-snowball shape. The dark green leaves have a slight luster and may develop reddish purple fall color. Use in the border. Grows 6 to 10 ft. high. Zones (5)6 to 8.

Viburnum ×*burkwoodii* 'Eskimo'

Viburnum ×*burkwoodii* 'Mohawk' flowers

Viburnum ×*carlcephalum*, Fragrant Viburnum

Viburnum ×*carlcephalum* flower

Viburnum carlesii
Koreanspice Viburnum

Along with *Viburnum* ×*burkwoodii*, this is the most familiar viburnum species because of the excellent spicy-sweet fragrance of its flowers. Koreanspice Viburnum develops into a dense, rounded shrub with stiff, upright-spreading branches. The 2- to 4-in.-long, dull dark green leaves may develop reddish to wine-red fall color. Pink- to reddish budded flowers open white and offer a wonderful fragrance. The 2- to 3-in.-diameter, semi-snowball inflorescences are at their best in late April and May when the leaves are about one-half to two-thirds their mature size. Use in a foundation planting, in the border, or in a grouping. Grows 4 to 8 ft. high and wide. Zones 4 to 7. Korea.

Cultivars and Varieties. 'Compactum' has exceptionally dark green leaves, and its flowers are about the same size as those of the species. Grows 2½ to 3½ ft. high and wide.

Viburnum carlesii, Koreanspice Viburnum

Viburnum carlesii flowers

Viburnum carlesii fall color

Viburnum dentatum flowers

Viburnum dentatum
Arrowwood Viburnum

In any landscape, Arrowwood Viburnum feels as comfortable as an old shoe. It has a durable nature and offers glossy dark green leaves, white flowers, and bluish fruit. It becomes a large, rounded shrub with spreading, finally arching branches. The lustrous dark green, 2- to 4½-in.-long leaves may turn yellow to red in fall. The white flowers are borne in 2- to 4-in.-diameter, flat-topped cymes in May and June. The bluish to blue-black fruit mature in September and October and are a favorite food of birds, and plants can be stripped in short order. Valued for its durability and utility, it makes a good hedge or screen and is useful in groupings, masses, and barriers. Displays excellent salt tolerance and is evident in New England coastal areas. Variable in size. Grows 6 to 8 (to 15) ft. high, 6 to 15 ft. wide. Zones 2 to 8. New Brunswick to Minnesota, south to Georgia.

Viburnum dentatum, Arrowwood Viburnum

Viburnum dentatum fruit

Viburnum dentatum fall color

Viburnum dilatatum, Linden Viburnum

Viburnum dilatatum
Linden Viburnum

Certainly one of the best fruiting shrubs for American gardens. Habit is variable; most often upright and somewhat stiff, others are densely rounded. The 2- to 5-in.-long, lustrous dark green leaves change to inconsistent russet-reds in fall. White flowers are borne in 3- to 5-in.-diameter, flat-topped cymes in May and June. The real show follows in September and October when the ⅔-in.-long, ovoid fruit ripen to bright red, cherry-red, or scarlet. The fruit often persist into winter. A great plant for groupings, borders, or large masses around commercial buildings. Don Egolf's breeding work at the National Arboretum in Washington, DC, has resulted in several superior cultivars. Grows 8 to 10 ft. high, variable spread. Zones (4)5 to 7. Eastern Asia.

MORE ➤

Viburnum dilatatum continued

Cultivars and Varieties. 'Asian Beauty', 'Catskill', 'Erie', and 'Iroquois' are some of the better selections for contemporary landscapes.

Viburnum dilatatum fall color

Viburnum dilatatum flowers

Viburnum dilatatum 'Erie' fruit

Viburnum farreri

Fragrant Viburnum

A delightfully fragrant, early blooming shrub that foreshadows the advent of spring, yet it is nowhere common in gardens. The habit is loose, unkempt, and unruly, possibly a reason for the plant's scarcity. The leaves emerge bronzy green, turn dark green, and finally take on reddish purple hues in fall. The 1½- to 4-in.-long leaves have deeply pleated veins. Fragrant pink flowers occur in 1- to 2-in.-long panicles in March and April, before the leaves. The flowers are randomly produced, and the shrub never quite jumps out and says "hello." Prefers moist, acid, well-drained soils, but plants did prosper in the higher pH soil of my Illinois garden. Use in the border; definitely not for single-specimen use. Grows 8 to 12 ft. high and wide. Zones (4)5 to 8. Northern China.

Cultivars and Varieties. 'Candidissimum' has white flowers and bright green leaves.

'Nanum' is a compact form, smaller in all its parts, with pinkish buds that open to fragrant, pinkish white flowers. It is tidier than the species. Grows 2 to 3 (to 4) ft. high, 4 to 6 ft. wide.

Viburnum farreri, Fragrant Viburnum

Viburnum farreri foliage

Viburnum farreri flowers

Viburnum ×juddii flowers

Viburnum farreri 'Nanum'

Viburnum ×juddii

Judd Viburnum

Gardeners have debated the fragrance strength of this species as compared to that of *Viburnum carlesii*, but to my olfactory senses, there is little difference. Judd Viburnum is a full, rounded shrub with dark green, almost blue-green leaves. Pink buds open to fragrant, white flowers in 2½- to 3¼-in.-diameter, semi-snowball inflorescences in late April and May. Has displayed better heat tolerance than *V. carlesii*. Exhibits better resistance to bacterial leaf spot than most other viburnums. Grows 6 to 8 ft. high and wide. Zones 4 to 8.

Viburnum ×juddii, Judd Viburnum

Viburnum lantana

Wayfaringtree Viburnum

An old standby in the Midwest and Northeast because of its ironclad adaptability and reliable performance over time. The habit is distinctly rounded with stout, coarse branches. The dull dark green, 2- to 5-in.-long leaves seldom develop good fall color. White flowers are borne in 3- to 5-in.-diameter cymes in May. The fruit are extremely handsome, beginning yellow and changing to red and black, often with all colors on the same infructescence. Fruiting is maximized when several different clones are in close proximity. One of the best viburnums for calcareous, clay-based soils. Use in the border, as a screen, or in groupings. It is coarse in winter and, for that reason, is best mixed with other shrubs. Grows 10 to 15 ft. high and wide. Zones 4 to 8. Europe, western Asia.

Cultivars and Varieties. 'Mohican' is more compact than the species and has darker green leaves and heavy, orange-red fruit set. Original selection was 8½ ft. high and 9 ft. wide after 15 years.

Viburnum lantana, Wayfaringtree Viburnum

Viburnum lentago

Nannyberry Viburnum

In its finest form, this is an attractive large shrub or small tree. Unfortunately, it is often disfigured by mildew. Nannyberry Viburnum offers 2- to 4-in.-long leaves that emerge soft yellow-green, turn glossy dark green, and may change to purplish red in fall. The 3- to 4½-in.-wide, white inflorescences open in May. They are followed by green, yellow, rose, and pink fruit that mature to purplish black. Plant where air movement is excellent to best deter mildew. Use in a naturalized planting. Grows 15 to 18 (to 30) ft. high, quite variable in spread. Zones 2 to 7. Hudson Bay to Manitoba, south to Georgia and Mississippi.

Viburnum lentago, Nannyberry Viburnum

Viburnum lantana flowers

Viburnum lantana 'Mohican' fruit

Viburnum opulus
European Cranberrybush Viburnum

Viburnum lentago flowers

Viburnum lentago fruit

An old favorite that is at home from Fargo, North Dakota, to Boston, Massachusetts. It is a large, coarse, rounded shrub that is quite imposing in the winter landscape. In leaf, however, it is significantly less intense. The three-lobed, maplelike leaves average 2 to 4 in. long and wide. The lustrous dark green leaves may develop yellow-red to purplish red autumn tints. Flowers occur in 2- to 3- (to 4-) in.-diameter, flat-topped cymes. The outer flowers are white and showy, the inner ones fertile and rather inconspicuous, and the entire effect is pinwheel-like. The ¼- to ⅜-in.-diameter fruit change from yellow to bright red and give the plant its common name. Fruit may persist into winter but will develop the appearance of dried raisins. Excellent shrub for fruit effect. Always use in borders. Tolerates wet or boggy areas better than many plants. Grows 8 to 12 (to 15) ft. high and wide. Zones 3 to 7(8). Europe, northern Africa, northern Asia.

Cultivars and Varieties. 'Compactum' matures to about half the size of the species and offers similar flowers and fruit. Good choice where space is a problem.

'Nanum' is a dwarf form with fine branches and smaller leaves. This form usually does not flower or fruit. Grows 1½ to 2 ft. high, 2 to 3 ft. wide; I have observed 4- to 5-ft.-high plants.

'Roseum', European Snowball or Guilder-Rose, has the same growth characteristics as the species, except its flowers are sterile and occur in 2½- to 3-in.-diameter, white, snowball-shaped inflorescences.

Viburnum opulus flowers

Viburnum opulus fruit

Viburnum opulus, European Cranberrybush Viburnum

MORE ➤

Viburnum opulus 'Roseum' flowers

Viburnum opulus 'Compactum'

Viburnum plicatum

Japanese Snowball Viburnum

Much like the next entry, except this species has a more upright growth habit and its flowers open about two to three weeks later than those of Doublefile Viburnum. The sterile, semi-snowball, 2- to 3-in.-diameter, white, carnationlike flowers last for two to three weeks. Grows 15 ft. high. Zones 5 to 8.

Viburnum plicatum flowers

Viburnum plicatum, Japanese Snowball Viburnum

Viburnum plicatum var. *tomentosum*

Doublefile Viburnum

An aristocrat among flowering shrubs. In its finest form, Doublefile Viburnum is a graceful, horizontally branched shrub. The 2- to 4- (to 6-) in.-wide, white flower cymes, similar in appearance to those of *Viburnum opulus*, are raised on 2-in.-high stalks above the foliage, resulting in a Milky Way effect. The flowers open in May. The 2- to 4- (to 5-) in.-long, dark green leaves are deeply veined and appear pleated. Fall color is often a good wine-red. The bright cherry-red fruit ripen in July and August, changing to black, and are a favorite food of birds. In my experience, this variety resents dry soil and heat stress more than any other viburnum. Provide ample moisture. Surprisingly, plants flower as well in shade as in sun. Use as an understory shrub, in borders, or as a specimen. It is virtually impossible to err when utilizing this variety or one of its excellent cultivars. Grows 8 to 10 ft. high, 9 to 12 ft. wide. Zones 5 to 8. China, Japan.

Cultivars and Varieties. 'Lanarth', 'Mariesii', and 'Shasta' are among the best of the numerous available cultivars.

Viburnum plicatum var. *tomentosum*, Doublefile Viburnum

Viburnum plicatum var. *tomentosum* fruit

Viburnum plicatum var. *tomentosum* fall color

Viburnum plicatum var. *tomentosum* 'Lanarth' flowers

Viburnum ×pragense
Prague Viburnum

Prague Viburnum is a hybrid between *Viburnum rhytidophyllum* and *V. utile* and embodies the best features of both parents. It is an oval-rounded shrub with 2- to 4-in.-long, waxy, dark green evergreen leaves. In May, pink buds open to white, pleasantly fragrant flowers. I have not observed fruit set. This species is extremely fast growing and occasionally requires pruning to fatten it up. It makes a great foliage mass or screen and can serve as an excellent background shrub for other plants. This hybrid is more cold hardy than *V. rhytidophyllum*, by 5 to 8°F, and should remain evergreen at –10°F. Grows 10 ft. high or more, 8 to 10 ft. wide. Zones 5 to 8.

Viburnum ×pragense, Prague Viburnum

Viburnum ×pragense foliage

Viburnum prunifolium
Blackhaw Viburnum

A great native species that has been described by Florence Robinson as a "puritan with a rigidity of character similar to some of the hawthorns." Blackhaw Viburnum develops into a large, stiffly branched shrub or small tree. The 1½- to 3½-in.-long, dark green leaves change to bronze, dull deep red, and shining red in fall. White flowers occur in 2- to 4-in.-diameter, flat-topped cymes in May. The fruit are quite similar to those of *Viburnum lentago*, and they pass from pinkish rose to bluish black at maturity. Very adaptable. Much like *V. lentago*, but this species is preferable because of its mildew resistance and superior foliage. Grows 12 to 15 ft. high, 8 to 12 ft. wide; can grow to a 20-ft.-high tree. Zones 3 to 9. Connecticut to Michigan, south to Florida and Texas.

Viburnum prunifolium, Blackhaw Viburnum

Viburnum prunifolium foliage

Viburnum prunifolium flowers

Viburnum prunifolium fruit

Viburnum ×*rhytidophylloides* 'Allegheny' foliage

Viburnum ×*rhytidophylloides*

Lantanaphyllum Viburnum

This is another useful hybrid viburnum, with *Viburnum rhytidophyllum* and *V. lantana* as parents. In my estimation, this plant and especially its cultivars are superior to either parent in ornamental quality and cultural adaptability. It is often confused with *V. rhytidophyllum*, but the leaves of the hybrid are much wider in the middle and are tardily deciduous. Flowers and fruit are similar to those of *V. lantana*. Requires another clone for cross-pollination. Excellent large shrub for screens, groupings, and backgrounds. Grows 10 to 15 ft. high and wide. Zones 4 to 8.

Cultivars and Varieties. 'Allegheny' is a superior selection, with dark green, coriaceous leaves, abundant inflorescences, and a vigorous, dense, globose growth habit. It is resistant to bacterial leaf spot. Appears slightly more cold hardy than the typical species. The original plant was 10½ ft. high, 11 ft. wide after 13 years.

'Willowwood' offers excellent lustrous, rugose, dark green foliage and an arching habit. Leaves may be more persistent than those of 'Allegheny'. Has the odd trait of flowering in the fall. A good selection, but no match for 'Allegheny'.

Viburnum ×*rhytidophylloides*, Lantanaphyllum Viburnum, flowers

Viburnum ×*rhytidophylloides* fruit

Viburnum ×*rhytidophylloides* 'Allegheny'

Viburnum rhytidophyllum
Leatherleaf Viburnum

For textural quality, this large-leaved evergreen shrub is a fine addition to the border. Although somewhat out of place in modern gardens because of its massive, rounded outline and coarse texture, it still functions for screening or as a background shrub. The leathery, lustrous dark green leaves are 3 to 7½ in. long and 1 to 2½ in. wide and heavily veined. Creamy flowers are borne in 4- to 8-in.-wide inflorescences in May. The flower buds are formed the previous summer and appear as small, brownish spheres in fall and winter. The fruit are spectacular and rival those of *Viburnum lantana* for effect and color. The oval, ⅓-in.-long fruit pass from yellow to red to black at maturity. For maximum fruiting, cross-pollinate with other clones or seedlings. This species grows best in heavy shade and should be sheltered from winter wind and sun. Prefers a more organic matter–laden, moist, well-drained soil than many viburnums. Grows 10 to 15 ft. high and wide. Zones 6 to 8. Central and western China.

Viburnum rhytidophyllum, Leatherleaf Viburnum

Viburnum rhytidophyllum flowers

Viburnum rhytidophyllum foliage

Viburnum rhytidophyllum fruit

Viburnum rufidulum
Rusty Blackhaw Viburnum

A beautiful plant with creamy white flowers, pink to blue-black fruit, reddish purple fall color, and blocky, blackish bark. The habit is oval to rounded, and full-grown specimens are behemoths (in the wild, plants can grow 30 to 40 ft. tall). The 2- to 4-in.-long, leathery, glossy dark green leaves are exquisite. Flowers occur in 2- to 4-in.-diameter, flat-topped cymes in May and June. Tolerates heavy shade, but maximum flowering and fruiting occur in full sun. Adaptable to dry soils. Use in the border, for screening, or in large groupings. Grows 10 to 20 ft. high and wide. Zones 5 to 9. Virginia to Illinois, south to Florida and Texas.

Viburnum rufidulum, Rusty Blackhaw Viburnum

Viburnum rufidulum flowers

Viburnum rufidulum foliage

Viburnum rufidulum fall color

Viburnum sargentii
Sargent Viburnum

Sargent Viburnum is a robust, large, coarse shrub, not unlike *Viburnum opulus* or *V. trilobum* in general characteristics. The habit is distinctly upright-rounded to rounded. The three-lobed, 2- to 5-in.-long, dark green leaves are leathery in texture and assume yellowish to reddish hues in autumn. The leaves have a longer central (terminal) lobe than those of *V. opulus* and *V. trilobum*. The flowers have the same configuration as those of the other species, but the anthers are purple, compared to the yellow color of *V. opulus* and *V. trilobum*. Flowers usually open in May, perhaps slightly later than *V. opulus*. The scarlet, ½-in.-long fruit are effective from August into October. Sargent Viburnum is definitely not heat tolerant and should be reserved for the cooler northern states. Uses are similar to that of *V. opulus*. Grows 12 to 15 ft. high and wide. Zones 3 to 6(7). Northeastern Asia.

Cultivars and Varieties. 'Onondaga' and 'Susquehanna' are two National Arboretum introductions, possibly better than the typical species. 'Onondaga' has dark maroon new growth and a more compact growth habit. 'Susquehanna' is a heavily branched form with corky bark and leathery, dark green foliage. It fruits heavily. Grows 12 to 15 ft. high and wide.

Viburnum sargentii, Sargent Viburnum

Viburnum sargentii fall color

Viburnum sargentii 'Onondaga' flowers

Viburnum sargentii fruit

Viburnum setigerum
Tea Viburnum

Gardening aficionados rave about the supposed sculptural quality of the branches and the handsome, persistent red fruit. Try to sell this plant on the open market, however, and you probably wouldn't do too well. If used in a border where the bare stems can be masked by facer plants, it can serve a wonderful function. Typically, plants are upright-arching in habit, with foliage only on the upper half of the shrub. Inconspicuous white flowers occur in 1- to 2-in.-diameter, flat-topped cymes in May and June, and one has to look pretty hard to see if plants are actually in flower. The ⅓-in.-long, egg-shaped, bright red fruit ripen in September and October and persist into late fall. This species prefers full sun for best fruit set, but reasonable fruiting does occur in shady environments. Grows 8 to 12 ft. high, 6 to 10 ft. wide. Zones 5 to 7. China.

Cultivars and Varieties. 'Aurantiacum' offers orange fruit and provides a pleasing color element in the shrub border.

Viburnum setigerum flowers

Viburnum setigerum, Tea Viburnum

Viburnum setigerum fruit and fall color

Viburnum sieboldii
Siebold Viburnum

Siebold Viburnum is one of the largest viburnum species, easily topping 20 ft. tall, and is suitable as a large shrub or small tree. This viburnum, possibly more so than any other, deserves specimen use. The lustrous dark green leaves average 2 to 6 in. long and have the odor of green pepper when bruised. Leaves hold late, and fall color seldom develops. Creamy white flowers open in May and June in 3- to 6-in.-diameter, flat-topped clusters. The flowers are borne in great profusion and mask the bright green foliage. The fruit, which ripen in October, can be spectacular, especially as they change from rose to red to black. The fruit stalks are a rich, almost fluorescent rose-red and remain effective for two to four weeks after the fruit have fallen. Requires sufficient moisture; leaf scorch will develop under stress of high heat and drought. Utilize as a small tree against buildings or walls or in the open. The nice rigidity of habit provides a texture different from that of dogwood or redbud. Grows 15 to 20 ft. high, 10 to 15 ft. wide; can reach 30 ft. high. Zones 4 to 7(8). Japan.

Viburnum sieboldii, Siebold Viburnum

Viburnum sieboldii flowers

Viburnum sieboldii fruit and fruit stalks

Viburnum trilobum
American Cranberrybush Viburnum

For the casual observer, separating this species from European Cranberrybush Viburnum *(Viburnum opulus)* is exceedingly difficult. Habit, flowers, and fruit are all quite similar. One major reliable difference is the stalked or raised petiolar glands of *V. trilobum*, as compared to the squatty, concave glands of *V. opulus*. For general landscape use in the northern states, *V. trilobum* is a better choice because of its superior fall color and greater resistance to aphids. Provide moist soils and a cool climate for best growth. I have seen it used to define property boundaries, as a hedge or screen, and in groupings. A handsome plant with multiseason ornamental characteristics. Grows 8 to 12 ft. high and wide. Zones 2 to 6(7). New Brunswick to British Columbia, south to New York and Oregon.

Cultivars and Varieties. 'Compactum' offers fine-textured branches and smaller leaves. Flowering and fruiting characteristics are quite good. Grows 5 to 6 ft. high and wide. 'Alfredo' and 'Bailey Compact' are other compact forms.

'Andrews', 'Hahs', and 'Wentworth' are good fruiting forms selected for their edible fruit. 'Andrews' fruits early in the season, 'Hahs' in midseason, and 'Wentworth' late. 'Hahs' and 'Wentworth' are excellent ornamental shrubs and are preferable to the typical species.

Viburnum trilobum, American Cranberrybush Viburnum

Viburnum trilobum fruit

Viburnum trilobum flowers

Viburnum trilobum fall color

Viburnum trilobum 'Compactum'

Vitex agnus-castus
Chastetree

I never fully appreciated the merits of this species until I saw 20-ft.-high shrubs covered with lilac-purple flowers in June and July. Truly a most magnificent experience! In the North, the species is a dieback shrub, but it will flower on new growth of the season. The habit is rounded to broad-rounded. On old specimens, the gray-brown bark develops a blocky, alligator-hide texture. The dark gray-green, aromatic leaves are composed of five to seven 2- to 4- (to 5-) in.-long leaflets that hold late and are usually killed by the first heavy frost. Flowers occur in 12- to 18-in.- high and wide panicles at the ends of the branches. Keep plants well fertilized and watered in the early part of the growing season to encourage vigorous shoots and, eventually, large flowers. Plant in full sun. Use as a herbaceous perennial in Boston, a large shrub in Baltimore, or a small tree in Atlanta. White- and pink-flowered forms are known; however, the white form is a weaker grower. Grows 6 to 10 ft. high or more, often wider at maturity. Zones (6)7 to 8(9). Southern Europe, western Asia.

Vitex agnus-castus, Chastetree

Vitex agnus-castus flowers

Vitex agnus-castus foliage

Vitex negundo
Chastetree

This species is not as widely planted as *Vitex agnus-castus*, and based on my observations, it is not as robust or large flowering. Larger plants are open, airy, and fine textured and have smaller, 5- to 8-in.-long panicles of lilac or lavender flowers. Cultural requirements are similar to that of the previous species. This species is possibly cold hardy to one more zone. Grows 10 to 15 ft. high and wide. Zones (5)6 to 8(9). Southeast Africa, Madagascar, eastern and southeastern Asia, Philippines.

Cultivars and Varieties. 'Heterophylla', with finely cut, gray-green leaves, provides an excellent foliage effect. Ideally it should be cut to the ground in late winter to induce long shoot extensions.

Vitex negundo, Chastetree

Vitis

Grape

Vitex negundo 'Heterophylla' foliage

Few gardeners in the United States consider grapes to be ornamental plants, but in Europe they are often used as wall plants to provide foliage color and texture. I will describe here a few species worthy of note. The two species I see most often are *Vitis cognetiae*, Gloryvine Grape, and *V. rotundifolia*, Muscadine Grape. Gloryvine Grape has 4- to 10-in.-wide, dull green, leathery leaves that turn rich scarlet in fall. I was given a small dormant plant of this species, or so I was told, only to find out when the leaves emerged that it was, in fact, *V. rotundifolia*. *Vitis rotundifolia* bears large, coppery green to purple, edible fruit and displays yellow fall color. *Vitis vinifera*, Wine Grape, is another common garden species. Its 3- to 6-in.-wide, rich green leaves have three to five lobes. *Vitis vinifera* 'Purpurea' has attractive new leaves that mature to dull reddish purple. Grape plants climb by means of tendrils and require support. Most prosper in moist, acid, well-drained soils, in sun or partial shade. Many grape species exist as understory vines in the wild. Zones 5 to 7(8).

Vitis, Grape, growing along a stone wall

Vitis fruit

Vitis vinifera 'Purpurea'

Weigela florida
Old-Fashioned Weigela

My negative sentiments toward this species were formed in my youth, when I saw the old, dirty, lavender-pink form haunting virtually every garden in the Midwest. Ugly! Times have changed, however, and breeders have improved upon the species by offering a variety of flower colors, more compact forms, and greater cold hardiness. I counted some 39 cultivars in the latest edition of my *Manual of Woody Landscape Plants*. The typical species is a spreading, dense, rounded shrub, with coarse branches that arch to the ground. The 2- to 4½-in.-long leaves are a nondescript green and are even worse in fall. The rosy pink flowers average 1 to 2 in. long, with an extended tubular corolla that flares at the mouth. The flowers occur in great profusion during May and June and sporadically throughout the growing season. Provide well-drained soils of moderate fertility and full sun for best growth. Prune after flowering. Shrubs often retain dead branches and require tidying. Use in masses or in a shrub border. Grows 6 to 9 ft. high, 9 to 12 ft. wide. Zones (4)5 to 8. Japan.

Weigela middendorffiana is a similar species with yellow flowers.

Cultivars and Varieties. Some of the better cold-hardy selections include: 'Minuet', with ruby-red flowers; 'Newport Red', ruby-red; 'Pink Princess', lavender-pink; 'Polka', pink outside, yellow inside; 'Red Prince', red; 'Rumba', dark red with a yellow throat; 'Samba', red, yellow throat; and 'Tango', red, yellow throat.

Weigela florida, Old-Fashioned Weigela

Weigela florida 'Newport Red' flowers

Weigela florida 'Red Prince' flowers

Weigela florida 'Pink Princess' flowers

Wisteria floribunda
Japanese Wisteria

Gardeners in the North labor intensely to successfully flower this species, while southerners with pruning equipment attempt to eradicate it. One gardener's flower is another's weed. Japanese Wisteria is a wild, twining vine that crushes any plant or wooden structure in its path in a boa constrictor–like fashion. The rich green leaves are composed of (11 to) 13 to 19 leaflets, each 1½ to 3 in. long. Fragrant, violet-blue, ½- to ¾-in.-long flowers are borne in 8- to 20-in.-long racemes that open from the base to the apex. The flowers open before or as the leaves develop in April and May. The fruit are 4- to 6-in.-long pods that contain multiple green bean–like seeds. The species thrives with minimal care and is quite adaptable to soil conditions. Provide full sun to partial shade and a suitable structure, preferably one that is metal. Use with the knowledge that considerable pruning is necessary to keep it in bounds. It is sometimes trained as a small tree and then pruned to maintain this shape. Many cultivars are available in a variety of flower colors, from white to pink-rose, violet, and deep purple. Can grow 30 to 50 ft. high; I have seen 80- to 90-ft.-high vines in oak trees along the South Carolina coast. Zones 4 to 9. Japan.

Wisteria floribunda, Japanese Wisteria

Wisteria sinensis
Chinese Wisteria

Arguably, Chinese Wisteria is superior to Japanese Wisteria as a landscape vine because of its less-rampant growth. The flowers open along the 6- to 12-in. length of the raceme at more or less the same time as those of *Wisteria floribunda*. Leaves are composed of 7 to 13 leaflets. Grows 20 to 30 ft. high. Zones 5 to 8. China.

Wisteria sinensis fruit

Wisteria floribunda flowers

Wisteria sinensis, Chinese Wisteria

Wisteria sinensis flowers

Xanthoceras sorbifolium
Yellowhorn

A virtual unknown in American gardens. Perhaps the best specimen resides at Winterthur Gardens in Delaware. The habit is not unlike that of *Koelreuteria paniculata*, Panicled Goldenrain Tree, developing an ultimately rounded outline of rather coarse branches. The lustrous dark green leaves are compound pinnate, with 9 to 17 sharply serrated, 1½- to 2½-in.-long leaflets that remain late into fall. Fragrant white flowers, each ¾ to 1 in. in diameter, occur in 6- to 10-in.-long racemes in May. Each flower has a yellow basal blotch that matures to red. The fruit are three-valved, 2- to 4-in.-long capsules, each containing several dark brown, pea-sized seeds. Adaptable to any well-drained soil of acid or high pH. Requires full sun for maximum growth. Use as a small flowering tree, either free standing or in a border. Grows 18 ft. high, 24 ft. wide. Zones (3)4 to 6(7). Northern China.

Xanthoceras sorbifolium foliage

Xanthoceras sorbifolium flowers

Xanthoceras sorbifolium, Yellowhorn

Xanthorhiza simplicissima
Yellowroot

The absence of this fine native species in the American landscape has always been a mystery to me. In the wild, this robust, suckering, woody groundcover occurs along shady watercourses. Under cultivation, it develops into a full, dense groundcover mass, particularly when sited in full sun. The leaves are composed of three to five 1½- to 2¾-in.-long, lustrous bright green leaflets that hold late and turn golden yellow to orange in fall. Flowers and fruit are not showy. The purple flowers appear in March and April. For best growth, provide moist, well-drained soils and ample light, although magnificent plantings will develop under less-than-ideal conditions. Could be used effectively in shady nooks and crannies around buildings. Grows 2 to 3 ft. high. Zones 3 to 9. New York to Kentucky and Florida.

Xanthorhiza simplicissima, Yellowroot

Xanthorhiza simplicissima flowers

Yucca

Yucca

Although seldom considered as shrubs, the yuccas are acaulescent or caulescent evergreen plants with swordlike leaves and reliable adaptability. The species are much confused taxonomically, but they are more or less the same for landscape considerations. They offer creamy white flowers in large inflorescences above the leaves in July and August. For textural effect, the 1- to 2½-ft.-long, 1½- to 3-in.-wide leaves provide a desert Southwest atmosphere. Yuccas thrive in infertile, dry, sandy soils, in full sun. Transplant from a container. *Yucca filamentosa*, Adam's-Needle Yucca, *Y. flaccida*, Weakleaf Yucca, *Y. glauca*, Small Soapweed, and *Y. smalliana*, Small Yucca, are the most cold-hardy and the most landscape-worthy species. Yuccas are hardy to at least –15 to –20°F. Grows 2 to 3 ft. high. Zones (4)5 to 9. Eastern and midwestern United States.

Cultivars and Varieties. 'Golden Sword', with green-margined, yellow-centered leaves, and 'Bright Edge', just the opposite, are rather soul-stirring selections; both are probably cultivars of *Yucca filamentosa*.

Yucca 'Bright Edge'

Yucca 'Golden Sword' foliage

Zelkova serrata
Japanese Zelkova

Japanese Zelkova has become a major player in the shade-tree market in recent years. Much of this success resulted from the introduction of superior forms like 'Village Green' and 'Green Vase'. Typically, seedling zelkovas grow like a rabbit's hind legs—crooked and uneven. They make respectable trees, however, if properly pruned. Habit is typically vase-shaped, with branches diverging at 45° angles to the central axis. The habit is similar to that of American Elm *(Ulmus americana)*, but without the dignity and grace. Dark green, strongly serrated, 2- to 5-in.-long leaves give way to yellow, golden bronze, and reddish purple fall colors. The brown bark on young trees has a polished, almost cherrylike quality, becoming gray and exfoliating with age, somewhat like that of *Ulmus parvifolia*, Chinese Elm. Adaptable to varied soils and climates. Displays tolerance to high heat and drought. Resistant to Dutch elm disease and the elm leaf beetle. Makes a fine street and park tree. Grows 50 to 80 ft. high, similar spread. Zones 5 to 8. Japan.

Cultivars and Varieties. 'Green Vase' is an excellent cultivar with upright-arching branches, resulting in a more graceful tree than 'Village Green'. Excellent dark green foliage turns orange-brown to bronzy red in fall. Faster growing than 'Village Green'. Grows 60 to 70 ft. high, 40 to 50 ft. wide.

'Village Green' was one of the first named selections, and it is still justifiably popular. The crown is more dense and stiff than that of 'Green Vase'. Old trees that I have observed were equal in height and width. The leathery, dark green foliage may develop a wine-red fall color. At maturity, probably smaller than 'Green Vase'.

Zelkova serrata, Japanese Zelkova

Zelkova serrata 'Green Vase', in a formal allée

Zelkova serrata bark

Zelkova serrata fall color

Zenobia pulverulenta
Dusty Zenobia

Dusty Zenobia is another underutilized native species that is more culturally adaptable than is generally believed. Plantings in full sun, in moist sites, at the Arnold Arboretum were successful. The habit is rounded-mounded with gracefully arching, slender branches. Plants tend to sucker and colonize. The typical bluish green to grayish green foliage is quite handsome and usually persists into winter. I have seen selections with almost silvery blue summer foliage that, if propagated in any numbers, would become popular plants. In autumn, leaves may turn yellowish with a tinge of red. The white, ⅜-in.-wide, anise-scented flowers arrive in May and June. The standard cultural recommendation is for acid, moist, well-drained soils, but again it is more adaptable than it is generally given credit. Use this species in mass plantings, along streams, or in a perennial or shrub border. Variable in almost all characteristics. Grows 2 to 3(6) ft. high and as wide. Zones 5 to 9. North Carolina to Florida.

Zenobia pulverulenta flowers

Zenobia pulverulenta, Dusty Zenobia

Zenobia pulverulenta fall color

Zenobia pulverulenta foliage

PART II

Selecting Plants for Specific Characteristics or Purposes

Many readers require ready access to information on specific plants for specific purposes. In compiling the following lists of the plants best suited to certain commonly desired characteristics or purposes, I have limited the number of entries to those plants that are most appropriate. Certainly a tad of personal bias is evident, but in the main, I erred on the side of objectivity. Use these lists as ready references to possible solutions for planting design problems. Perhaps salt tolerance is a criterion for landscaping a beach house; *Rosa rugosa, Myrica pensylvanica,* and *Prunus maritima* appear on the list of salt-tolerant shrubs. Look them up in the plant listings, read the text, peruse the photographs, and decide which plants will create the desired effects.

This information is categorized by Trees, including deciduous conifers and ginkgo; Shrubs, including broadleaf evergreen shrubs; Needle Evergreens; and Vines.

Plant Lists

Flower Color and Fragrance

The following trees bear flowers with notable color and/or fragrance. Flower color has been categorized according to general color groups: white, yellow, pink/rose, red, and purple. The primary flower color(s) is indicated for each species or genus. Variations of flower color will exist in certain cultivars or varieties of a plant, and flowers can often be ornamented with stripes or blotches of a different color.

TREE	COLOR					FRAGRANCE	COMMENTS
	WHITE	YELLOW	PINK/ROSE	RED	PURPLE		
Acer ginnala	★					★	
Acer platanoides		★					
Acer rubrum				★			
Acer tataricum	★					★	
Acer truncatum		★					
Aesculus ×carnea				★			
Aesculus hippocastanum	★						
Aesculus pavia				★			
Albizia julibrissin			★			★	
Amelanchier	★						
Aralia	★						
Asimina triloba					★		
Castanea mollissima	★						Malodorous
Catalpa	★						
Cercis canadensis			★				Magenta buds
Chionanthus	★					★	
Cladrastis kentukea	★					★	
Cornus alternifolia	★						
Cornus florida	★						
Cornus kousa	★						
Cornus mas		★					
Cornus officinalis		★					
Crataegus	★						Somewhat malodorous
Evodia daniellii	★						
Halesia	★						
Hovenia dulcis	★						
Kalopanax pictus	★						
Koelreuteria paniculata		★					
Laburnum ×watereri		★					
Maackia amurensis	★					★	
Magnolia	★	★	★		★	★	
Malus floribunda	★					★	Red buds
Malus hupehensis	★					★	Pink buds
Malus sargentii	★					★	Red buds
Malus sieboldii var. *zumi*	★					★	Red buds
Malus cultivars	★		★	★		★	Red or pink buds
Oxydendrum arboreum	★					★	
Parrotia persica				★			
Paulownia tomentosa					★	★	
Prunus avium	★					★	

TREE	COLOR					FRAGRANCE	COMMENTS
	WHITE	YELLOW	PINK/ROSE	RED	PURPLE		
Prunus cerasifera	★		★			★	
Prunus ×incam 'Okame'			★			★	
Prunus maackii	★					★	
Prunus padus	★					★	
Prunus persica	★		★	★		★	
Prunus sargentii			★			★	
Prunus serotina	★					★	
Prunus serrulata	★		★				
Prunus subhirtella	★		★				
Prunus virginiana	★					★	
Prunus ×yedoensis	★					★	Pink buds
Pyrus	★						Somewhat malodorous
Robinia pseudoacacia	★					★	
Sassafras albidum		★					
Sophora japonica	★					★	
Sorbus	★						
Stewartia	★						
Styrax japonicus	★					★	
Styrax obassia	★					★	
Tilia	★	★				★	
Xanthoceras sorbifolium	★					★	

TREES: DESIGN CHARACTERISTICS
Fruit

The following trees offer ornamental fruit. The primary fruit color(s) is indicated for each plant, although variations will occur within a species or genus, and many fruit change color as they mature.

TREE	COLOR	EDIBLE	COMMENTS
Acer ginnala	red		
Acer rubrum	red		
Acer tataricum	red		
Amelanchier	purple-black	★	
Aralia	purple-black		
Asimina triloba	black	★	Matures from greenish yellow to black
Castanea mollissima	brown	★	Nuts edible, but messy
Cornus alternifolia	purple-black		Pinkish red fruit stalks
Cornus florida	red		
Cornus kousa	red		
Cornus mas	red	★	
Cornus officinalis	red		
Crataegus	red		
Euonymus bungeanus	pinkish		Orange seeds
Euonymus europaeus	pink, red		Orange seeds
Evodia daniellii	black		Matures from red to black
Halesia	brown		Matures from green to light brown
Hippophae rhamnoides	orange		

Trees: Design Characteristics, *Fruit,* continued

TREE	COLOR	EDIBLE	COMMENTS
Hovenia dulcis	red		Edible fruit stalk
Kalopanax pictus	blue-black		
Koelreuteria paniculata	brown		Matures from green to yellow to brown
Magnolia acuminata	pinkish red		
Magnolia macrophylla	rose		
Magnolia virginiana	red		
Malus floribunda	yellow, red		
Malus hupehensis	yellow, red		
Malus sargentii	red		
Malus sieboldii var. *zumi*	red		
Malus cultivars	red		
Oxydendrum arboreum	brown		
Paulownia tomentosa	brown		Fruit messy
Prunus avium	reddish black	★	
Prunus cerasifera	purple, red	★	
Prunus maackii	black		Matures from red to black
Prunus padus	black		
Prunus persica	yellow, red	★	
Prunus sargentii	purple-black		
Prunus serotina	black		Matures from red to black
Prunus subhirtella	black		Matures from red to black
Prunus virginiana	purple-black		
Prunus ×yedoensis	black		
Sophora japonica	yellow, brown		Matures from green to yellow and brown
Sorbus	orange, red		
Xanthoceras sorbifolium	brown		Matures from green to brown

TREES: DESIGN CHARACTERISTICS

Fall Color

The following trees exhibit attractive fall foliage color. Many of these trees will display the full range of fall colors, from pale yellows to deep reds and purples, often on the same tree or even on the same leaf. For the purposes of this list, fall color has been broken down into the most common broad categories of yellow, orange, red, purple, and brown; therefore, "red" can signify anything from pinks to deep maroon tints.

TREE	COLOR				
	YELLOW	ORANGE	RED	PURPLE	BROWN
Acer buergerianum	★		★		
Acer ginnala	★	★	★		
Acer griseum			★		
Acer japonicum	★	★	★	★	
Acer mandschuricum			★		
Acer maximowiczianum	★		★	★	
Acer palmatum	★	★	★		
Acer pensylvanicum	★				
Acer platanoides	★				
Acer rubrum	★	★	★		
Acer saccharum	★	★	★		
Acer triflorum		★	★		
Amelanchier	★	★	★		
Asimina triloba	★				
Betula	★				
Carya	★				★
Cercidiphyllum japonicum	★	★			
Cladrastis kentukea	★				★

TREE	COLOR				
	YELLOW	ORANGE	RED	PURPLE	BROWN
Cornus alternifolia			★	★	
Cornus florida			★	★	
Cornus kousa			★	★	
Cotinus obovatus	★	★	★	★	
Crataegus crusgalli			★		
Crataegus phaenopyrum		★	★	★	
Fagus	★				★
Fraxinus americana	★		★	★	
Fraxinus pennsylvanica	★				
Ginkgo biloba	★				
Larix	★				
Liquidambar styraciflua	★	★	★	★	
Liriodendron tulipifera	★				
Metasequoia glyptostroboides		★			★
Nyssa sylvatica	★	★	★		
Oxydendrum arboreum	★	★	★		
Parrotia persica	★	★	★		

TREE	COLOR				
	YELLOW	ORANGE	RED	PURPLE	BROWN
Phellodendron	★				
Prunus sargentii			★		
Pyrus calleryana		★	★	★	
Quercus acutissima	★				★
Quercus alba			★		
Quercus coccinea			★		
Quercus palustris			★		
Quercus rubra			★		
Sassafras albidum	★	★	★		
Sorbus alnifolia	★	★			★
Sorbus aucuparia	★		★	★	
Stewartia		★	★		
Taxodium		★			★
Tilia	★				
Ulmus americana	★				
Zelkova serrata	★		★	★	

TREES: DESIGN CHARACTERISTICS

Bark

The following trees have bark with interesting texture or color.

Acer buergerianum
Acer griseum
Acer mandschuricum
Acer maximowiczianum
Acer palmatum
Acer pensylvanicum
Acer pseudoplatanus
Acer triflorum
Aesculus hippocastanum
Aesculus octandra
Amelanchier
Aralia
Betula alleghaniensis
Betula jacquemontii
Betula lenta
Betula maximowicziana
Betula nigra
Betula pendula
Betula platyphylla var. *japonica*
Betula populifolia
Carpinus
Carya laciniosa
Carya ovata
Cedrela sinensis
Celtis laevigata
Celtis occidentalis
Cercidiphyllum japonicum
Cladrastis kentukea
Cornus florida
Cornus kousa
Cornus mas
Cornus officinalis
Corylus colurna
Cotinus obovatus
Davidia involucrata
Diospyros virginiana
Evodia daniellii
Fagus
Gymnocladus dioica
Halesia
Hovenia dulcis
Kalopanax pictus
Maackia amurensis
Magnolia
Malus
Metasequoia glyptostroboides
Nyssa sylvatica
Ostrya virginiana
Oxydendrum arboreum
Parrotia persica
Phellodendron
Platanus
Populus alba
Prunus avium
Prunus ×incam 'Okame'
Prunus maackii
Prunus padus
Prunus sargentii
Prunus serotina
Prunus serrulata
Prunus subhirtella
Prunus ×yedoensis
Quercus acutissima
Stewartia
Styrax japonicus
Styrax obassia
Taxodium
Ulmus parvifolia
Zelkova serrata

TREES: DESIGN CHARACTERISTICS

Weeping Habit

The following trees display a weeping habit or offer gracefully arching branches.

Acer palmatum var. *dissectum*
Alnus glutinosa 'Imperialis'
Carpinus betulus 'Pendula'
Cercidiphyllum japonicum 'Pendula'
Cercidiphyllum magnificum 'Pendulum'
Cornus florida 'Pendula'
Cornus kousa 'Lustgarten Weeping'
Euonymus bungeanus
Fagus sylvatica 'Pendula'
Laburnum alpinum 'Pendulum'
Laburnum anagyroides 'Pendulum'
Larix decidua 'Pendula'
Malus 'Red Jade'
Morus alba 'Pendula'
Parrotia persica 'Pendula'
Prunus subhirtella 'Pendula'
Prunus ×*yedoensis* 'Perpendens'
Quercus robur 'Pendula'
Salix alba 'Tristis'
Salix babylonica
Styrax japonicus 'Pendula'
Ulmus glabra 'Camperdownii', 'Horizontalis'

TREES: DESIGN CHARACTERISTICS

Columnar or Fastigiate Habit

The following trees are columnar or fastigiate in habit.

Acer platanoides 'Columnare', 'Erectum'
Acer rubrum 'Armstrong', 'Bowhall'
Acer saccharum 'Monumentale'
Alnus cordata
Alnus glutinosa 'Pyramidalis'
Betula pendula 'Fastigiata'
Carpinus betulus 'Columnaris', 'Fastigiata'
Corylus colurna
Fagus sylvatica 'Fastigiata'
Ginkgo biloba 'Fastigiata', 'Princeton Sentry'
Koelreuteria paniculata 'Fastigiata'
Larix laricina
Liriodendron tulipifera 'Fastigiatum'
Metasequoia glyptostroboides
Populus alba 'Pyramidalis'
Populus nigra 'Italica'
Prunus sargentii 'Columnaris'
Pyrus calleryana 'Capital', 'Chanticleer'
Quercus robur 'Fastigiata'
Taxodium ascendens
Taxodium distichum
Tilia americana 'Fastigiata'

TREES: DESIGN CHARACTERISTICS

Principal Species of Commerce

The following trees have the greatest number of cultivars or the greatest volume of sales in the landscape trade.

Acer campestre
Acer palmatum
Acer platanoides
Acer rubrum
Acer saccharinum
Acer saccharum
Aesculus hippocastanum
Amelanchier
Cercis canadensis
Cornus florida
Cornus kousa
Cornus mas
Crataegus
Fagus sylvatica
Fraxinus
Ginkgo biloba
Gleditsia triacanthos var. *inermis*
Liquidambar styraciflua
Liriodendron tulipifera
Magnolia
Malus
Morus alba
Phellodendron amurense
Platanus ×*acerifolia*
Prunus
Pyrus calleryana
Quercus palustris
Quercus phellos
Quercus robur
Quercus rubra
Salix alba
Sophora japonica
Sorbus aucuparia
Syringa reticulata
Taxodium distichum
Tilia cordata
Ulmus
Zelkova serrata

TREES: DESIGN CHARACTERISTICS
Underutilized Species and Cultivars

The following trees are underutilized but deserve greater consideration for landscape use.

Acer buergerianum
Acer saccharum 'Legacy'
Acer truncatum
Alnus cordata
Celtis laevigata
Chionanthus retusus
Cornus controversa
Evodia daniellii
Hovenia dulcis
Koelreuteria paniculata 'September'
Maackia amurensis
Magnolia kobus var. *borealis*
Magnolia ×*loebneri* 'Ballerina', 'Merrill', 'Spring Snow'
Magnolia stellata 'Centennial'
Platanus ×*acerifolia* 'Yarwood'
Pyrus ussuriensis Prairie Gem™
Sorbus alnifolia
Stewartia monadelpha
Styrax japonicus 'Emerald Pagoda'
Ulmus parvifolia Allee®, Athena®, 'Milliken'

TREES: DESIGN CHARACTERISTICS
A Guide to Tree Sizes

SMALL (15 TO 30 FT.)

Acer buergerianum
Acer ginnala
Acer griseum
Acer japonicum
Acer mandschuricum
Acer maximowiczianum
Acer palmatum
Acer pensylvanicum
Acer tataricum
Acer triflorum
Acer truncatum
Aesculus pavia
Albizia julibrissin
Amelanchier
Aralia
Asimina triloba
Betula populifolia
Carpinus caroliniana
Cercis canadensis
Chionanthus retusus
Chionanthus virginicus
Cornus alternifolia
Cornus kousa
Cornus mas
Cornus officinalis
Crataegus
Elaeagnus angustifolia
Euonymus bungeanus
Euonymus europaeus
Hippophae rhamnoides
Laburnum ×*watereri*
Maackia amurensis
Magnolia ashei
Magnolia denudata
Magnolia fraseri
Magnolia ×*loebneri*
Magnolia ×*soulangiana*
Magnolia stellata
Magnolia virginiana
Malus
Morus australis
Parrotia persica
Prunus ×*blireiana*
Prunus cerasifera
Prunus ×*cistena*
Prunus ×*incam* 'Okame'
Prunus maackii
Prunus persica
Prunus serrulata
Prunus virginiana
Pyrus salicifolia
Stewartia
Styrax japonicus
Styrax obassia
Xanthoceras sorbifolium

MEDIUM (30 TO 50 FT.)

Acer campestre
Aesculus ×*carnea*
Aesculus glabra
Alnus glutinosa
Carpinus betulus
Castanea mollissima
Catalpa bignonioides
Cedrela sinensis
Cornus controversa
Corylus colurna
Cotinus obovatus
Davidia involucrata
Diospyros virginiana
Eucommia ulmoides
Evodia daniellii
Gleditsia triacanthos var. *inermis*
Halesia
Hovenia dulcis
Juglans regia
Kalopanax pictus
Koelreuteria paniculata
Larix laricina
Maclura pomifera
Magnolia kobus var. *borealis*
Magnolia macrophylla
Magnolia tripetala
Morus alba
Morus rubra
Paulownia tomentosa
Populus nigra 'Italica'
Populus tremuloides
Prunus avium
Prunus padus
Prunus sargentii
Prunus subhirtella
Prunus ×*yedoensis*
Pyrus calleryana
Pyrus communis
Pyrus pyrifolia
Pyrus ussuriensis
Salix babylonica
Salix matsudana
Sorbus

LARGE (50 FT. AND GREATER)

Acer platanoides
Acer pseudoplatanus
Acer rubrum
Acer saccharinum
Acer saccharum
Aesculus hippocastanum
Aesculus octandra
Ailanthus altissima
Betula alleghaniensis
Betula jacquemontii
Betula lenta
Betula maximowicziana
Betula nigra
Betula papyrifera
Betula pendula
Betula platyphylla var. *japonica*
Carya
Catalpa speciosa
Celtis occidentalis
Cercidiphyllum japonicum
Cladrastis kentukea
Fagus

LARGE (50 FT. AND GREATER), continued

Fraxinus
Ginkgo biloba
Gymnocladus dioica
Juglans nigra
Larix decidua
Larix kaempferi
Liquidambar styraciflua
Liriodendron tulipifera
Magnolia acuminata
Metasequoia glyptostroboides
Nyssa sylvatica
Phellodendron
Platanus
Populus alba
Populus deltoides
Quercus
Robinia pseudoacacia
Salix alba
Sassafras albidum
Sophora japonica
Taxodium
Tilia
Ulmus
Zelkova serrata

TREES: CULTURAL CHARACTERISTICS

Tolerance to Compacted Soils, Drought, and Heat

The following trees offer tolerance to compacted, infertile soils and other environmental stresses such as heat and drought.

Acer buergerianum
Acer campestre
Acer negundo
Acer truncatum
Ailanthus altissima
Alnus cordata
Aralia
Carpinus betulus
Catalpa
Cedrela sinensis
Celtis
Crataegus
Elaeagnus angustifolia
Eucommia ulmoides
Evodia daniellii
Fraxinus pennsylvanica
Ginkgo biloba
Gleditsia triacanthos var. *inermis*
Kalopanax pictus
Koelreuteria paniculata
Liquidambar styraciflua
Maackia amurensis
Maclura pomifera
Morus
Paulownia tomentosa
Platanus
Pyrus calleryana
Pyrus ussuriensis
Quercus acutissima
Quercus palustris
Quercus phellos
Quercus robur
Taxodium
Tilia cordata
Ulmus parvifolia
Zelkova serrata

TREES: CULTURAL CHARACTERISTICS

Street and Urban Planting

The following species and cultivars offer the genetic plasticity to produce offspring that are better able to adapt to a variety of environmental stresses. From these trees, tomorrow's cultivars will be bred and selected.

Acer buergerianum
Acer campestre Queen Elizabeth™
Acer rubrum
Acer saccharum 'Legacy'
Acer truncatum
Betula nigra 'Heritage'
Carpinus betulus 'Columnaris', 'Fastigiata'
Chionanthus retusus
Cornus mas
Cornus officinalis
Evodia daniellii
Ginkgo biloba
Gleditsia triacanthos var. *inermis*
Koelreuteria paniculata 'September'
Maackia amurensis
Platanus ×*acerifolia* 'Bloodgood', 'Columbia', 'Liberty', 'Yarwood', and other disease-resistant cultivars
Prunus sargentii
Pyrus calleryana 'Chanticleer' and certain other cultivars
Quercus
Sophora japonica
Taxodium distichum
Tilia
Ulmus parvifolia Allee®, Athena®, 'Milliken'
Zelkova serrata 'Green Vase'

TREES: CULTURAL CHARACTERISTICS

Tolerance to Moist to Wet Soils

The following trees are tolerant of moist to wet soil conditions.

Acer negundo
Acer rubrum
Acer saccharinum
Alnus cordata
Alnus glutinosa
Betula nigra
Carpinus caroliniana
Carya illinoinensis
Celtis occidentalis
Fraxinus pennsylvanica
Gleditsia triacanthos var. *inermis*
Larix laricina
Liquidambar styraciflua
Liriodendron tulipifera
Magnolia virginiana
Metasequoia glyptostroboides
Nyssa sylvatica
Platanus
Populus alba
Populus deltoides
Quercus palustris
Salix alba
Salix babylonica
Salix matsudana
Taxodium
Ulmus americana

TREES: CULTURAL CHARACTERISTICS

Salt Tolerance: A Review of the Literature

The inconsistency in rating the salt tolerance of trees is the result of many factors. No trees are wholly resistant to salt. Different degrees of resistance are apparent in species and cultivars, but rarely is there consensus among plant authorities as to the level of salt tolerance displayed by a particular tree. The table presented here, derived from a paper I published in the *Journal of Arboriculture* 11: 209–216 (1976), serves to indicate how trees have most commonly been cited with regard to their salt tolerance. Each ★ represents the number of times the tree was cited as having good, moderate, or poor salt tolerance by various authorities. A dash means no citations occurred. Several species included in this compilation are not in the main body of the text but are included here for purposes of comparison. Use this table only as a guide.

TREE	SALT-TOLERANCE RATING		
	GOOD	MODERATE	POOR
Abies balsamea	–	★	★
Acer campestre	★	★	–
Acer ginnala	–	–	★
Acer negundo	–	★★	★
Acer platanoides	★★★★	★	–
Acer pseudoplatanus	★	–	★
Acer rubrum	–	★	★★★
Acer saccharinum	★	★	★
Acer saccharum	★	–	★★★
Acer tataricum	–	–	★
Aesculus hippocastanum	★★★	–	–
Ailanthus altissima	★★	–	–
Alnus glutinosa	–	–	★★
Alnus incana	–	–	★
Alnus rugosa	–	★★	★★
Amelanchier canadensis	★	–	–
Amelanchier laevis	–	–	★
Amelanchier	–	–	★
Betula alleghaniensis	★	–	–
Betula lenta	★	–	–
Betula papyrifera	★	★★	–
Betula pendula	–	★★	–
Betula populifolia	★	★	–
Betula	–	★	–
Caragana arborescens	★★	–	–
Carpinus betulus	–	–	★★
Carpinus caroliniana	–	–	★★
Carya ovata	★	–	★
Carya	–	–	★
Catalpa speciosa	–	★	–
Celtis occidentalis	–	–	★
Cercis canadensis	–	–	★
Chamaecyparis pisifera	–	–	★
Corylus	–	–	★★
Crataegus crusgalli	★	–	★
Crataegus	–	–	★★

★ = A rating by a particular researcher or evaluator.
– = No citations occurred.

Trees: Cultural Characteristics, *Salt Tolerance*, continued

TREE	SALT-TOLERANCE RATING		
	GOOD	MODERATE	POOR
Elaeagnus angustifolia	★★★	–	–
Euonymus	–	–	★
Fagus grandifolia	–	★	★★★
Fagus sylvatica	–	–	★★★
Fraxinus americana	★	★★	–
Fraxinus excelsior	★	–	–
Fraxinus pennsylvanica	★	★★	–
Gleditsia triacanthos var. *inermis*	★★★★	–	★
Hippophae rhamnoides	★★	–	–
Ilex opaca	★	–	–
Juglans nigra	★	–	★★
Juglans regia	★	–	★★
Juniperus virginiana	★★	★★	–
Larix decidua	★	–	–
Larix kaempferi	★	–	–
Larix laricina	★	–	–
Larix	–	–	★★
Liriodendron tulipifera	–	–	★
Magnolia grandiflora	★	–	–
Malus baccata	–	★★	–
Malus	–	★★	★
Metasequoia glyptostroboides	–	–	★
Morus alba	★★★★	–	★
Nyssa sylvatica	★	–	–
Picea abies	–	★★	★
Picea asperata	★	–	–
Picea glauca	–	★	★
Picea pungens	★	–	–
Picea pungens var. *glauca*	★★	★	–
Pinus banksiana	★	–	–
Pinus cembra	★	–	–
Pinus mugo	★	–	–
Pinus nigra	★★	–	–
Pinus ponderosa	–	★	–
Pinus resinosa	–	–	★★★
Pinus rigida	★	–	–
Pinus strobus	–	–	★★★
Pinus sylvestris	★	★	★★
Pinus thunbergii	★	–	–
Platanus ×*acerifolia*	–	–	★
Populus alba	★★★★★	–	–
Populus alba 'Pyramidalis'	★	–	–
Populus angustifolia	★	–	–
Populus deltoides	★	★	–
Populus grandidentata	★	★	–
Populus nigra 'Italica'	–	★	★★
Populus tremuloides	★	★★★	–
Populus	–	★	–
Prunus avium	–	★	–
Prunus padus	★	–	–
Prunus serotina	★★	–	★
Prunus virginiana	★	–	–
Pseudotsuga menziesii	–	★★	★
Pyrus	–	★	–
Quercus alba	★★★	–	★
Quercus bicolor	–	–	★
Quercus macrocarpa	★	★	★
Quercus marilandica	★	–	–
Quercus muehlenbergii	–	–	★
Quercus palustris	–	–	★
Quercus robur	★★	–	★
Quercus rubra	★★★★	–	–
Rhamnus cathartica	★★★	–	–
Rhamnus davurica	★	–	–
Rhamnus frangula	★	★	–
Rhus typhina	★★★	–	–
Robinia pseudoacacia	★★★★★★★	–	–
Robinia pseudoacacia 'Umbraculifera'	★	–	–
Salix alba	–	★	★
Salix alba 'Tristis'	★	★	–
Salix matsudana 'Tortuosa'	★	–	–
Salix	★★	–	–
Sorbus	–	★★	–
Syringa reticulata	★	–	–
Tamarix ramosissima	★★★★★	–	–
Taxus cuspidata	–	★	★
Thuja occidentalis	–	★	★
Tilia americana	–	★	★★
Tilia cordata	–	–	★★
Tilia ×*euchlora*	–	–	★
Tilia platyphyllos	★	–	–
Tsuga canadensis	–	–	★★★
Ulmus americana	–	★★	★
Ulmus glabra	★★	–	–
Ulmus pumila	★	★	–

★ = A rating by a particular researcher or evaluator.
– = No citations occurred.

TREES: CULTURAL CHARACTERISTICS

Shade Tolerance

The following trees have moderate to good shade tolerance.

Acer ginnala
Acer japonicum
Acer palmatum
Acer pensylvanicum
Aesculus glabra
Aesculus octandra
Aesculus pavia
Amelanchier
Aralia
Asimina triloba
Carpinus betulus
Carpinus caroliniana
Cercis canadensis
Chionanthus
Cornus alternifolia
Cornus florida
Cornus kousa
Cornus mas
Cornus officinalis
Euonymus bungeanus
Euonymus europaeus
Fagus
Halesia
Magnolia ashei
Magnolia fraseri
Magnolia macrophylla
Magnolia tripetala
Magnolia virginiana
Morus rubra
Ostrya virginiana
Oxydendrum arboreum
Parrotia persica
Stewartia
Styrax japonicus
Styrax obassia

SHRUBS: DESIGN CHARACTERISTICS

Showy Flowers, by Color

The following shrubs display showy flowers. Flower color has been categorized into five basic color groups: white, yellow, pink/rose, orange/red, and blue/lavender/purple (blue/purple). The primary flower color(s) is indicated for each species or genus. Variations of flower color will exist in certain cultivars or varieties of a plant, and flowers can often be ornamented with stripes or blotches of a different color.

SHRUB	COLOR					COMMENTS
	WHITE	YELLOW	PINK/ROSE	ORANGE/RED	BLUE/PURPLE	
Abeliophyllum distichum	★					Faintly pink tinged
Aesculus parviflora	★					
Amorpha					★	
Aronia arbutifolia	★					
Aronia melanocarpa	★					
Berberis		★				
Buddleia alternifolia					★	
Buddleia davidii	★		★	★	★	Variation in cultivars
Buddleia ×weyeriana 'Sun Gold'		★		★		
Calluna vulgaris			★			Variation in cultivars
Calycanthus floridus				★		
Calycanthus floridus 'Athens'		★				
Caragana		★				
Caryopteris ×clandonensis					★	
Ceanothus americanus	★					
Cephalanthus occidentalis	★					
Cercis chinensis			★			
Chaenomeles japonica				★		
Chaenomeles speciosa	★		★	★		Variation in cultivars
Clerodendrum trichotomum	★					
Clethra acuminata	★					
Clethra alnifolia	★					
Colutea arborescens		★				
Cornus alba	★					
Cornus amomum	★					
Cornus racemosa	★					

Shrubs: Design Characteristics, *Showy Flowers, by Color*, continued

SHRUB	COLOR: WHITE	YELLOW	PINK/ROSE	ORANGE/RED	BLUE/PURPLE	COMMENTS
Cornus sanguinea	★					
Cornus sericea	★					
Corylopsis		★				
Cotoneaster adpressus			★			
Cotoneaster apiculatus			★			
Cotoneaster dammeri	★					
Cotoneaster divaricatus			★			
Cotoneaster horizontalis			★			
Cotoneaster lucidus	★		★			
Cotoneaster multiflorus	★					
Cotoneaster salicifolius	★					
Cytisus scoparius	★	★	★	★		Variation in cultivars
Daphne ×burkwoodii	★					Pink buds
Daphne caucasica	★					
Daphne cneorum			★			
Daphne mezereum					★	
Daphne mezereum var. *alba*	★					
Deutzia gracilis	★					
Deutzia ×kalmiiflora			★			
Deutzia ×lemoinei	★					
Deutzia scabra	★					
Diervilla sessilifolia		★				
Dirca palustris		★				
Elaeagnus	★	★				
Elsholtzia stauntonii			★			
Enkianthus campanulatus		★		★		Veined with red
Enkianthus cernuus	★					
Enkianthus perulatus	★					
Erica carnea	★		★			
Exochorda racemosa	★					
Forsythia		★				
Fothergilla	★					
Franklinia alatamaha	★					
Genista		★				
Hamamelis ×intermedia		★		★		Variation in cultivars
Hamamelis japonica		★				Purple calyx cup
Hamamelis mollis		★				Reddish brown calyx cup
Hamamelis vernalis		★		★		
Hamamelis virginiana		★				
Heptacodium miconioides	★					
Hibiscus syriacus	★		★	★	★	Variation in cultivars
Hydrangea arborescens	★					
Hydrangea macrophylla	★		★		★	Variation in cultivars
Hydrangea paniculata	★					
Hydrangea quercifolia	★					
Hypericum		★				
Indigofera kirilowii			★			
Indigofera kirilowii var. *alba*	★					
Itea virginica	★					
Kalmia latifolia	★		★	★		
Kerria japonica		★				
Kolkwitzia amabilis			★			

SHRUB	COLOR					COMMENTS
	WHITE	YELLOW	PINK/ROSE	ORANGE/RED	BLUE/PURPLE	
Leiophyllum buxifolium	★					
Leucothoe	★					
Ligustrum	★					
Lonicera fragrantissima	★					
Lonicera korolkowii			★			
Lonicera maackii	★					
Lonicera tatarica	★		★			Variation in cultivars
Lonicera xylosteum	★	★				
Mahonia aquifolium		★				
Neillia sinensis			★			
Neviusia alabamensis	★					
Philadelphus coronarius	★					
Philadelphus Hybrids	★					
Photinia villosa	★					
Physocarpus opulifolius	★					
Pieris floribunda	★					
Pieris japonica	★		★			Variation in cultivars
Poncirus trifoliata	★					
Potentilla fruticosa	★	★	★	★		Variation in cultivars
Prinsepia sinensis	★	★				
Prinsepia uniflora	★					
Prunus besseyi	★					
Prunus glandulosa			★			
Prunus 'Hally Jolivette'			★			
Prunus maritima	★					
Prunus tenella				★		
Prunus tomentosa	★					
Prunus triloba var. *multiplex*			★			
Pseudocydonia sinensis			★			
Pyracantha coccinea	★					
Rhododendron atlanticum	★					
Rhododendron calendulaceum		★		★		
Rhododendron carolinianum			★			
Rhododendron catawbiense					★	
Rhododendron maximum	★					Pink buds
Rhododendron mucronulatum					★	
Rhododendron periclymenoides	★		★		★	
Rhododendron 'PJM'			★		★	
Rhododendron prinophyllum			★			
Rhododendron schlippenbachii			★			
Rhododendron vaseyi			★			
Rhododendron viscosum	★		★			
Rhododendron yakushimanum	★					Pink or red buds
Rhododendron yedoense			★		★	
Rhodotypos scandens	★					
Rhus aromatica		★				
Rhus chinensis	★					
Rhus copallina		★				
Rhus glabra		★				
Rhus typhina		★				
Ribes odoratum		★				
Robinia hispida			★			
Robinia pseudoacacia	★					
Rosa			★	★	★	

Shrubs: Design Characteristics, *Showy Flowers, by Color,* continued

SHRUB	COLOR					COMMENTS
	WHITE	YELLOW	PINK/ROSE	ORANGE/RED	BLUE/PURPLE	
Salix caprea	★					Grayish male catkins
Salix gracilistyla	★					Grayish male catkins, pinkish tinged
Salix sachalinensis	★					Grayish male catkins
Sambucus	★					
Shepherdia argentea		★				
Shepherdia canadensis		★				
Skimmia japonica	★					Red buds
Sorbaria	★					
Spiraea albiflora	★					
Spiraea ×*bumalda*			★			
Spiraea cantoniensis	★					
Spiraea japonica	★		★			
Spiraea nipponica	★					
Spiraea prunifolia	★					
Spiraea thunbergii	★					
Spiraea ×*vanhouttei*	★					
Stephanandra incisa	★					
Styrax americanus	★					
Symphoricarpos orbiculatus			★			
Syringa ×*chinensis*					★	
Syringa laciniata					★	
Syringa meyeri			★			
Syringa microphylla			★		★	
Syringa oblata					★	
Syringa patula					★	
Syringa ×*persica*					★	
Syringa reticulata	★					
Syringa villosa	★				★	
Syringa vulgaris					★	
Tamarix ramosissima			★			
Vaccinium angustifolium			★			
Vaccinium corymbosum	★					
Vaccinium vitis-idaea	★		★			
Viburnum	★					Often pink in bud
Viburnum farreri			★			
Vitex agnus-castus					★	White forms available
Vitex negundo					★	
Weigela middendorffiana		★				
Yucca	★					
Zenobia pulverulenta	★					

Fragrant Flowers

The following shrubs have notably fragrant flowers, and they are rated from light to medium to strong. Marks in more than one rating column indicate a range of fragrance strength.

SHRUB	DEGREE OF FRAGRANCE			COMMENTS
	LIGHT	MEDIUM	STRONG	
Abeliophyllum distichum	★			
Buddleia		★	★	
Calycanthus floridus		★	★	
Cephalanthus occidentalis	★			
Clerodendrum trichotomum		★	★	
Clethra alnifolia			★	
Corylopsis	★	★		
Daphne			★	
Elaeagnus	★	★	★	
Forsythia ×intermedia	★			Almost undetectable at times, but still present
Fothergilla			★	Honey scent
Hamamelis		★		Strong in some cultivars, like 'Arnold Promise'
Heptacodium miconioides		★		
Ligustrum			★	Sickeningly sweet
Lindera benzoin	★			Minimal in flowers; bruised stems smell great
Lonicera fragrantissima			★	Sweet
Mahonia aquifolium	★			
Philadelphus		★	★	
Pieris japonica	★	★		
Rhododendron atlanticum			★	
Rhododendron Exbury Hybrids			★	
Rhododendron periclymenoides		★	★	
Rhododendron prinophyllum			★	
Rhododendron viscosum			★	
Rosa		★	★	
Sarcococca hookerana			★	
Skimmia	★			
Syringa		★	★	
Viburnum ×burkwoodii			★	
Viburnum ×carlcephalum			★	
Viburnum carlesii			★	
Viburnum farreri			★	
Viburnum ×juddii			★	
Viburnum ×pragense	★	★		
Zenobia pulverulenta	★			

Flowering Sequence

The following table serves as a guide to the flowering habits of shrubs. Many shrubs flower over extended periods, providing color for several months at a time, and they are listed here for each of the months that they are in bloom. These dates are for Zones 5 and 6, and are only approximate. Because from year to year spring may come two weeks earlier or later than the norm and bloom times will change accordingly, this table should be used only as a guide.

JANUARY

Erica carnea
Hamamelis ×intermedia, early cultivars such as 'Jelena', 'Pallida', and 'Ruby Glow'
Hamamelis vernalis

FEBRUARY

Erica carnea
Hamamelis ×intermedia
Hamamelis japonica
Hamamelis mollis
Hamamelis vernalis

MARCH

Abeliophyllum distichum
Buxus microphylla
Cercis chinensis
Chaenomeles speciosa
Corylus americana
Corylus avellana
Corylus maxima var. *purpurea*
Daphne mezereum
Dirca palustris
Erica carnea
Forsythia ×intermedia
Hamamelis ×intermedia
Hamamelis japonica
Hamamelis mollis
Lindera benzoin
Lonicera fragrantissima
Mahonia aquifolium
Myrica pensylvanica
Pieris japonica
Rhododendron mucronulatum
Rhus aromatica
Salix caprea
Salix gracilistyla
Sarcococca hookerana
Skimmia japonica
Spiraea prunifolia
Spiraea thunbergii
Stachyurus praecox
Viburnum farreri
Xanthorhiza simplicissima

APRIL

Abeliophyllum distichum
Berberis ×gladwynensis
Berberis ×mentorensis
Berberis thunbergii
Buxus microphylla
Buxus sempervirens
Cercis chinensis
Chaenomeles japonica
Chaenomeles speciosa
Comptonia peregrina
Corylopsis glabrescens
Corylopsis gotoana
Corylopsis pauciflora
Corylopsis platypetala
Corylopsis spicata
Dirca palustris
Elaeagnus multiflora
Exochorda racemosa
Forsythia 'Arnold Dwarf'
Forsythia ×intermedia
Forsythia suspensa var. *sieboldii*
Forsythia viridissima
Fothergilla gardenii
Fothergilla major
Kerria japonica
Leucothoe axillaris
Lindera benzoin
Lonicera fragrantissima
Mahonia aquifolium
Myrica pensylvanica
Pieris floribunda
Pieris japonica
Poncirus trifoliata
Prinsepia sinensis
Prinsepia uniflora
Prunus besseyi
Prunus glandulosa
Prunus 'Hally Jolivette'
Prunus tenella
Prunus tomentosa
Prunus triloba
Pseudocydonia sinensis
Rhododendron mucronulatum
Rhododendron periclymenoides
Rhododendron 'PJM'
Rhus aromatica
Ribes alpinum
Ribes odoratum
Salix caprea
Salix gracilistyla
Sarcococca hookerana
Shepherdia argentea
Shepherdia canadensis
Skimmia japonica
Skimmia reevesiana
Spiraea prunifolia
Spiraea thunbergii
Spiraea ×vanhouttei
Stachyurus praecox
Syringa oblata var. *dilatata*
Vaccinium angustifolium
Viburnum ×burkwoodii
Viburnum ×carlcephalum
Viburnum carlesii
Viburnum ×juddii
Xanthorhiza simplicissima

MAY

Acanthopanax sieboldianus
Aronia arbutifolia
Aronia melanocarpa
Berberis candidula
Berberis ×gladwynensis
Berberis koreana
Berberis ×mentorensis
Berberis thunbergii
Buxus sempervirens
Calycanthus floridus
Caragana arborescens
Caragana frutex
Colutea arborescens
Comptonia peregrina

Cornus alba
Cornus racemosa
Cornus sanguinea
Cornus sericea
Cotoneaster adpressus
Cotoneaster apiculatus
Cotoneaster dammeri
Cotoneaster divaricatus
Cotoneaster horizontalis
Cotoneaster lucidus
Cotoneaster multiflorus
Cytisus scoparius
Daphne caucasica
Deutzia gracilis
Deutzia ×*kalmiiflora*
Deutzia ×*lemoinei*
Elaeagnus multiflora
Elaeagnus umbellata
Enkianthus campanulatus
Enkianthus cernuus
Enkianthus perulatus
Euonymus alatus
Exochorda racemosa
Fothergilla gardenii
Fothergilla major
Genista lydia
Ilex crenata
Kalmia latifolia
Kerria japonica
Kolkwitzia amabilis
Leiophyllum buxifolium
Leucothoe axillaris
Leucothoe fontanesiana
Ligustrum amurense
Lonicera alpigena
Lonicera korolkowii
Lonicera maackii
Lonicera tatarica
Lonicera xylosteum
Neillia sinensis
Neviusia alabamensis
Philadelphus coronarius
Philadelphus ×*cymosus*
Philadelphus ×*lemoinei*
Philadelphus ×*virginalis*
Photinia villosa
Physocarpus opulifolius
Poncirus trifoliata
Prunus besseyi
Prunus glandulosa
Prunus 'Hally Jolivette'
Prunus maritima
Pseudocydonia sinensis
Pyracantha coccinea
Rhamnus frangula
Rhododendron atlanticum
Rhododendron calendulaceum
Rhododendron carolinianum
Rhododendron catawbiense
Rhododendron Exbury Hybrids
Rhododendron periclymenoides
Rhododendron prinophyllum
Rhododendron schlippenbachii
Rhododendron vaseyi
Rhododendron viscosum
Rhododendron yedoense
Rhodotypos scandens
Robinia fertilis
Robinia hispida
Rosa spinosissima
Sambucus racemosa
Shepherdia argentea
Shepherdia canadensis
Spiraea nipponica
Spiraea ×*vanhouttei*
Stephanandra incisa
Styrax americanus
Symplocos paniculata
Syringa ×*chinensis*
Syringa laciniata
Syringa meyeri
Syringa microphylla
Syringa oblata var. *dilatata*
Syringa patula
Syringa ×*persica*
Syringa villosa
Syringa vulgaris
Vaccinium corymbosum
Vaccinium vitis-idaea
Viburnum ×*carlcephalum*
Viburnum carlesii
Viburnum dentatum
Viburnum dilatatum
Viburnum ×*juddii*
Viburnum lantana
Viburnum lentago
Viburnum opulus
Viburnum plicatum
Viburnum plicatum var. *tomentosum*
Viburnum prunifolium
Viburnum ×*rhytidophylloides*
Viburnum rhytidophyllum
Viburnum rufidulum
Viburnum sargentii
Viburnum setigerum
Viburnum sieboldii
Viburnum trilobum
Weigela florida
Zenobia pulverulenta

JUNE

Acanthopanax sieboldianus
Aesculus parviflora
Amorpha fruticosa
Berberis candidula
Buddleia alternifolia
Buddleia davidii
Callicarpa americana
Callicarpa bodinieri
Callicarpa dichotoma
Callicarpa japonica
Calycanthus floridus (sporadically)
Caragana frutex
Ceanothus americanus
Colutea arborescens
Cornus alba
Cornus amomum
Cornus racemosa
Cornus sanguinea
Cornus sericea
Cotinus coggygria
Cotoneaster adpressus
Cotoneaster apiculatus
Cotoneaster divaricatus
Cotoneaster horizontalis
Cotoneaster salicifolius
Cytisus scoparius
Daphne caucasica
Deutzia scabra
Diervilla sessilifolia
Elaeagnus umbellata
Enkianthus campanulatus
Euonymus alatus
Euonymus fortunei
Genista lydia
Genista pilosa
Genista tinctoria
Hydrangea arborescens
Hydrangea macrophylla
Hydrangea quercifolia
Hypericum frondosum
Hypericum prolificum
Ilex crenata
Indigofera kirilowii
Itea virginica
Kalmia latifolia

JUNE, continued

Kolkwitzia amabilis
Leiophyllum buxifolium
Ligustrum amurense
Ligustrum obtusifolium
Ligustrum ×*vicaryi*
Ligustrum vulgare
Lonicera maackii
Philadelphus coronarius
Philadelphus ×*cymosus*
Philadelphus ×*lemoinei*
Philadelphus ×*virginalis*
Photinia villosa
Physocarpus opulifolius
Potentilla fruticosa
Pyracantha coccinea
Rhododendron atlanticum
Rhododendron calendulaceum
Rhododendron maximum
Rhododendron viscosum
Rhododendron yakushimanum
Rhodotypos scandens
Rhus glabra
Rhus typhina
Robinia fertilis
Robinia hispida
Rosa carolina
Rosa moyesii
Rosa rubrifolia
Rosa rugosa
Rosa spinosissima
Rosa virginiana
Sambucus canadensis
Sambucus nigra
Sorbaria aitchisonii
Sorbaria arborea
Sorbaria sorbifolia
Spiraea albiflora
Spiraea ×*bumalda*
Spiraea japonica
Spiraea nipponica
Stephanandra incisa
Symphoricarpos albus
Symphoricarpos ×*chenaultii*
Symphoricarpos orbiculatus
Symplocos paniculata
Syringa microphylla
Syringa patula
Syringa reticulata
Syringa villosa
Tamarix ramosissima
Vaccinium vitis-idaea
Viburnum acerifolium
Viburnum dentatum
Viburnum dilatatum
Vitex agnus-castus
Vitex negundo
Weigela florida
Zenobia pulverulenta

JULY

Aesculus parviflora var. *serotina*
Amorpha canescens
Callicarpa americana
Callicarpa bodinieri
Callicarpa dichotoma
Callicarpa japonica
Calluna vulgaris
Calycanthus floridus (sporadically)
Caryopteris ×*clandonensis*
Ceanothus americanus
Clethra alnifolia
Colutea arborescens
Diervilla sessilifolia
Euonymus fortunei
Euonymus kiautschovicus
Franklinia alatamaha
Genista tinctoria
Hibiscus syriacus
Hydrangea arborescens
Hydrangea macrophylla
Hydrangea paniculata
Hydrangea quercifolia
Hypericum frondosum
Hypericum prolificum
Indigofera kirilowii
Potentilla fruticosa
Rhus copallina
Rhus glabra
Rhus typhina
Rosa carolina
Rosa moyesii
Rosa rugosa
Sambucus canadensis
Sorbaria aitchisonii
Sorbaria arborea
Sorbaria sorbifolia
Spiraea albiflora
Spiraea ×*bumalda*
Spiraea japonica
Symphoricarpos orbiculatus
Tamarix ramosissima
Vitex agnus-castus
Vitex negundo
Yucca

AUGUST

Callicarpa americana
Callicarpa bodinieri
Callicarpa dichotoma
Callicarpa japonica
Calluna vulgaris
Caryopteris ×*clandonensis*
Cephalanthus occidentalis
Clethra alnifolia
Diervilla sessilifolia
Euonymus kiautschovicus
Franklinia alatamaha
Genista tinctoria
Hibiscus syriacus
Hydrangea macrophylla
Hydrangea paniculata
Hypericum prolificum
Potentilla fruticosa
Rhus chinensis
Rhus copallina
Rosa rugosa
Sorbaria aitchisonii
Sorbaria arborea
Spiraea ×*bumalda*
Vitex agnus-castus
Vitex negundo
Yucca

SEPTEMBER

Calluna vulgaris
Elsholtzia stauntonii
Franklinia alatamaha
Hibiscus syriacus
Hydrangea paniculata 'Tardiva'
Potentilla fruticosa (until frost)
Rhus chinensis
Vitex agnus-castus (sporadically)

OCTOBER

Disanthus cercidifolius
Elsholtzia stauntonii
Hamamelis virginiana

NOVEMBER

Hamamelis virginiana

Fruit

The following shrubs have colorful ornamental fruit. The primary fruit color(s) is indicated for each plant, and color is arranged in the following general color categories: yellow, pink/rose, red, blue, purple, black, and white. Many fruit will change color as they mature; this is indicated in the comments by, for example, "red to black," meaning that the fruit mature from red to black.

SHRUB			COLOR					COMMENTS
	YELLOW	PINK/ROSE	RED	BLUE	PURPLE	BLACK	WHITE	
Aronia arbutifolia			★					
Aronia melanocarpa						★		
Berberis koreana			★					
Berberis thunbergii			★					
Callicarpa					★			Magenta
Chaenomeles japonica	★							
Chaenomeles speciosa	★	★						Often speckled rose
Clerodendrum trichotomum				★	★			Red sepals
Cornus alba							★	Slightly blue-tinted
Cornus amomum				★				White blotches
Cornus racemosa							★	
Cornus sanguinea						★		
Cornus sericea							★	Slightly blue-tinted
Corylus maxima var. *purpurea*					★			
Cotoneaster adpressus			★					
Cotoneaster apiculatus			★					
Cotoneaster dammeri			★					
Cotoneaster divaricatus			★					
Cotoneaster horizontalis			★					
Cotoneaster lucidus						★		
Cotoneaster multiflorus			★					
Cotoneaster salicifolius			★					
Daphne mezereum			★					
Elaeagnus multiflora			★					
Elaeagnus umbellata			★					
Euonymus kiautschovicus			★					
Heptacodium miconioides		★						Rose sepals
Ilex ×*aquipernyi*			★					
Ilex ×*attenuata*			★					
Ilex crenata						★		
Ilex decidua			★					
Ilex glabra						★		Some white forms
Ilex ×*meserveae*			★					
Ilex opaca			★					
Ilex pedunculosa			★					
Ilex serrata			★					
Ilex verticillata			★					
Ligustrum						★		
Lindera benzoin			★					
Mahonia aquifolium				★	★			
Myrica pensylvanica							★	Gray

Shrubs: Design Characteristics, *Fruit,* continued

SHRUB	COLOR							COMMENTS
	YELLOW	PINK/ROSE	RED	BLUE	PURPLE	BLACK	WHITE	
Poncirus trifoliata	★							
Prinsepia sinensis			★					
Prinsepia uniflora			★					
Prunus besseyi						★		
Prunus maritima	★		★		★			Yellow-orange to red and purple
Prunus tomentosa			★					
Pseudocydonia sinensis	★							
Pyracantha coccinea			★					
Rhamnus frangula			★			★		Red to black
Rhodotypos scandens						★		
Rhus			★					
Ribes alpinum			★					
Rosa			★					Some orange
Sambucus canadensis					★	★		
Sambucus nigra						★		
Sambucus racemosa			★					
Shepherdia argentea			★					Some orange
Skimmia japonica			★					
Symphoricarpos albus							★	
Symphoricarpos orbiculatus		★						
Vaccinium angustifolium				★		★		
Vaccinium corymbosum				★		★		
Vaccinium vitis-idaea			★					
Viburnum acerifolium						★		
Viburnum ×burkwoodii			★			★		Red to black
Viburnum carlesii			★			★		Red to black
Viburnum dentatum				★		★		Blue to blue-black
Viburnum dilatatum			★					
Viburnum lantana	★		★			★		Yellow to red and black
Viburnum lentago		★		★		★		
Viburnum opulus	★		★					Yellow to red
Viburnum plicatum var. *tomentosum*		★				★		
Viburnum prunifolium		★				★		Pink to blue-black
Viburnum ×rhytidophylloides			★			★		Red to black
Viburnum rhytidophyllum			★			★		Red to black
Viburnum sargentii	★		★					Yellow to red
Viburnum setigerum			★					
Viburnum sieboldii			★			★		Red to black
Viburnum trilobum	★		★					Yellow to red

Fall Color

The following shrubs have foliage with notable fall color. For the purposes of this table, fall color has been broken down into the three most common broad categories of yellow, orange, and red.

SHRUB	COLOR		
	YELLOW	ORANGE	RED
Aesculus parviflora	★		
Aronia			★
Berberis koreana			★
Berberis ×*mentorensis*			★
Berberis thunbergii			★
Calycanthus floridus	★		
Clethra alnifolia	★		
Cornus alba			★
Cornus amomum			★
Cornus racemosa			★
Cornus sericea			★
Cotinus coggygria	★	★	★
Cotoneaster			★
Dirca palustris	★		
Disanthus cercidifolius		★	★
Enkianthus campanulatus	★	★	★
Enkianthus cernuus	★	★	★
Enkianthus perulatus			★
Euonymus alatus			★
Fothergilla	★	★	★
Franklinia alatamaha		★	★
Hamamelis ×*intermedia*	★	★	★
Hamamelis japonica	★	★	★
Hamamelis mollis	★	★	
Hamamelis vernalis	★		
Hamamelis virginiana	★		
Hydrangea quercifolia			★
Itea virginica	★	★	★
Kerria japonica	★		
Photinia villosa	★	★	★
Poncirus trifoliata	★		
Prunus besseyi	★		★
Prunus 'Hally Jolivette'	★		
Prunus tenella	★		★
Prunus tomentosa	★		★
Prunus triloba	★		★
Pseudocydonia sinensis	★		★

SHRUB	COLOR		
	YELLOW	ORANGE	RED
Rhododendron calendulaceum	★		★
Rhododendron mucronulatum	★		★
Rhododendron periclymenoides	★		
Rhododendron prinophyllum	★		★
Rhododendron schlippenbachii	★	★	★
Rhododendron vaseyi			★
Rhododendron Hybrids	★	★	★
Rhus aromatica		★	★
Rhus chinensis	★	★	★
Rhus copallina			★
Rhus glabra	★	★	★
Rhus typhina	★	★	★
Rosa	★	★	★
Spiraea ×*bumalda* cultivars	★		★
Spiraea japonica cultivars	★		★
Spiraea prunifolia		★	★
Spiraea thunbergii	★	★	
Syringa oblata			★
Tamarix ramosissima	★		
Vaccinium angustifolium			★
Vaccinium corymbosum	★		★
Viburnum acerifolium			★
Viburnum ×*burkwoodii*			★
Viburnum ×*carlcephalum*			★
Viburnum carlesii			★
Viburnum dentatum	★		★
Viburnum dilatatum			★
Viburnum farreri			★
Viburnum opulus	★		★
Viburnum plicatum			★
Viburnum prunifolium			★
Viburnum rufidulum			★
Viburnum sargentii	★	★	★
Viburnum trilobum	★	★	★
Xanthorhiza simplicissima	★	★	
Zenobia pulverulenta	★		

SHRUBS: DESIGN CHARACTERISTICS

Evergreen, Semi-Evergreen, or Tardily Deciduous Foliage

The following shrubs are grouped into the categories of evergreen/semi-evergreen shrubs and tardily deciduous shrubs. Evergreen shrubs have foliage that remains green (alive) for at least a year and through more than one growing season; semi-evergreen implies leaf loss in winter, but this quality is variable; the foliage of tardily deciduous plants will die at the end of the growing season, but the leaves tend to persist for a prolonged period and are resistant to shed.

EVERGREEN OR SEMI-EVERGREEN FOLIAGE

Berberis candidula
Berberis ×*gladwynensis* 'William Penn'
Berberis julianae
Buxus microphylla
Buxus sempervirens
Calluna vulgaris
Cotoneaster salicifolius
Erica carnea
Euonymus fortunei
Gaylussacia brachycera
Ilex ×*aquipernyi*
Ilex crenata
Ilex glabra
Ilex ×*meserveae*
Ilex opaca
Ilex pedunculosa
Kalmia latifolia
Leiophyllum buxifolium
Leucothoe axillaris
Leucothoe fontanesiana
Ligustrum ovalifolium
Pieris floribunda
Pieris japonica
Pyracantha coccinea
Rhododendron carolinianum
Rhododendron catawbiense
Rhododendron maximum
Rhododendron 'PJM'
Rhododendron yakushimanum
Rhododendron yedoense
Sarcococca hookerana
Skimmia
Viburnum ×*pragense*
Viburnum rhytidophyllum
Yucca

TARDILY DECIDUOUS FOLIAGE

Daphne ×*burkwoodii*
Euonymus kiautschovicus
Viburnum ×*rhytidophylloides*
Xanthorhiza simplicissima
Zenobia pulverulenta

SHRUBS: DESIGN CHARACTERISTICS

Winter Stem Color and Texture

The following shrubs have notable stem color or texture during the winter season.

Cornus alba
Cornus amomum
Cornus sanguinea
Cornus sericea
Cytisus
Euonymus alatus
Heptacodium miconioides
Kerria japonica
Poncirus trifoliata
Robinia
Rosa
Salix caprea
Salix chaenomeloides
Salix elaeagnos
Salix gracilistyla
Salix purpurea
Salix sachalinensis

A Guide to Shrub Sizes

Note that shrubs may appear in more than one size category. This is to emphasize that, while the plant will tend to grow to within a size range, there is the possibility of attaining greater size. An asterisk (*) next to the plant name indicates that it is more commonly found in the smaller size range.

SMALL (6 FT. OR LESS)

Abeliophyllum distichum
Amorpha canescens
Berberis candidula
Berberis ×gladwynensis
Berberis ×mentorensis
Berberis thunbergii
Buxus microphylla
Callicarpa dichotoma
Calluna vulgaris
Caragana frutex
Caryopteris ×clandonensis
Ceanothus americanus
Chaenomeles japonica
Clethra alnifolia
Comptonia peregrina
Corylopsis pauciflora
Cotoneaster adpressus
Cotoneaster apiculatus
Cotoneaster dammeri
Cotoneaster divaricatus
Cotoneaster horizontalis
Cytisus scoparius
Daphne ×burkwoodii
Daphne caucasica
Daphne cneorum
Daphne mezereum
Deutzia gracilis
Deutzia ×kalmiiflora
Deutzia ×lemoinei
Diervilla sessilifolia
Dirca palustris
Elsholtzia stauntonii
Enkianthus cernuus
Enkianthus perulatus
Erica carnea
Euonymus fortunei
Forsythia 'Arnold Dwarf'
Forsythia viridissima
Fothergilla gardenii
Genista lydia
Genista pilosa
Genista tinctoria
Hydrangea arborescens
Hydrangea macrophylla
Hydrangea quercifolia
Hypericum
Ilex crenata
Ilex glabra
Indigofera kirilowii
Itea virginica
Kerria japonica
Leiophyllum buxifolium
Leucothoe axillaris
Leucothoe fontanesiana
Mahonia aquifolium
Pieris floribunda
Pieris japonica
Potentilla fruticosa
Prinsepia uniflora
Prunus besseyi
Prunus glandulosa
Prunus tenella
Rhododendron carolinianum
Rhododendron 'PJM'
Rhododendron yakushimanum
Rhododendron yedoense
Rhodotypos scandens
Rhus aromatica
Ribes alpinum
Ribes odoratum
Rosa carolina
Rosa rugosa
Rosa spinosissima
Rosa virginiana
Salix gracilistyla
Salix purpurea
Sarcococca hookerana
Shepherdia canadensis
Skimmia japonica
Skimmia reevesiana
Sorbaria sorbifolia
Spiraea albiflora
Spiraea ×bumalda
Spiraea japonica
Spiraea nipponica
Spiraea thunbergii
Stephanandra incisa
Symphoricarpos
Vaccinium angustifolium
Vaccinium vitis-idaea
Viburnum acerifolium
Xanthorhiza simplicissima
Yucca
Zenobia pulverulenta

MEDIUM (6 TO 12 FT.)

Acanthopanax sieboldianus
Aesculus parviflora
Amorpha fruticosa
Aronia
Berberis julianae
Berberis koreana
Buddleia
Buxus sempervirens
Callicarpa americana
Callicarpa bodinieri
Callicarpa japonica
Calycanthus floridus
Caragana arborescens
Cephalanthus occidentalis
Cercis chinensis
Chaenomeles speciosa
Clerodendrum trichotomum
Clethra acuminata
Clethra alnifolia
Colutea arborescens
Cornus alba
Cornus amomum
Cornus racemosa
Cornus sanguinea
Cornus sericea
Corylopsis glabrescens
Corylopsis gotoana
Corylopsis platypetala
Corylopsis spicata
Cotoneaster lucidus
Cotoneaster multiflorus
Cotoneaster salicifolius
Deutzia scabra
Disanthus cercidifolius
Elaeagnus
Enkianthus campanulatus
Euonymus kiautschovicus
Forsythia ×intermedia
Forsythia suspensa var. *sieboldii*
*Forsythia viridissima**
Fothergilla major
Hamamelis vernalis
Hibiscus syriacus
Hydrangea paniculata
*Hydrangea quercifolia**
*Ilex glabra**
Ilex ×meserveae
Ilex serrata
Ilex serrata × I. verticillata Hybrids
Ilex verticillata
Kalmia latifolia
Ligustrum
Lindera benzoin
Lonicera alpigena
Lonicera fragrantissima
Lonicera korolkowii
Lonicera maackii
Lonicera tatarica
Lonicera xylosteum
Myrica pensylvanica
Neillia sinensis
Neviusia alabamensis
Philadelphus
Physocarpus opulifolius
*Pieris japonica**
Poncirus trifoliata
Prinsepia sinensis
Prunus maritima

* More commonly found in the smaller size range.

MEDIUM (6 TO 12 FT.), continued

Prunus tomentosa
Prunus triloba
Pyracantha coccinea
Rhododendron atlanticum
Rhododendron calendulaceum
Rhododendron catawbiense
Rhododendron Exbury Hybrids
Rhododendron mucronulatum
Rhododendron periclymenoides
Rhododendron prinophyllum
Rhododendron schlippenbachii
Rhododendron vaseyi
Rhododendron viscosum
Robinia
Rosa moyesii
Rosa rubrifolia
Salix caprea
Salix elaeagnos
Salix sachalinensis
Sambucus
Shepherdia argentea
Sorbaria aitchisonii
Sorbaria arborea
Spiraea cantoniensis
Spiraea prunifolia
Spiraea ×vanhouttei
Styrax americanus
Syringa ×chinensis
Syringa meyeri
Syringa microphylla
Syringa oblata
Syringa patula
Syringa ×persica
Syringa villosa
Vaccinium corymbosum
Viburnum ×burkwoodii
Viburnum ×carlcephalum
Viburnum carlesii
Viburnum dentatum
Viburnum dilatatum
Viburnum farreri
Viburnum ×juddii
Viburnum lantana
Viburnum plicatum
Viburnum plicatum var. *tomentosum*
Viburnum setigerum
Weigela florida
Weigela middendorffiana

LARGE (12 FT. AND GREATER)

*Amorpha fruticosa**
*Caragana arborescens**
Corylus americana
Corylus avellana
Corylus maxima var. *purpurea*
Cotinus coggygria
*Cotoneaster multiflorus**
Euonymus alatus
Exochorda racemosa
Franklinia alatamaha
Hamamelis ×intermedia
Hamamelis japonica
Hamamelis mollis
Hamamelis virginiana
*Hydrangea paniculata**
Ilex ×aquipernyi
Ilex ×attenuata
Ilex decidua
Ilex opaca
Ilex pedunculosa
*Ilex verticillata**
Kolkwitzia amabilis
*Lonicera fragrantissima**
*Lonicera korolkowii**
*Lonicera maackii**
Photinia villosa
*Poncirus trifoliata**
Prunus 'Hally Jolivette'
Pseudocydonia sinensis
Rhamnus
Rhododendron maximum
Rhus chinensis (treelike)
Rhus copallina
Rhus glabra
Rhus typhina
*Salix caprea**
Symplocos paniculata
Syringa reticulata
Syringa vulgaris
Tamarix ramosissima
Viburnum lentago
Viburnum opulus
Viburnum prunifolium
Viburnum sargentii
Viburnum sieboldii
Viburnum trilobum
Vitex

* More commonly found in the smaller size range.

SHRUBS: CULTURAL CHARACTERISTICS AND MAINTENANCE

Tolerance to Dry Soils

The following shrubs are good plants for dry soil conditions.

Acanthopanax sieboldianus
Amorpha
Berberis
Caragana
Ceanothus americanus
Colutea arborescens
Comptonia peregrina
Cotinus coggygria
Cotoneaster
Cytisus
Deutzia
Elaeagnus
Gaylussacia brachycera
Heptacodium miconioides
Ligustrum
Lonicera alpigena
Lonicera fragrantissima
Lonicera korolkowii
Lonicera maackii
Lonicera tatarica
Lonicera xylosteum
Photinia villosa
Physocarpus opulifolius
Potentilla fruticosa
Prinsepia
Prunus maritima
Pyracantha coccinea
Rhamnus
Rhodotypos scandens
Rhus
Robinia
Rosa rugosa
Shepherdia
Spiraea ×bumalda
Spiraea cantoniensis
Spiraea japonica
Spiraea prunifolia
Spiraea ×vanhouttei
Symphoricarpos
Syringa laciniata
Syringa meyeri
Syringa oblata
Syringa reticulata
Tamarix ramosissima
Viburnum acerifolium
Viburnum dentatum
Viburnum lantana
Viburnum rufidulum
Yucca

SHRUBS: CULTURAL CHARACTERISTICS AND MAINTENANCE
Tolerance to Moist Soils

The following shrubs are tolerant of moist soil conditions.

Aronia
Cephalanthus occidentalis
Clethra alnifolia
Cornus alba
Cornus amomum
Cornus sanguinea
Cornus sericea
Ilex glabra
Ilex opaca
Ilex serrata × *I. verticillata* Hybrids
Ilex verticillata
Itea virginica
Leucothoe
Lindera benzoin
Neviusia alabamensis
Rhododendron atlanticum
Rhododendron periclymenoides
Rhododendron viscosum
Salix caprea
Salix elaeagnos
Salix gracilistyla
Salix purpurea
Salix sachalinensis
Sambucus canadensis
Styrax americanus
Vaccinium corymbosum
Xanthorhiza simplicissima
Zenobia pulverulenta

SHRUBS: CULTURAL CHARACTERISTICS AND MAINTENANCE
Salt Tolerance

The following shrubs are tolerant of salinity. A distinction is made here between tolerance to saline conditions in the soil and tolerance to salt spray.

Amorpha	Soil
Caragana	Soil
Cytisus	Spray
Elaeagnus	Soil and spray
Hydrangea macrophylla	Spray
Ilex, especially *I. glabra*, *I. opaca*	Spray
Ligustrum	Spray
Lonicera	Spray
Myrica pensylvanica	Spray (some soil tolerance)
Prunus maritima	Soil and spray
Rhus	Soil and spray
Rosa rugosa	Soil and spray
Rosa virginiana	Soil and spray
Shepherdia	Soil
Sorbaria	Spray
Tamarix ramosissima	Soil and spray
Viburnum dentatum	Spray
Yucca	Soil and spray

SHRUBS: CULTURAL CHARACTERISTICS AND MAINTENANCE
Shade Tolerance

The following shrubs are tolerant of conditions of medium shade or greater. Some plants will produce diminished flowers or fruit in shady environments.

Acanthopanax sieboldianus
Aesculus parviflora
Callicarpa
Calycanthus floridus
Clerodendrum trichotomum
Clethra alnifolia
Cornus alba
Cornus amomum
Cornus racemosa
Cornus sanguinea
Cornus sericea
Corylopsis
Daphne
Dirca palustris
Disanthus cercidifolius
Enkianthus
Euonymus alatus
Euonymus fortunei
Euonymus kiautschovicus
Fothergilla
Hamamelis
Hydrangea arborescens
Hydrangea macrophylla
Hydrangea quercifolia
Ilex
Itea virginica
Kerria japonica
Leucothoe
Lindera benzoin
Mahonia aquifolium
Pieris
Rhododendron
Rhodotypos scandens
Rhus aromatica
Ribes
Sarcococca hookerana
Skimmia
Stephanandra incisa
Styrax americanus
Symphoricarpos
Vaccinium corymbosum
Viburnum
Xanthorhiza simplicissima
Zenobia pulverulenta

Hedges and Parterres

The following shrubs are particularly amenable to pruning and are among the better choices for hedging. Pruning is a dwarfing process and often results in loss of flower buds (see following table, "Pruning Times").

Acanthopanax sieboldianus
Berberis
Buxus
Caragana
Cotoneaster divaricatus
Cotoneaster lucidus
Elaeagnus
Euonymus alatus
Ilex ×aquipernyi
Ilex ×attenuata
Ilex crenata
Ilex glabra
Ilex ×meserveae
Ligustrum
Lonicera alpigena
Lonicera fragrantissima
Lonicera korolkowii
Lonicera maackii
Lonicera tatarica
Lonicera xylosteum
Physocarpus opulifolius
Poncirus trifoliata
Prinsepia
Rhamnus
Rhodotypos scandens
Ribes alpinum
Rosa
Salix elaeagnos
Salix purpurea
Shepherdia
Spiraea cantoniensis
Spiraea ×vanhouttei
Viburnum dentatum
Viburnum lentago
Viburnum prunifolium

SHRUBS: CULTURAL CHARACTERISTICS AND MAINTENANCE

Pruning Times

The following table is a guide to the best time to prune shrubs. Very often people prune either too early or too late, removing flower buds or young fruit before they can develop. For plants that produce outstanding flowers and fruit, there is seldom a best time to prune. Flowers (and the fruit that follow) are formed either on the previous season's wood or on new growth of the season. For shrubs that flower on old wood, pruning should be done after flowering. Shrubs that flower on new growth can be pruned either before or after flowering.

SHRUB	FLOWERS ON
Abeliophyllum distichum	Old Wood
Acanthopanax sieboldianus	Old Wood
Aesculus parviflora	Old Wood
Amorpha canescens	Old Wood
Amorpha fruticosa	Old Wood
Aronia arbutifolia	Old Wood
Aronia melanocarpa	Old Wood
Berberis candidula	Old Wood
Berberis ×gladwynensis	Old Wood
Berberis koreana	Old Wood
Berberis ×mentorensis	Old Wood
Berberis thunbergii	Old Wood
Buddleia alternifolia	Old Wood
Buddleia davidii	New Growth
Buddleia ×weyeriana 'Sun Gold'	New Growth
Buxus microphylla	Old Wood
Buxus sempervirens	Old Wood
Callicarpa americana	New Growth
Callicarpa bodinieri	New Growth
Callicarpa dichotoma	New Growth
Callicarpa japonica	New Growth
Calluna vulgaris	New Growth
Calycanthus floridus	Both (primarily Old Wood)
Caragana arborescens	Old Wood
Caragana frutex	Old Wood
Caryopteris ×clandonensis	New Growth
Ceanothus americanus	Old Wood
Cephalanthus occidentalis	Old Wood (some New Growth)
Cercis chinensis	Old Wood
Chaenomeles japonica	Old Wood
Chaenomeles speciosa	Old Wood
Clerodendrum trichotomum	New Growth
Clethra acuminata	Old Growth
Clethra alnifolia	Old Growth
Colutea arborescens	New Growth
Comptonia peregrina	Old Wood
Cornus alba	Old Wood (some New Growth)
Cornus amomum	Old Wood
Cornus racemosa	Old Wood
Cornus sanguinea	Old Wood
Cornus sericea	Old Wood (some New Growth)
Corylopsis glabrescens	Old Wood
Corylopsis gotoana	Old Wood
Corylopsis pauciflora	Old Wood

SHRUB	FLOWERS ON
Corylopsis platypetala	Old Wood
Corylopsis spicata	Old Wood
Corylus americana	Old Wood
Corylus avellana	Old Wood
Corylus maxima var. *purpurea*	Old Wood
Cotinus coggygria	Old Wood
Cotoneaster adpressus	Old Wood
Cotoneaster apiculatus	Old Wood
Cotoneaster dammeri	Old Wood
Cotoneaster divaricatus	Old Wood
Cotoneaster horizontalis	Old Wood
Cotoneaster lucidus	Old Wood
Cotoneaster multiflorus	Old Wood
Cotoneaster salicifolius	Old Wood
Cytisus scoparius	Old Wood
Daphne ×*burkwoodii*	Old Wood
Daphne caucasica	Old Wood and New Growth (flowers into fall)
Daphne cneorum	Old Wood
Daphne mezereum	Old Wood
Deutzia gracilis	Old Wood
Deutzia ×*kalmiiflora*	Old Wood
Deutzia ×*lemoinei*	Old Wood
Deutzia scabra	Old Wood
Diervilla sessilifolia	Old Wood (some New Growth)
Dirca palustris	Old Wood
Disanthus cercidifolius	New Growth
Elaeagnus multiflora	Old Wood
Elaeagnus umbellata	Old Wood
Elsholtzia stauntonii	New Growth
Enkianthus campanulatus	Old Wood
Enkianthus cernuus	Old Wood
Enkianthus perulatus	Old Wood
Erica carnea	Old Wood
Euonymus alatus	Old Wood
Euonymus fortunei	Old Wood
Euonymus kiautschovicus	Old Wood
Exochorda racemosa	Old Wood
Forsythia 'Arnold Dwarf'	Old Wood
Forsythia ×*intermedia*	Old Wood
Forsythia suspensa var. *sieboldii*	Old Wood
Forsythia viridissima	Old Wood
Fothergilla gardenii	Old Wood
Fothergilla major	Old Wood
Franklinia alatamaha	New Growth
Gaylussacia brachycera	Old Wood
Genista lydia	Old Wood
Genista pilosa	Old Wood
Genista tinctoria	Old Wood (some New Growth)
Hamamelis ×*intermedia*	Old Wood
Hamamelis japonica	Old Wood

SHRUB	FLOWERS ON
Hamamelis mollis	Old Wood
Hamamelis vernalis	Old Wood
Hamamelis virginiana	New Growth
Heptacodium miconioides	New Growth
Hibiscus syriacus	New Growth
Hydrangea arborescens	New Growth
Hydrangea macrophylla	Old Wood (some New Growth)
Hydrangea paniculata	New Growth
Hydrangea quercifolia	Old Wood
Hypericum frondosum	New Growth
Hypericum prolificum	Old Wood (some New Growth)
Ilex ×*aquipernyi*	Old Wood
Ilex ×*attenuata*	Old Wood
Ilex crenata	Old Wood
Ilex decidua	Old Wood
Ilex glabra	Old Wood
Ilex ×*meserveae*	Old Wood
Ilex opaca	Old Wood
Ilex pedunculosa	Old Wood
Ilex serrata	Old Wood
Ilex serrata × *I. verticillata*	Old Wood
Ilex verticillata	Old Wood
Indigofera kirilowii	Old Wood (some New Growth)
Itea virginica	Old Wood
Kalmia latifolia	Old Wood
Kerria japonica	Old Wood (some New Growth)
Kolkwitzia amabilis	Old Wood
Leiophyllum buxifolium	Old Wood
Leucothoe amurense	Old Wood
Leucothoe axillaris	Old Wood
Ligustrum amurense	Old Wood
Ligustrum obtusifolium	Old Wood
Ligustrum ovalifolium	Old Wood
Ligustrum ×*vicaryi*	Old Wood
Ligustrum vulgare	Old Wood
Lindera benzoin	Old Wood
Lonicera alpigena	Old Wood
Lonicera fragrantissima	Old Wood
Lonicera korolkowii	Old Wood
Lonicera maackii	Old Wood
Lonicera tatarica	Old Wood
Lonicera xylosteum	Old Wood
Mahonia aquifolium	Old Wood
Myrica pensylvanica	Old Wood
Neillia sinensis	Old Wood
Neviusia alabamensis	Old Wood
Philadelphus coronarius	Old Wood
Philadelphus ×*cymosus*	Old Wood
Philadelphus ×*lemoinei*	Old Wood
Philadelphus ×*virginalis*	Old Wood
Photinia villosa	Old Wood

SHRUB	FLOWERS ON
Physocarpus opulifolius	Old Wood
Pieris floribunda	Old Wood
Pieris japonica	Old Wood
Poncirus trifoliata	Old Wood
Potentilla fruticosa	New Growth
Prinsepia sinensis	Old Wood
Prinsepia uniflora	Old Wood
Prunus besseyi	Old Wood
Prunus glandulosa	Old Wood
Prunus 'Hally Jolivette'	Old Wood
Prunus maritima	Old Wood
Prunus tenella	Old Wood
Prunus tomentosa	Old Wood
Prunus triloba	Old Wood
Pseudocydonia sinensis	Old Wood
Pyracantha coccinea	Old Wood
Rhamnus frangula	Old Wood
Rhododendron atlanticum	Old Wood
Rhododendron calendulaceum	Old Wood
Rhododendron carolinianum	Old Wood
Rhododendron catawbiense	Old Wood
Rhododendron Exbury Hybrids	Old Wood
Rhododendron maximum	Old Wood
Rhododendron mucronulatum	Old Wood
Rhododendron periclymenoides	Old Wood
Rhododendron 'PJM'	Old Wood
Rhododendron prinophyllum	Old Wood
Rhododendron schlippenbachii	Old Wood
Rhododendron vaseyi	Old Wood
Rhododendron viscosum	Old Wood
Rhododendron yakushimanum	Old Wood
Rhododendron yedoense	Old Wood
Rhodotypos scandens	Old Wood
Rhus aromatica	Old Wood
Rhus chinensis	New Growth
Rhus copallina	New Growth
Rhus glabra	New Growth
Rhus typhina	New Growth
Ribes alpinum	Old Wood
Ribes odoratum	Old Wood
Robinia fertilis	Old Wood
Rosa carolina	New Growth (some Old Wood)
Rosa moyesii	New Growth (some Old Wood)
Rosa rubrifolia	New Growth (some Old Wood)
Rosa rugosa	New Growth (some Old Wood)
Rosa spinosissima	Old Wood (some New Growth)
Rosa virginiana	New Growth (some Old Wood)
Rosa Hybrids	New Growth (some Old Wood)
Salix caprea	Old Wood
Salix elaeagnos	Old Wood

SHRUB	FLOWERS ON
Salix gracilistyla	Old Wood
Salix purpurea	Old Wood
Salix sachalinensis	Old Wood
Sambucus canadensis	Old Wood
Sambucus nigra	Old Wood
Sambucus racemosa	Old Wood
Sarcococca hookerana	Old Wood
Shepherdia argentea	Old Wood
Shepherdia canadensis	Old Wood
Skimmia japonica	Old Wood
Skimmia reevesiana	Old Wood
Sorbaria aitchisonii	New Growth
Sorbaria arborea	New Growth
Sorbaria sorbifolia	New Growth
Spiraea albiflora	New Growth
Spiraea ×bumalda	New Growth
Spiraea cantoniensis	Old Wood
Spiraea japonica	New Growth
Spiraea nipponica	Old Wood
Spiraea prunifolia	Old Wood
Spiraea thunbergii	Old Wood
Spiraea ×vanhouttei	Old Wood
Stachyurus praecox	Old Wood
Stephanandra incisa	Old Wood
Styrax americanus	Old Wood
Symphoricarpos albus	Old Wood
Symphoricarpos ×chenaultii	Old Wood
Symphoricarpos orbiculatus	Old Wood
Symplocos paniculata	Old Wood
Syringa ×chinensis	Old Wood
Syringa laciniata	Old Wood
Syringa meyeri	Old Wood
Syringa microphylla	Old Wood
Syringa oblata var. *dilatata*	Old Wood
Syringa patula	Old Wood
Syringa ×persica	Old Wood
Syringa reticulata	Old Wood
Syringa villosa	Old Wood
Syringa vulgaris	Old Wood
Tamarix ramosissima	New Growth
Vaccinium angustifolium	Old Wood
Vaccinium corymbosum	Old Wood
Vaccinium vitis-idaea	Old Wood
Viburnum acerifolium	Old Wood
Viburnum ×burkwoodii	Old Wood
Viburnum ×carlcephalum	Old Wood
Viburnum carlesii	Old Wood
Viburnum dentatum	Old Wood
Viburnum dilatatum	Old Wood
Viburnum farreri	Old Wood

SHRUB	FLOWERS ON	SHRUB	FLOWERS ON
Viburnum ×*juddii*	Old Wood	*Viburnum sieboldii*	Old Wood
Viburnum lantana	Old Wood	*Viburnum trilobum*	Old Wood
Viburnum lentago	Old Wood	*Vitex agnus-castus*	New Growth
Viburnum opulus	Old Wood	*Vitex negundo*	New Growth
Viburnum plicatum	Old Wood	*Weigela florida*	Old Wood (some New Growth)
Viburnum plicatum var. *tomentosum*	Old Wood	*Weigela middendorffiana*	Old Wood
Viburnum ×*pragense*	Old Wood	*Xanthorhiza simplicissima*	Old Wood
Viburnum prunifolium	Old Wood	*Yucca filamentosa*	New Growth
Viburnum ×*rhytidophylloides*	Old Wood	*Yucca flaccida*	New Growth
Viburnum rhytidophyllum	Old Wood	*Yucca glauca*	New Growth
Viburnum rufidulum	Old Wood	*Yucca smalliana*	New Growth
Viburnum sargentii	Old Wood	*Zenobia pulverulenta*	Old Wood
Viburnum setigerum	Old Wood		

NEEDLE EVERGREENS: DESIGN AND CULTURAL CHARACTERISTICS

Single Specimens, Groupings, Screens, and Groves

In many landscapes, a grouping of three, five, seven, or more evergreens provides both visual privacy and a more aesthetically pleasing feeling than tight, boxy hedges. When positioning evergreens, whether as single specimens or in groups, screens, or hedges, be careful to provide ample space to spread.

Abies
Calocedrus decurrens
Cedrus
Chamaecyparis nootkatensis
Chamaecyparis obtusa
Chamaecyparis pisifera
Cryptomeria japonica
×*Cupressocyparis leylandii*
Juniperus, tree types
Picea
Pinus, except *P. aristata*, *P. mugo*, *P. pumila*
Pseudotsuga menziesii
Sciadopitys verticillata
Thuja occidentalis
Thuja plicata
Thujopsis dolobrata
Tsuga canadensis
Tsuga caroliniana

NEEDLE EVERGREENS: DESIGN AND CULTURAL CHARACTERISTICS

Hedging

The following needle evergreens can be used as hedges.

Abies. This genus (along with the genera *Picea* and *Pinus*) is not the best for hedges, although it is often used in displays at arboreta and botanical gardens. Plants can be extremely variable, particularly in needle color, because they are grown from seed. Prune when the needles of the new spring shoots are half normal size. New buds will form behind the cuts and insure a full, dense plant the next year.

Calocedrus decurrens

Cedrus. I have observed *Cedrus atlantica* var. *glauca* used as a hedge, but it is a tragic waste of a great plant. Also, it is an expensive approach.

Chamaecyparis. All species can be pruned into hedges. The slower growing forms of *Chamaecyparis obtusa*, if planted close, make handsome hedges without much pruning.

×*Cupressocyparis leylandii*

Juniperus. Any upright juniper can be fashioned into a hedge.

Picea. See *Abies* entry.

Pinus. See *Abies* entry. *Pinus mugo*, *P. pumila*, *P. strobus*, and *P. sylvestris* are the best pines for hedging purposes.

Taxus. Overused for hedging, but excellent in sun or shade.

Thuja. Easily pruned and maintained.

Thujopsis dolobrata. A handsome but expensive hedge.

Tsuga canadensis. Where it can be grown, there are no rivals.

NEEDLE EVERGREENS: DESIGN AND CULTURAL CHARACTERISTICS
Groundcovers and Massing

The following needle evergreens are good selections for groundcovers and low masses. Particular cultivars or varieties listed for species are among the better selections, but other forms as well as the species form will often serve just as well. *Juniperus procumbens* 'Nana' and *Taxus baccata* 'Repandens' are particularly good choices for groundcover; *Pinus mugo* var. *mugo* and *Taxus* are among the best for low masses.

Chamaecyparis obtusa, dwarf cultivars
Chamaecyparis pisifera, dwarf cultivars
Juniperus chinensis forms such as 'Armstrong', 'Pfitzeriana Compacta', and var. *sargentii*
Juniperus communis 'Depressa', 'Effusa'
Juniperus conferta 'Blue Pacific', 'Emerald Sea', 'Nana'
Juniperus davurica 'Parsoni', also yellow- and white-variegated types.
Juniperus horizontalis cultivars
Juniperus procumbens 'Nana'
Juniperus sabina 'Broadmoor', var. *tamariscifolia*
Juniperus scopulorum 'Table Top Blue', and other low-growing types
Juniperus squamata 'Blue Carpet', 'Blue Star'
Juniperus virginiana 'Grey Owl', 'Silver Spreader', and other low-growing types
Pinus mugo var. *mugo*
Taxus
Taxus baccata 'Repandens'

NEEDLE EVERGREENS: DESIGN AND CULTURAL CHARACTERISTICS
Salt Tolerance

The following needle evergreens do well in saline environments.

Abies. Generally not considered very salt tolerant, but research has shown that the bluer the needles—i.e., the more wax on the needle surface—the more resistant the plant is to salt deposition.
Cedrus atlantica var. *glauca*
Chamaecyparis thyoides
×*Cupressocyparis leylandii*
Juniperus, particularly the following species and their cultivars:
- *Juniperus conferta*
- *Juniperus chinensis*
- *Juniperus horizontalis*
- *Juniperus virginiana*

Picea glauca
Pinus nigra
Pinus parviflora
Pinus thunbergii

NEEDLE EVERGREENS: DESIGN AND CULTURAL CHARACTERISTICS
Shade Tolerance

The following needle evergreens can tolerate shady siting. Distinctions are made here for tolerance to light shade or to medium to heavy shade.

Chamaecyparis obtusa	Light
Cryptomeria japonica	Light
Sciadopitys verticillata	Medium to Heavy
Taxus	Medium to Heavy
Thujopsis dolobrata	Light
Tsuga	Medium to Heavy

VINES: DESIGN AND CULTURAL CHARACTERISTICS
Flowers, Fruit, and Fall Color

The following vines have notably colorful or fragrant flowers, attractive fruit, and/or interesting fall color.

VINE	FLOWERS		FRUIT	FALL COLOR
	COLOR	FRAGRANCE		
Actinidia	white	★	★	
Akebia quinata	maroon	★	★	
Ampelopsis brevipedunculata			★	
Bignonia capreolata	orange	★		★
Campsis	orange-red			
Celastrus			★	
Hydrangea anomala subsp. *petiolaris*	white	★		
Lonicera ×*brownii*	red			
Lonicera caprifolium	yellow-white, purple	★	★	
Lonicera ×*heckrottii*	red, yellow	★		
Lonicera japonica	white to yellow	★		
Lonicera periclymenum	yellow-white, rose	★	★	
Lonicera sempervirens	red		★	
Lonicera ×*tellmanniana*	yellow-orange			
Schizophragma hydrangeoides	white	★		
Vitis cognetiae				★
Wisteria	lavender	★		

VINES: DESIGN AND CULTURAL CHARACTERISTICS
True Clinging Vines

The following vines do not require support for growth, i.e., they are true clinging vines.

Bignonia capreolata
Campsis radicans
Campsis ×*tagliabuana*
Hedera helix
Hydrangea anomala subsp. *petiolaris*
Parthenocissus
Schizophragma hydrangeoides

VINES: DESIGN AND CULTURAL CHARACTERISTICS
Shade Tolerance

The following vines grow well in shady conditions.

Akebia quinata
Ampelopsis brevipedunculata
Aristolochia durior
Bignonia capreolata
Campsis
Hedera helix
Hydrangea anomala subsp. *petiolaris*
Lonicera ×*brownii*
Lonicera caprifolium
Lonicera ×*heckrottii*
Lonicera japonica
Lonicera periclymenum
Lonicera sempervirens
Lonicera ×*tellmanniana*
Menispermum canadense
Parthenocissus
Schizophragma hydrangeoides
Wisteria

U.S. Department of Agriculture Hardiness Zone Map

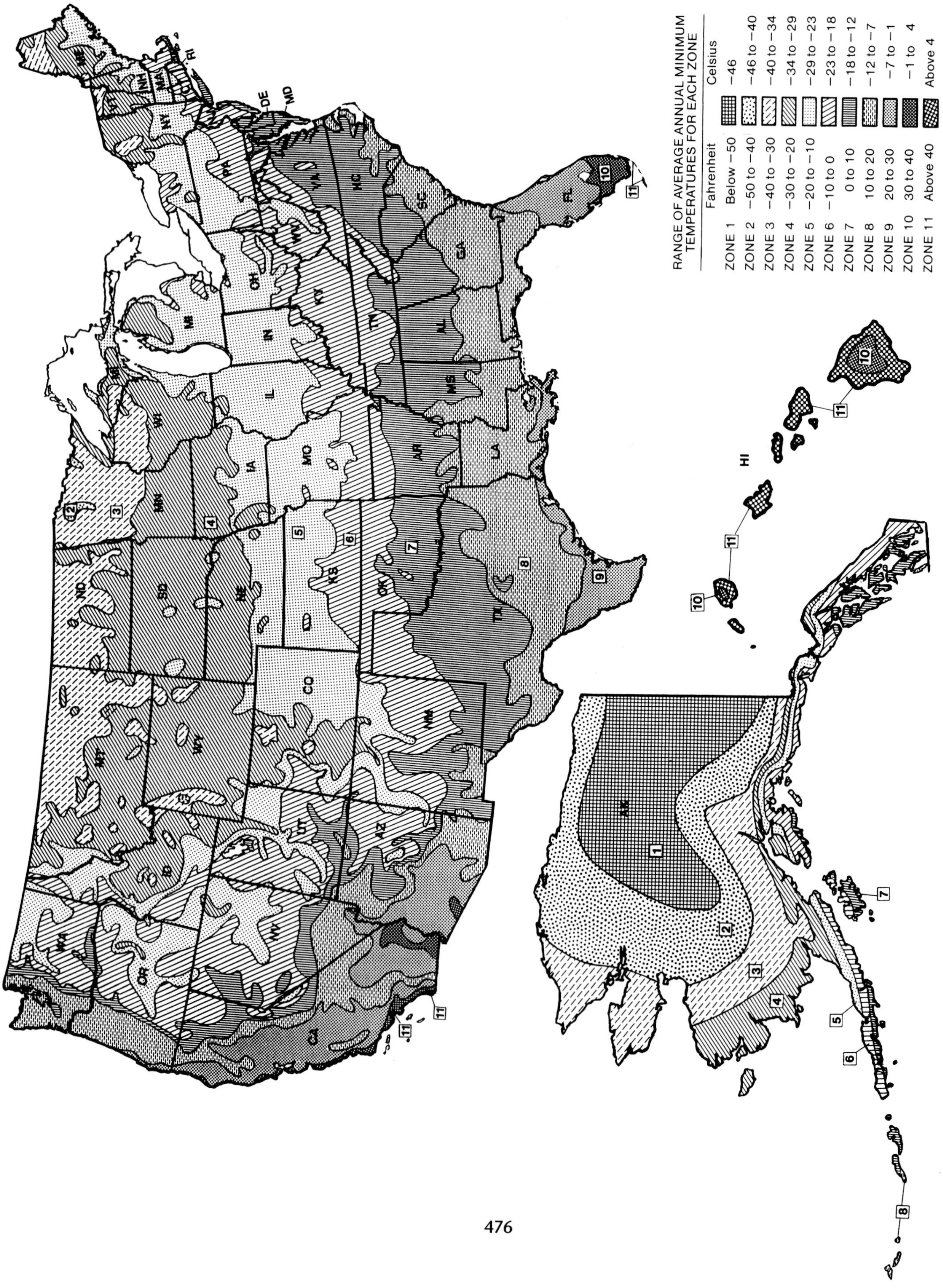

Conversion Table for Metric Measurements

INCHES	CENTIMETERS	FEET	METERS
1/8	0.3	1/4	0.08
1/6	0.4	1/3	0.1
1/5	0.5	1/2	0.15
1/4	0.6	1	0.3
1/3	0.8	1 1/2	0.5
3/8	0.9	2	0.6
2/5	1.0	2 1/2	0.8
1/2	1.25	3	0.9
3/5	1.5	4	1.2
5/8	1.6	5	1.5
2/3	1.7	6	1.8
3/4	1.9	7	2.1
7/8	2.2	8	2.4
1	2.5	9	2.7
1 1/4	3.1	10	3.0
1 1/3	3.3	12	3.6
1 1/2	3.75	15	4.5
1 3/4	4.4	18	5.4
2	5.0	20	6.0
3	7.5	25	7.5
4	10	30	9.0
5	12.5	35	10.5
6	15	40	12
7	17.5	45	13.5
8	20	50	15
9	22.5	60	18
10	25	70	21
12	30	75	22.5
15	37.5	80	24
18	45	90	27
20	50	100	30
24	60	125	37.5
30	75	150	45
32	80	175	52.5
36	90	200	60

$$°C = 5/9 \times (°F - 32)$$

$$°F = (9/5 \times °C) + 32$$

Index of Plant Scientific Names

Page numbers in **boldface** indicate a main text entry and illustration.

Index of Plant Common Names

Page numbers in **boldface** indicate a main text entry and illustration.